Pastoral Counseling Across Cultures

Pastoral Counseling Across Cultures

David W. Augsburger

The Westminster Press
Philadelphia

Scripture quotations from the Revised Standard Version of the Bible are copyrighted 1946, 1952, © 1971, 1973 by the Division of Christian Education of the National Council of the Churches of Christ in the U.S.A. and are used by permission.

Quotations from *The Moral Context of Pastoral Care* by Don S. Browning are copyright © 1976 The Westminster Press. Used by permission.

Book design by Gene Harris

First edition

Published by The Westminster Press®
Philadelphia, Pennsylvania

PRINTED IN THE UNITED STATES OF AMERICA

9 8 7 6 5 4 3 2 1

Library of Congress Cataloging-in-Publication Data

Augsburger, David W.
  Pastoral counseling across cultures.

  Bibliography: p.
  Includes index.
  1. Pastoral counseling. 2. Cross-cultural counseling. I. Title.
BV4012.2.A875 1986   253.5   86-13343
ISBN 0-664-21272-7

Contents

Foreword

If you're looking for a succinct statement of simple guidelines and how-to methods for counseling with people of cultures, classes, ethnic backgrounds, or gender different from your own, this book isn't it. But if you need and are ready for an in-depth exploration of the psychological, cultural, therapeutic, and theological complexities of doing counseling and psychotherapy in an increasingly diverse society, you've come to the right place. If the communications revolution, the jet age, and the massive transplantation of people from other cultures have increased the impact of the global village on your village or town or city, this is a book you'll find incredibly helpful—as well as somewhat shaking at times. In its pages you'll encounter an immense variety of ideas, images, stories, questions, and conceptual maps that will be useful resources for understanding and counseling with those in and from the "two-thirds" world, as well as with persons in the many subcultures that exist in what may appear to be a relatively homogeneous community. You'll also gain insights about counseling with people in your own community whose psyches are reeling from the impact of contact with persons and groups with radically different life-styles and aspirations.

David Augsburger has created a useful volume full of insights on cross-cultural counseling and therapy. And in doing so, he has given us much more. He offers a psychologically sophisticated and theologically grounded view of the human situation understood from a global perspective—a perspective from which we may view ourselves and our own society with increasing transcultural awareness. Such a perspective and such an awareness can expand our cultural horizons and enable us to take another step toward fuller liberation from the unconscious ethnocentrism that makes us captive to our culture-bound socialization and values.

In a world challenged by threats of nuclear annihilation and environmental catastrophe, any awareness that lets us transcend the identities and loyalties of our culture's socialization process, even to a limited degree, may make a small but significant contribution to human survival on a livable planet. It's becoming increasingly dangerous in our world to live "like the frog under the coconut shell" (in the words of a Malay proverb cited by the author), fused with one's own culture. Becoming more global in our commitments may be the most essential as well as the most difficult survival task for the human family in the remaining years of this millennium. I am delighted to affirm the importance of this book. It is an invaluable resource for those who desire to move ahead with this task, within themselves and in their families, their work, and their world.

As far as the literature of the pastoral and counseling field is concerned, this book makes an original and timely contribution. The vigorous process of internationalization within the pastoral care movement in the last fifteen years has made it increasingly multicultural. The two most recent meetings of the International Congress of Pastoral Care and Counseling have provided evidence that the field is moving beyond its North American–European white, largely male, middle-class origins. The voices and perspectives of persons with advanced clinical and academic training in pastoral care from cultures in Asia, Africa, and, to a lesser extent, Latin America have become more prominent in the presentations and dialogue at these meetings. And the need for indigenous and clinically based literature on pastoral care in various non-Western cultures has also become apparent. This book is written by a white male North American. It does not diminish the need for pastoral care literature written by those who know other cultures as insiders. But this book makes a different contribution, which is also urgently needed. It is written from a multicultural and, in a sense, a transcultural point of view. Its author is a brilliant student and theoretician of cross-cultural pastoral care. Perhaps more important, his receptive, noncondescending mind and warm, appreciative heart make him a refreshing example of what he describes so effectively in the first chapter, a "culturally aware" and "culturally effective" person and counselor. His examples and insights grow out of his search for greater understanding of persons in and from radically diverse cultures.

It would be true, though a gross understatement, to say that touching minds with David Augsburger in the pages of this book is an "experience." If your experience is anything like mine, encountering his many-faceted, remarkably innovative theory building may make you feel at times that your circuits are overloaded. His ability to draw on scholarly findings from a wide variety of disciplines—among them, biblical studies and liberation theology, cross-cultural research findings by anthropologists, historians, psychologists, therapists, and healers (both Western and indigenous), family experts and sociologists, linguists, and folk-story scholars—is impressive, even dazzling. Yet there is a systematic ordering and integration of this material that gives coherence to the flow of the book. I like particularly his use of charming folk tales from around the planet to launch each chapter and his frequent summaries and diagrams, which, with the stories, help to activate right-brain involvement to balance the left-brain theoretical material that is presented in such profusion and clarity.

Knowing David's style, I expected before reading the book that he would do his homework with breadth and thoroughness to prepare his mind for such a challenging writing task. This expectation is more than confirmed. His background preparation included some thirteen years at the Mennonite Board of Missions and, more recently, the continuing stimulation of teaching in a theological seminary where international issues and transcultural service by the faculty and a high percentage of students are major emphases. In addition, David has consulted, interviewed, and done research in some fourteen third-world countries in the last five years. These included the eight countries in which, during a recent sabbatical year, he did focused field research for this book, learning from a host of culturally knowledgeable people in each country. Although he incorporates many insights, stories, and case illustrations from these countries, the book is not a kind of ideological travelog. Its strength flows from the fact that he took what must have been a voluminous mass of experiences, images, and data and wove together the most relevant material with an integrating conceptuality that can sparkle like waves in the sunlight as it reflects his knowledge and his skill in communicating.

Each chapter is an exploration of universal human themes that are highlighted in new ways when viewed from an intercultural perspective. Among the themes he explores are these:

The importance of distinguishing and learning from the three aspects in all of us—the universal, which we share with all other humans; the culturally programmed, which we learn from our own culture of origin; and our individual uniqueness, which distinguishes each of us from all other people

The cross-cultural variations in dependence, independence, and interdependence

The constructive as well as destructive roles of anxiety, shame, and guilt as a society's ways of controlling behavior and forming personality structure

The variety and power of the central values and guiding worldviews in different cultures

The interplay of the culturally unique and the universal motifs in marriage and family life and in relationships between women and men

The universality of patriarchal, sexist treatment of women in all cultures and the differences of the goals of women's liberation in the third world

Moral development from a cross-cultural perspective, and the role of storytelling and story living in guiding ethical decision making

The communal nature of much healing power in cultures, which produces communal rather than individualistic personality structure

Alternative ways of understanding and treating demonic possession

Cultural determinants and variations in defining what is mentally healthy and what is pathological

I was particularly intrigued by the author's ten universal metaphors for counseling and therapy from a cross-cultural perspective.

Although this book is specifically addressed to the issues and concerns of those of us in the field of pastoral care and counseling, I predict that it will prove to be a valued resource for a much broader readership, including scholars and students of cross-cultural studies and the role of religions in various cultures; those in the secular helping, counseling, and teaching professions who deal with people from multicultural backgrounds; persons who are interested in the relationships between society and personality and in cross-cultural insights regarding the disciplines of psychology and sociology of religion; women and men who wish to understand how relationships between the two genders in the same culture have many of the characteristics and problems of intercultural relationships; and persons living and working in other countries who decide to learn from rather than seek to escape from the severe pain of their culture shock.

As you can tell, I like this book! On a more personal level, let me say that my heart is warmed indeed by knowing that a colleague and friend has produced a book of the quality, richness, and helpfulness of this volume. As so often happens in my experience as a teacher, our roles were reversed as I read David's book. Although I began to read mainly so that I could write this introduction, I soon became an eager and appreciative learner, as David helped his former teacher understand with greater clarity some striking but unclear experiences that I have had while working in non-Western cultures during the past two decades. For this I am most grateful.

Crossing over to another culture with openness and reverence and then coming back is the spiritual adventure of our time, according to David Augsburger. In his view, crossing over with this mind-set and heart-set enables one to return to one's own culture enriched, more aware, more humble, and more alive. In a real sense, the power of this book is that it can enable us as readers to cross over, experience a stunning array of diverse cultural realities, and then return home with the treasure and growth-in-personhood that comes from interpathic caring in different worlds. Exciting travels await you, as you use the book on your own journeys.

Howard Clinebell
Professor of Pastoral Psychology and Counseling
School of Theology at Claremont, California

Acknowledgments

The listing of contributors who deserve special appreciation is long and stretches back over a decade of conversations on intercultural counseling, but especial gratitude must be expressed to Philemon Choi and the Breakthrough Center Counseling staff, Paul Clasper, Ira and Evelyn Kurtz, Wilson Chou, and Tim Sprunger in Hong Kong; to Mohan Isaac and the National Institutes of Mental Health and Neurosciences in India, who welcomed me as a fellow; to Dayanand Pitamber and Roslyn Karaban of the United Theological College, Bangalore; to Mesach Krisetya, Charles Christano, and Willi Toisuta and the counseling center staff of Universitas Kristen Satya Wacana in Indonesia; to Kyohei Minaga, Tetsuo Kashiwagi, Takio Tanase, Suichi Kaku, Waldemar Kippes, Kenneth Dale, and Charles and Ruth Shenk in Japan; to Anthony Yeo and the Counseling and Care Center staff of Singapore; to John Williamson in Nepal, Tai Ki Chung and Keun-Won Park in Korea, and to many others, in Africa, Central and South America, and the Caribbean Islands; to my many students with international experience, and to seminar members at the Associated Mennonite Biblical Seminaries, especially Janet Brenneman, Ann Gingrich, James Metzler, Juliette Kuitse, Ken Litwiller, Takeji Nomura, Rick Janzen, Shirley Yoder, and Betty Hochstetler; to my colleagues Marlin Miller, Gerald Kauffman, Willard Swartley, Daniel Schipani, Gayle Gerber Koontz, and Leroy Friesen; to John Hinkle, John Paton, Dale Schumm, and Paul76iebert for their criticism and assistance; to Howard Clinebell for his encouragement and foreword; to Keith Crim for his editorial counsel; and most of all to Nancy Wert Augsburger, co-traveler, research associate, copy editor, typist, and partner in many experiences of crossing over.

Goshen, Indiana   *D.A.*
January 1986

Pastoral Counseling Across Cultures

Introduction

The time has come for the pastoral counseling movement to function from an expanded, intercultural perspective. The counseling theories and therapies that have emerged as modes of healing and growth in each culture, useful and effective as they are in their respective locales, are too limited, too partial to serve human needs in a world community where peoples of many cultures meet, compete, and relate.

It is time to cross over into other perspectives and return with the broadened vision of humanness that emerges only along the cultural boundaries. Western individualism, as it spreads along with urbanization and technological change, brings with it a fragmentation of traditional family solidarity, a weakening of social controls, and a loss of historic stability and security in community. As these changes occur across cultures, many common features emerge in urban life-styles, in modern youth culture, and in self-actualization values, for example, but great variations, contrasts, and contradictions are also created as traditional and contemporary worlds collide.

The pastoral counselor in a world of accelerated change must be an intercultural person. "Intercultural" is a better designation than the more frequently used "international," "universal," "multicultural," or "marginal." These imply that one "knows" or "possesses" multiple cultures, or is competent in all groups, or is on the boundary but not belonging to any people.

The intercultural person is not culture-free (a hypothetical and undesirable state). Rather, the person is culturally aware. Awareness of one's own culture can free one to disconnect identity from cultural externals and to live on the boundary, crossing over and coming back with increasing freedom. Disidentification of the self from old cultural identifications leads to rediscovery of the self in at least three contexts—one's own culture, a second culture, and in that unique third culture that always forms on the boundary between the two. This third-culture perspective enables the intercultural person to make communication easier, interpret cultural conflict, and function with acceptable competence without any inappropriate switching or confusing of behavior.

The intercultural counselor develops a special skill that we will call "interpathy." Interpathy enables one to enter a second culture cognitively and affectively, to perceive and conceptualize the internal coherence that links the elements of the culture into a dynamic interrelatedness, and to respect that culture (with its strengths and weaknesses) as equally as valid as one's own. This interpathic respect, understanding, and appreciation makes possible the transcendence, for a moment in a particular case, of cultural limitations.

The training of pastoral counselors must be broadened to include alternate worldviews. The world situation has changed around us, while we in Western education have persistently continued to teach as though Western models, values, and views of human nature and community were normative. The mystique of Western psychotherapy viewed through Eastern eyes can be seen as more than a phenomenon; it is an institution of Western society. Its roots are deep in the Western cultural heritage, and in turn it affects and transforms the soil and the era in which it thrives. The greater movement for mental health may be viewed as both a symbolic and a substantive cultural undertaking to meet the deficits in the Western way of life and to attempt to cope with the negative implications of its premises (Pande 1968:425).

Two central issues in training pastoral counselors are, first, the belief in the fundamental importance of seeing individual development as embedded in and inseparable from its social and cultural context; and, second, the development of ministry models and training programs which appreciate the validity of "the second culture" equally with that of the dominant culture. Individual and group differences must be seen not just as the products of different environments but as existing now in the context of a particular setting of cultural traditions, perspectives, and norms. Any therapeutic intervention must be in harmony with the context in which it occurs. Any psychology or theology that pretends to be acultural or ahistorical in its conception of "the individual" is reductionistic, regardless of its breadth or depth. Tragically, the acultural, ahistorical, apolitical conception of individuals remains the favorite in counseling theories and in much theology. Training and practice models must be grounded in sociocultural systems thinking. All human psychology is embedded in its cultural context, and all counseling must take the personal and the contextual with equal seriousness.

This book moves from an initial description of the intercultural counselor to explorations of culture, individuality, controls, values, family systems, sexual roles, ethics, possession, psychopathology, and models of psychotherapy. Each chapter is focused toward central theological concerns that arise among pastoral counselors working on the boundaries. There is no attempt to include all such theological concerns but, rather, to touch issues most frequently raised in interviews with pastoral counselors, educators, and congregational leaders in the two-thirds world. Such issues are presence and dialogue, culture and faith, the nature of humanness, grace and human failure, values, the family, sexuality and liberation, the demonic and human suffering, and the nature of evil. Pastoral theology must address on each cultural boundary the unique concerns and conflicts faced within each particular culture.

The book seeks to identify central elements needed in order to construct an integrative model for intercultural counseling. Not only must certain key variables be included in such a design, such construction must be done by each counselor in each cultural context. The construction of not one model but many models, by many readers, is the goal. The hope of this text, as of any survey of a field that has been so little explored, is to serve foundationally and heuristically as a stimulus for further reflection and more creative writing. The next decade, one hopes, will see increasing development in the theory and practice of intercultural pastoral care-giving.

It is important at the start to set forward three definitions that will be operative as we examine (1) pastoral counseling in its (2) Western practice and its development in the (3) third world.

Pastoral counseling is a liberating and healing ministry of the faith community that is based on a relationship between a pastor (or a pastoring team) with counseling skills and a family or person who come together to engage in conversation and interaction. The relationship is a dynamic process of caring and exploration, with a definite structure and mutually contracted goals, and occurs within the tradition, beliefs, and resources of the faith community that surrounds and supports them.

The West refers to a state of mind, more than a geographical region, that includes the individualism, scientism, social evolutionism, egalitarianism, and self-actualization referred to as modern thought. References to Western views and values will include not only North American and European cultures but also those who espouse similar perspectives in virtually every country.

The third world does not refer to "third-class" or "third-rate" but to the original meaning of the French expression *tiers monde,* a third world that is not involved with either the first (capitalist) or second (socialist) worlds and does not participate in the controversy between the two. In other words, "third" means "the outsider, the other" (Katoppo 1981:1). Contrasting the non-Western and Western worlds tends to ignore the fact that the gaps between non-Western countries, or even within one country, are often much wider than those between them and the West. Most properly, we should speak of non-Western worlds always in the plural form and, when gathering them into one grouping, always remember their diversity.

Viewed interculturally, the pastoral counselor or caregiver has many different images, whose work takes a rich variety of forms, whose task is accomplished in a wide spectrum of styles, and whose role requires a great breadth of definitions. It is difficult to name a common denominator. One-to-one counseling, marital and familial therapy, and group therapy models are similar in most settings, but the forms of care-giving become unrecognizable to the Western eye in cultures where most problems are resolved within the joint family, where the vertical patterns of filial piety depend on the wisdom of the elders, and where the conversations on problems of living occur in informal rather than formal contractual settings. Christian caring is altered radically by its context, whether in Christian, secular, or non-Christian cultures. For example, the work of a pastor in the Chinese Christian subgroup within the 98-percent Javanese Muslim majority of Indonesia's Java will require a subtlety unimagined and unrequired in Manila, Singapore, or Hong Kong, where secularization and materialism present an overt challenge to all cultural and religious traditions.

In this book, we will be exploring those cultural, social, and familial differences that demand these radically varied forms of care-giving. Where personalities are sociocentric rather than egocentric, where familial esteem is more crucial than self-esteem, where identity is more rooted in village (land), in tribe (kinship), in patrilineal solidarity (filial piety) than in individual self-actualization, counseling and care will have different beginning points, processes, and ends. Pastoral care around the world is, as it must be, as varied as is the human family.

1

The Cross-Cultural Counselor

A Theology of Presence

"Hitherto most people have accepted their cultures as fate, like climate or vernacular; but our empathic awareness of the exact modes of many cultures is itself a liberation from them as prisons. We can now live, not just amphibiously, in divided and distinguished worlds, but in many worlds and cultures simultaneously. We are no more committed to one culture—to a single ratio among the human senses—any more than to one book or language or technology. Compartmentalizing of human potential by single cultures will soon be as absurd as specialism in subject or discipline has become."

—*Marshall McLuhan, 1962*

EMPATHY–INTERPATHY
Two Classic Chinese Stories

Once upon a time, I, Chuang-tzu, dreamed I was a butterfly, fluttering hither and thither, to all intents and purposes a butterfly. I was conscious only of following my fancies as a butterfly, and was unconscious of my individuality as a man.

Suddenly, I awoke, and there I lay, myself again.

Now I do not know whether I was then a man dreaming I was a butterfly, or whether I am now a butterfly dreaming I am a man.

Chuang-tzu the philosopher and Hui-tzu the logician were strolling one day on the bridge over the river Hao.

Chuang-tzu said, "Look how the minnows dart hither and thither where they will. Such is the pleasure that fish enjoy."

Hui-tzu said, "You are not a fish. How do you know what gives pleasure to fish?"

Chuang-tzu said, "You are not I. How do you know that I do not know what gives pleasure to fish?"

Hui-tzu said, "If because I am not you, I cannot know whether you know, then equally because you are not a fish, you cannot know what gives pleasure to fish. My argument still holds."

Chuang-tzu said, "Let us go back to where we started. You asked me how I knew what gives pleasure to fish. But you already knew how I knew it when you asked me. You knew that I knew it by standing here on the bridge at Hao."

Chuang-tzu said, in gathering all wisdom into unity, "Heaven and earth live with me; the ten thousand things and I are one." We do not watch the Way, we participate in it. We do not observe nature and life, we enter it empathically so that subject and object are one.

"One who knows but one culture knows no culture." We are born into culture as we are born to the atmosphere of planet Earth. The biosphere welcomes us, surrounds us, sustains us. It makes life possible, even as it nourished and supported those who gave us birth. Yet just as our life-giving atmosphere is invisible to us until we meet another one (a smoke-filled room perhaps, a smog-clouded city, or a temple filled with incense), so culture becomes visible on the boundary, in comparison, in contrast.

Anyone who knows only one culture knows no culture. In coming to know a second or a third culture, one discovers how much that was taken to be reality is actually an interpretation of realities that are seen in part and known in part; one begins to understand that many things assumed to be universal are local, thought to be absolute are relative, seen as simple are complex; one finds that culture shapes what we perceive, how we perceive it, and which perceptions will be retained and utilized; one realizes that culture defines both what is valued and which values will be central and which less influential.

Knowing another culture may free one from or freeze one to the culture of origin. When the knowledge of contrasting perspectives shatters illusions and perforates old boundaries, the collision of cultures may forge new central commitments that weld old assumptions into new patterns. But the encounter with another culture can result in freezing old boundaries, in confirming biases, in asserting the superiority of one's own assumptions, and thus in reinforcing the cultural encapsulation of an unexamined worldview. Cultural values held as central commitments can free us and provide a flexible resilience. Cultural views maintained as external boundaries isolate and encapsulate us.

Culture is a given to the human person. It simply is in our origins. To become culturally effective is a gift, a gift received through learning from other cultures, through being teachable in encounters with those who differ, and through coming to esteem other worldviews equally with one's own.

If we are to continue life on this planet, we cannot exist within isolated cultural, national, or racial boundaries. Industrialization, the communications revolution, the exploding population, and the resultant economic interdependency of all nations have brought us to the point where we are indispensable to one another across all boundaries. This awareness is dawning on us slowly and has not yet permeated education, psychology, or (obviously) political science, although it is already self-evident in the world of economics. The old nationalism, we are coming to recognize, is an obsolete residue of nineteenth-century romanticism that is of no help in the emerging interdependent world. A new nationalism is evolving that expresses a people's longing to live self-directed political lives in concert with other nations, to direct their economic and social improvement in cooperation with other nations, to protect their interests against imperialism from other nations. Ethnic, cultural, religious, and racial backgrounds can become heritages to be prized, protected, nourished, and cherished, as guides for life-style, but not as boundaries, barriers, or blocks to communication and cooperation between peoples.

Every discipline must contribute to this movement from a mutually exclusive world of competing nations to an inclusive world of collaborating peoples. The snail's pace of ideological change, compared to rapid shifts in technological and economic realms, must incite us to revolutionary thinking and excite radical caring about the future of humankind. Psychological anthropology has laid the groundwork for an interface of the studies of personal, interpersonal, cultural, and intercultural dynamics. Pastoral counseling has barely begun to think about the contribution it can offer from its standpoint at the conjunction of psychology, psychotherapy, theology, philosophy, ethics, missiology, sociology, and anthropology. No other field stands at the conjoint boundaries of eight great disciplines. Pastoral counseling's opportunity and responsibility at the end of the twentieth century are great if it is to contribute not to the end of this millennium but to the beginning of the next.

Other fields are recognizing the absolute necessity of such creative work on the boundaries of our discipline. Harry Triandis, a cross-cultural psychologist, writes (1979:392):

> If humankind survives, cross-cultural psychology will become a central activity for all psychology. Psychological theories will have to use universally valid propositions. However, such theories may well include parameters that reflect the major ecological, economic, and sociocultural variations.

This is a time for pastoral theologians to claim the unique vantage point offered by their integrative stance and multidisciplinary training and vision. It is a crucial position for contributing to the central agenda of our age. And it must begin with a shift in the way we define the essential nature of pastoral counseling and a broadened model of the pastoral counselor as a person, as a professional, and as a culturally capable therapist.

The Culturally Capable Counselor

The ability to join another in his or her culture while fully owning one's own requires a broadened vision of the task of facilitating human growth and healing. Clinical skills within a culture are not sufficient. Cultural skills that transcend and thus can participate in transforming culture are equally crucial.

Culturally capable counselors are distinguished by five measurable and teachable characteristics that protect them, the counselee, and the counseling process from being culturally oppressive.

1. *Culturally aware counselors have a clear understanding of their own values and basic assumptions.* They recognize which human behaviors they view as appropriate or inappropriate, desirable or undesirable, life-enhancing or destructive. They are fully aware that others may hold different values and assumptions, which are legitimate even when they are directly opposite to their own. This understanding has been internalized as both insight (cognitive) and awareness (affective) so that the counselor will not unwittingly impose values or unconsciously influence others into accepting directions alien to their own community.

For example: Inducing guilt in a counselee is seen as undesirable in Western counseling ("You should feel guilty about refusing to obey your mother"). And suppressing a counselee's communications is seen as nontherapeutic ("You should not talk about this"). But in Japan, guilt induction and suppression of communication are central to the two most effective and widely recognized counseling theories.

2. *Culturally aware counselors have a capacity for welcoming, entering into, and prizing other worldviews without negating their legitimacy.* They can go beyond empathy, which assumes a common cultural base, and feel at home on the boundary between worldviews. They can enter into another's world, savor its distinctness, and prize its differentness while holding clearly to the uniqueness of their own.

For example: A counselor who assumes that persons ought to become autonomous individuals as they mature toward adulthood may suspend, or "bracket," these values while listening to a member of a culture in which family solidarity and a collective sense of personhood leads to a mature dependency within the family unit. Seeking to inculcate Western individualism as a means of increasing autonomy violates the integrity of the person and his or her system. Integrity—the integrating core of the person—is what makes autonomy a desirable characteristic to begin with.

3. *Culturally aware counselors seek sources of influence in both the person and the context, both the individual instance and the environment.* Having come to appreciate the impact of the historical, social, religious, political, and economic forces that have shaped the identity and values of all human beings, they are sensitive to the effects of racism, economic exploitation, political oppression, historic tragedy, religious prejudice, or the absence of these on the person's personality or interpersonal adjustment. The action *and* the actors, the behavior *and* the context, the particular counseling interaction *and* the cultural environment must be seen, understood, and respected.

For example: To a counselor from another context, the first interview with a male Palestinian Arab might suggest strong paranoid formation, decided anti-Semitism, and radical loss of control of self and personal environment. Further empathy might reveal that the persecutory ideas are related to the recent confiscation of his home by Israeli settlers and to the imprisonment of his son for accepting a scholarship to study law in Jordan; his "anti-Semitism" is not generalized and racial but based on specific complaints against certain persons, offices, and acts of discriminatory practice; the loss of control is found to be actual and the sense of impotence a correct appraisal because he has no recourse for any of these perceived injustices.

4. *Culturally aware counselors are able to move beyond counseling theory, orientation, or technique and be effective humans.* They are truly eclectic in their counseling, not in a random selection of techniques that work but in a disciplined flexibility that allows them to select a particular set of counseling skills as a considered decision about its appropriateness to the life experience of the particular counselee. They can be critical of each methodology, theory, and orientation, recognizing that "no theory of counseling is politically or morally neutral" (Sue 1978:451).

For example: A counselor who sees an American couple may choose to be noninterpretive and offer primarily experiences and exercises for their mutual discovery of self and other. When asked for evaluation, the counselor may return the question and elicit their awareness of what has occurred and ask for their insight into its meaning. In the next hour, the same counselor may see an Oriental couple and choose to be interpretive, directive, and behaviorally focused. To the Oriental couple, the exercises, experiences, and refusal to interpret would be seen as disinterest, as being cold and aloof.

5. *Culturally aware counselors see themselves as universal citizens, related to all humans as well as distinct from all of them.* They live in the world, not just in their own community or country. Aware as they are of what is culture-bound and class-bound, they refuse to allow what is local to be valued as universal, or to trivialize what is universal by identifying it with any local application. The world is their home, humankind have become their kind. Thus they prize differences as well as similarities, uniqueness as well as commonality. Recognizing that enemy love is the central pastoral task of this century, they hold cultures in respect that are antithetical to their own at points of high value; they extend understanding to nations whose actions are hostile to their own native country.

For examples we may look to black pastoral counselors in Zimbabwe who offered care to revolutionary and loyalist alike, while holding their own convictions about justice, or to pastoral counselors in South Africa who live on the boundary, recognizing that maintaining trust with either one or both sides is a fragile process possible only for a time, yet offering care to people regardless of race or their oppressed place in society. They are not alone. In Latin America, South America, India, Southeast Asia, the Muslim states, Russia, and countries new and old, pastoral care crosses over boundaries and brings people to oneness within and with each other.

The Culturally Encapsulated Counselor

"Among the 500 or so classical Malay proverbs I had to memorize as a child," writes theologian Marianne Katoppo, "one of my favorites was this: *Seperti katak di bawah tempurung*—'Like the frog under the coconut shell.' The image was clear: the frog, never having escaped the boundaries of the coconut shell, could not but conceive of the world as dark, silent, limited" (Katoppo 1981:v).

Perhaps there is no clearer metaphor for the culturally encapsulated counselor. It is the natural tendency among humans to see the world as stretching only from horizon to horizon or to feel at one only with those between familiar boundaries. When such boundaries become—consciously or unconsciously—taken for granted and seen as givens, they function as if absolutized.

Encapsulation then, becomes a useful word for human sin. As Katoppo writes (1981:6), "Sin, all sin, is by nature an all-encompassing absolute. When we sin we think we are all that there is and are therefore divine. We deny the Other and believe that our own totalized order is the kingdom of heaven. Or, as the Malays put it, we are like the frog under the coconut shell."

Counselors are especially susceptible to cultural encapsulation. Their intense specialization in learning the nonverbal language of their counselees—the gestures, facial signals, voice tones, silences, eye movements—and their skill in intuiting expectations, multilevel communications, and denied or concealed emotions may lead them to trust their culturally bound interpretations of these expressions even when they are aware that the same signal may mean the reverse in another culture. However, these same skills of observation and interpretation can help them break out of encapsulation once it is recognized and confronted.

Cultural encapsulation, as described so well by Wren (1962:444–449), results from three unconscious choices, motivated by the desire to reduce the complexity of the world and simplify its confusing and contradictory variety. (1) The culturally encapsulated counselor is one who has substituted symbiotic model stereotypes for the real world. The need to create reliable cognitive maps of the world has been carried to the point where the person prefers the map to the territory, the menu to the meal, the model to the reality. (2) The encapsulated counselor has disregarded cultural variations among clients. A counseling focus on the individual, a preference for examining internal dynamics, and the dismissal of social, environmental, and situational forces as equally significant all contribute to seeing persons as having little significant variation. (3) The culturally encapsulated counselor has dogmatized technique-oriented definitions of counseling and therapy. This trust in technique leads to a self-reinforcing process of moving from symptom to intervention without first examining the symptom for its unique meaning for this person in this specific cultural situation.

Encapsulation functions for the counselor in a way similar to the addictive process. One can become "addicted" to one system of cultural values, resulting in the same disorientation and dependency as for any other addiction. Automatic reliance on a network of meanings subscribed to by the parent culture reduces the capacity for independent thought and case-by-case creativity. This loss of sensitivity is the natural result of addictive attachment in the counselor's worldview—or lack of worldview and resulting satisfaction with a local view (Morrow 1972: 30–32).

In systems language, the culturally encapsulated counselor is fused to the culture of origin, with no distinct boundary between self and society. The necessary differentiation process that makes reflection, awareness, insight, and understanding possible has not yet begun. Thus the counselor's worldview is unconsciously coterminous and continuous with the cultural context. Cultural values and perspectives are mixed with the counselor's view of human nature and understandings of personality dynamics, with no practiced ability for separating fact from fiction or for differentiating feelings about how the human person functions from observations tested cross-culturally. As in a fused family, the culturally encapsulated counselor is surrounded by a rubber wall of boundary assumptions from which new ideas effectively rebound. The person with few independent reflective ideas may function effectively and empathically with others who share the identical cultural perspectives and so facilitate appropriate adjustment within that culture, but such a counselor will be culturally oppressive to persons from another world of experience.

The culturally effective counselor has differentiated a self from the culture of origin with sufficient perceiving, thinking, feeling, and reflecting freedom to recognize when values, views, assumptions, and preferences rise from an alternate life experience. Such a counselor feels a measure of inner freedom to float these differences to the surface and discuss them with more objectivity than the immediate subjective feelings of evaluation, prejudice, threat, or defensiveness.

It is often assumed that training programs will facilitate this differentiation of the person and his or her unexamined context with its many maps of reality, pictures of other cultures, patterns of thinking about other life-styles, feelings attached to other ethnic groups, and clichés and stereotypes about racial, social, religious, or political groupings, but it is too rarely so. The process of encapsulation is frequently built into the very training programs that should be culturally integrative. In becoming a pastoral counselor, one seeks to achieve an understanding of personality theory, therapeutic theory, and theological values and insights and to consolidate these into a centered identity and a core definition of reality. Through one's own personal therapy and growth, this is internalized into a clear set of central convictions. These basic assumptions, well tested in a monocultural setting, become the measure of reality that anchors the person when walking with others along the narrow boundaries between illusion and reality. Such assumptions contain, of necessity, many stereotypes that condense reality into perceivable units, and because of early developmental learnings and unconscious rooting, the stereotype is more readily trusted than new conflicting data from the real world. Thus it is inevitable that all humans have a natural insensitivity to cultural variations and contrasts and will prefer views tested and trusted in the past. Even after years of work across cultures, the most skilled person will still be threatened by interaction with unexpected cultural values, political views, or religious perspectives and react with defensiveness or dogmatism.

Although we may move free from much cultural encapsulation, we cannot fully escape the limitations of our past experiences, or our anxiety before the unknown and unpredictable, or radically alter our present capacities to tolerate ambiguity and contradiction.

> In working with persons from different ethnic, cultural, or sexual backgrounds, it is essential to be aware of the universal tendency to feel, on some level, that one's own experiences and culture are the norm for all human beings. Each of us judges cultural differences as inferior, according to the degree this tendency operates in us. It may blind us to subtle but significant differences in the ways counselees from other backgrounds perceive, conceptualize, feel, solve problems, and create their world-view. (Clinebell 1984:101)

It is a demanding task to transcend the values, biases, and convictions that form our cultural contexts; it is far more difficult to recognize, own, and modify the cultural roots, depths, and patterns that shape our unconscious and automatic behavior. We are limited, finite beings, and the limitations that protect our sanity also inhibit our capacity to perceive an alternate world. As Clinebell concludes after several decades of consulting cross-culturally (1984:101):

> When counseling with a person from a different gender or cultural background, it is helpful to say: "I realize that, much as I would like to understand what you are saying, I won't understand at times because of the differences in our backgrounds. Our work together will be more helpful if you will tell me when you sense I'm not really understanding what you are saying."

In spite of our persistent struggles with cultural, racial, sexual, and religious prejudices, the most we can achieve is a deepened awareness of our ethnocentrism and some appreciable degree of liberation from our unconscious and conscious programming toward cultural superiority. (See Boundary Checklist, p. 39.)

Toward Cultural Awareness

Movement from unawareness to awareness is facilitated best by encounter with more than just information about another culture. Nothing dissolves old assumptions like salt water, particularly crossing a large amount of it and finding oneself in a totally unfamiliar situation. Accelerated learning and unlearning occur as one discovers the immediate need to discard old givens and assimilate new options.

Traditional peoples in tribal or local settings had little or no need to develop an awareness of more than superficial differences. The primary values, common denominators of the group or culture, bound members together with profound and basic similarities. Secondary values create the individual differences that distinguish members from each other to balance and complete the variety of humankind.

Modern peoples in the expanded context of a varied and heterogeneous society were forced to develop capacities for awareness that appreciated more significant differences in secondary values and occasionally penetrated to primary levels. This requires an expanded psychological flexibility for the learning of new roles and the acceptance of contrasting others (Hanvey 1979:55).

As accelerated change in communications systems, increased interaction through travel and migrations, growing interdependency in economic development, and proliferating interchange in multinational corporations all join to demand a new level of awareness, we must be capable of visualizing and understanding the roles, rules, and life routines of persons in other cultures sharing fewer common basic assumptions. This change comes from encounter, contact, and interaction, not from programmic education or social engineering. It occurs on the boundary, not in the cultural enclave.

Cross-cultural awareness comes gradually to persons who remain in monocultural communities. But with repeated encounters, the strange becomes familiar, the exotic becomes accepted, the unbelievable becomes believable, and then the second culture becomes a second home.

Paul Hanvey suggests we can discriminate between four levels of cross-cultural awareness, as seen in Table 1-1.

At level 1, tourists may note the "exaggerated" politeness and gestures of deference practiced in the Japanese culture. At level 2 they become frustrated at the hesitance of a Japanese friend to disagree or correct them when they have reached a false conclusion. At level 3 they may come to understand that the really distinctive aspect of the Japanese culture has little to do with the many levels of politeness and their linguistic and behavioral forms and much to do with the intense sense of mutual obligation between superior and inferior. At level 4, intellectual insight and emotional understanding of this cultural trait become assimilated and appreciated.

Cultural immersion does not guarantee achievement of both cognitive and affective understanding and awareness. Many expatriates, living within a host culture but not coming to value and respect it, may over time slip back to level 2. The crucial factors are the capacity to experience empathy for the differentness and the willingness to value others' perspectives alongside one's own.

According to this model, the person comes to "believe" the other culture and its forms only at levels 3 and 4. Without "believability," persons do not accept other groups as fully equal members of humanity. Affectively, those in levels 1 and 2 rarely feel that exotic others share the same biological species as truly human others. Thus level 3 is a worthy goal for all persons in the context of our present world community. The tendency to deny the full humanness of the enemy in times of war is painfully familiar; the less obvious ways of relegating others to "primitive," "aborigine," "savage," "uncivilized," or "nonmoral" categories facilitate the objectification of persons who are not seen as equal subjects. The subtle forms of such valuations emerge in numerous psychological theories that place childhood and cultural development schema in parallel lines, with childlike and primitive equated on the low end and adulthood and Western thought forms at the top. The epigenetic (child-to-adult cycle) is seen as parallel to the phylogenetic (history of human species development) and to the ethnogenetic (cultural development from primitive peoples to technological society). The implicit hierarchies within these structures, all indebted to the system of eighteenth-century German philosopher Immanuel Kant, invite conscious relegation of the "less developed nations" to the lower end of the developmental charts and unconscious reduction of their value.

The capacity not only to "believe" the second culture but to come to understand it both cognitively ("thinking with") and affectively ("feeling with") is necessary before one enters cross-cultural counseling.

Table 1-1. Four Levels of Cross-Cultural Awareness

Level	Information	Mode	Interpretation
1	Awareness of superficial or very visible cultural traits: stereotypes	Tourism, textbooks, *National Geographic*	Unbelievable, i.e., exotic, bizarre
2	Awareness of significant and subtle cultural traits that contrast markedly with one's own	Culture-conflict situations	Unbelievable, i.e., frustrating, irrational
3	Awareness of the meanings of the cultural traits that contrast sharply with one's own	Intellectual analysis	Believable cognitively
4	Awareness of how another culture feels from the standpoint of the insider	Cultural immersion: living the culture	Believable because of subjective familiarity

(Hanvey 1979:53)

The Empathic–Interpathic Counselor

All understanding begins in a movement from within oneself to enter the world of another; being understood is opening and enlarging one's experience to make room for another. Such movements toward another, in both insight and feeling, may be automatic and unconscious, as in sympathy; or they may be intentional and active, as in empathy; or they may require the envisioning of another's thoughts and feelings from within a different culture, worldview, and epistemology. We are only beginning to conceptualize this third level of identification with differing others, and we lack words to name it from our past vocabularies. Since it is a pathos, or "feeling-level way of knowing," as well as insight into a radically different perspective, we shall call it "interpathy,"* as compared to sympathy and empathy.

Sympathy is the spontaneous response to another's emotional experience, which wells up as the other's pain evokes memories of similar hurts in the past. It is a co-suffering; one sufferer knows just how the other feels by connecting parallel injuries through projective identification. Sympathy is a kind of projection of one's own inner feelings upon another, for in judging that your suffering is understandable because I have suffered in similar fashion, my emotion is felt to be one with yours. When the other person's tragedy evokes feelings connected to my own tragic past, or another's loss triggers feelings once attached to losses in my life, then my own feelings function as a barometer to measure and reflect the pressure of emotion within the other. As the Chinese proverb expresses it, "When your own tooth hurts you can understand how another's toothache feels."

In the shock of deep losses, persons often reach out for those who have suffered in similar ways. The first phase of grief work is to come to terms with the numbness and allow the realization "This has actually happened to me" to slowly take shape. Sympathy assists as one finds co-travelers who are co-sufferers. This emotive state is one of union, with little or no differentiation for healing to progress. One needs more than sympathetic union; there must be genuine contact with persons who exercise the next level of "feeling with" we call empathy, in which both union and separation, connectedness and respect for the other's uniqueness, are offered in authentic encounter.

Empathy is sharing another's feelings, not through projection but through compassionate active imagination. Empathy is an intentional affective response rather than the spontaneous automatic reaction of sympathy; it is the choice to transpose oneself into another's experience in self-conscious awareness of the other's consciousness. Thus it is enriched by similarities between the observer and the observed, but it is based on differences. Empathy respects the distinctness of self and other and seeks to enhance rather than diminish these boundaries. In empathic caring, I enter your feeling and thinking world in an effort to understand

---

*I am indebted for the suggestion of this word to Willi Toisuta, Rector of Universitas Kristen Satya Wacana, Salatiga, Indonesia.

your perceptions, thoughts, feelings, muscular tensions—even the temporary states that come and go as you speak. I seek to share your joy or pain while recognizing that it is uniquely yours, and in seeking to share it with you I do not lay claim to it as my own. I share it as I am present with you, but I recognize that it is your feeling.

Empathy, as the perception of the cognitive and affective world of a separate other, is based upon common linguistic and cultural assumptions. It is grounded in the joint worldview and the shared patterns of thinking that provide a base for the encoding and decoding of percepts. Thus a balance of union and separation, of caring closeness and clarifying distance, is maintained. Empathy is the capacity to imagine oneself into another person or role within the context of one's own culture. In a mobile community, with the rich variety of persons met and known briefly or intimately in modern society, empathy has become a necessary ability for all effective human relations. Daniel Lerner writes in *The Passing of Traditional Society* (1958:50–51):

> Empathy . . . is the capacity to see oneself in the other fellow's situation. This is an indispensable skill for people moving out of traditional settings. Ability to empathize may make all the difference, for example, when the newly mobile persons are villagers who grew up knowing all the extant individuals, roles, and relationships in their environment. Outside his village or tribe, each must meet new individuals, recognize new roles, and learn new relationships involving himself. . . .
>
> High empathic capacity is the predominant personal style only in modern society, which is distinctively industrial, urban, literate, and participant. Traditional society is nonparticipant—it deploys people by kinship into communities isolated from each other and from a center. . . .
>
> Whereas the isolated communities of traditional society functioned well on the basis of a highly constrictive personality, the interdependent sectors of modern society require widespread participation. This in turn requires an expansive and adaptive self-system, ready to incorporate new roles and to identify personal values with public issues. This is why modernization of any society has involved the great characterological transformation we call psychic mobility. . . . In modern society *more* individuals exhibit *higher* empathic capacity than in any previous society.

Some psychologists have attempted to construct continua of empathy from unconscious reflections of posture and gesture to the complete mystical union of the one with the All and of all with the One. Gordon Allport's eight levels (1954:13) are the classic definition of a scale of empathic feeling from the subliminal to the sublime.

1. Motor mimicry, as in an aesthetic response to a work of art. The lowest level of empathy, it is shown by tilting the head to match the portrait or taking the posture of the statue, in an unconscious effort toward understanding. The similarity is in the act, not the feeling.

2. Simultaneous feelings occurring in two persons in response to each other or to a situation or event. This is a spontaneous sympathy, triggered by the depth or intensity or beauty of a shared experience.

3. Emotional contagion sweeping from person to person in a crowd.

It is the emotion that brings the people together, not the commitment of the persons themselves (as in level 6).

4. Identification between persons. The similarities between persons are noted, and a feeling of common identity is shared, but not a joint identity of the two feeling boundaries dissolving into oneness.

5. Persons who know how others feel, but the understanding of the other is conscious and detached, distinguishing the self from others. The self understands how others feel but does not necessarily endorse their actions.

6. Affiliative fellow feelings. Though the feelings themselves are separated, the persons are connected in a common emotional bond.

7. Sensing the state of mind of the other by the self, which prizes and respects it fully as one's own. Boundaries are disappearing and a profound sense of oneness, of joint personhood, is felt, but it is an intentional choice of prizing the separate other.

8. The mystical union of all with the One. The empathic sense of joint experiencing of spiritual oneness connects both to each other and to the Transcendent and the universal.

A review of these eight levels reveals a rhythm between difference and similarity. The even-numbered levels suggest states of similarity, summarized as simultaneous feelings, identification between persons, affiliative fellow feelings, and the unity of all in the One. These contrast with the odd numbers, which refer to differences and to the lack of the common bond of the even levels. Thus the even numbers show movement from simple attraction, to temporary fusion of self with others, to a complete mystical union. The odd numbers indicate the need for detachment, separation of self and other, in transcendence or differentiation. Thus empathy has complex roots in both unity and uniqueness, in similarity and difference, in union and separation.

Within this scale, Allport has included sympathy as the first three levels, empathy as it is used in both social and clinical definitions in levels 4 through 6, and intimacy, unity, and shared mysticism in levels 7 and 8. All this presupposes a common base of experience that can be mutually shared and celebrated, a cultural platform for encounter and interaction. But the needed direction for stages 7 and 8 is in moving beyond empathy to an interpathic caring that can value and view the world through the experience of one who is distinctly, culturally, and epistemologically other.

Interpathy is an intentional cognitive envisioning and affective experiencing of another's thoughts and feelings, even though the thoughts rise from another process of knowing, the values grow from another frame of moral reasoning, and the feelings spring from another basis of assumptions.

In interpathic caring, the process of "feeling with" and "thinking with" another requires that one enter the other's world of assumptions, beliefs, and values and temporarily take them as one's own. Bracketing my own beliefs, I believe what the other believes, see as the other sees, value what the other values, and feel the consequent feelings as the other feels them.

Viewing an other from within, empathically, is not a skill unique to counselors and therapists. As Thomas Oden has pointed out (Oden and others 1974:40–43), such decentering of the self and entering of another frame of reference is necessary for the artist, archaeologist, anthropologist, historian, sociologist, author, actor, translator, political scientist, even geologist. However, the degree to which this moves from analytic entertaining of the other to empathic experiencing of the other varies widely from person to person as well as situation to situation.

In interpathic caring, I, the culturally different, seek to learn and fully entertain within my consciousness a foreign belief. I take a foreign perspective, base my thought on a foreign assumption, and allow myself to feel the resultant feelings and their cognitive and emotive consequences in my personality as I inhabit, insofar as I am capable of inhabiting, a foreign context. Interpathy is the voluntary experiencing of a separate other without the reassuring epistemological floor of common cultural assumptions; it is the intellectual invasion and the emotional embracing of what is truly other.

Anthropologist and philosopher Magoroh Maruyama names this process "transspection," as a step beyond analytic inspection of another culture.

> Transspection is an effort to put oneself into the head (not shoes) of another person. One tries to believe what the other person believes and assume what the other person assumes. For example, if someone claims that he sees a ghost and is scared, you try to visualize his ghost and see how scared you become. If you have questions about his ghost, you ask these questions not as an interviewer but as someone who visualizes the same ghost. Transspection differs from analytical "understanding." Transspection differs also from "empathy." Empathy is a projection of feelings between two persons with one epistemology. Transspection is a trans-epistemological process which tries to *experience* a foreign belief, a foreign assumption, a foreign perspective, feelings in a foreign context, and consequences of feelings in a foreign context, as if these have become one's own. It is an understanding by practice. (Maruyama and others 1978:55)

This capacity to join others in their world offers a bidirectional strength: one, the ability to see as others—who are truly other—see; and, two, the ability to see ourselves as others—who are fully other—see us.

Looking at ourselves from outside our own culture is a possibility for those who learn to look through the eyes of the outgroup. As Paul Hanvey comments, "Native social analysts can probe the deep layers of their own culture, but the outside eye has a special sharpness: if the native for even a moment can achieve the vision of the foreigner, he/she will be rewarded with a degree of self-knowledge not otherwise obtainable" (Hanvey 1979:55).

Western culture, with individualism assumed as a given, prizes similarities as the point of meeting, the basis of understanding, the evidence of co-feeling. Eastern cultures, with traditional cultural mores guaranteeing similarities, find differences in the new element to be discovered and the source of excitement to bring people into conversation. So sympathy is the more natural Western response, empathy more automatic in the East, and interpathy a new step to be learned by both as we build bridges between us. (See Table 1-2.)

In interpathic "feeling with," empathy is extended beyond known borders to offer a grace that draws no lines, refuses limits, claims universal humanness as sufficient foundation for joining another in a unique world of experience. Interpathic listening strives for co-perception in recognition that the perceiver and the percepts are a radically ("from the roots") foreign viewer and vision. Interpathic caring awaits the discovery of how caring is given and received within that culture before initiating

Table 1-2. The Boundaries Between Sympathy, Empathy, and Interpathy

Sympathy	*Empathy*	*Interpathy*
Sympathy is a spontaneous affective reaction to another's feelings experienced on the basis of perceived similarity between observer and observed.	Empathy is an intentional affective response to another's feelings experienced on the basis of perceived differences between the observer and the observed.	Interpathy is an intentional cognitive and affective envisioning of another's thoughts and feelings from another culture, worldview, epistemology.
In sympathy, the process of "feeling with" the other is focused on one's own self-conscious awareness of having experienced a similar event.	In empathy, the process of "feeling with" the other is focused on the imagination, by which one is transposed into another, in self-conscious awareness of another's consciousness.	In interpathy, the process of knowing and "feeling with" requires that one temporarily believe what the other believes, see as the other sees, value what the other values.
In sympathy, I know you are in pain and I sympathize with you. I use my own feelings as the barometer; hence I feel my sympathy and my pain, not yours. You are judged by my perception of my own feelings. You are understood by extension of my self-understanding. My experience is both frame and picture.	In empathy, I empathically make an effort to understand your perceptions, thoughts, feelings, muscular tensions, even temporary states. In choosing to feel your pain with you, I do not own it; I share it. My experience is the frame, your pain the picture.	In interpathy, I seek to learn a foreign belief, take a foreign perspective, base my thought on a foreign assumption, and feel the resultant feelings and their consequences in a foreign context. Your experience becomes both frame and picture.
Sympathy is a kind of projection of one's own inner feelings upon another as inner feelings are judged to be similar to experiences in the other.	Empathy is the perception of a separate other based on common cultural assumptions, values, and patterns of thinking that provide a base for encoding and decoding percepts.	Interpathy is the experience of a separate other without common cultural assumptions, values, and views. It is the embracing of what is truly other.

care-giving on patterns from one's own tradition. Interpathic identification prizes the meeting of humanness in which universals of life experience coincide, but without assuming that the interpretation or the emotional savoring of these universals will overlap or necessarily even touch. Interpathic presence enters another world of human energies and risks, making the self available to entertain what was formerly alien, to be hospitable to what is utterly new.

Interpathic Understanding

Interpathic "thinking and feeling with" another across cultural boundaries requires a willingness to bracket one's own way of knowing —one's epistemology—and enter another. This may require exploring notions completely foreign to one's assumed or preferred rational process, which must be suspended in the effort to undergo the change necessary to stand with and understand a citizen of another worldview. Most counseling training is grounded in empiricism or phenomenology. Either approach focuses on observable phenomena that are replicable, measurable, and definable by either naturalistic observation or objective self-description. Neither approach offers a useful perspective on mystic, cultic, folk religious, and commonly believed perspectives that shape many cultures.

CASE STUDY: The Gold Talisman (Indonesia)

A counselee, recently converted from Islam to Christianity, is troubled by the magical talisman that has given him power, success, and prosperity in the past. It is a gold coin, visible beneath the skin on the underside of the forearm. There is no scar, no sign of an incision. He reports that it was placed there by a Muslim priest who laid the coin on the arm, covered it with his hand, chanted the incantation, and when he took away his hand the coin was beneath the skin. The young man, having now rejected such magic, wishes to have the coin and its powers removed. He leaves the counseling interview, having decided to request prayer in the public worship service. The next Sunday he goes forward asking that this symbol and its powers be removed. The pastor shows the arm and visible coin to the congregation, then lays hands on the talisman while all pray. At the end of the prayer, the coin is in the hand of the pastor; the arm is clear, scarless, and with no sign of the previous implantation.

In other cases, the pastoral counselor reports, prayer removes the special powers experienced by the person with the embedded coin, then a surgeon at the Christian hospital removes the coin but stitches mark the operation scar.

Such actual material phenomena are outside the categories of hypnotic, hysteric, or psychosomatic description which we use to label symptoms from psychologically induced blindness to psychosocial death. But the insertion of coins in the arm, or diamonds in the temples, or the ability to walk barefoot over live coals, or pouring boiling oil over oneself from head to foot in temple ceremonies with no visible burn damage, these have been empirically verified by witnesses from within and without the culture. Such persons must be counseled from within the reality of their experience, though one possesses no scientific explanation for the phenomena observed.

(Krisetya 1984)

The case study of the Gold Talisman presents a public event that is beyond any explanations of a common scientific worldview. Gold coins do not pass through skin without rupturing tissue, sleight-of-hand does not explain what is beyond reach. The intercultural counselor, working in a culture that accepts a rich variety of experiences from the mesocosmos, must be capable of interpathic entertainment of new possibilities and their emotional consequences.

The discussion of this case focuses on the contrasting epistemologies and the capacity to transcend such boundaries interpathically in the counseling relationship. Chapter 9 will explore the relationships of magic, of shamanism, of healing in folk religions, and of witchcraft and the demonic to cross-cultural pastoral counseling.

Western scientific thought since the eighteenth century has increasingly accepted a Platonic dualism that has resulted in a two-tier world, as psychological anthropologist Paul Hiebert has described the secularization of science and the mystification of religion. These two levels exclude the traditional middle zone that is central in the epistemological model for the majority of the earth's peoples on the popular or folk level of observation.

The two-tiered view of reality offers only two levels, the religious level, based on faith, manifest in miracles, and concerned with otherworldly problems; and the scientific level, based on experience and manifest in the natural order dealing with the problems of this world (Hiebert 1982: 90; see Table 1-3).

The excluded middle leaves a vacant area in the epistemology, which causes dismay when one encounters unexplainable phenomena in another culture that violate the natural laws of the scientific realm.

In many traditional societies a three-tiered view of reality provides explanation for many of life's puzzling dilemmas. This zone of "low religion" offers answers to why the unpredictable patterns of nature— storms, lightning, rains, floods—strike one person or group and not another, why prosperity and good fortune fall on one family and misfortune and calamity on another, why a child dies or a pregnancy miscarries. It offers ways to prevent accidents, to ensure success, to guarantee the happiness of a marriage, to safeguard the health of one's children. In a Western culture these things are dismissed as luck, accidents, unforeseeable events, or tragedies that fall by the law of averages with no

Table 1-3. Two Views of Reality

The Western Two-tiered View	*The Historic and Multicultural Three-tiered View*
Religion	*High Religion*
Faith in God The spiritual dimension The Sacred Miracles and exceptions to the natural order	Cosmic beings: God, gods, angels, demons, of a world separate from this one Cosmic forces: kismet, fate, karma, or impersonal cosmic forces
	Low Religion, Magic, Mana
(Excluded Middle)	Folk religion: local gods and goddesses, ancestors, spirits, demons, ghosts Psychic phemomena: curses, blessings, special powers, astrological forces, evil eye Physical phenomena: magical rites, charms, amulets, firewalking, embedded charms, psychic surgery
Science	*Natural and Social Science*
Sight and experience The natural order Secular definition Empirical methodology Mechanical analogies Sense experience Experimentation and proof	Directly observable sensory phenomena, knowledge based on experimentation and replication. Interaction of human beings or interaction of natural objects based on natural forces

(Adapted from Hiebert 1982)

respect for persons. "But many people are not content to leave so important a set of questions unanswered, and the answers they give are often in terms of ancestors, demons, witches, and local gods, or in terms of magic and astrology" (Hiebert 1982:92).

When Raymond Firth was doing fieldwork in Tikopia, one of the Santa Cruz Islands in the Pacific Ocean, a house collapsed, causing the death of a man. Immediately the villagers set about discovering the shaman who caused it, threatening to kill the witch or sorcerer. The anthropologist gathered the people and showed them the rotten and termite-eaten poles, which everyone recognized had collapsed in the accident. They admitted the poles should have been replaced as they regularly were when poles rotted. But they saw no logic in Firth's argument of natural causation. For them the question was not "Why did the poles collapse?" as it was for Firth. They asked, "Why was this particular man sitting under this particular house at this particular time when the poles gave way?" The Western answer that these factors are simply a matter of chance or accident is neither more nor less satisfactory than the Tikopian understanding that a shaman was responsible (Firth 1957:244). We may accept the laws of statistical averages, but this evades the questions of the middle zone: "Why? To what end? For what purpose? By what power?" These are the questions that trouble the soul "when tragedy strikes," as we say—expressing the same process of reasoning rather than concluding that a random event of calamity has occurred.

The puzzling phenomena of fire walking, bathing in hot oil, extraordinary physical powers, embedded talismans, psychic surgery, healing of visible physical symptoms, invoking illness, tragedy, or death through curses, incantations, spells, dark magic—all these belong to the middle zone. In Western cultures such things are considered empty rituals or sleight of hand, effective largely by the power of suggestion or by deceit. In other cultures, these practices figure prominently in the emotional lives of a high percentage of its people. In Jakarta, Indonesia, a pastoral counselor reports that an early diagnostic question of most Christian pastoral counselors at the outset of personal, marital, or family counseling is, "Do you have any charms or amulets in your home?" In an outer-directed culture with a rich middle zone, counseling that deals only with inner-directed or interpersonal issues may be avoiding a crucial part of the counselee's reality. Holistic treatment takes the social, spiritual, and cultural forces as seriously as the developmental, emotional, familial, or marital factors. When the reported phenomena contradict the rational explanations taken as givens within the counselor's culture, the ability to suspend judgments and evaluations and interpathically enter an alternate way of knowing is necessary if there is to be communication on the primary anxieties of the counselee.

Interpathic caring enters a foreign epistemology to evaluate it not by extracultural values but rather by its own internal consistency and by its contextual congruency. When the belief system of the counselee possesses an integrity within and a congruence with the cultural field, it can have integrative power for that person, and healing and growth will emerge from using that system, not from contradicting it.

At the same time, *the counselor is not value-free; no theory of therapy is, no effective therapist will be, no human being of integrity can be.* Values are central to all truly human existence; values are essential to all healing and maturing in the therapeutic process.

The interpathic process involves an assumption of the other person's values, an experiencing of their emotional impact when fully entertained within the self, and an envisioning of their consequences within the self and between self and other. Simultaneously one's own values, although suspended for the moment, are within awareness but bracketed, to allow full hospitality to the other stance. Equal concern for the values of both self and other thus rises from the ethical commitment to prize the other's values equally with one's own, but all the while maintaining one's own value center.

Crossing Over

A theology that functions on the boundary requires a commitment to presence, to dialogue, to crossing over and coming back between worlds.

Pastoral counseling across cultures is rooted in an incarnational theology that is truly present to others and a dialogical theology that is open to others in agape.

Presence embodies grace. Dialogue actualizes mutuality and humility. Pastoral theology unites both presence and dialogue in fleshing out grace through authentic encounter that invites growth, healing, and liberation.

John Dunne has given a clear description of this dimension in the encounter of persons, cultures, and faiths. In *The Way of All the Earth* he has described the journey of "passing over" and "coming back" as the most important religious fact of our times. He writes:

> What seems to be occurring is a phenomenon we might call "passing over," passing over from one culture to another, from one way of life to another, from one religion to another. Passing over is a shifting of standpoint, a going over to the standpoint of another culture, another way of life, another religion. It is followed by an equal and opposite process we might call "coming back," coming back with new insight to one's own culture, one's own way of life, one's own religion. The holy man of our time, it seems, is not a figure like Gautama or Jesus or Mohammed, a man who could found a world religion, but a figure like Gandhi, a man who passes over by sympathetic understanding from his own religion to other religions and comes back again with new insight to his own. Passing over and coming back, it seems, is the spiritual adventure of our time. . . . The course such an adventure follows is that of an odyssey. It starts from the homeland of [one's] own religion, goes through the wonderland of other religions, and ends in the homeland. . . . One has to pass over, to shift standpoints, in order to enter into the life of Jesus, even if one is a Christian, and then one has to come back, to shift standpoints again, to return to one's own life. (Dunne 1972:ix–x)

Passing over, into an "other world," is possible for us because we share the common experience of being human. Nothing human is alien. Each of us holds within the self, potentially, a part of any other person. We share the richness and the poverty, the vastness and the finitude of being human. However, these potentials may be possessed in fragmentary or rudimentary form. All true relational growth rises from our experience of seeing through another's eyes, entertaining another's thoughts, and interpathically sensing another's feelings. It is, Dunne argues (1972:180), the means of our becoming completed as persons.

> Passing over, therefore, entering sympathetically into other lives and times, if we are on the right track, is the way to completeness. This is not an unlikely hypothesis. For whenever [one] passes over to other lives or other times, [one] finds on coming back some aspect of her or his own life or times which corresponds to what was seen in others. Passing over has the effect of activating these otherwise dormant aspects of oneself.

The benefits of this two-way pilgrimage across boundaries are described by Clasper as a personal transformation that occurs as persons move in the free air of new worlds and then return with a second wind.

> To "pass over" is to enter a new world; to "come back" is to return a different person. One is bound to look at one's own world with fresh eyes and with fresh questions once the journey of friendship has been taken. It is easy to see why a narrow, fearful sect-mentality always urges a careful restriction of personal contacts. One can be "contaminated" by alien perspectives! Friendships are risky and threatening adventures. They can draw us out of our isolation and our restricted worlds. They force new concerns, new questions, and new priorities upon us. If we want to "remain the same" it is best not to venture out in significant friendships. (Clasper 1982: 126–127)

Presence

Presence is a primary word for pastoral care and for pastoral psychotherapy. A counselor is pastoral when she or he is truly there for others, is fully present to others, and recognizes that this presence is in the name of God, who has called the counselor to be available at a depth beyond normal association. The pastoral therapist is one who has answered the call to be present with all of the self that can be owned by that person —the conscious experiences of being and the unconscious experiences as they rise to awareness. When one is truly there for another, a depth of communication occurs that is beyond words or style, or technique, or theory, or theology. It is presence gifted by Presence.

In cross-cultural pastoral counseling, the greatest gift the counselor may have to offer is the opening of the self to receive another in authentic presence. John V. Taylor, in his reflection on Christian presence amid African religion, writes, "The Christian, whoever he (she) may be, who stands in the world in the name of Christ, has nothing to offer unless he (she) offers to be present, really and totally present, really and totally in the present" (Taylor 1963:107).

Presence requires an integration of self-awareness with an awareness of the other. The consciousness of being "with" another is not a superficial association but an openness from the center of one's existence. As one is transparent to his or her own experience, the feelings, intuitions, thoughts, desires, resistances, anxieties, impulses, fantasies, and images that rise from the unconscious depths can be admitted into conscious awareness. Such self-awareness permits more complete attending to others and a willingness to perceive as much of the other's experience as he or she is free to reveal. Thus one can talk of being only partially present or of being authentically present to the depths of one's lived experience. Out of suffering, depression, and despair can come a knowledge of the dark side of experience, which, when claimed with healing acceptance, can open levels of communication and communion with fellow sufferers that is presence from the core of existence.

Presence and dialogue must not be undertaken as a means or methodology for reaching an ulterior end; each is a good in itself, like work for charity, for social justice, and for healing of alienation. The pastoral counselor is called to embody grace, to incarnate agape, to flesh out the steadfast love of God.

Incarnation and embodiment are the inevitable direction of the love of God. The solidarity of God with humanity is a central motif of the biblical history of God's relation to creatures and creation—from the accounts of creation, the pursuit of humans throughout history, the event of incarnation, to the ongoing presence of God within the believing community and the world.

God is justified by this presence, solidarity, and incarnation. In this radical solidarity with us, God accepts fully the responsibility for creating finite beings who are vulnerable to evil and remains in loving relationship with us. The abandonment we fear is ungrounded. The solidarity and community we need are the basic guarantee of grace. We are secured by the very nature of the God who created us.

God is present for us in those persons and that community which embody grace and enflesh unconditional love. The power of the pastoral is grounded in this experiencing and expression of the presence of God in human relationship.

Presence is central to all forms of ministry. Being and doing are inseparable. It is being which authenticates doing, doing which demonstrates authentic being. A theology of presence, writes Calvin Shenk, is central to any truly biblical theology.

> If we presume to approach [incarnation and presence] biblically, we are not free to choose or reject a theology of presence. Presence as incarnation is fundamental to all witness. All ministries of the church are rooted in "being present." . . . It is not enough to suggest that Christian presence is a kind of pre-evangelism but that it is not evangelism. It is not enough to see presence only as a first step in identification. Presence has an intrinsic value in itself. (Shenk 1983:32–33)

Dialogue

"Dialogue is an encounter between people, mediated by the world in order to name the world," Paulo Freire has written. An encounter between persons who name and own a private world and seek to impose it upon others is inimical to dialogue. "Mediation by the world" accepts the reality of the world as third party to the conversation, as the reality that transcends, critiques, corrects both our subworlds.

Such genuine encounter is difficult when there is a power differential between the persons or parties. When all power and authority flows one way, it is impossible (Freire 1970b:76).

Can a white "think black"? Can a Christian "think Buddhist"? Can the rich "think poor"? Can a man "think woman"? Lawrence Howard, an Afro-American writer, has suggested this important impossibility:

BOUNDARY CHECKLIST

Living on the boundary demands a repentant attitude toward one's automatic preferences for or instinctive loyalty to one's own culture, religion, or community.

Check those automatic instinctive responses which you have experienced.

Yes   No

____ ____ 1. I find I sometimes compare the worst of the other culture/religion with the best examples of my own.

____ ____ 2. I see the abuses of the other group and instinctively contrast it with my group's graces. (I avoid contrasting our abuses with their graces.)

____ ____ 3. I often note the lack of social concern by others at the point where my own group is most concerned. (I do not immediately see where they show concern that is missing among us.)

____ ____ 4. I see the lack of compassion for the poor among other religious leaders and compare it with such Christians as Mother Teresa, but I do not contrast their noblest examples with our apathetic majority.

____ ____ 5. I frequently contrast the ideal Christianity with the real Islam, Buddhism, or Hinduism, but I overlook the real contradictions in my own community.

____ ____ 6. I sometimes pit the internal consistency of Christian theology at its best against the visible contradictions of the popular or folk practices of the other faith.

____ ____ 7. I remember the other faith's tragedies of history while recalling only the wisdom, art, and beauty of my own tradition.

From safe inside one's own territory, such comparisons may go unnoticed, but on the boundary they become transparent.

> Black consciousness is open to anyone who . . . will operate in black categories. . . . Blacks, in the deepest sense, are people of any color who are dedicated to emancipation, national interdependence, freedom from fear and human fulfillment—whose priority is always people over property or machines. Blacks are all those who affirm the species in its deepest psychic dimensions. (Quoted in L. Russell 1974:165)

The choice to think black or Buddhist or poor or woman requires one to move from identity to mutuality. Mutuality means entering another's worldview, sharing that consciousness, exploring its interior, looking out at the wider world through its windows while retaining one's own worldview. One does not become identical with the other, but mutual. Identity has been joined with another's identity in reciprocal interchange and transformation.

Dialogue and hierarchy are contradictory. When one person insists on defining or describing reality in exclusive terms and possesses the power to impose the definition and description on the other, a vertical violence dehumanizes both. For the oppressor to learn the ways of dialogue, especially in communication with the oppressed, requires a series of changes. (1) Members of oppressing groups can trust the oppressed to work for liberation and to decide when they have been empowered. (2) People of the oppressor group can learn to play a support role to those working to liberate themselves and wait for the oppressed to take the lead. (3) Oppressors can become advocates, helping to break the barriers in the society. (4) Persons of oppressed groups and of oppressing groups can learn to understand the things that oppress their own lives and begin their own process of conscientization in coming to understand their own history, identity, and dignity (Russell 1974:69–70).

Dialogue is a conversation on a common subject between two or more persons who hold differing views. The goal is for both sides to learn from the other, to enter into the other's perspective and seek to understand the opposing position from within. It is as deeply committed to strengthening the other's position by contributing to any discovered point of weakness as it is to clarifying and improving one's own stance. Dialogue can begin only when there is an openness to being fully confronted and perhaps persuaded by the other view. Thus it carries the risk of change.

Two contrasting movements take place in dialogue between Eastern and Western persons. The individualist Westerner must leave the self center and go out to meet the other. The Eastern person, already at the boundary in joint identity, must withdraw into the self in order to listen.

To hear another, the individualist must open the self to admit another's consciousness, perspectives, and vision of reality with its otherness. The movement is outward; it is encountering; it is the meeting of two separate individuals.

To hear another, the corporate personality must return to the self to experience the self as perceiver, listener, separate agent.

In Japanese, the word *ningen* as "person" is compounded from *nin* ("man") and *gen* ("the space between"), which emphasizes the space between persons as central to an encounter. The two previously joined in social solidarity must withdraw into the selves in order to encounter the other as Other.

In the West, encounter means to step out of one's own self in order to meet the other person, who is doing the same. In Japan, the person is already in "the space between." In order to meet the other person, one must first come back to self, while the other person is doing the same (Kimura 1927:107).

We are concerned here with a specialized kind of dialogue, that which gradually emerges in the counseling encounter, as the initial power differential is equalized and the counselee claims his or her full privilege and responsibility in the pastoral conversations. As the pastoral therapist and the counselee grow toward more accurate perception and more complete understanding of each other, the transference and countertransference exchange decreases. As the authentic encounter of two persons apprehending and comprehending each other's self presentations grows toward full mutuality, dialogue becomes the sign of emerging maturity and health in the relationship. In cross-cultural exchange, the need for each party to own her or his worldview and to affirm solidarity with it is central to the task of inviting healing. Since the unconscious processes speak in the language, metaphor, and myth of one's people and place of birth, growth proceeds as one can freely reconnect with, reclaim, and reconcile the present with the depths of the past.

> If one is to truly hear what the other person has to say in its own integrity, there must be a breaking through of the barrier that stands between the language world of the hearer and that of the speaker. Stated more fundamentally, to "know" another means to enter that person's world in such a way that a merging of experienced reality can take place. The ancient Old Testament image that associates knowing with intercourse between the sexes expresses the truth that an intimate merger or interpretation must take place if one is to truly know another. Theologically speaking, we encounter here the primordial sense of incarnation. To know another in the incarnational sense is to enter that other's world and to have the other enter our world. Hermeneutically speaking, this is possible only because of and to the extent that we are able to enter the other's language world, the world of the other's meanings. In the same way, if we are to be known by the other person, the other must in some degree enter our world, the language of meaning we bring to the encounter. (Gerkin 1984:43)

There is a special relationship between the observed and the observer, like that between the reader and the text read. The interpretive process is reciprocal; the text interprets the reader as well as the reader the text. Just as a person reading a biblical text may discover the text is searching and disclosing new insights about the self, so every encounter with a significant document "discloses a world" that the reader appropriates. The world disclosure power of a text calls the reader to reorient the self. In understanding a text, one's own world lights up, and the situation, experienced in a new light, enlarges into a world. A broader world is opened up for us (Ricoeur 1971:536).

In cross-cultural encounter and interpretation, each person brings a "horizon of understanding" into the new situation. Within the limits of that horizon we can experience empathy; as we encounter the horizon we must reach out with interpathic openness.

> Care involves the opening of the horizon of our understanding to admit the intrusion of the world of the other in the hope and expectation that something truly new may be shared in the encounter—a "fusion of horizons" in which the other is permitted to speak, to question our understanding and vice versa. (Gerkin 1984:45)

This reciprocal process of interpreting and being interpreted, reading and being read, creates an intersubjective process of joint hermeneutics. Each is seeking to know and be known by the other. In knowing the other, one comes to know the self more deeply; in knowing oneself, one is opened to perceive and receive the other more fully.

Five basic ground rules of intercultural or interreligious dialogue must be observed if dialogue is actually to take place. First, each participant must come to the dialogue with complete sincerity and honesty. No deception, evasion, or presentation of false fronts have any place in dialogue. Second, each participant must assume a similar complete sincerity and honesty in the other partner. Either pretension of sincerity or suspicion of insincerity in the other will make dialogue impossible. No trust, no dialogue. Third, each participant must define himself or herself. Only the Buddhist can define from within what it means to be a Buddhist; another can only observe. This definition will continually deepen, expand, and modify as the dialogue progresses. Fourth, each participant must approach the dialogue without hard-and-fast assumptions as to where points of disagreement are. Each listens openly and sympathetically, agreeing as far as is possible without violating the integrity of her or his own tradition. This can proceed until an absolute impasse is reached. This, the real point of disagreement, is rarely the same as those assumed in advance. Fifth, dialogue is grounded in trust, so it is advisable to begin with those issues that are most universal and consolidate common ground to establish trust. Then dialogue can move to more thorny issues of disagreement.

Dialogue usually proceeds through three states. The first is a discovery and dispelling of misinformation and faulty assumptions as we come to know each other as we are. The second is seeing values in the other's tradition and wishing to appropriate them for our own. Third comes the discovery of new areas of reality and meaning we were not aware of before (Swidler 1981:10–12).

Dialogue is urgent and essential to repudiate the arrogance, aggression, and negativism of those evangelistic crusades that obscured the gospel and caricatured Christianity as an aggressive and militant religion. Above all, dialogue is essential for us to discover the Asian, African, or Aborigine face of Jesus Christ as the Suffering Servant, so that the church itself may be set free from self-interest and play the role of a servant in building community (de Silva 1981b:50).

Interfaith Dialogue

Japanese theologian Kosuke Koyama stresses the need for a dialogue that lays aside pretensions to superiority and practices the crucified mind of its Leader.

> If the Christian message is formulated into a chauvinistic Christianity, that is, a "superiority Christianity," "the-best-religion Christianity," and "finality Christianity," then [those of other religions] at once detect arrogance, superficiality, and unreligiousness in *our* understanding of Christianity. (Koyama 1977:88)

Koyama argues that (1) religions are not objectively comparable, since such comparison would require vast knowledge and profound religious experience of each. (2) Religious commitments belong to the world of I-Thou relationships. An "I" can be treated comparatively, a "Thou" can be compared subjectively but not objectively. (3) To judge all other religions as inferior faiths is arrogance, not an observation made by "a crucified mind." (4) Theological perception is primarily grace-grasped instead of date-grasped; it is symbolical, sacramental, and revelatory instead of being comprehensive and comparative. It is story-oriented rather than rationally and sequentially argued.

> The Christian faith would lose nothing if Christians stopped calling their faith the superior or the best religion. . . . Up to now the discussion of the finality of Christ has been predominantly formulated within the framework of Joseph's sweet dream of my-sheaf-stood-up theology. All other religions are supposed to bow down to the upright sheaf of Christianity. (Koyama 1977:88–92)

The dialogue between faiths is of particular concern to the pastoral counselor, because faith issues, faith values, and the practice of faith are the central issues in healing and wholeness. Everyone enters dialogue, particularly interreligious dialogue, with presuppositions, and it is necessary to recognize these from the outset.

Lesslie Newbigin, Bishop of the Church of South India (1947–1975), has noted four streams of assumptions:

1. All religions must make good their claims at the bar of reason. This post-Enlightenment school of comparative religion evaluates religious experience by criteria from other fields and sees it as a functional illusion. There are theories of a Hegelian type that see religion as a primitive anthropomorphic science, theories of a Schleiermacher type that see religion as a product of human psychology, and theories of a Kantian type that see religion as the result of the moral pressure of the community on the individual.

2. All religions rise from a common core of reality: from the ancient voice of the Rig Veda, "the real is one, though sages name it variously," to the Thomist "All truth is God's truth," to W. Cantwell Smith, who suggests we cease talking of different religions and speak of human religiousness (Smith 1962:48).

3. All religions can provide a practical and necessary social and political unity. As old as ancient Egypt or China, this view subordinates religious truth to other values.

4. All religions must embrace their own values, both those that are inclusive and those that are exclusive. The integrity of dialogue depends, first of all, on the extent to which participants take seriously the full reality of their own faiths as the ground of their total life experience. It is this fourth position that Newbigin recommends (Newbigin 1981:13, 15–16).

The understanding of one faith by another varies widely from group to group, but several dominant patterns do appear. I shall discuss and illustrate these from the perspective of the Christian, although the converse perceptions are appropriately held by persons in the other world religions.

Exclusivism: Other religions and ideologies are wholly false and have nothing to offer. (This refuses to see that every faith can be my teacher in its unique view of truth. Every translation of the Bible uses the traditional word for god from that culture's heritage.)

Demonic: Other religions are evil, the work of the demonic, and only distort or cleverly mimic the Truth. (This either-or thinking extends the paranoid dualism of concrete thought to cosmic extent.)

Preparatory: Other religions serve as preparations for our faith, which fulfills them. (In reality, the different religions turn on different axes. The questions Hinduism asks and answers are not the primary concerns of Christianity.)

Value balance: All religions possess many values, but only in Christ are all values found in proper relationship, balance, and unity.

Concentric: All world religions are concentric circles with the Roman Catholic Church at the center and other Christians, Jews, Muslims, other theists, other religionists, and atheists at progressively greater distances. (*Ecclesiam Suam* 1964—This fails to understand religions from within, or the paradoxical fact that those closest to the Truth may be the bitterest opponents of the gospel.)

Anonymous Christians: All believers of all faiths are anonymous Christians, since all religions are the means through which God's saving will reaches those who have not been touched by Christ (Rahner 1978:115). An expert Christian has a much greater chance of salvation than an anonymous one. (Other religionists insist this does not take them seriously; it assumes salvation is in religion and not, for example, in lived faith.)

Witness to Christ: All religions bear witness to a unique vision of the truth, and the Christian is one who has been laid hold upon by Jesus Christ to be his witness, a witness to the uniqueness of Jesus, the kindness and justice of God revealed through him, his central place in history, his position as Lord of the Church and of all humanity (Newbigin 1981: 21–24).

Models of Dialogue

There are multiple models for encounter between the Christian way and the Asian paths to spirituality—Theravada Buddhism, Hinduism, Zen. Paul Clasper depicts these as the metaphors of the dungeon, the round table, the graduation, the higher synthesis, and the crown.

The dungeon model, one of the oldest and most persistent, views all other religions as imprisoned in darkness, in a dungeon of slavery. The dungeon may be decorated, furnished, even made quite livable, but it is still inferior, inadequate, and condemned to a tragic end.

The round table model, at the opposite extreme, sees all as equal, as a genial, open "parliament of religions." The conviction is that no one has all the truth, that each is completed by all others, since all are variations on a single theme.

The graduation model, equidistant from both preceding, suggests that all religions are traditional heritages which are now fulfilled, surpassed by scientific ideology. Communism as an applied scientific sociology, secularism as a life perspective, and psychology and psychiatry when practiced as a religious worldview all offer themselves as a new vision beyond religion.

The higher synthesis, an inclusive merging of all faiths, hails the coming of a new world faith as a basis for a coming world civilization. The hope of reconceiving the Judaic and Buddhaic traditions into a common path of Being and Blessedness is largely the dream of intellectuals who hope to create a harmonizing force for world unity.

The crown of all faiths, a midpoint between the exclusive view of the dungeon and the inclusive view of the round table, notes both the similarity and the uniqueness of Christ (not Christianity) to all other faiths and sees Jesus the Christ as the completion, the crown of other paths. This perspective, from Indian writer J. N. Farquhar in *The Crown of Hinduism* (1913), sees Jesus the Christ as the summation and crystalization of the richest tendencies and highest insights of Hinduism. Christ came to fulfill, not to destroy the best of Judaism, Hinduism, Buddhism, and other faiths; he is not the enemy of other worldviews but one who challenges, clarifies, completes, and consummates the healing, liberation, and transformation (Clasper 1982:101–110).

The most useful metaphor for visualizing interfaith dialogue is that of *multiple staircases,* all of which rise from a common landing on which stands a cross. The staircases represent the many ways by which humans learn to rise toward the fulfillment of God's purpose—all the ethical, aesthetic, and religious achievements of each culture. But at the common foot stands the symbol of a historical deed of God. In total vulnerability, God exposed God self to human purposes. The cross revealed that, at the religious highest and lowest, humanity is still the enemy of God. God comes to meet us not at the top of our stairways but at the bottom. Our ascent, real and genuine as it is in search of God's purposes, takes us farther from the real point of meeting. We meet with other religions not at the peak of our insights and achievements but at the bottom of the stair in self-emptying, not in the security of systematized truth and ritualized holiness but on the common landing of human suffering, where God suffers among us, with us, in us (Freytag 1958:21).

> The Christian attitude is not ultimately one of bringing Christ *in,* but of bringing him *forth,* of discovering Christ; not one of command but of service. . . . The Christian instinctively falls in love with the positive aspects of other religions . . . because he believes that he discovers there the footprints of God's redemption, and some veiled sometimes disfigured grace which he believes he must unveil and reformulate, out of love for the neighbor and a sense of responsibility for the faith God has given him. (Panikkar 1964:45)

This openness to the presence of God in all creation, cultures, and creatures sends the Christian theologian searching for the spore of the

Spirit. There are signs of the Presence in the myths and stories of every people, so the universal mythical heritage is to be appreciated, not denigrated. The writings of C. S. Lewis offer a case study in sensing the presence of God in all human cultures. He wrote:

> God sent the human race what I call good dreams; I mean those queer stories scattered all through the heathen religions about a god who dies and comes to life again and, by his death, has somehow given new life to men. (Lewis 1952:39)

Elsewhere he notes:

> We must not be nervous about "parallels" and "pagan Christs"; they ought to be there—it would be a stumbling block if they weren't. (Lewis 1952:67)

And again:

> If my religion is erroneous then occurrences of similar motifs in pagan stories are, of course, instances of the same or similar error. But if my religion is true, then these stories may be a *preparatio evangelica,* a divine hinting in poetic and ritual form at the same central truth which was later focused and (so to speak) historicized in the Incarnation. (Lewis 1970:132)

The uniqueness of Christianity is that in the gospel "myth" has become "fact."

> By becoming fact it does not cease to be myth: that is the miracle. . . . To be truly Christian we must both assent to the historical fact and also receive the myth, fact though it has become, with the same imaginative embrace which we accord to all myths. The one is hardly more necessary than the other. (Lewis 1970:66–67)

But the real meeting point is in spirit, not doctrine, Lewis suggests.

> It is at her center, where her truest children dwell, that each communion is really closest to every other in spirit, if not in doctrine. And this suggests that at the center of each there is a something, or a Someone, who against all divergencies of belief, all differences of temperament, all memories of mutual persecution, speaks with the same voice. (Lewis 1952:9)

There is a place of crossing over, even in our most valued and sacred regions of faith. One can cross over in openness and reverence and return more rich, more humble, more alive, and more deeply centered in one's own faith in the God who is present in our midst.

Summary

Cultural awareness is a necessity in this age of global interchange, interaction, and interdependency. The survival of humankind depends on our developing increasing capacities to understand and appreciate other cultural values and views.

The intercultural pastoral counselor has definable skills that can be taught and learned. Cultural encapsulation can be transcended as one differentiates an intercultural self, develops an enriched cognitive aware-

ness of other's experience, and exercises interpathic insight and awareness.

The intercultural pastoral counselor who is at home on the boundary
crosses over and returns with effectiveness, freed by theological groundedness to function as a mediating and reconciling person. Theology on
the boundary is committed to authentic presence and genuine dialogue
between cultures, faiths, and values.

2

The Universal, the Cultural, the Unique

A Theology of Culture

"Culture is dictatorial unless understood and examined. It is not that humans must be in sync with or adapt to culture, but that cultures grow out of sync with us. When this happens, people go crazy and they don't know it. In order to avoid mass insanity, people must learn to transcend and adapt their culture to the times and to their biological organisms. To accomplish this task, since introspection tells you nothing, we need experience of other cultures; i.e., to survive, all cultures need each other."

—*Edward Hall, 1976*

THE MAKING OF FIRE
ARABIAN FOLKTALE

Once there was a man who discovered how to make fire.

This man, named Nour, traveled from one community to another teaching his discovery. Some received the knowledge gladly; others drove him away thinking he must be dangerous before they could learn how valuable fire could be; finally a tribe became so panic-stricken by the fire that they killed him, fearing that he was a demon.

Centuries passed, and a wise man and his disciples passing through the lands discovered that one tribe reserved the secret of fire for their priests, who were warm and wealthy while the people froze; another tribe had forgotten the art but worshiped the instruments and the ashes; a third worshiped the image of Nour, who once made fire, but had forgotten the secret; a fourth retained the story and the method in their legends but no one believed or tried it; a fifth used the fire to cook, to give warmth, and to manufacture all kinds of useful goods, even bronze and iron.

The disciples were amazed at the variety of rituals and said, "But all these procedures are in fact related to the making of fire, nothing else. We should reform these people." The teacher said, "Very well, then. We shall retrace our journey. By the end of it, those who survive will know the real problems in teaching people and how to suggest change."

So the teacher and disciples attempted to teach as Nour had taught. They too were scorned, abused, driven away. At the end of their journey, the master said, "One must learn how to teach, for no one wants to be taught. First you must teach people that there is still something to be learned. Then you must teach them how to learn. Then you must wait until they are ready to learn. Then you will find that they learn what they imagine is to be learned, not what they really must learn. When you have learned all this, then you can devise a way to teach." (Adapted from Shah 1967)

"Every person is in certain respects (a) like all others, (b) like some others, (c) like no other." With these oft-quoted words, Kluckhohn and Murray (1948) defined the three dimensions of being human: the universal, in which a person is "like all others"; the local or cultural, in which one is "like some others"; and the individual, in which each is "like no other." These three dimensions allow us to examine our essential humanness, our cultural embeddedness, and our individual uniqueness: human nature, culture, and personality.

Every human being is like every other. We are much more alike than we are different. Nothing that happens in one human person is totally foreign to another. There are commonalities, shared responses that rise from our essential humanness. We are all born helpless, we grow from dependence toward self-management, we relate to other beings and to a physical environment, we age, and one out of one dies.

Every human being is shaped, formed, patterned by the community that calls him or her into personhood. This matrix of values, beliefs, customs, religion, and basic life assumptions which we call culture is shared with and similar to those who share that community.

Every human being is unique, a unique world of perceptions, feelings, and experience. No other person will ever see, think, feel, celebrate, or suffer in the identical way. Each has a unique genetic code, one-of-a-kind voice patterns, fingerprints, dental patterns; each a distinctive life history and developmental sequence and a particular life-style.

Some counseling theories focus predominantly on the uniqueness—the *ideographic*—and reject the imposition of culturally defined expectations or universally true natural laws. Other theories focus on common experiences and the similar characteristics of all persons—the *nomothetic*—and put less stock in individual peculiarities. We shall maintain in this chapter that the culturally effective pastoral counselor is informed by all three dimensions and differentiates among them with insight and clarity. Only when the universal is clearly understood can the cultural be seen distinctly and the individual traits respected fully; only when the person is prized in her or his uniqueness can the cultural matrix be seen clearly and the universal frame be assessed accurately. The universal unites us as humans, the cultural identifies us with significant persons, and the individual affirms our identity. (See Figure 2-1.)

"Like All Others":
The Universals of Human Nature

We are all much more alike than unalike.

> Men and women differ, one from another, within each society. And certainly they differ even more radically from one culture to another. Yet certain aspects of the human situation remain common to us all. In the final analysis, perhaps we are all more alike than we are different. (Kopp 1971:3)

The simple equivalence of cultural variability and behavioral variety with personality diversity is not appropriate. There is, affirms Michael Spiro, a much greater constancy in the area of personality—"the system of cognitive, perceptual, motivational, and affective dispositions 'underlying' behavior" (Spiro 1978:355).

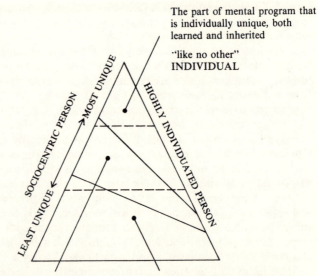

The part of mental program that is individually unique, both learned and inherited

"like no other"
INDIVIDUAL

The culturally shared part of mental program, virtually all learned from the context

"like some others"
CULTURAL

The universal elements of mental program, shared by all humans and almost entirely inherited

"like all others"
UNIVERSAL

Figure 2-1. Model of human commonality and uniqueness.

Persons along the right side of the model are much more differentiated as individuals, those on the left more collective—culturally and biologically determined.

However much societies differ, they all must cope with common biological features, especially prolonged infantile dependency; the adaptively viable means for coping with this exhibit common social and cultural features across a narrow range of social and cultural variability; these common biological, social, and cultural features are a set of constants which, in their interaction, produce a universal human nature. (Spiro 1978:355)

After surveying the cross-cultural search for universals stretching across the last half century, Walter J. Lonner concludes:

There is ample evidence that striking similarities, if not an avalanche of universals in human behavior, far outweigh substantive differences. For that matter culture(s) may be viewed as an opaque veneer covering an essential universality of "psychic and somatic unity." (Lonner 1980:147)

The great number of universals are evidenced by the work of Yale University's Human Relations Area Files, which from their beginnings in 1936 have collected ethnographic source material from over three hundred cultural groups. These files now list eighty-eight categories of universals in human nature (Murdock 1961). Table 2-1 offers such a listing, arranged in alphabetical order to emphasize their variety.

Table 2-1. Human Universals

Age grading	Food taboos	Mournings
Athletic sports	Funeral rites	Music
Bodily adornment	Games	Mythology
Calendar	Gestures	Numerals
Cleanliness training	Gift giving	Obstetrics
Community	Government	Penal sanctions
organization	Greetings	Personal names
Cooking	Hair styles	Population policy
Cooperative labor	Hospitality	Postnatal care
Cosmology	Housing	Pregnancy usages
Courtship	Hygiene	Property rights
Dancing	Incest taboos	Propitiation of
Decorative art	Inheritance rules	supernatural beings
Divination	Joking	Puberty customs
Division of labor	Kin groups	Religious ritual
Dream interpretation	Kinship nomenclature	Residence rules
Education	Language	Sexual restrictions
Eschatology	Law	Soul concerns
Ethics	Luck superstitions	Status differentiation
Ethnobotany	Magic	Surgery
Etiquette	Marriage	Toolmaking
Faith healing	Mealtimes	Trade
Family	Medicine	Visiting
Feasting	Modesty concerning	Weaning
Fire making	natural functions	Weather control
Folklore		

(Adapted from Murdock 1945:124)

From a review of studies of human universals, a pattern emerges. Similarities are most pronounced on the biological level, increased variation appears in the psychological, greater variety exists in the interpersonal and social, with the greatest contrasts occurring in the institutional and the broader worldview levels (Figure 2-2).

Luzbetak describes human needs as falling into three groupings: biological needs, derived needs, and integrative needs.

> The primary needs are those which the human organism shares with other animals. . . . The second class of imperatives is termed "derived" because the various needs are "derived" or arise from man's social nature. Man cannot survive except collectively. . . . The third category of needs is called "integrative" because the needs in question do not seem to be absolutely necessary for the purely biological or social nature of man but rather emanate from man's intellectual and moral nature. (Luzbetak 1970:173–179)

Social Constants

Any society must have ten functional prerequisites if it is to survive, and every society exists as a system balanced by at least these functions. It must (1) deal effectively with the environment, (2) provide for its sexual reproducibility, (3) make role differentiations and role assignments, (4) have learned systems of symbolic communication, (5) have a populace with shared cognitive orientations, (6) share an unarticulated set of goals, (7) have a normative regulation of means to achieve the shared goals, (8) regulate affective expression so that it is mutually communicable and comprehensible, (9) provide for the socialization of its new members by transmitting the essentials of the social structure, and (10) effectively control forms of behavior that are disruptive to the society (Aberle and others 1950:100).

If a culture emerged in complete isolation from any other, hypothetical as this may be, a number of functions and social structures would appear: language, property rules, incest and marriage rules, myths, legends, music, dancing, neuroses, and psychoses, to begin the list. These would be present, says Fox, because we are the kind of beings who do these things (Fox 1971:284).

Thus we may conclude that five dimensions are universally present among humans: *biologically* we are a common species, *socially* we have common relational prerequisites; *ecologically* we must adjust to a common atmosphere and a limited number of climates; *spiritually* we invariably seek to touch the numinous, the transcendent, the meaning of our existence; and *psychologically* we have an intraspecies sameness of processes.

Bronislaw Malinowski (1944:91) postulated seven basic biological and psychological needs common to all humans. These seven needs are seen as impulses to act. The act is a cultural function leading to biological and psychological satisfaction. This process he called the "permanent vital sequence" (see Figure 2-3).

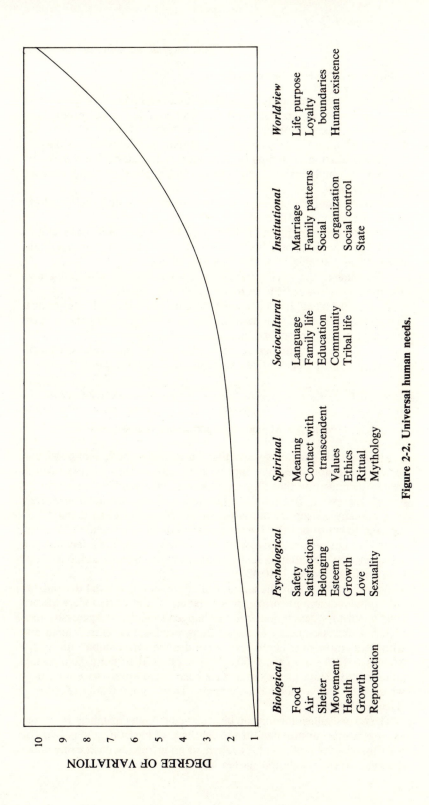

Figure 2-2. Universal human needs.

Malinowski's seven basic needs are:

1. Metabolism, the needs for oxygen, liquid, and food. This need is met in every society by an organized behavior system for the production, distribution, and consumption of food and liquid. Humans vary in what is eaten, when, how often, how, with whom, and by what customs.

2. Reproduction, including the sexual drive, the survival of the society, and marriage and kinship customs that connect, place, and train a person for that society.

3. Bodily comforts, a range of temperature, humidity, shelter, clothing, and protection of the body.

4. Safety, the prevention of bodily injuries by mechanical accident or attack from animals or other humans. This includes defense methods, weapons, and strategies or the rejection of these.

5. Movement, the activity necessary to all organisms, which functions instrumentally toward the satisfaction of other needs.

6. Growth, from the dependency of childhood through the gradual maturation process to the defenselessness of old age, and the support necessary to sustain or facilitate it.

7. Health, the maintenance and repair of the biological organism, including hygiene, preventive care, and cures for illnesses.

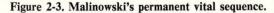

IMPULSE ————————→ ACT ————————————→ SATISFACTION
(Drive or need)   (Cultural)   (Biological and psychological)

Figure 2-3. Malinowski's permanent vital sequence.

Although all people have similar basic needs, both biological and social, aggression does not appear to be one of them. Cross-cultural studies demonstrate that all people do *not* have similar dispositions to act out aggression. In a number of societies, violent conflict is extremely rare, and any concept of war is absent. As Margaret Mead noted, "Neither the Eskimos nor the Lepchas in the Himalayan mountains understand war, not even defensive warfare. The idea of warfare is lacking, and this idea is as essential to really carrying on a war as an alphabet . . . is to writing" (Mead 1940:403).

What is clear is that the amount of aggression displayed depends on cultural values and historical circumstances. Cultures that were historically pacifist for generations can be changed to violently aggressive peoples. Semar tribesmen of Malaysia, long pacifistic in temperament and with little knowledge about war, were drafted into combat during the Malaysian civil war of the 1950s. "Taken out of their nonviolent society and ordered to kill, they seem to have been swept up in a sort of insanity which they called blood drunkenness. They thought only of killing" (Dentan 1968:142).

The reverse phenomenon can be observed in many instances in history as long-hostile cultures can turn to centuries of harmony and peace. The warring tribes of tenth-century Japan, as an intriguing case, came under a largely peaceful rule that lasted almost nine hundred years.

Four Global Constants

Basic human needs, similar as they are, create a great area of human experience, shared across cultures, with a significant degree of commonality in the biological, psychological, spiritual, and sociocultural realms.

1. *Human beings are biologically similar.*

> *Homo sapiens* is one unitary species to which all living humans belong. There are indeed physical differences among the people of certain global areas, but the differences between groups in the same area may be of even greater magnitude. Thus the Watutsi, the tallest people on earth, and the Pygmies, the shortest, live within a few hundred miles of each other. Both have black skin, which seems to be the sine qua non of race for those who think the concept "race" has any significance. (Murphy 1979:18)

Various scholars argue that the very attempt to classify human populations according to race is not worthy of discussion (Montagu 1964:14). The term should be forgotten as useless since there is much more variety within than between "color" groups. The stereotyped differences of color, features, and stature are inconsequential when one notes that human anatomy, reproduction, and all bodily functions of physiology are virtually the same the world over. The only major biological difference among humans is sexual, and that difference is within, not between, races and cultures. United as we are by a common biological constitution, we humans share problems common to members of all societies. These needs are cared for in vastly different ways, but the biological imperatives provide a basic framework for the construction of the first level of all cultures.

2. *Psychologically, there are major areas of commonality.* Often called "the psychic unity of humankind," the basic processes of perception, memory, reasoning, emotion, and volition are essentially identical among humans, as are such psychic defenses as rationalization, projection, attribution, denial, and reaction formation. Maslow's analyses of the sequence of levels of psychological needs appear to have universal applicability on the first three levels. The need for esteem and for actualizing life's meanings takes a more corporate form in many cultures in contrast to Maslow's assumed individualism. This hierarchy of needs rises from deficiencies in the organism and requirements from the emerging self. As such, they can be seen as biologically based or, as he suggests, "instinctoid." As physical needs and safety needs are satisfied, social-relational motivations become prominent. As these are fulfilled, personal-esteem needs and life-meaning needs reach toward actualization.

3. *Humans are united by spiritual similarities.* The interrelationship of a sense of the transcendent, of moral values, of some kind of a symbolic eternity, of explanations for the presence of good and evil in existence, and of some means for understanding the forces of destiny when "encountering the beyond" appear in the religious formations of every cul-

ture. The essential self-interest of the human individual—what is seen as
the root of sin in all major world religions—appears to be universal in
all humans from an early age.

4. *Socioculturally, humans create structures with intriguingly parallel
patterning.* Biological, psychological, and spiritual needs elicit a great
number of cultural forms and functions performed by every culture. The
similar cognitive capacities of all humans, coupled with the common
biophysical needs, are related to the resemblances between the institutions of different cultures. The major differences in institutions do not
seem to lie in variations in basic human needs or in differences in the
fundamental reasoning processes, but in the selection of different premises for logic and of different parameters for its exercise and conclusions.
So each society, with its common needs and reasoning capacities, creates
institutions that maintain the social system, unite the group by inhibiting
the fracturing caused by individual self-interest, and harness the strength
of persons to facilitate corporate action. "Human society . . . is the means
by which the ego-centered psychobiological needs of the individual are
both given satisfaction and held in check, for these ego-oriented needs
—whether they are food and protection, sexual gratification, or personal
self-satisfaction—can only be attained by man in a social interaction
system" (Goldschmidt 1966:59).

Homo sapiens is a "sapient" or knowing animal, but the forms of logic
vary from one culture to another, with some prizing linear sequential
thought or tightly propositioned rationality, and others a holistic intuitive assessing of reality. However, certain processes of thinking consecu-
tively and analytically and the organization of the human mind have a
uniformity across cultures.

Structural Constants

The conviction that certain structures or modes of organization are
hereditarily human and common to all humankind has been growing
through the convergence of structural psychology and linguistics. The
first strand comes from the structural thought of Jean Piaget, who suggests that there are regular and inherent pathways for the development
of reason that are ascertainable at various levels of child development.
This accommodation-assimilation model of brain functioning sees the
child as encountering new experiences and incorporating them into its
mental organization of data by a process of accommodating to the new
reality, then assimilating the information into a new, more advanced
schema, only to encounter additional data, which leads to further accommodation, and so on. This is based on Kantian and Hegelian
thought and its philosophical empiricism is patently Western, but with
correction and clarification by other cultures it is opening new understandings of our shared primary rationality, though varied in its secondary forms.

A second strand grows from the linguistics of Noam Chomsky (1960), who has found certain grammatical regularities suggesting that deep below the surface organization of conventional grammar there lies a basic infrastructure—a structure of structures—that is a hidden organizer of grammar. Grammar is not a totally learned facility; rather, one learns it according to an inbuilt predisposition and along prewired pathways. The acquisition of the formal rules of language is made possible by these deep human mental structures, and the grammars, though richly varied, conform to these primal structures. Since grammar is a form of logic, this postulation of latent patterns hypothesizes an inherent rationality that is a universal human capacity.

Humans possess an innate language ability that provides a language readiness in sequential development.

1. All children in all cultures learn their language at the same time; that is, between the ages of eighteen months and four years. The process begins between eighteen and twenty-four months of age. In no known society does it begin earlier or later.

2. All children in all cultures learn their language at the same rate. By age five, children in all societies have usually mastered the grammatical structure of their language.

3. There is no known primitive language; all are adequate for the task of communication. All known languages have a fully developed grammatical structure and are capable of expanding to incorporate any new technology or concepts that enter that society. Not only are there no known primitive languages now, there is no evidence that primitive languages ever existed.

Thus there is a readiness factor involved in language acquisition. Human beings have an innate language ability. There is no evidence for the evolution of language.

The school of thought known as structuralism, developed by Claude Lévi-Strauss, suggests that the structure of the psyche is universally the same, and the essential working of the human mind involves a continual sorting of perceptions into paired opposites, which are then reconciled. The mind is a dialectical faculty. So we define what an object is by contrast with what it is not, thus producing a panhuman logic rooted in the neurophysiology of the brain. This binary process may be accounted for from the essential nature of language and words, since a word is both inclusive and exclusive, or from the dual and symmetrical structures of anatomy and sense organs. But the parallels beneath the many varied expressions of logic point to common cognitive capacities in all humankind. We are truly one species.

Psychological Constants

Seen from the counselor or therapist's chair, the human personality seems to show a pattern or configuration of psychological needs, like vectors, which move the person in a basic rhythm, inward and outward: toward making the center firm and toward contacting the boundaries, toward understanding the past and envisioning the future, toward self-affirmation and toward intimacy or relatedness with others, toward stability or consolidating the present and toward mobility and a growth or change. The character of each of these poles is culturally shaped, as is the absence of emphasis on either pole in some settings. But the rhythm is constant. Human beings think by sorting things into opposites, positives and negatives. Some groups think preferably in dialectic, others in dualisms, still others in a polar sort of holism. This universal tendency toward binary logic, as Durkheim concluded, is present in all reasoning and rationality, and it is evidenced in the personality rhythms, which may move freely or be stuck and frozen.

In every person, culture, and group, there are four basic psychological universals, as Frank Kimper, professor of pastoral care at the School of Theology at Claremont, teaches. These four thrusts are central to humanness. They are expressed in varying degrees and in richly different ways in each culture, but they are invariably present. There is a thrust toward *self-affirmation;* every being senses his or her own worth, rejoices when it is recognized by another, and responds with hurt or anger when it is negated. There is a thrust toward *relatedness;* to be human is to be related to significant others, and we both need and need to be needed. There is a thrust toward *individuation;* every human possesses and prizes distinctiveness, uniqueness, a differentness from all others, although this is expressed in contrasting ways, from Western individualism to personhood within the group. There is a thrust toward *growth,* the movement from the helplessness of infancy through maturity to the defenselessness of old age. These thrusts, when trusted, are self-regulating. They are trustworthy. To come to trust them, honor them, and express them in balance is to be centered, to be whole, to be human (Kimper 1971).

"Like Some Others": The Commonalities of Human Culture

Human beings are both inventors of and inventions of culture. The effective pastoral counselor is a constant student of her or his own culture and the cultures of others being served. He or she must move constantly and without apology across the boundary into the parallel discipline of anthropology, because its skills and contributions are indispensable for all therapy.

Anthropology is the study of the phenomenon of humanness—the human mind, body, origins, development, tools, art, and groups and the patterns or configurations that these form. These patterns of human experience we call "culture," with the word used variously to designate the global "human culture" or narrowly to define the specific historical and geographical patterns of human existence in a particular group or locale.

Anthropological study of human culture is done only by humans from within or without that culture, but not by persons without culture. Absolute objectivity must be recognized as a pretense; the most one can hope for is relative objectivity based on the characteristics of one's own culture. "Absolute" objectivity would require that the anthropologist have no biases and hence no culture at all (Wagner 1981:2).

Since each person belongs to a culture, each stands in a position of equality with every other. Thus the observer and the observed respond from equivalent cultures. No absolute, infallible method exists for grading, ranking, or grouping cultures into types or levels, so the position of "cultural relativity" enables us to bring together two cultures as parallel varieties of human phenomena and to seek understanding by valuing each equally.

"We might actually say that an anthropologist 'invents' the culture he or she believes her/himself to be studying. In the act of inventing another culture, the anthropologist invents his own, and in fact he reinvents the notion of culture itself" (Wagner 1981:4). The relation that the anthropologist builds between two cultures is through the invention of a set of analogies that translate one group of basic meanings into the other, participating in both systems of meanings in the same way that their inventor does. In experiencing this second culture, the student also comes to realize new potentialities and possibilities for the living of life that may trigger significant personality changes through the process of coming to understand a new worldview. (See Figure 2-4.)

This is, of course, parallel to the way in which each person becomes a self within the constraints and freedoms of the surrounding and nurturing culture. We create a self out of the world of cultural convention. The invention of personality is a dialectic, a movement between and a synthesis of our voluntary choices and the expectations and demands of the environment.

> The trick of learning personality is that of learning not to take oneself (one's personality) seriously, of mastering the technique of creating and responding to guilt (in ourselves and in others) in such a way that the conventional distinction between what one is and what one does is maintained. It is the art of invention in a world whose serious business is the articulation of convention. (Wagner 1981:82)

The conventions of culture, representing "the way of thinking, feeling, believing of a group (the group's knowledge stored up for future use)" provide the directions for the person's growth, the family's life cycle, the community's existence (Kluckhohn 1948:54). We are born without culture, although the act of birthing begins the imprinting process. Within three years the child will be largely enculturated as Japanese, Javanese, Chinese, or African. The interaction between what are biological and hereditary givens and what are cultural, social, and familial gifts stamps the child's emerging personality indelibly.

Our social, cultural, natural "worlds" shape our world of perceptions and our way of perceiving. A classic illustration comes from the work of Colin Turnbull. While investigating the "world" of the B Mbuti Pygmies in a tropical forest of such density that one could see only a few yards in any direction, he chose to test the contrast of an open "world." He took one of the Pygmies, Kenge, to a clearing where a herd of a

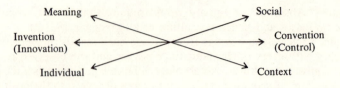

Invention	*Convention*

Invention	*Convention*
The individual's own choices and actions are a significant input in determining the self. We create the world of convention out of the needs, values, and views of our inner selves.	The individual is a product of the society. We create the self out of the world of convention, the expectations, values, and beliefs of our culture.
The self in Western culture is skewed toward the individual and the particularistic and prizes the inventive. (Yet this is patterned by cultural convention.)	The self in Eastern culture is skewed toward the collective and the corporate and values the conventional. (Yet this provides a context for invention.)
The invention of personality is a dialectic between voluntary choice and the constraints and guilts of convention.	The conventions of being "a self" define our understandings of "innate," "instinctual," "natural," and what is social or communal.
Invention is possible only for one anchored in the context of convention.	Convention is only sustained and carried forward by acts of invention.
When convention predominates: neurosis	When invention is exaggerated: hysteria

Invention and convention must be kept in creative tension
and stabilizing balance.

DIALECTIC

Figure 2-4. Cultural relativity.

Culture rises from a dialectic between the individual and the social world, between invention and convention, between innovation and control, between meaning and context.

hundred buffalo was grazing a mile away. Kenge asked what kind of *insect* they were. He insisted that they were insects, even when Turnbull took him by car to drive through the herd. As they came close to the animals and they appeared increasingly larger, Kenge became frightened. Even after recognizing the buffalo, Kenge was puzzled about how they had suddenly grown larger and wondered if some kind of witchcraft were being worked on him (Zimbardo 1977:235).

The nature vs. nurture controversy, which seeks to differentiate the contributions of heredity and environment, inevitably resolves into the acknowledgment of each person's dual heritage—our biological physical endowment and the cultural context that surrounds us from the beginning of each life. The interrelationship of the inner potentials and the family's possibilities, of the hereditary tendencies and the environment's opportunities and reinforcements, make these two aspects of the same developmental reality. Like the two sides of a coin, nature and nurture are the faces of the same reality which we call humanness. We humans are both given in our origins and gift from our environment. To be human is to experience and express both.

We are shaped by culture but not determined, just as we are endowed by heredity but not determined. This perspective corrects theories of cultural determinism. As Goldschmidt notes:

> While it is true that no human can ever be truly culturally innocent, it is still not true to say that human behavior is culturally determined. While it may be true that it is possible, out of cultural motives, to make *some* individuals do almost anything and many individuals do *some* things, it is not true that culture can make *all* persons do *anything*. (Goldschmidt 1966:133)

We are directed by the flowering of our prewired potential, but the potential becomes actual within the forms of culture. Culture is so inevitably present and pervasive that even in the most desperate attempts to flee from its power, such as in experiences of insanity, the madness is still patterned by the culture's norms and rituals.

Four assumptions on the acquisition, character, and dynamic of culture by George Foster offer a widely accepted summary of anthropological thought.

1. *Culture is learned.* The patterns of behavior that form a culture are not genetically or biologically determined. At birth, every normal infant has the potential to learn any culture.

2. *A culture is organismic.* As a logically integrated, functional, sense-making whole, culture is not an accidental collection of customs and habits. It is more like an organism, with all parts related to each other in relationships of both harmony and conflict, of both complementary unity and stress and strain.

3. *Culture is dynamic.* All cultures are constantly changing; no culture is completely static. Change rises from inventors and discoverers within, but more frequently from exposure to ideas, tools, and techniques of other groups.

4. *Culture is transacted through symbols.* A symbol is some form of fixed sensory sign to which meaning has been arbitrarily attached. Persons within a cultural tradition share common symbols with common understandings. Those outside this symbol system take great risks in inferring the meanings of symbols from the context of their own system. (Foster 1962:12–19)

The relationship between sociocultural variables and psychological variables is one of the most intriguing and important questions in intercultural research. Sociocultural forces shape the person's development; psychological dynamics direct the unfolding of the personality. How do these two relate?

Anthropologists have been primarily concerned with the impact of culture on personality, psychologists with the variables of psychic formation and functioning. What effects do these two varieties of variables have

each upon the other? Is either the determining factor, or are both interdependent? (Hunt 1967:xi)

Six different relationships between these two kinds of variables have
been hypothesized.

1. *Culture is personality.* The sociocultural variables are the dominant
determinants of personality, and the psychic variables are irrelevant. For
example, Durkheim argued that social factors are best explained by other
social factors, not by psychic variables (Durkheim 1951:310–311). Thus
culture is personality, personality is culture in miniature.

2. *Personality is culture.* The sociocultural variables are dominant, and
the psychic variables are dependent upon them. This has been a dominant position in cultural anthropology, so that it is axiomatic that most
psychic variables, including much of the personality, are largely determined by cultural conditioning; that is, shaped by tradition or custom.
Thus culture determines personality, not vice versa, which leads to anthropological reductionism.

3. *Personality creates culture.* The sociocultural variables are dependent upon the psychic. This places the psychological variables in the
dominant position to create and control culture. For example, Freud in
The Future of an Illusion and Malinowski in *Magic, Science and Religion*
both maintain that human anxiety about the life cycle and the encounter
with finitude in face of "the beyond" give rise to the complex of religious
rituals. Thus all human activity can be explained by studying individuals,
which leads to psychological reductionism.

4. *Personality mediates culture.* Personality is a connective or a mediator between two aspects of culture, the one made up of determinants of
personality, the other consisting of expressions of personality. *The primary institutions* consist of the socioeconomic structure and the child-
rearing practices, constraints, and influences; *the secondary institutions*
consist of religion, art, folklore, and expressive media. Thus primary
culture creates personality, which in turn creates secondary aspects of
culture.

5. *Personality and culture are parallel systems.* Psychic and cultural
variables are distinct separate elements but interdependent and mutually
influencing and cannot be brought together in linear cause-and-effect
relationships. Thus culture and personality are linked in a kind of chain
reaction, each in turn changing the other. Gregory Bateson exemplified
this view in 1936 when he defined *ethos* (the culturally standardized
mode of cognition) and *cultural structures* as two parallel phenomena
that he called the "essential elements" of patterned human behavior
(Bateson 1936:118), but in later writing he moved to position 6.

6. *Personality and culture are parts of an organic system.* Psychic and
cultural variables are interacting elements of a living system in a continuous interaction and constant collaboration and compromise. The system
is composed of society, culture, economics, and personality, all of which
co-relate in interdependence. These abstractions are energy fields and are
not to be handled as concrete entities. This view models the relation

between ethos and cultural structure as being like a river and its banks: the river molds the banks, and the banks guide the river. So ethos molds the cultural structure and is in turn guided by it. "In fact, 'ethos' and the rest . . . are labels for points of view voluntarily adopted by the investigator" (Bateson 1972:84–87).

A systems perspective sees the multivalent patterns of all these elements as interrelated without arranging them in chains of causal sequence. This is the most satisfactory view for integrating all the variables in the patterns of personality, family, community, and society that compose the megapattern we are calling culture.

"Like No Other":
The Uniqueness of Human Personality

Every individual is a unique world of experience, with a personal history distinct from every other, a constellation of traits, gifts, strengths, and weaknesses differing from all others, and a self-conscious center of life experience never replicated by any other.

The uniqueness of a person—the clustering of traits, attitudes, values, actions, thoughts, and feelings characteristic of the individual—we call "personality." This personality is composed of both unique elements that are distinct from others and unifying elements that are shared in common. Each cultural group inculcates certain core or central elements in the earliest years of growth, but never with a unanimous regularity that produces core uniformity. There are options available for choice, from the earliest learning to the most complex, and although a culture leaves its imprint on every member, it is in the form of patterning rather than precise replication. As the child grows and personality takes more visible "character," the options increase with the broadening of cognitive ability, so we can speak of a primary personality core from early childhood, which is largely shared with others in the culture, and a secondary personality complex, which is constructed from the wider series of options in roles, relationships, and status ascribed or achieved in the social group. As Kluckhohn and Murray observe (1948:55), "Each individual's modes of perceiving, feeling, needing, and behaving have characteristic patterns which are not precisely duplicated by those of any other individual."

In cross-cultural studies of continuities and contrasts between persons, personality has been the most frequently examined psychological variable (among intelligence, perception, cognition, hostility, aggression, security, psychopathology, and social psychiatry). However, personality has been so variously defined that correlation of these studies is difficult.

The concept of personality has these common elements in most theories, whether psychological or anthropological in orientation (Hunt 1967:xiii):

1. Personality refers to the individual organism.
2. Personality refers to the long-term, relatively permanent constella-

tion of capacities, central tendencies, energies, and processes in the organism.

3. Personality is both innate (genetic and temperamental endowment) and acquired (learning on both conscious and unconscious levels).

4. Personalities are individually unique. No two personalities, even identical twins, are the same in every detail.

5. Personalities unfold through a unique sequence of developmental tasks and social experiences. The personality is the end result of this complex series of events.

6. Personalities share commonalities, similarities, virtually identical part processes.

Most psychological anthropologists have assumed that there are similarities between individuals in a given culture and that these similarities are important. However, research has failed to demonstrate such uniformity in more than 40 percent of a population. Thus societies do not replicate uniformity throughout the entire population; rather, a complex culture requires differentiation and contrast. A complex culture could not exist without a rich diversity of persons, personalities, and psychic traits. Instead of a model of replicated uniformity, we must look for a model of organized diversity. The division of labor in a culture demands a psychic division of types and traits (Wallace 1961:84ff.).

Every society demonstrates a wide distribution of personality types, inviting and rewarding uniqueness. The greater the individualism, the more overtly visible is the diversity. But in collective societies the variation, though covert and less visible, is still wide. Individuality exists even when individualism is not acceptable. Uniqueness is present even where uniformity is most valued.

With both similarities and differences present in each person, the ultimate uniqueness of each personality is the product of countless interactions between temperament, endowment, environment, and the process of development.

A systems view of the emergence of personality variation sees multiple factors interacting to create the one-of-a-kind configuration of each human person. (1) *Temperament* includes the constitutional variability of activity, sociability, emotionality, and impulsivity (Buss 1975:8). (2) *Endowment* reflects the differences in intellectual capacity: memory, verbal and quantitative skills, and abstract reasoning ability. (3) *Environment* refers to parental, familial, communal, social, and cultural variables. (4) *Development* traces the journey through the stages of life that each person marks out in a never-to-be-replicated pattern.

Although uniqueness is distinctly visible and crucial to the identity of each person, similarity is equally important. Human beings are, by and large, more similar than dissimilar. In spite of sharply contrasting cultural norms, customs, and mores, the members of those cultures may have more in common with each other—between cultures—than they have with some members of their own group.

There is much evidence to indicate "that people are more alike than are cultures; that the average behavior under any culture tends toward the center of the range for humans as a whole. There is a good deal of evidence that, for instance, the average Zuni and the average Kwakiutl man behave a good deal more like each other than the normative patterns of the two cultures are alike (Goldschmidt 1966:134).

Kardiner (1945:vi–viii) and Linton in the early studies of culture and personality offered four assumptions that have remained working propositions for many perspectives on culture and personality.

1. The individual's early experiences exert a lasting effect on lifelong personality formation, especially on the development of the projective system.

2. Similar experiences will tend toward producing similar personality configurations in the individuals who are subjected to them.

3. The techniques used by members of any society in the care and rearing of children are culturally patterned and will tend to be similar, although never identical, for various families within the society.

4. The culturally patterned techniques for the care and rearing of children differ from one society to another.

From these propositions, one may infer that members of any society will have many elements of early childhood experience in common, and thus there will be shared elements of personality. Yet within any society's patterns of child rearing the possibilities of variation offer great opportunities for personal idiosyncrasies and individual choice.

Universal, Cultural, Particular

The universal, the cultural, and the individual may be seen in the case study Stages of Dying. The universals are clear: Death is common to all persons, and the dying process elicits review, grief, and separation anxiety in every culture. "Death awareness is a natural sequel to the development of self-awareness—an intrinsic attribute of humankind. The consciousness of transience . . . is thus a universal phenomenon" (Palgi and Abramovitch 1984:385).

CASE STUDY: Stages of Dying

Japan	United States
A patient with stomach cancer undergoes surgery and is told he has an ulcer. After several years, he is hospitalized again for repeated "ulcer" surgery, but the cancer has metastasized and is inoperable. He is told the surgery "went well." The patient feels secure and hopes for recovery, but the condition worsens. Suspicion	A patient with a gastric disorder is suspected of cancer. The surgeon informs him of the possibility before surgery and of the malignancy hours after the patient regains consciousness. His immediate response is one of denial, followed several weeks later by a period of rage. As recovery from the operation

emerges, followed by anxiety, depression, resignation, and finally acceptance of impending death. At no point has open conversation on dying occurred.

progresses, he begins quietly bargaining with God for another ten years. The recurrence of symptoms triggers a period of depression. In two months, as his health deteriorates, he begins to view his approaching death with acceptance.

Stages Observed in Japan

1. Hope. A strong sense of hope for health, recovery, life is fostered by health care, family, physicians.
2. Suspicion. As the condition worsens, suspicion expands and concern about symptoms grows.

3. Anxiety. Suspicion grows into anxiety with insomnia, panic, and fear. Some extroverted persons ask about their condition, then express anger at the silence or answers given.
4. Depression. Most patients do not ask and move into depression. The irritable also grow quiet and depressed when rage passes.
5. Resignation and acceptance. Resignation is passive abandonment. Acceptance is positive calm, an open attitude toward death.

(Kashiwagi 1980:66–76)

Stages Observed in America

1. Denial. "No, not me!" The instant response is denial of reality. This cushions the impact of the inevitable.
2. Rage. "Why me?" The awareness of one's own death and of the going-on-as-usual elicits anger.
3. Bargaining. "Yes, me, but what if I . . . ?" The fact of death is accepted, but the time is negotiated, promises made.

4. Depression. "Yes, it is me." Mourning begins for past losses and life unlived, and grieving for the approaching end.
5. Acceptance. "My time is very close now, and it's all right." The final stage is peaceful acceptance of the finality of death.

(Kübler-Ross 1969:38–137)

The cultural patterns are more complex. They are interconnected with values, worldviews, social-relational patterns, and religious beliefs. In Japan, the deep respect for dignity and face reduces the amount of openness practiced by family and physicians. Americans prefer open confrontation, even with tragic news. Americans can't stand ambiguity, while Japanese are used to it. Westerners recognize and express open anger, while Japanese prefer subtle negation or cautious irritability. Where Westerners, whether theists or agnostics, still bargain with God, the Japanese do not. Their cosmology does not offer a sovereign power who can be swayed by human strategies of persuasion, so they move from hope and suspicion directly to depression.

Americans believe that they have the right to know everything that affects them and their destiny. Japanese prefer not to ask, even when "the doctor knows and the patient knows that the doctor knows that he knows" (Kashiwagi 1980:70).

The individual way of dying is as unique as are human personalities. In every culture, the introverted are less likely to express fears and grief; extroverts are more likely to question, protest, converse, and commune with others on their grief work. Variations in hostility, negativism, irritability, and sociability, for example, occur in every culture and become more distinct and pronounced in the dying experience.

The universal (human givens), the cultural (human context), and the individual (human uniquenesses) shape the dying process of each group as well as of each person. What is universal in caring is the longing for community, communion, and communication by all persons in the stages of dying, although what can be said about death and how it is shared varies culturally and individually.

Unity and Diversity

After examination of "fake universals"—religion, marriage, property—which are similar only in name, Geertz concludes:

> There is no such thing as a human nature independent of culture. . . . Without men, no culture, certainly; but equally, and more significantly, without culture, no men. We are, in sum, incomplete or unfinished animals who complete or finish ourselves through culture—and not through culture in general but through highly particular forms of it: Dobuan and Javanese, Hopi and Italian, upper class and lower class, academic and commercial. (Geertz 1973:49)

Humans live in the information gap between what the body reports and what they must know in order to function, and they fill that vacuum with the information and misinformation provided by culture. The boundary between what is innately controlled and culturally controlled is indistinct and in constant change. The capacity to speak is innate, but language and content are cultural. Ideas, values, acts, and emotions are cultural products composed of innate capacities, tendencies, and drives but manufactured all the same.

> If we want to discover what man amounts to, we can only find it in what men are: and what men are, above all other things, is various. It is in understanding that variousness—its range, its nature, its basis, and its implications—that we shall come to construct a concept of human nature that, more than a statistical shadow and less than a primitivist dream, has both substance and truth. (Geertz 1973:52)

We must locate humanity not "behind," "under," or "beyond" custom and culture but within it. Thus "humanity is as various in its essence as it is in its expression." This need not result in either cultural relativism or cultural evolution. The study of culture as a symbolic system can focus on what is, in all its variety and particulars, without seeing all as relative or ranking all toward a selected goal.

Throughout the history of cross-cultural studies, three major ways of accounting for human diversity have received wide support. The tendencies have been to minimize it, to rank-order it, or to see it systemically as relative and related.

The universalist view maintained that diversity is a superficial overlay, an opaque veneer covering an essential universality of psychic and somatic unity. It held that exotic intellectual approaches and idea systems, which appear totally alien at first glance, are seen upon analysis as more like our own than they initially appeared. This perspective, yielding to the impact of social evolutionist thought, tends now to be only one pole of a dialectic rather than considered an adequate inclusive view.

The evolutionary perspective is committed to the view that alien idea systems are different and that they differ in a progressive way that indicates rank ordering in a natural progression from primitive to advanced states. Thus other people's systems can be categorized as incipient and less adequate stages in the development of advanced humanity. The selection of the normative model to be considered the end point of the ideational ladder of development coincides with the observer's culture: Western anthropologists saw their own culture as the end product of a long development toward "the perfect culture"; Japanese and Chinese theorists did the same.

Cultural relativism emerged in reaction to such ethnocentric absolutizing of a particular culture, first with an exaggerated absolutizing of relativity, which stressed diversity to the point of denying underlying human universals, then moderating to a balanced relativity, which correlates both the universal and the culture-specific. Cultural relativism is committed to the view that alien idea systems, while fundamentally different from our own, display an internal coherency that can be understood but not judged by our own.

This correction of egocentric reasoning, as anthropologist Walter Goldschmidt of the University of California observes, moved us from seeing others as arrested or stunted in growth and allowed us to see them in their true wisdom and folly alongside our own insight and ignorance.

> For as astronomy moved the earth away from the center of the universe and biology moved man out of his unique position in the living world, so, too, anthropology has removed Western man from the pinnacle and quintessence of human perfectability and placed him with the Australian aborigine and the Hottentot as one of so many diverse cultural beings. (Goldschmidt 1966:ix)

A relativism that respects the integrity of cultural differences is essential to cross-cultural pastoral care, but also a relativism authentically related to each culture on its own terms *and at the same time* to transcultural values (see Table 2-2). We do not work in a value-free universe, but amid a basic regard for justice and a respect for the integrity and dignity of each cultural group. Three rules of thumb for a principled relativism are:

1. "The principle of contextualization." Every piece of behavior and every belief must be considered in "the framework within which" it takes

Table 2-2. Three Models of Interpretation of Human Diversity

Universalism	*Evolutionism*	*Relativism*
Views intellectual diversity as more apparent than real. Exotic idea systems, alien at first blush, are really more like our own than they appear.	Views alien idea systems as truly different from our own but in a special way: other people's systems are really incipient and less adequate stages in the development of our own understandings.	Views alien idea systems, while fundamentally different from our own, as displaying an internal coherency which can be understood but cannot be judged.
Homogeneity	*Hierarchy*	*Pluralism*
"Apparently different but really the same." Diversity is sacrificed to equality.	"Different but unequal." Diversity is not only tolerated, it is expected, then ranked.	"Different but equal." Equality and diversity are held in creative self-corrective tension.
When confronted by differences, there are two powerful ways to discover universals: 1. Emphasize general likenesses and overlook specific differences (the "higher-order generality" rule). 2. Examine only a subset of the evidence by restricting data (the "data attenuation" rule).	When confronted by differences, rely on a three-stage rule of thumb for ordering variety: 1. Locate a normative model. 2. Treat it as the end point of development. 3. Describe diverse beliefs and understandings as steps on an ideational ladder moving in the direction of the end point.	When confronting differences, relativists seek to preserve their integrity by establishing the coequality of the variegated "forms of life." Two rules of thumb are used: 1. Contextualization rule: The premises, standards, views, framework are crucial to all understanding. 2. Arbitrariness rule: Equally rational persons can look at the "same" world and yet arrive at different understandings.
Difficulties: The pursuit after a "higher-order generality" may lead to fragmentation that destroys the actual instance.	*Difficulties:* There is no normative model for many areas of social thought: viz., distribution—to each equally, to each according to need, or to each according to work. There is no guarantee that one does not judge in defense of the present, the status quo.	*Disadvantages:* Egalitarian as it may be, it offers no basis for common negotiation. Thus it supports intellectual domination or "force of arms" in subduing conflict; in a value-free universe, majority, might, or wit wins.

(Adapted from Schweder and Bourne 1982:99–103)

place. This includes the premises, the surrounding standards, the over-arching worldviews—what is beneath, around, and above the item or event.

2. "The principle of arbitrariness." Equally rational persons can look at the same world and yet arrive at different understandings. Multiple perspectives exist on the simplest of assertions as well as on the most complex.

3. "The principle of groundedness." All pluralism exists in polar relationship to particular values. Plural contexts can exist when pro-tected by safeguarding values such as justice, mutual concern for the integrity of the other, and the prizing of the other as Other. Relativism must be grounded in universal values, not in an absence of values. An uncritical pluralism that renders the observer incapable of seeing both the functions and dysfunctions of a particular social behavior or institu-tional pattern eliminates the ground of authentic observation. As Goldschmidt concludes:

> It was necessary for anthropology to go through a relativistic phase in order to relieve social philosophers of the habit of evaluating cultures in terms of our own culturally determined predilections. Yet by now we can certainly appreciate the contextual value of infanticide without advocating it, or can see the merits and demerits of polygamy without concern over our own convictions or regulations. . . . There are enough instances on record of primitive peoples not being happy in their own customs but (like many a married couple) not knowing how to escape them . . . so that we, too, should begin to understand the phenomenon of dysfunction and establish relevant criteria for functional efficacy. This means, among other things, that we anthropologists must rid ourselves of the Rousseauean "good savage," must cease to use ethnographic data either as an escape or as a vehicle for expressing our personal social discontent, and begin to look at primitive societies for what they can tell us not only about the possible but about the probable, and about the consequences—to individuals and to societies—of either. (Goldschmidt 1966:138)

Beyond Relativity

Relativity arises inevitably from the "shock experience" of encounter-ing an alien society. "All forms of culture shock are *ipso facto* relativiz-ing," Peter Berger notes. "Indeed, at the core of the shock is the insight that perceptions and norms previously taken for granted are now re-vealed to be highly relative in terms of space and time" (Berger and Kellner 1981:56).

Any encounter with a second culture may nudge one off the safe bank of monocultural superiority and into the stream where nothing is fixed and all is as relative as swimming with no footing or balance. One need not remain in this relativity indefinitely. Emerging on the far bank, one may discover a new sense of universals that embrace both the relative and the absolute, both the contextual and the universal.

Pascal's famous phrase that what is truth on one side of the Pyrenees is error on the other recognizes that our notions of truth and error are shaped by the accident of birth in a particular location of geography and history. On the northern slope, the French hold value A; on the southern the Spaniards espouse value B. Each group possesses a different *plausibility structure,* by which different definitions of reality are conceivable and believable. However, plausibility and validity are not identical. Although we all live in a world of relativities, no one is immune to actual consequences. This does not make scientific objectivity impossible. Its possibility is grounded in a person's ability to maintain multiple *relevance structures.* One may be a "cultural relevance structure," which is plausible because of its congruence with one's historical context; a second may be a "scientific relevance structure," which is plausible because of its tested congruence with objective, replicable, measurable reality (Berger and Kellner 1981:62).

A third reality structure may offer philosophical, theological, or ethical value positions, which allow judgments of rightness or wrongness, truth or error, fitness or unfitness. None of these are possible within the scientific plausibility structure, since they are simply outside its scope and process. The relativities of the social world must be transcended by the world of scientific observation, and the scientific realm must be transcended by the value structures. Thus a radical relativism that reduces all structures to a common relativity is neither operational nor defendable; rather, it is circular in logic as well as process and makes it impossible to compare anything with anything. Apples and oranges can be compared as varieties of fruit, fruits and vegetables can be compared as varieties of botanical foods, etc.

By transcending one plausibility structure we may enter another, which allows us to speak of both relativity and truth, of contextual variability and universal reality.

These become confused in modernity. Scientization prefers the descriptive and discards the normative. As Peter Berger expresses it, "Scientific value-freeness (perfectly proper within the scientific relevance structure) becomes value-freeness in everyday life (where it has no proper place)" (Berger and Kellner 1981:64).

Both the normative and the descriptive are essential, necessary to social, intellectual, scientific, and moral life. We must journey through cultural relativism, with all its insight and definitive power, and retain its strengths while entering succeeding levels of transcendence that allow historical, philosophical, ethical, and theological integrity to emerge.

Theology and Culture

Culture mirrors theology. Theology reflects culture. Consider this folk tale called "The Mirror," known in China as early as the Tang dynasty (A.D. 618–906).

> Wang the Third was a stupid man. One day his wife wanted him to buy her a wooden comb and, being afraid that he would forget it, she pointed at the narrow crescent moon and said, "Buy me a wooden comb, just like the moon in the sky."

A few days later, the moon shone full and round. Wang the Third remembered what his wife had told him and, since his purchase was to be like the moon in the sky, he bought a round mirror and took it home.

The moment his wife saw it, she burst into tears, stamped on the ground, fled back to her parents' house, and said to her mother, "My husband has taken a concubine."

The mother-in-law looked into the mirror and said with a sigh, "If only he had chosen a young woman! Why did he take such a hideous old hag? You should never return to him. Get a divorce!"

When they brought the mirror as evidence before the district judge, he looked into it and said, "How dare you mock me, dressing up someone else in my robes. It's unbelievable!" And he threw them out of court. (Eberhard 1965:179)

Theology reflects one's culture, but to use the reflection to conclude that this is all there is is to live in a house of mirrors. To see the reflection as a way of clarifying one's perceptions and correcting one's vision is to allow theology and culture to fulfill their common tasks.

As we examine universal humanness, cultural humanness, and the individual human being, each discipline employs a different language and focuses on its preferred level. Anthropology has dealt primarily with the second, psychology with the third. Theology seeks to define origin, meaning, and destiny on all three planes. A cross-cultural approach to pastoral counseling must respect the integrity of each language world. Each of the three disciplines—theology, anthropology, and psychology—interprets human experience from its particular vantage point—universal, local, individual—or from a synthesis of all three. A theology of culture must be rooted in multiple cultures corrected by universals and applied to individuals.

A theology of universals—such as grace, justice, love, power, mercy—has been the domain of systematic thinkers for centuries. Pastoral counselors reflect on such theological issues with breadth and richness. In therapy, these central concerns direct the healing relationships and correct the imbalances both in participants and in the process.

A theology of particulars—such as prizing the worth of each person, respecting the uniqueness of each personality, supporting the ethical choices of an individual, integrating the relationships of persons, families, and communities—has been the major focus of application in practical theology. Pastoral counselors specialize in theological reflection on such human situations.

A theology of culture—such as the meaning of being cultural beings and the significance of structures, institutions, and systems—has received much less attention and tends to be overlooked in practice. This excluded middle of human experience is theologically crucial in pastoral care and counseling across cultures.

Such theologizing must be open to a broadened historical past that includes all human history, to a broadened human experience that embraces all cultures, to a broadened future that opens theological thought to the ongoing work of God among the nations of the world. This is to build not a neutral theology but a responsibly inclusive one.

> There is no such thing as a theology immune from cultural and historical
> influences. Theology is culturally and historically not neutral. A neutral
> theology is in fact a homeless theology. It does not belong anywhere. But
> theology really begins in earnest when it identifies its home and discovers
> its belonging. (Song 1978:20)

The beginning point for pastoral theology must be both local—
with a particular case, person, instance—and universal—with all humankind, human culture, and human history. Awareness of both the
universal and the particular offers a constant corrective and directive to creative theologizing. Four basic beginning points can be affirmed.

1. *All human beings are the subjects of theology.* From being white,
male, and Teutonic, theology has been enlarged across the boundaries of
color, gender, geography, and culture. Black theology has shattered the
illusion that whites can speak for all other colors. Feminist theology has
revealed the male pretensions in portraying a God who is a sovereign,
power-oriented, male autocrat. Liberation theology from Latin America,
Oceania, and Korea has moved the frontiers of thought from Europe and
North America to the two-thirds world.

2. *All human life is the raw material of theology.* From dealing primarily with the sacred, the holy, the philosophical, the abstract, theological
frontiers have encircled all issues that affect life, all concerns that engage
human anxiety or create human pain. The focus is enlarged from the
church to include all creation, from the concerns of one Christian community to caring for all humankind.

3. *All human cultures are the locus of authentic theology.* From the
idolization of Western culture as the true expression of God's work with
humanity, theology has begun to see that all cultures are within God's
care for the nations; no culture or history is outside the reach or without
the presence of God. Every culture offers background to the saving work
of God, every culture is a God-given context for theological reflection
and direction.

4. *All human history is preparatory to, revelatory of, and hospitable to
theological thought.* From "the historical supremacy of the history of
Israel and Christianity," theology can be at home in all world history.
History is theologically meaningful, not simply as it records the advance
of the kingdom of God as defined by Israel and the church of Christ but
as it reveals the mystery of God's ways with the nations. Western theology has tended to see other streams of world history as meaningful only
insofar as they came within the onward movement of Christianity, but
every people's past, every cultural history, is both our common human
story and God's story of divine presence in creation. The decisive factor
in all history, from the Christian theologians' point of view, is Jesus
Christ. In Christ, God acted most fully, decisively, and self-revealingly
as compared with all history. Our simplistic, linear, culturally bound
views of history must be broadened to be both earth story and God's
story.

Theology is the work of interpreting God's presence and work with all humanity. Thus all persons must root their theologies firmly in their own culture while expanding that theology's vision and perspective. This alters the way in which one views humans as creators and creations of culture, tradition, and history.

Cultural Creations and Creators

Human beings are cultural beings. Humans create culture; humans are created by culture. As producer and produced, we exist in this circular pattern of causality. We are shaped by culture from the moment of birth, and we participate in reshaping our culture as we develop personally and evolve communally.

Much of a person's life is created by the givens of culture. One person can create comparatively little in a lifetime of change and growth. From birth we begin to walk pathways built by others long before. Our lives require little creativity because a wealth of options stretches to the horizon, inviting us to explore all that has been constructed by preceding generations. Signposts along the way guide us by the social, moral, and behavioral norms of those who traveled this way before. These pathways help us through virtually impassable terrain and make possible our assault on unexplored territory or unconquered peaks.

Cultural pathways provide the objective realities of life, the clearly defined, marked, traveled pathways of that piece of social terrain. The subjective realities of each individual—the perceptions, preferences, perspectives—fill the journey with meaning. This meaning content of values, beliefs, and commitments is the stuff of religion that fills the structures provided by culture.

The relationship between religion and culture is that of form and content, Paul Tillich argued.

> Religion is the substance of culture, culture is the form of religion. Every religious act, not only in organized religion, but also in the most intimate movement of the soul, is culturally formed. Religion as ultimate concern is the meaning-giving substance of culture, and culture is the totality of forms in which the basic concern of religion expresses itself. (Tillich 1959:42)

The temptations pull in both directions, worship of the form in cultural idolatry and obsession with the content in a religious domination of the culture. As Chinese theologian Song Choan-seng says:

> There is a dialectical relation between religion and culture. When the tension between the two is broken, then one of two things may happen, namely, either religion is culturalized, that is, becomes a part of culture, or culture is indiscriminately identified with religion. When this happens, religion loses its prophetic function. (Song 1979:13)

The identification of faith with culture is, sadly, a universal process. "Western culture" and "Judeo-Christian thought" are terms often used interchangeably. When cultural form and religious substance are seen as separate yet interlocking aspects of human existence, culture becomes more dynamic and adaptive without sacralization reifying its structures, and religion becomes more authentic and prophetic in challenging the culture's forms.

Culture and personality are related circularly. Each creates the other, and each is a creation of the other in six key elements.

1. *Humans are social beings.* We are created social persons by biological need, developmental necessity, cultural direction, emotional attraction, spiritual motivation, and communal interaction. To be human is to be of the group and in the group. To be mature requires inclusion in a tradition-bearing group. To be fully human requires even more—the gaining of history, tradition, morality, and spirituality through the medium of group membership.

2. *Humans are historical beings.* We record, define, and interpret history; we are directed and determined by it. We are formed as much by history as by nature. The sequence of historical faces that humans have taken reveals the multiplicity and the commonality of persons across the centuries. Any cultural imperialism that proclaims one face to be the only appropriate or fully satisfactory one is invalidated by its own as well as by all human history.

3. *Humans are traditional beings.* We learn tradition from the preceding generation, we teach it to the next. Our cultural forms and patterns are historical creations passed as by a bucket brigade down the fire line of generations by explicit instruction and implicit example. Language is exemplary as a cultural tradition, created in history, handed from parents to children. As persons, we are initiated by heredity but completed by culture and tradition.

4. *Humans are moral beings.* Moral capacity forms in childhood, but it is also formed by the moral values of the society, of tradition, of history. Subjective values—chosen by the person from inner preferences —and objective values—defined by the moral community—both contribute to the formation of moral conscience and direct moral choice. The development of ritual in early childhood provides the capacity for uniting history, tradition, sociality, and morality into political structures and the creation of law.

5. *Humans are political beings.* We are born into traditional structures of institutions—marriage, family, community, state. These form our relationships, and we in turn form or reform these structures in a search for both acquisition and security, avarice and justice, self-interest and altruism. As political creatures we live in, by, for, and under these structures of human existence.

6. *Humans are spiritual beings.* We are meaning makers, driven by a will to meaning. We are meaning seekers. We search for meaning in relationships, in community, in history, in life, and in death. We are goal-directed beings—we seek goals for life and choose values as both means and ends. We are worshiping beings. We feel awe, reverence, and

wonder for the transcendent, for "the beyond," and express it in respect for the sacred in its many forms. We are questioning beings, who can conceive of ultimate questions probing the origin, nature, and purpose of things.

Culture and Values

Cultures integrate themselves around a central cluster of values. These take the form of institutions, structures, and political establishments. Secular cultures and religious cultures alike have been constructed around values such as power, privilege, and patriarchy, values reserved for the few, preserved for those with special rights.

Alongside these cultures of the powerful stand the cultures of the poor, powerless, and oppressed. These suffering people form a culture separate from and over against the culture of systems and establishments. It is with this people's culture that Jesus identified the kingdom of God.

Jesus inaugurated a people's culture, a culture in which people— women, children, and men—matter more than anything. He initiated a culture that values justice, mercy, and love beyond all other values. His culture of shalom confronts all other cultures that build oppressive systems and justify power by coercive means.

The pastoral counselor who is culturally effective comes to respect and deeply value the cultures of both the powerful and the powerless. There is healing and mediation to be done in both since pain, estrangement, and the fracturing of persons and relationships are stranger to neither. But the pastoral counselor, because of profound theological rooting in the life, teaching, and movement begun by Jesus Christ, leans toward the side of the oppressed, the abused and misused. Thus the people's culture is a primary concern of the theologically guided helper.

The people's culture is a culture of protest. The suffering of great injustices has been woven through their customs and mores, through their stories and myths, through their values and visions of life's destiny. The women, even more than the men, have absorbed the injustice of centuries and woven from it a dynamic living pattern of cultural wisdom. It is a culture of conviction. Out of human pain rises commitment to life, to each other, to the possibilities of change, a revolution that can free the downtrodden and set a world right side up. It is a culture of conscience, for out of the bearing of injustice rises a cry for a new justice, a call for a new equality that redistributes opportunities and resources. It is this people's culture of suffering and protest, of oppression and conviction, of injustice and conscience to which the pastoral counselor instinctively belongs if the title "pastoral" is descriptive of the inner nature of the counselor's life.

Among the many cultures encountered, the pastoral person is drawn irresistibly, from the depth of theological rootedness, to embody acceptance where there has been rejection, to enflesh grace where there has been only a meritocracy, to extend equality where there has been exploitive hierarchy, to work for justice where injustice has reigned.

The pastoral counselor must be able to see the presence of God in the cultural development of groups from other worlds of religion, politics, and social philosophies. The ethnocentric assumption that God works among Christians or Jews alone must be questioned. The depth and richness of cultures of great profundity and creativity are no less gifts from the Creator than are our own. God's exclusiveness is not to be stressed to the point where it diminishes God's inclusiveness. God has included the whole of humanity within the circle of divine judgment and grace.

The pastoral counselor must also be able to determine what is truly human and what is inhuman in cultures. For the Christian, this discerning arises from the comparing of cultural manifestations with the life and model of Jesus Christ. Christ is the center, culture the context. In Jesus Christ, God has said "yes" to all that is human and "no" to all that is inhuman. As cultures develop in creative or destructive directions, the counselor finds in the Christ a personified basis for judgment and evaluation.

The pastoral counselor finds the goal of cultural growth, the power for change, and the means of redeeming cultures from their destructive forces in the truth modeled in the life, teaching, death, and living presence of Christ. This transforming power of Christ is demonstrated in the community of faith, which incorporates people of different cultural traditions and backgrounds into a true fellowship with one another in Christ. The task of the faith community is not to create a Christian cultural system; the church is sent to live within and do its transforming mission through the existing cultural system.

John Howard Yoder has written of the mediating, bridge-building, transcultural role of Jesus in a way which clarifies the uniqueness of the vision that gives power to pastoral counselors as they cross over in ministry.

> Jesus participates in localizable, datable history, as many religious hero figures do not. Jesus intervenes in the liberation from violence and he identifies with the poor, as many savior figures do not. He contributes to the nuts-and-bolts reconstruction of forgiving community, as many people planning to change the world do not. His memories have created, despite much betrayal by his disciples, a nearly worldwide communion, as some of the great culture religions have not yet done. His message interpenetrates with the realms of politics and culture, as some forms of devotion do not. Let these specimens stand for the longer list of traits of *relative* fruitfulness of Jesus as mediator in cultural clashes and changes. (Yoder 1983:70)

Summary

The intercultural pastoral counselor is sensitive to what is universal, cultural, and individual. The universals—those biological, psychological, social, and spiritual elements that are essential to humanness—are shaped, filtered, and channeled by the cultural context, and out of these emerge individual uniqueness and particular specialization.

The universal, the cultural, the particular are visible in every area of human behavior; for example, in the stages of dying. What is shared can be differentiated from what is distinct to the person. The variety in human diversity on the cultural and individual levels can be interpreted from the viewpoints of universalism, evolutionism, and relativism. Each offers strengths, although relativism is the most widely accepted approach.

The pastoral counselor views the universe, its cultures, and its peoples from a theology that addresses both universals and particulars. Culture is the form, theology is the content of human experience.

An intercultural theology values humans as social, traditional, moral, political, historical, and spiritual beings whose life together reflects and creates meaning out of joy and pain, relatedness and alienation, life and death.

3

Individualism, Individuality, and Solidarity

A Theology of Humanness

"Traditional culture defines the individual's identity in the following onto-logical formula: Cognatus ergo sum: I belong, therefore I am. To belong is to participate in and contribute to the life and welfare of the family. This is in opposition to the individualistic dictum of Descartes: Cogito ergo sum: I think, therefore I am. It is not the individual's capacity to think which is the prime source of his or her identity formation, but rather the reality and the ability of belonging, participating, and sharing. The sharing of one's life with another's leads to wholeness and guarantees health."

—*Masamba Ma Mpolo, 1985*

A WISE MAN SOLVES HIS OWN PROBLEMS
AFRICAN FOLKTALE, YORUBA TRIBE

In the older days there lived a man called Alatishe. He had huge money and many wives. The first wife had borne him three children. The rest were yet childless. One day Alatishe's eyes began to pain him, and he began to spend money to cure his eyes, but all was in vain and he became blind.

Then a second misfortune befell him that brought even greater sadness than the first. He became impotent and lost the privilege of sleeping with his wives. He ran from one herbalist to another, who told him lies and robbed him of much money. Still he continued, thinking, A man who refuses to buy lies will never buy a truth. When his money came to an end, all his wives left him except for the senior wife and the junior one. The senior wife thought in her stomach, Now only my children will remain to divide Alatishe's land after his death. But the junior wife loved him and wept with him for his sorrows.

One day Alatishe was sitting in front of his house when a wood pigeon flew into his lap, panting and frightened. "My blind father," it said, "do not suffer me to die a hot death. Save me from the hawk that pursues me. If you help me, I will open your eyes again." Immediately Alatishe hid the bird in his robes.

Then the hawk appeared. "I am dying of hunger," he said. "If you give me the pigeon I shall give you great power to sleep with your wives again."

Alatishe was confused. Was it good to have many children but never see them? Or to see his beautiful young wife but not be able to enter her?

Then he called his senior wife and asked her advice. Immediately she answered, "You must save the pigeon. It is not good to walk in darkness. Your children shall bear you children and that is enough. You shall have eyes to see them. If your power returned you would lose it in growing old. Let the hawk find other food. Save the pigeon from the bitterness of death."

This did not satisfy Alatishe, so he called for his junior wife. She said, "I beg of you, my husband, give up the pigeon and regain your power with a woman. I want to bear you children. And what is the sun, moon, and stars to you compared to sons and daughters?"

Alatishe hung his head like a banana leaf thinking of the different advice from his two wives. He said to himself, "I, Alatishe, must solve my own problem." Then wisdom entered his head. He sent his young wife to buy another pigeon and hid it under his cloak. Then he said to the hawk, "If I satisfy your hunger with a pigeon will you fulfill your promise?" "Yes," cried the hawk, and pounced instantly on the offered bird. Alatishe, to his delight, felt his blunt knife grow sharp again. Then he freed the first pigeon and regained his sight. When all his wives heard that he had regained sight and strength they returned and bore him many children.

Thus the man who succeeds in the end is always the wise one who does not listen to much advice from others, but who knows how to solve his own problem. For no other person ever has your own interest fully at heart. Even your own wife may not care whether you go blind or impotent. (Condensed from Gbadamosi 1969:365–370)

All Western thought about human beings begins with "the individual." Eastern thought is more likely to begin with the family, African with the tribe. Each finds it difficult to understand the basic assumptions of the others.

In Western thought, our two cardinal ideals are equality and liberty. These assume as their common principle and primary exemplification the idea of the human individual. Humanity is made up of individual humans, and each is conceived as representing both her or his uniqueness and, at the same time, the essence of humanity. This individual is quasi-sacred, absolute, the final irreducible unit of value in society. There is nothing over and above the individual's legitimate demands; her or his rights are limited only by the identical rights of other individuals (Dumont 1970:5).

The individual is, in short, a monad (a self-contained independent unit), and every group is an aggregate of monads. This stands in polar contrast to the views of collective humanity, a society in which persons are corporately linked to one another. As the young Marx wrote in youthful exaggeration, "It is society which thinks in me." The truth in this assertion is as profound as is also the freedom of choice it denies. We do think the thoughts, perceive the perceptions, and choose from the options offered us consciously and unconsciously by our society. We are free, in part, because we are obliged to be free by our society. Westerners have a greater obligation to think and act freely than do members of many other groups.

We humans, and to an exaggerated degree among Western humans, "have a strange need to imagine that what happens to us is unique in order to recognize it as our own, whereas it is the bread and tears of our particular collectivity or humanity. When a hackneyed truth, hitherto foreign to me, becomes a truth of experience for me, I am apt to imagine that I have invented it" (Dumont 1970:6).

Persons are persons, each with an individual and unique experience but made up of many common elements. It takes nothing from our humanness to recognize this. Tear yourself away from the social fabric that has created and nurtured you, and you are left not with an individual person but with the potential for organizing a person. Personhood rises from peoplehood. Individual consciousness does not spring fully capable, already equipped, from the affirmation of self; it is enriched and supplied by the enveloping culture.

In traditional society, the society is the end and the human individual is the means. In Western society, society is the means and the life of each individual is the end. Ontologically, the society no longer exists; it is no more than an association of beings who contract to cooperate to reach their individual ends. In traditional cultures, the society is a *people,* which exists as a whole greater than the sum of its individual parts and from which each individual draws life, receives being, continues family, learns personhood, and expresses the culture's wisdom.

Tribal Identity

Dr. Jacob Loewen once asked a group made up of Africans and Western missionaries to decide on the main point of the story of Joseph in the Old Testament. The Westerners all pointed to Joseph as an individual who remained faithful to God even when rejected and cut off from all human ties, who was an island of strength no matter what happened to him. The Africans, in contrast, saw Joseph as a person who, no matter how far he traveled or what he endured, never forgot his family. Both meanings are legitimate understandings of the passage, but the culture of each group led them in their interpretation (Kraft 1979:9).

The Westerner, since Descartes, defines the self by saying, "I think, therefore I am." The African says, "I participate, therefore I am"; the Oriental, "I belong, therefore I am"; the Palestinian villager, "I reside in this village, therefore I am."

The basic philosophy of the African, writes John Mbiti (1980:56), is, "I am because we are, and since we are therefore I am." This is the exact reverse of the Jewish tradition of individuation in community, as Rabbi Mendel of Kiosk wrote:

> I am I. You are you.
> But if I am I because you are you
> then I am not I.
> And if you are you because I am I
> then you are not you.
> So I shall be I and you must be you.

The African lives in both vertical and horizontal solidarity with others. Vertically, the child, the parent, the grandparent, the ancestors are seen as a continuous generational unity. Horizontally, "each person is related to others so closely that one has literally hundreds of 'fathers,' 'mothers,' 'brothers,' 'sisters,' and so on even if there is no immediate blood or biological link. This is what has developed the tribal system in which the tribe is organized in clans which are divided into sub-clans, then into families, homesteads, and households. Each person exists because others exist" (Mbiti 1980:57).

> The African child is brought up in an atmosphere which does not freely sanction individuality but emphasizes group activity. This is observed early in life when [the child] is greatly influenced by maternal "uncles" and "classificatory fathers"; that is, father's brothers who, like the father, are called "father." Identification with a father-figure or mother-figure, which normally forms the matrix for individuality in Western culture, is lost in the vast anonymity of the extended family circle. The child learns to identify and integrate with groups. Aggression, love, hate, identification normally directed towards parents are therefore displaced to the group. (Amara 1972:10)

Tribal life, initiation rites, participation in secret societies all reinforce this group solidarity. The African tends to regard personal problems as group problems. The loss of group solidarity through the move to the city means the loss of group protection, the normal psychological prop, and leaves the person isolated and vulnerable. Return to the village for treatment by traditional methods is thus a powerful renewal of lost psychic structures and leads to an immediate and marked anxiety reduction.

One of the essential elements of the African's traditional beliefs is the awareness of others. The African is fundamentally concerned with establishing good relations, not only with significant people here and now (empirical humans) but also with those who have vanished from mortal sight (transcendental humans, the basis of ancestor worship). Ancestor worship strengthens all family bonds, enabling the departed father to retain his role as a powerful leader of the group (a spiritual force) and at the same time to become a being of far more than human excellence (Lambo 1964:445).

Communal Identity

"Where are you?" not "Who are you?" is the question of identification in many areas of the People's Republic of China. A person is known by his or her unit, not by an individual name. The group, or *danwei,* is the basic building block of the society. One is more likely to be asked for a *danwei* than a name.

> Every Chinese belongs to a *danwei* through his office, factory, school, or commune. Although technically a person's place of work, the *danwei* also often provides the housing where a Chinese lives, the school where his children get an education, clinics for when he gets sick, and ration cards for his rice, cooking oil, and soap. Before a Chinese can get married, he must get permission from the Party secretary of his *danwei;* if a couple want to get divorced, their *danwei* must first approve. (Butterfield 1982:323)

Where the West is oriented toward the individual, to satisfying a person's needs and catering to the tastes of each, the Chinese center of gravity is in the group or the family. The pursuit of conformity and the acceptance of authority are assumed as normal experiences of humanness. The proverbs that reflect these millennia of group-centric values are many: "The tall tree is crushed by the wind"; "A rock that protrudes on the riverbank will be washed away by the current." There is no equivalent word in Chinese for conformity, it is only doing what is expected, acting in propriety, fulfilling *Li,* the laws of ritual and etiquette. One does not show talents, express uniqueness, take independent positions, but is all things to all people. As the proverb puts it, "When in a herd of elephants, trumpet; when in the company of cocks, crow; when in a flock of goats, bleat."

Relational patterns are absorbed very early and shape the ways of perceiving, understanding, and classifying incoming data. As Chiu's study contrasting Chinese and American children indicates (1972:242):

> Chinese children preferred to categorize external stimuli on the basis of their interdependence or relationships, while American youngsters preferred to differentiate or analyze the components of the stimulus complex as well as to classify stimuli on the basis of inference made about the stimuli which are grouped together.

This suggests that interdependence and independence as foci of interest and as bases for inference are learned early and act unconsciously in the selectivity of perception and the automatic patterns of accommodation to new information and assimilation of it into existing schemata.

Village Identity

The sociocentric personality does not live by roots alone, it is connected, like rhizome grasses, by a fibrous network of runners that unite, nourish, and sustain all the shoots together, and the matting of roots and earth surrounding and beneath are inseparable from the selfhood and existence of the whole.

> "What do you mean, I must 'know myself'?" the Palestinian Arab asks the pastoral counselor. "How can I know myself in another land? How can I find myself if I am not in my village?"
>
> "You are you. You are here, now," replies the counselor.
>
> "No, you do not see me. To see me, you must see me in my village. You must see me among my people. You must see me on my land. They are all parts of me. Without them, I am nothing. This is not me you see."
>
> "But this is you that I hear expressing your values, your beliefs, your own self-understanding so forcefully and clearly."
>
> "No, these are the beliefs of my people, the human rights of my sisters and brothers to the land that has cared for their families for many generations. You cannot speak to me without speaking to the whole of me, and you cannot see the whole of me when I am driven out into the desert." (Name withheld)

Of the sociocentric personality in Indonesia, Van der Kroef writes:

> The village (desa) is regarded as a community of one big family, within which all of its members share together one common ancestor, are related to a definite area of communal soil, and inseparably linked with one another within one religious communion. . . . Societies such as these naturally draw a sharp distinction between the in-group of the village and the outside world of foreigners, because of the religious unity of the in-group. Within such a frame of thought, concern and compassion for humankind as a whole and/or loyalty to something beyond the boundaries of their particular communities are, at least in theory, absent. (Van der Kroef 1956:199,203)

The uprooting of the village person leads to the fragmentation of the personality as well. The movement from the solidarity of an organically connected community to the isolation of an urban metropolis leaves persons with a sociocentric self-organization consciously (and to a far greater extent unconsciously) incomplete, isolated from their sources of life, severed from their essential values.

V. S. Naipaul, in *Among the Believers* (1981:358), quotes an Indonesian official, Darma-Sastro:

> Among us there are now people who have lost their personalities or their identity. They don't belong to the village anymore. They have become too rich or too important. To them going back to the village would be a degeneration. They have lost the sense of security provided by the mutual-help society of the village. At the same time they are not individuals in the western sense. They cannot stand on their own and as individuals interact on an equal basis with others.
>
> Some of them have been abroad, but there are many people whose bodies have been abroad but whose minds have stayed in the country. . . . They

remain villagers. They are there in the west only to get that diploma and to return to Indonesia with that ascriptive dignity.

But here they are not members of the nobility. They don't have the feudal values of noblesse oblige. So, with their new dignity, they seek power and wealth mainly. This is the cancer. In the old days important people had a responsibility to the society. If you were nobility you were supposed to give an example. The people I'm talking about cannot function now as arbiters of right and wrong because they themselves cannot distinguish between right and wrong anymore. Why? In their loss of identity they have lost all values except those associated with power. They are people continuing to look for their own security.

Individual Identity

Individualism is a remarkable belief. The "individual" sees the self as autonomous, as an island of experience distinct from every other human. The autonomous individual imagines an unimaginable thing (for most of the world's population)—that he or she lives in a private, inviolate protected territory (the enclosing boundaries of the self) where he or she is "free to choose," free to undertake projects of personal expression, free to live a private life with a personal history separate from all others, free to believe that what is chosen is "my own business" (Schweder and Bourne 1982:129).

Individualism is an isolating belief system. Each person is visualized as a microcosm, a particular instance or personification of "humanity," a self both like and unlike all other selves. This single human being is seen as an inviolate unit of value, a supreme value in and of itself. Social relationships arise not from any corporate solidarity but from the consent of autonomous individuals and the social contracts they pledge with one another. Society is an association of parties whose privacy is protected from invasion by a system of laws that treat property as an extension of the person and safeguard as inviolable both persons and property.

In Western traditions, the self is ego, an independent observer and potential controller of a world that is experienced as profoundly separate from self. Other traditions stand in sharp contrast, with their emphasis on self-transcendence rather than self-assertion, on harmony with nature rather than utilization and control of the natural order, and on integration into a social totality rather than autonomy from social solidarity (Pedersen 1981:326).

Individualism and group centeredness are two poles of all human experience. The first is often simplistically equated with independence, the second with conformity. The terms are not synonymous. Group-centered societies do invite or require a good deal of conformity, but they also permit a significant measure of independence. And individualists conform more than they know, and they too must sacrifice independence to be a part of society. The group-centric person often possesses greater individuality than the "rugged individualist."

Individualism, as found among Western peoples and particularly among Americans, is quite different from individuality. The two are often confused. This is not a distinction without a difference. Westerners who exaggerate individualism tend not to assert their individuality. A separate sense of self (individualism) is quite different from the freedom to express many different sides of the self in varied contexts (individuality).

Individualism refers to one's self-concept, to the image of oneself as an individual unit whose motivations and behavior are aimed at individual goals, as opposed, for instance, to a member of a group whose behavior is directed toward smooth harmonious interpersonal relations.

Individuality, in contrast, refers to the development of differences within the personality, the cultivation of versatility, the exercise of adaptability in various contexts. It is the freedom to exhibit a variety of behavior patterns in different social situations, as opposed, for example, to a rugged individualist, whose behavior shows high consistency in the responses given in family intimacy, in cooperative work, or in casual friendships (Stewart 1972:69).

Much imprecision and confusion arise from failing to distinguish two different uses of the term "individual": (1) the empirical agent, present in every society, the person expressing his or her own *individuality;* and (2) the rational private being who is the normative social unit and subject of institutions, protected by equality and liberty, an individualistic idea and ideal.

"Individuality" in Thai life, for a specific cultural example, allows persons to express both group centeredness and individuality. Each "self" seeks to merge into the group identity by avoiding nonconformist dress, assertive physical movements, or open emotional expression that draws undue attention. This reduces friction and facilitates a sense of harmony, as each person "takes the other person's feelings into account at all times." Yet the Thai is known for independence, versatility, and creative adaptability in many different situations.

Individualism in American life asserts the autonomy of each person, yet the culture affects all areas of behavior; that is, the person is mature when he or she acts consistently in all social contexts or is seen to have integrity when behaviors in family, work, and community are congruent. The cultural patterns cover all areas of behavior, and their constant presence and pressure inhibits idiosyncratic nonconformist behavior. This is not to imply that complete conformity is required at all times. There is room for differences within a person's behavioral repertoire, but the impact of the individualistic culture on the individual, though less strong than in traditional societies, is more pervasive (Fieg 1979:28).

In a group-centered culture, individuality is fostered by the restrictedness within the group, family, or tribal unit and by the wide latitude in behavior outside the tribe or family. Thus the person may display more conformist behavior in the family, but since the culture does not follow the person outside this basic group, strong personality, firm personal convictions, and idiosyncratic behavior occur. "The contradiction is only apparent. In some cultures where the individual is subject to the norms of family or tradition he [she] is allowed considerable room to cultivate individuality, as long as these [actions] do not interfere with obligations to family or tradition" (Stewart 1972:70).

> To members of western societies, the importance and power of the group over the individual sounds pathological, as it may be when it occurs in a western society in which the culture demands individualism. But to a corporate culture, such as the Javanese, the individual and the group are not mutually exclusive categories; in fact they are not seen on a continuum but are intimately related. There is an absence of emphasis on individual identity *per se,* and a recognition of the constant conforming and adjusting to the opinions of others necessary for social life. In contrast, there is great emphasis on society, social honor, social rank, social prestige, social power. . . . Social prestige and social power are the achievement motivations prized above all else. . . . Individual autonomy is seen as the greatest danger to any desirable order, whether it occurs on a macro or micro scale. The individual must be controlled, cannot be trusted, should be watched and guided by the group. (Mulder 1978:108–110)

Dependence, Independence, Interdependence

"Your mental health is our mental illness; our mental health is your mental illness. Our therapy only makes your patients worse, and your therapy is destructive to ours."

This conclusion, terse and oversimplified, came near the end of an evening of conversation with a psychiatrist of the Davis Hospital in Ranchi, India.

"We see people who are breaking out of effective social life as well as breaking down in thought and feeling disorders. They are often wildly independent in a social context that requires interdependence, or what is better described as responsible dependence. So our therapy is designed to move them back into proper dependence in their family and community. That is quite different from your Western therapies."

Different? It is the exact reverse. The interpersonal and intrapersonal breakdowns in an individualistic society frequently occur as a return to dependence, a regression to feelings of helplessness compounded with judgments of hopelessness. So Western therapies are designed to invite, teach, and reinforce independence once more.

Mature health, for both systems, is found in interdependence. Although the social form of interdependence to which the Indian psychiatrist's clients return is hierarchical in structure, and my counselees resume a place in a more equalitarian context, it is interdependence we both seek. The doors we enter, to assume interdependence, are from opposite directions. Two contrasting paths toward maturity are clinically visible in the persons he counsels and observes and in those to whom I minister in the West.

Born helpless, the human infant is dependent upon the mothering figures that nourish and protect the emerging person. In Western cultures, that dependence is frustrated at an early age and training in independence nudges the child toward autonomy and independence. In Eastern cultures the childhood dependency is accepted as the appropriate model for life in society, and the person is invited to mature through sequential stages of responsible dependency until adulthood admits the person into interdependency.

We can chart the two contrasting paths from infantile dependency to adult interdependency (Figure 3-1). The Western one leads from early autonomy via responsibility-for-self training to identity formation as an individual self whose choices, actions, and behavior are "his own busi-

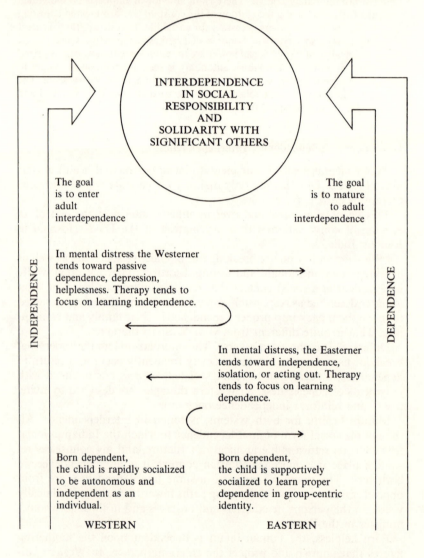

Figure 3-1. Contrasting paths of development, east and west.

ness" or "her private responsibility"; the Eastern path leads from infantile dependency to appropriate childhood conformity to adolescent familial responsibility to young adult corporate solidarity with the group. Both then, as adults, are equipped to enter the social arena of interdependence but through opposite doorways.

The Western perspective prizes the development of autonomy and the internalization of the parent in the budding superego, so that the child will be self-directing at as early an age as possible. It is reinforced by multiple parenting practices, such as a parent asking a three-year-old, "What do you want to eat for dinner?" Or in the parent's polite knock on the door before entering the six-year-old child's personal space, the private bedroom. Or the careful respect given a teenager's diary, which no Western parent of integrity would read uninvited. When a child is naughty, a Western mother says, "I'll make you stay in"; a Japanese mother, "I make you stay out." The ego's view of its "self" is the product of the culture's collective self-understandings. We socialize deep "intuitions" about the indecency of external intrusions, regulations, or invasions of our inviolable private self (Schweder and Bourne 1982:132). The boundaries of privacy, personal space, and individual dignity all combine to cultivate our intuitions about what is modest, decent, tasteful, polite, or appropriate body language, proxemics, or behavior. A Westerner in an Oriental queue finds that invisible boundaries assumed elsewhere are being penetrated and single-file priorities violated. These intuitions of privacy, responsibility, dignity, and security all support the individualist notions of "free to choose," "autonomy in decision making," "doing one's own thing," "minding my own business." The highly redundant socialization practices unite to confirm the rights of the individual to a body, mind, room, life-style, career, and destiny of his or her own.

The Indian and the Euro-American sociocultural systems are, as Dumont has shown, in many important respects the mirror image of each other. In the Euro-American case, the person is conceived of as an individual, ontologically prior to any collectivity and containing within the self all the attributes of humanity. Conversely, in the "individualistic universe," society as a whole is regarded as "in principle two things at once: a collection of individuals and a collective individual" (Dumont 1971:33).

In the contrasting Indian case, the social whole, informed by the hierarchical opposition of pure and impure, is ontologically prior to any empirical actor. In this holistic universe, particular human beings are regarded as possessing different and unequal attributes of humanity, and each finds his or her station in the social hierarchy, the communal order, the familial unity. "To members of sociocentric organic cultures the concept of the autonomous individual, free to choose and mind his (her) own business, must feel alien, a bizarre idea cutting the self off from the interdependent whole, dooming it to a life of isolation and loneliness" (Kakar 1978:86).

The goal of maturity in India may be described as satisfying and continuous dependency within the family unit (Pedersen 1977:375; Carstairs 1957:75). Dependence in Indian life has its origin in social hierarchy, vertical communication patterns, and authoritarianism. Parents are respected, their opinions have power, the children owe them obedience. In the wider community, seniority bestows power, status, and authority, so authority not only of parents but of all superiors in the hierarchically arranged society is accepted without reservation. Such social dependence is seen as healthy and adaptive in the Indian culture.

Indian authoritarianism in families is a cultural pattern and the individuals do not match the "authoritarian personality" of the West, which clusters the traits of preference for dominance-submission in social relationships, an aversion to insight into one's own personality, and a tendency to externalize. Similarly, Indian children do not develop the developmental defect seen in the "dependent personality" of the West.

The unique social dependence of the Indian culture invites the person to excel in the given role but not to exceed the limits of that role. The well-developed personality exercises full independence within the status-authority-responsibility boundaries of the role, and dependence to those outside, particularly in roles above. Total dependence is not normal in Indian society; dependence is selective and in the service of the ego.

> Fulfilling one's goals and potentials is one of the goals of psychotherapy. However, in Indians, the technique has to be different. As an Indian is always an ambassador of the family, achievements, ambitions, and aspirations are merely the reflections of those of the family. This is not unconscious and not related to identification but conscious and deliberate. He (she) cannot get away from this behavior without feeling ashamed. In Western psychiatry, helping the patient to achieve autonomy and to separate his (her) needs from that of the family is the goal of psychotherapy, and the goal is the opposite in Indian psychotherapy. (Ananth 1981:124)

The child born into a sociocentric culture finds dependency trusted, not feared; rewarded, not frustrated. Within the security of parental protection, the person internalizes the intuitions of solidarity with others in the family system. Linked to others in a network of dependencies, the members of an organic culture take an active interest in one another's affairs. They feel comfortable with controlling and being controlled, with regulating and being regulated. Others are the means to one's own satisfactions, and one becomes the means to others' functioning and fulfillment.

Dependency relationships are most frequently hierarchical, with each person's place, role, and relationships defined with the obligations and rights assigned within the group context. By adolescence the person has come to know her or his place as ascribed by the community. In adulthood, the person feels herself or himself a necessary part of the "organic social body" of community.

> The human body is often taken as a metaphor for society (and society, conceived as an organic whole, is sometimes taken as a metaphor for nature). The human body is a pregnant metaphor. It has its ruler (the brain), its servants (the limbs), etc. Political affairs, interpersonal dyads,

family organization are all easily conceived after a model of differentiated parts arranged in a hierarchy of functions in the service of the whole. (Schweder and Bourne 1982:129)

Internal Control or External Control

Based on many life experiences, people learn one of two worldviews about the nature of personal power; either the locus of control rests within the individual or the locus of control rests with some external force. One is either in control of life or feels controlled by life.

Julian Rotter utilized the internal-external control dimension to measure a personality trait shaped by the belief that reinforcements (rewards) are dependent on one's own actions so a person can shape his or her own fate vis-à-vis the belief that reinforcing events (rewards) occur independently of one's actions and the future is determined more by chance and luck (Rotter 1966). Research findings from populations of Western peoples correlated high internality of control with (1) greater attempts at mastering the environment, (2) superior coping strategies, (3) better cognitive processing of information, (4) lower predisposition to anxiety, (5) higher achievement motivation, (6) greater social action involvement, and (7) placing greater value on skill-determined rewards. Brief reflection on these seven traits will show that they are highly valued by Western—and particularly American—society and constitute the accepted core features of mental health (Rotter 1975:66).

But all is not well with this dimension as an indicator of mental health; it does not take into account the different cultural values and social experiences of persons and groups. Early research in the West indicated that ethnic group members, lower-class persons, and women score significantly toward the external end of the continuum. Thus it hardly measures authentic mental health, just one subgroup's ideal (Strickland 1971; Tulkin 1968; Levenson 1974; Wolfgang 1973; Lefcourt 1966; Battle and Rotter 1963; Sanger and Alker 1972). Although the theory behind the internal-external measure may be sound, the interpretation is clearly culture bound. Not only do women and the less privileged minority groups learn that control functions differently for them than it does for the whole middle-class male group in Western society, so also do large segments of the world's population, who live in very different contexts with sharply contrasting power structures. External control not only has different meanings for different persons, it functions in vastly different ways—as illustrated by the following cases.

A is a white middle-class male in an American urban setting who is experiencing significant depression. "I have just lost my job, and I don't think there's any use trying to find one. Once it's on my record that I was fired, it's no use applying. I'm marked and there's nothing I can do about it." (Depressiveness with strong external control and feelings of helplessness.)

B is a black minority female in a major American city. "I went in to apply for a job at this hospital in the medical records department, and they handed me a form that listed all kinds of requirements for this clerical job and asked me if I could read them. I glanced down over the list and I said to myself, Sure I can read this; it says no black need bother applying for this job." (Recognition of external control which may be depressive or may be the reality of the social situation.)

C is a Chinese villager from near Zhongshan. "I wish to have a son, but it is not possible. I have a daughter, and one child is all that is permitted. I shall be content, since that is the way the authorities have decreed." (Active, not passive, acceptance of external control, as is characteristic of his community.)

D is a Malayan businessman with a small food stall in a suburb of Kuala Lumpur. "The year has not been prosperous for me. Bad fortune has struck down all my profits. Perhaps the new year will be a more auspicious one. I have consulted a dukan for an amulet to bring better fortune." (External control related to impersonal forces, chance, and luck. Another external-control person might have attributed it to powerful authorities or inflation and a depressed economy. An internal-control subject would have seen it as a personal failure to control the economic crisis.)

External-control beliefs may be based on political realities as well as psychological tendencies, on prejudicial oppression as well as suspicion or superstition, on religious belief in divine predestination or a philosophy of fatalism. Thus it has many meanings, which may represent health or unhealth, positive or negative valuation.

The sociocentric perspective of the Chinese culture places great value on the group (an individual is not defined apart from membership in the family); it stresses tradition, social expectations, appropriate roles, and harmony with the universe. Thus the worldview of the traditional Chinese culture elevates external scores. However, this external orientation is highly valued by the community and maintains social and mental health (Sue 1981:76). Mao Zedong's comment, "There is no human nature, there is only class nature," united Marxist theory and traditional cultural values.

Research comparing Chinese, American-born Chinese, and Anglo-Americans showed variations in the degree of internal control experienced. The Chinese scored lowest in internality, followed by the Chinese Americans and finally by the Anglo-Americans. The individual-centered American culture with its stress on independence, self-reliance, and individual efforts was in contrast with the situation-centered Chinese culture with its high regard for group harmony (Hsieh, Shybut, and Lotsof 1969:122).

For the Chinese, the external controls are visualized as benevolent forces—the family, the group, the community of origin—but many persons scoring high on external control—blacks under apartheid, women in male-dominant societies, minorities oppressed by a hostile majority—may experience it as malevolent power.

The internal-external continuum offers a helpful way of understanding an important dimension in culture, but it is useful in therapy only as the counselor makes clear distinctions about its meaning. High externality may be seen as due to (1) chance, luck, or fate, (2) cultural dictates experienced as benevolent, (3) a political force of totalitarianism, or (4) social forces of racism, or discrimination that is realistically malevolent (Sue 1981:77).

The crucial issue for the counselor is going beyond the preferences in his or her culture for a particular understanding of control functions and perceiving interpathically the nature of control in the counselee's situation. Mental health is not defined by either end of the continuum but by the appropriate balance within the person and congruence with the cultural context. Thus what is healthy for an Indian of lower caste will be unhealthy for a higher-caste family, or what is appropriate for an Indonesian Chinese in an oppressive situation is different for the Javanese neighbor secure in his cultural homeland.

Internal Responsibility or External Responsibility

Responsibility—credit or blame—may be located in the person or in the system. This is a second major continuum in understanding persons and cultures. We can refer to it as the locus of responsibility, either internal or external. This dimension measures the degree of responsibility or blame that is placed on the individual for problems in living, achieving, or relating; or the degree placed on the system, which either fosters or frustrates success in problem solving. This dimension emerges from research in attribution theory that contrasts person-centered and system-centered assigning of credit or blame (E. Jones and others 1972).

Person-centered definitions of problems have characterized the field of counseling. In most theories of therapy the responsibility for change invariably ends with the individual. This reinforces the belief in a person's ability to command his or her own fate by rewarding middle-class persons who "climbed the ladder to success" or "made it on their own." It also increases complacency about and judgment of those who "can't measure up" or "didn't make the grade."

Those who hold a person-centered orientation tend to (1) emphasize the understanding of a person's motivations, values, feelings, and goals, (2) believe that success or failure is attributable to individual skills or personal inadequacies, and (3) believe that there is a strong relationship between ability, effort, and success in society. In essence, these people adhere strongly to the Protestant ethic that idealizes "rugged individualism" (Sue 1981:78).

Those who hold a situation-centered orientation of defining responsibility see the individual and the environment as virtually inseparable in understanding the causes of any problem situation and see the sociocultural influences as much more potent than the individual. Recognizing the power of political, social, economic, and family group forces, they attribute success or failure to the surrounding situation rather than to personal attributes possessed by the individual.

Western society tends to hold individuals responsible for their problems. Blacks, for example, are often categorized by whites as inadequately motivated in view of their lower standard of living, whereas within the minority group the discrepancy is attributed to racial discrimination, economic oppression, and the absence of opportunities.

> What is done about a problem depends on how it is defined, on assumptions about the causes of a problem and where they lie. If the causes of delinquency, for example, are defined in person-centered terms (e.g., inability to delay gratification, or incomplete sexual identity), then it would be logical to initiate person-change treatment techniques and intervention strategies to deal with the problem. Such treatment would take the form of counseling or other person-change efforts to "reach" the delinquent, thereby using his potential for self-control to make his behavior more conventional.
>
> If, on the other hand, explanations are situation-centered, for example if delinquency were interpreted as the substitution of extra legal paths for already pre-empted, conventionally approved pathways for achieving socially valued goals, then efforts toward corrective treatment would logically have a system-change orientation. Efforts would be launched to create suitable opportunities for success and achievement along conventional lines; thus, existing physical, social, or economic arrangements, not individual psyches, would be the targets for change. (Caplan and Nelson 1973: 200–201)

The responsibility continuum must be viewed differently for groups within a culture, and much more so between cultures. An internal response of accepting blame for one's failure may be both "normal" and appropriate for a middle-class white American, but for a black American in a lower economic setting such an internal responsibility process may be inaccurate, intrapunitive, and extreme. It is often inappropriate for a black male who is last hired and first fired to blame himself for the discrimination by asking, "What's wrong with my work, or with me as a person?" And a counselor who stresses internal responsibility is both psychologically oppressive and situationally unrealistic. In fact, external responsibility may indicate higher mental health in such situations. Research findings indicated that Blacks who scored high in external responsibility (system blame) showed the following traits: (1) exhibited more innovative coping behavior, (2) more often aspired to nontraditional occupations, (3) were more in favor of group rather than individual action for dealing with discrimination, (4) engaged in more civil rights activities (Gurin and others 1969).

Responsibility, in many cultures, is automatically externalized. In Spanish linguistic forms, one says "the dish broke itself" or "the door slammed itself on my sister's hand." In Egyptian culture responsibility is immediately deferred to any external factors in self-protection so there is no attack from the offended party, no loss of face. The listing of cultures that externalize responsibility is long, whether it occurs as an effective strategy in evading shame, or in accounting for luck, fate, or kismet, or in extending responsibility to the family, group, or community, or in recognition of the dominance of the political, religious, or social system. The counselor must be aware of the locus of responsibility in the counselee's culture and family group and in his or her personal management of successes and defeats, of good fortune and bad.

> Nigerian taxi drivers commonly drove at horrendous speeds (up to 150 kph) on the open highway and flew through the villages that straddled the highway at virtually the same speed. The only concession they would make for the safety of the villagers was to blow their horns continuously while going through a village. If anyone happened to be hurt or killed, it was seen as the will of Allah. The person [whose] "time had come" was destined to die at that particular moment—if not in an automobile accident then in some other way. The vehicle was the agent of death but not the cause. (Paradoxically, though, a driver who had killed a pedestrian was in serious danger of being beaten to death by the mob gathering at the scene of the accident.) (R. Janzen 1985)

The Control and Responsibility Context

These two psychological orientations, locus of control and locus of responsibility, can both be placed on a continuum at right angles to each other so that they form four quadrants: internal control–internal responsibility (IC-IR), external control–external responsibility (EC-ER), and the two combinations, IC-ER and EC-IR (Figure 3-2). Each quadrant, suggests Derald Sue, the originator of this theoretical diagram, represents a different worldview or orientation to life (Sue 1981:80).

Internal Locus of Control–External Responsibility (IC-ER)

This describes individuals who are high in internal control and have a strong belief that the context is responsible for opportunities and outcomes. Such persons believe in their ability to shape their future and

4 IC-IR	INTERNAL CONTROL		1 IC-ER
	Individual Responsibility and achievement orientation	Collective Action and social concern	
INTERNAL RESPONSIBILITY			EXTERNAL RESPONSIBILITY
	Biculturalism and cultural flexibility	Ability to compromise and adapt to life conditions	
3 EC-IR	EXTERNAL CONTROL		2 EC-ER

Figure 3-2. Four different orientations to life.

manage events if given the chance. They refuse to believe that present difficulties are caused by their own inability or weakness. They have a clear and realistic view of the barriers that block the reaching of goals —whether these are discrimination, prejudice, rigidity of their system, economic depression, or social exploitation.

Minority groups within a dominant and oppressive society often see their world with IC-ER eyes. Pride in one's own racial and cultural heritage may be expressed by the relabeling of identity with phrases such as "Black is beautiful." This claiming of internal control to define oneself as over against the majority society's negative definitions and to think courageously, act militantly, and demand justice firmly is done in the face of a system that is exclusive and oppressive (external responsibility indicates that the blocked opportunities are caused by the system). In the United States, militancy reached the explosive point with riots in the major cities from 1964 to 1967 as Blacks came to the full recognition of their internal control (their power to speak, act, protest, revolt against conditions) and the external responsibility for the situation. The message to the white community was, "Our ghetto existence, denial of jobs, exclusion from education, and discrimination in housing are all the result of racism, not some inherent weakness. We can and will take control of our own lives."

The conscientization process used by Paulo Freire among the oppressed peoples of South America is a means for, among other educational goals, internalizing control and coming to full recognition of the external responsibility for much of the injustice experienced. Women's consciousness-raising groups perform the same function for persons discriminated against and economically, sexually, and relationally abused by male-dominated society.

In Latin America, Africa, India, Korea, and Indonesia, to name a few places, liberation theology summons humanity to claim active, committed control of their situation and confront the powers and systems who are responsible for limiting the lives and destiny of people within their domain. The IC-ER vision, when aroused to feeling and apprised of its situation, can be a force for initiating change.

In counseling practice, IC-ER clients tend to be action-oriented. They expect involvement and active participation from the counselor. As persons desiring change, they prefer a therapist who is capable of change-agent strategies, who offers explorative questions, options, directions, and suggestions rather than nondirective reflection, rephrasing, and feeling-oriented work.

External Locus of Control–External Responsibility (EC-ER)

This describes the person who feels that control lies outside the self —"I really have no options; my place is pretty well set no matter what I do"—and recognizes that responsibility lies in the system, not in the self.

In Western society, this typifies the minority peoples who are squeezed into marginal status, discriminated against in such total ways that passivity, learned helplessness, and depression result. The high rates of unemployment, poverty, suicide, delinquency, tuberculosis, alcoholism, and crime in many black ghettoes and in the Chinatowns of both New York City and San Francisco indicate the effects of cumulative powerlessness (Sue and Sue 1973).

A person high in external control convictions and system blame (external responsibility) believes there is little one can do in the face of the pressures (discrimination in the West, position and station in life in the East) or in breaking free of the powers that determine things (prejudice and oppression in the West, tradition and cultural expectations in hierarchical societies of the East). This is not to equate the psychological impact of the EC-ER situation in East and West; they can be vastly different. For the minority person in a closed marginal position in the midst of an open society the EC-ER stance is oppressive; for the person who lives in the security of a traditional community in a hierarchical society such as an Indian or Chinese rural village, this is accepted as one's station in life, one's karma, one's calling.

Thus what indicates depressive learned helplessness in an Amerindian can be vastly different for an Asian Indian. Native Americans have been the victims of widespread massacres that reduced their population from 3,000,000 to 600,000. Their life expectancy is 44 years, compared to 72 for white Americans. The danger of extinction is high (Wrightsman 1972). An EC-ER stance rises in part from the culture's essential values and in part from the oppression and near genocide suffered. But an EC-ER worldview of an Indian villager is a positive dependency that is contextually congruent with the person's own learnings and the culture's traditional patterns.

In counseling practice, external control and external responsibility place special demands on both counselor and counselee. The individual-oriented therapist will miss the central problems faced by the counselee in his or her living situation. The external responsibility perspective gives the counselee a clear understanding of the oppressive social, political, or economic forces. The culturally aware counselor will help the counselee (1) to assess the situation accurately through consciousness-raising, (2) to discover and learn new coping behaviors and strategies, (3) to experience personal successes and negotiate group and system change, and (4) to strengthen ties with the support community. Thus the counselor works with both the person and the system, both the individual and the community.

External Control–Internal Responsibility (EC-IR)

Persons in Western cultures who show these personal worldviews are highly likely to accept the dominant culture's definition of being personally responsible for their situation, but they have very little control over their lives, or believe they have no control. They see themselves as defined by others and unable to change an undesirable situation. This unites powerlessness and self-blame, a combination that is rarely sustained except when imposed by dominant others.

One such situation is the "cultural racism" practiced by the broader American culture upon minorities who live on the margins of the society, accepting the other group's view that their problems are caused by binding traditions, laziness, or inferiority, but see no way to be included (Jones 1972:159). Such persons reject their own cultural heritage, evidence self-hatred, accept the standards and values of the dominant culture as superior, and internalize these feelings passively, since acceptance and inclusion must come from an external source. The attempt to adjust one culture to another, in the hope of avoiding inferiority and feelings of isolation, actually produces the ambivalence and inner malevolence it seeks to evade in the society.

This marginal EC-IR position occurs with subgroups in every culture and with individuals (such as rural persons) seeking entry into urban settings of social mobility where inclusion is largely denied. The necessary dynamics for creating cultural racism, according to Jones, are (1) belief in the superiority of one's cultural heritage over all others, (2) belief in the inferiority of another or all other life-styles, and (3) the power to impose such standards on a less powerful group (Jones 1972:148).

In counseling, it is crucial that the counselor not assume that marginality and self-hatred are the person's own internal conflicts, arising from the pathology of the individual. Paulo Freire writes (1970a:10–11):

> Marginality is not by choice, marginal man has been expelled from and kept outside of the social system and is therefore the object of violence. In fact, however, the social structure as a whole does not "expel." Nor are marginal men "beings outside of," they are "beings for another." Therefore the solution to their problems is not to become "beings inside of," but men freeing themselves; for, in reality, they are not marginal to the structure, but oppressed men within it.

The counselor who is culturally capable will not assist the counselee in acculturating at the expense of his or her own cultural values. Maintaining a sense of the dignity and worth of one's own heritage while making positive attempts to adjust to the new culture can foster authentic bicultural adjustment, but without the loss of one's past, one's core, one's essential cultural identity.

What is defined as marginal in Western society is a central personality form in Japanese society. External control is the pattern of Japanese males from childhood dependency (amae) to adult allegiance to the company. Internal responsibility is grounded in the deeply buried sense of guilt, reinforced by the high value placed on honor. It is exemplified by an executive who accepts full responsibility for a scandal in the company and commits suicide out of loyalty to the institution and responsibility turned against the self in self-destruction (Kashiwagi 1985).

The complexity of the Japanese personality is in part derived from this inner tension between control from without and responsibility within.

Marginal personalities in Japan fall into the individualist quadrant (IC-IR) or the active dependent (EC-ER).

Internal Control–Internal Responsibility (IC-IR)

People with high internal personal control believe that they are in charge of their own lives and that their choices and actions determine the consequences and outcomes; their high sense of internal responsibility leads them to credit success to or blame failure on their own efforts and abilities. This focuses both control issues and responsibility attitudes on the individual, not on the social system, so it is the central belief structure of individualism. Western cultures, which place a premium on self-reliance, achievement, and power and control over life, nature, and others, all focus on these factors internal to the individual as decisive and necessary. The individual, however, is held accountable for whatever occurs, so frustrated goals mean a lack of ability, and failure evokes self-blame, guilt, depression, and feelings of inadequacy.

In counseling practice, Western therapists stress autonomy in decision making, independence in life-style, individualism in separating from family of origin, responsibility that is a response to one's own potential ability rather than obligations to others, and self-therapy as the goal of individual therapy. Individualism is the single most pervasive influence and the undeniable evidence of cultural encapsulation in Western counselors. The inability to move beyond a "doing" orientation to work at "being," the focus on activism, competition, achievement, and personal independence rather than supporting cooperation, ascribed status, and group-centered values, can severely limit the pastoral counselor in understanding, supporting, or intervening in the problems of counselees from a contrasting culture. IC-IR counselees are often struggling with the pain of self-blame, the intrapersonal abuse of deeply internalized punitive structures, and the chronic depressiveness that result in part from the worldviews of control and responsibility. A broadened understanding of the self-in-community as the basic unit of humanness, and the establishing of a meaningful network of relationships, can turn the person outward and invite the creation of a healthy context for personal healing.

Cross-Cultural Comparison of IC-ER/IR-ER

The essential assumptions of Western cultures, particularly of white middle-class majority groups, strongly emphasize—perhaps we should say exaggerate—the internal control–internal responsibility beliefs. In sharp contrast, many major groups in the two-thirds world value the reverse beliefs to a significant degree. For the purpose of contrasting, these two will be referred to as individualistic cultures vis-à-vis group-centric cultures. The two are charted in Figure 3-3. The areas within the dotted lines indicate the dominant grouping valued within the culture with the majority of the population indicated, excluding the marginal, resistant, and depressed and the isolate, deviant, and depressed that occur in the respective configurations.

The strong skewing of Western culture toward the internal control–internal responsibility quadrant follows the core values of individualism as it has developed in the West since the Renaissance. Its primary characteristics are as follows.

Individualism as a life-style stresses doing over being, action over reflection, equality instead of hierarchy, informality rather than formality, and functional friendships above long-term loyalties or obligational commitments to friends. Group membership is by renewable contract, with rights and duties defined by one's own goals, instead of group membership by virtue of one's social and familial place in society, with one's behavior in the group dictated by the group's mores and sanctions or the authority of the leader. Achievement and competition are seen as motivational necessities and norms, rather than being disruptive of social harmony. The worth of a person is measured by objective, visible social achievements (education, appointments, memberships, certifications) or material possessions (wealth, property, status symbols) instead of by familial status, social position, class, and caste; personal accomplishments are more important than birth, family prestige, heritage, or traditional prominence. Achieved status is valued over ascribed status. The individual self is seen as separate from both the physical world and from other persons instead of organically connected to the earth and to fellow humans. Decision making and responsibility are posited in the person, not in the group, in contrast to decisions being shared events with significant others and responsibility to and for fellow group members making one fully accountable. For individualists, the group is not a social unit but an aggregate of individual units, whereas in sociocentric societies the group is an organismic unity. Where Western society socializes the person by pressing for a crisis formation of individual identity leading to autonomy, privatism, and asserting one's own rights, other cultures socialize for dependent collaboration, familial identity, personal responsibility to the group, collective solidarity, and submission of individual rights to the harmonious interaction of the larger whole (Stewart et al. 1969:69).

Thus it is clear that effective interpersonal and intrapersonal adjustment in the two settings is in sharp contrast, the one proceeding from the social contract of discrete individuals, the other from the group solidarity of committed persons. Western counseling theories prize the individualistic forms of IC-IR so wholly that they are used as criteria for mental health and form the basic working assumptions in most theories of abnormal psychology and psychopathology. We must recognize that fully functioning persons do exist in all other quadrants and that the primary criteria must be the correspondence between inner congruence and contextual congruence.

This is not to suggest that all cultures are equivalent in their fostering of mental health and of the realization of human potential. The incidence

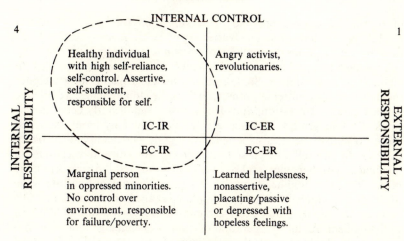

WESTERN URBAN

INTERNAL CONTROL

4   1

Healthy individual with high self-reliance, self-control. Assertive, self-sufficient, responsible for self.

Angry activist, revolutionaries.

IC-IR   **IC-ER**

EC-IR   **EC-ER**

Marginal person in oppressed minorities. No control over environment, responsible for failure/poverty.

Learned helplessness, nonassertive, placating/passive or depressed with hopeless feelings.

EXTERNAL CONTROL

3   2

(INTERNAL RESPONSIBILITY — left axis; EXTERNAL RESPONSIBILITY — right axis)

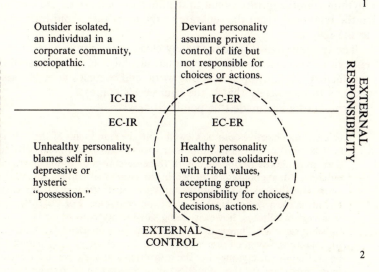

EASTERN TRIBAL

INTERNAL CONTROL

4   1

Outsider isolated, an individual in a corporate community, sociopathic.

Deviant personality assuming private control of life but not responsible for choices or actions.

IC-IR   **IC-ER**

EC-IR   **EC-ER**

Unhealthy personality, blames self in depressive or hysteric "possession."

Healthy personality in corporate solidarity with tribal values, accepting group responsibility for choices, decisions, actions.

EXTERNAL CONTROL

3   2

(INTERNAL RESPONSIBILITY — left axis; EXTERNAL RESPONSIBILITY — right axis)

Figure 3-3. Contrasting views of health and unhealth.

of repression, oppression, and dehumanization for over half of the world's population—women—varies significantly from culture to culture. In many settings the function of women is largely limited to biological, manual, and menial task performance, although exceptions exist in virtually all communities. Some cultures, such as Ireland, show a higher incidence of schizophrenias; others, such as the United States, a tendency toward greater depression. Suicide rates vary significantly between cultures. Certain groups evidence greater individual hysteric responses; more collective societies experience the same personality disturbance external to the self as "possession." There are cultural variations in incidence, type, behavior, and recovery rate in mental illnesses. But none of the data on mental health or illness suggest that any one culture is the ideal toward which other groups should be shaped or modified, and this includes the highly publicized—around the world—culture of Western individualism. As an exaggeration of human distancing from other humans, individualism needs the balancing of more complete relatedness within community.

Individualism, inadequate as a view of humanness, is even more inadequate as a criterion for judging mental health and mental illness. Francis Hsu (1972:11) rejects individualism as a measure and describes mental health in terms of an "interpersonal nexus" in his theory of psychosocial homeostasis (PSH). His alternative is to emphasize the individual-in-context as primary. It is the person-with-relationships-to-significant-others that is the basic irreducible unit of humanness.

The counselor who has come to think in systems language sees the person not as an individual in need but as a person in pain-producing relationships. Thus the counseling objectives will move in a continuous rhythm from the intrapersonal to the interpersonal, from the individual to the relational, from the separate to the corporate, from the personal to the familial.

The systems approach immediately envisions multiple goals. It is not enough to visualize increasing personal satisfaction; there must also be satisfactory relationships, satisfying work, and being a source of satisfactoriness to the society that is the counselee's context.

Rene Dawis has made this point strongly:

> Counseling objectives can be viewed from the standpoint of the individual (satisfaction) or of the institution or society (satisfactoriness). The counselor may choose to optimize both these outcomes or to maximize either outcome. Most counselors trained in the American culture would almost automatically seek to maximize counselee satisfaction; in other words, to attend to the psychological needs of the counselee. For counselees from many other cultures, however, being satisfactory is much to be preferred to being satisfied. That is to say, the institution or society's evaluation of the counselee is valued much more than the counselee's evaluation of the institution or society; meeting the institution's or society's requirements is more important (to the counselee) than meeting the counselee's requirements. (Dawis 1978:465)

Internal Worth and Internal Identity

A second major pairing of continua crucial to the process of healing, growth, and healthy human functioning is the intersection of scales showing the location of a sense of worth and a center of identity.

The locus of worth may be experienced as internal, as intrinsic to the person regardless of whether he or she is held in esteem by others in the immediate context; or worth may be experienced as external, as extrinsic to the person and dependent on the reflected esteem of the group or community.

The concept of personal worth has been variously described: as intrinsic or extrinsic, as ascribed or achieved, as inherent or earned, as personal worth or performance worth. All these are alternate descriptions of the poles of the internal-external worth continuum. Approaches to western psychotherapy vary across the scale, with Gestalt, Rogerian, transactional analysis, and psychosynthesis at the internal pole; behaviorism, social learning theory, and some schools of psychoanalysis at the external pole. Within Eastern cultures the same variety occurs, with Confucian philosophy at the center between the poles ("jen" is reverence for the worth of each human as a human, but etymologically the word *jen* is composed of two parts, "person" and "two," meaning goodness in interpersonal relationships [Teng and Hsu 1971]). Buddhism falls at the external pole (enlightenment means the dispelling of the illusion of personal identity and the recognition that one has no essence, but is energy of life in process and transformation).

The locus of identity may be experienced as internal, as centered within the person, or as external, in the family, group, or tribal unit. This has been variously termed egocentric vs. group-centric identity, or individual vs. sociocentric identity, or personal vs. familial identity. All these are seeking to locate identity on a continuum that reaches from the one to the many, from private autonomy to corporate solidarity.

Identity, whether as a centered sense of selfhood (personal) or as a corporate sense of peoplehood (collective), shares two common processes of definition (self definition/group definition). First, the self or group defines its boundaries—this is I, this is not I, and these are in, those are out. Second, the self or group locates itself in the environment—I am I, you are you, and we are we, and we exist in this context, as contrasted to those others, and sharing these commonalities or those differences. (See Figure 3-4.)

A Theology of Humanness

Human nature—its complexity and contradictions—has been the subject of reflection for centuries, as revealed by this ancient Chinese folktale.

> Long ago in a certain place, one of the immortals saw a man and his dog struck dead by lightning and decided to bring them back to life. He first

Quadrant no. 1 is valued in many Chinese cultural groups. The self is seen as good, valuable, of intrinsic worth; identity is conferred from family, tradition, ancestral place, and rank.

Quadrant no. 2 is assumed in strongly sociocentric groups where both worth and identity are located in the family or the tribal/village/ethnic group.

Quadrant no. 3 represents persons such as those in transition from a rural 2 to an urban 4, who are forced to claim an identity but see worth as a "success to be achieved."

Quadrant no. 4 is prized in Western individualistic cultures. The individual is the highest unit of value, inviolable in worth, and identity is internal, separate, distinct from others.

> examined the man, and found the man's heart completely destroyed. So he took the dog's heart and gave it to the man, and made a heart out of earth for the dog. Then he pronounced the words which brought them both to life again. The dog raised its head, licked the Immortal One's hand, and wagged its tail in gratitude. The man, however, not only offered no thanks to his benefactor, he cursed him. (Eberhard 1965:2)

What is human nature? What is truly human existence? These are not repetitive questions. The word "human" has multiple meanings, as in the statement "Human life must be kept human." The first usage is descriptive of all in the species; the second is evaluative, meaning "truly or authentically human." Or the reverse usage—"What an inhuman rascal!"—reveals that only a human being can be called inhuman,

INTERNAL WORTH

4	1
Individualistic self-definition with an internal sense of self-esteem and an egocentric sense of centered identity.	Internal sense of intrinsic worth as a person; ascribed identity from solidarity with others in a group-centered culture.
IW-II	IW-EI
EW-II	EW-EI
Ascribed or achieved worth or esteem conferred or earned in the group; internal sense of egocentric identity as an individual.	Ascribed or achieved worth or esteem conferred or earned in the group; identity from solidarity with others in a group-centric collective culture.

| 3 | EXTERNAL WORTH | 2 |

Figure 3-4. Quadrants of internal and external worth and identity.

and even an inhuman person deserves to be treated as a human. Thus we may, as Macquarrie argues (1983:2), speak of "human becoming" rather than "human being." Although we already are human, we are constantly discovering what the potentialities of humanness are within us. Our humanness is composed of both actualities and possibilities.

The pastoral counselor's understanding of humanness—the nature, origin, process, and destiny of human existence—is a core determinant of where therapy begins, how it proceeds, and toward what vision of health, maturity, and wholeness it is directed. The vision of making human nature truly human provides direction for both therapist and client.

Western pastoral counseling, during the first three fourths of the twentieth century, looked to psychological theory for its sources of new knowledge. The impact of psychoanalytic thought, the rise of behavioral psychology, and the rapid change in cultural models led to the psychologizing of Western society. The therapeutic view was replacing other ways of perceiving personal, familial, and relational problems. Pastoral counseling took on the language of psychotherapeutic theory and practice.

Central to this societal change was a shift in views of human nature. The impact of widely varied psychological images of humanness led many to discard theological roots and incorporate the sharply contrasting perspectives of the new "human sciences."

Psychology as a behavioral science has been described as "objective, mechanistic, materialistic, behavioralistic, fatalistic, reductionistic" (Sperry 1965:76). The mechanistic or existential model sees humans as passive beings subject to the determinisms of environmental forces. The focus of the model is on adjustment, with mental illness seen as maladjustment. Psychology as a humanistic science defines itself as subjective, organismic, existential, intentional, responsible, inclusive. It sees humans as active deciding agents with authentic choice and a wide measure of freedom. Psychoanalytic psychology viewed humans as determined by instinctual drives, yet capable of choice and change; as controlled by unconscious processes, yet responsible to choose, decide, and act in movement toward rationality. Psychology as a systems approach sees all these factors and more as correlated in a network of interrelated elements—such as behavior, self-system, family, community, culture.

All these streams—behavioral, existential, humanistic, psychoanalytic, and systems—offered new views of the human situation that had formative impact on the various theorists of pastoral care and counseling. The views of humans as passive and reactive or active and self-regulating, as individual and existentially isolated or as communal and socially solidaric; as biologically defined and determined or as bio-social-spiritual unities—these hardly begin the listing of contrasting polar options offered to counselors by the information explosion of the many streams of psychological research and writing.

The Westernization of the pastoral counseling movement resulted from the rapid inclusion of the blend of philosophy and psychology that made up the new secular therapies. The historically grounded, universally owned roots of biblical and theological theory became secondary sources to be correlated with the more primary empirical and phenomenological data drawn from the "living human document." Theological reflection on the diagnostic data allowed the pastoral counselor to criticize or correct the scientific worldview by a return to the categories and convictions of biblical and historical values.

The recovery of theological and biblical roots for pastoral counseling has been a major effort of the final quarter of the twentieth century. This return to the resources of theology is made even more necessary by the attempt to view humans transculturally. Any intercultural perspective reveals how dominated by Western philosophy and culture are the pastoral counseling models built on the psychological theories of this modern era. (See Case Study: Malaysian Dilemma.)

Biblical Views of Humanness

The biblical writings have no formal descriptions of human nature. Theologians may synthesize an analysis of humanness from the narratives and writings, but this, though accurate in quotation, may yet be unfaithful to the scriptures, because the image of humans in the Bible is a dynamic image-in-action, selfhood-in-relationships, and person-in-community that resists a systematic construction.

The central element of the Hebrew view of humans is a fundamental sense of unity in the person. No dualisms exist between nature and spirit, mind and body, or other part processes. The human is a unitary organism. It is the total person who acts, thinks, feels, relates, chooses, sins, and repents. Divisions within or between constitute disorder, disease, or the disruption of relationships called evil. This unity is not a reductionistic monism. Instead, it is rich in paradox. All these part processes fit together as an organic whole, so that the various parts are aspective yet unitive.

The nature of human beings from biblical perspective is multidimensional, too complex for simple definition, too compound for linear description. The biblical story of humanity is inclusive, not reductionistic. It is best seen as polar and paradoxical (Stagg 1973). To explore these polar elements of the nature of humans we shall look at seven central contrasts in the biblical view of humanness.

1. *Human beings are in the image of God* yet *co-images of God.* To be created in the image of God (Gen. 1:26; 2:7; 5:3) is both a gift (the gift of likeness) and a task (the privilege of dominion). It is both being and doing, both responsivity and responsibility. *Yet* the image is not in our individuality but in our relatedness, not in our separateness but in our responsible co-humanity with each other, not in our autonomy but in our responsive co-existence before God.

CASE STUDY: Malaysian Dilemma

An unmarried Malaysian woman, a Christian, became pregnant by a Muslim man. For the sake of the unborn child, she went to the Muslim court and registered her marriage. She then felt sharp conflict between her betrayal of her Christian faith and her desire to remain related to her lover. She knew that if she were to renounce the Muslim faith, which she had needed to affirm in the registration, she could precipitate a riot between the predominantly Muslim community and the minority Christian congregation.

Western response: In Western cultures, this woman's dilemma would be considered largely in terms of her own ability to handle the unwanted pregnancy, the options available to her, and her own perspectives and ego strength. The marital-communal-interfaith issues would be given little significance.

Malaysian response: In an Eastern setting, friends, the extended family, and the entire Christian congregation play major roles. The pregnant woman confided in a close friend at her place of work. The friend went to her pastor and informed him of the situation. The pastor arranged for the friend to invite the woman's oldest brother to her home, to inform him of the facts, and to suggest that both a Muslim wedding and a Christian service in the bride's home be arranged. The brother reacted violently, but the friend encouraged the expression of anger over a two-hour period, then supported his plans to inform the family. The immediate family, after hearing of the pregnancy, invited the entire extended family to assist in finding a resolution. In a very heated session, several members of the clan threatened to kill the sister. The key person offering understanding was the grandmother. The brother, supported by the grandmother, absorbed much of the familial anger. Two months later a wedding of Muslim rites was held, followed by a service that gathered the whole Christian congregation in the home of the bride. A relative gave a talk pointing out that even though it had all started out wrong, the family stood by the bride and the future was hopeful.

No formal counseling took place. The bride's support came largely from a friend. The whole community was mobilized to resolve the problem by changing the context, not by seeking to alter only the person.

(Adapted from Leslie 1979:17)

2. *Human beings are created creatures* yet *co-creators.* As creatures, we link creation and its Creator, we unite spirit and nature (Gen. 1:26; Ps. 8), Yet we are called to continue the Creator's work of bringing order from chaos, of creating meaning from events and experiences.

3. *Human beings are personal* yet *communal.* As individual persons, one identity is not confused with another (Gen. 5:1–3; Ex. 20; Gen. 12). One is other from each other individual. Personhood is distinct from

peoplehood. *Yet* solitude exists in polar relation to solidarity, individual identity to corporate identity.

4. *Human beings are aspective* yet *unitive.* Humanness has multiple aspects—physical, mental, emotional, rational, moral, spiritual, social, volitional, cyclical, sequential, intentional. *Yet* these aspects are unitive, not partitive; they are composed of dualities, not dualisms. No aspect can be extracted but as part process in holistic, not monistic, unity of aspects (psyche, soma, nous, kardia, sarx, pneuma).

5. *Human beings are complex/contradictory* yet *polar/complementary.* Humans are multiplex and self-reflective, multi-motive and contradictory, multifaceted and capable of isolation from parts or distortion of poles (1 Cor. 6:3; 7:34; 1 Thess. 5:23). *Yet* the multiplicity strives for integration, the polar part processes drive for completion, the separated returns for union, the empty yearns for satisfaction.

6. *Human beings are finite beings* yet *free becomings.* All human being exists within the bounds of finite possibilities, within range of familial-social opportunities, within limits of frailty and fallibility (Heb. 2:6–9; 1 Peter 2:21; Micah 6:8; Mark 12:29; Gal. 5:1; John 8:31–36). *Yet* a human being is always a human becoming; the actual person is also a potential person. Choice is real, not illusory. Freedom is authentic, not determined.

7. *Human beings are valuing subjects* yet *valued objects.* In personal, subject-subject (I-thou) relationships we meet each other, we encounter God in loving mutuality and reciprocity of grace (Matt. 22:37; 1 Cor. 13; 1 John 4). *Yet* we can transcend self, body, behavior in objectified accountability, prizing self and other equally, recognizing that persons are irreducibly valuable in the equal regard of agape.

The Individual-in-Community

The individual-in-community is the primary unit of humanness. Any description of the individual apart from his or her community deals only with part process, with a fragment of a unitary whole. Humanness is not individually defined, nor is it a description of all the uniqueness, variation, or possibilities within community. Thus definition does not move from what is the individual essence of a particular human to what is the nature of humans collectively. The trajectory is not from ontology to identity to depravity to morality to community. Rather, the movement is from truly human community to the true humanness of the individual-in-community. The proper direction is from communal integrity to moral responsibility, to personal identity, to individual actions and transactions.

Persons, as individuals in their respective communities, are irreducibly valuable, of unalterable worth, and are to be prized as ends in themselves. Thus neither the community nor the individual is to be valued above the other. Both find maturity in the balanced prizing and integration of each with the other.

Developmentally, the individual-in-community is a contracting-covenanting being who lives by the promises made and the commitments kept in relationship. These covenants are both implicit and explicit, conscious and unconscious, voluntary and coerced, unilateral and multilateral (Table 3-1). These covenants are the means for the protection of values,

---

Table 3-1. Humans as Covenanting Beings

"We are our contracts and covenants." As all social relationships are contractual relations, so the individual-in-community is a multilayer pattern of covenants.

1. Infancy: Primal Covenants
  (Trust of the mothering other)
The infant makes intuitive promises to the self on basic trust of self and other and on primal hope and orientation toward life.

2. Childhood: Familial Covenants
  (Trust of self with parents, siblings, family)
The young child makes emotive promises to the self on risking shame, guilt, doubt and on choosing between good and evil, resistance and submission, aggression and withdrawal.

3. School Child: Educational Covenants
  (Trust of self with tasks and structures)
The child makes performance promises to the self and to others on being capable or feeling incapable, on achieving competence or accepting incompetence, on being industrious or apathetic.

4. Youth: Personal Covenants
  (Trust of self with peers, community, world, God)
The youth makes interpersonal promises to both self and others on identity, friendship, sexuality, ideology, responsibility, and the acceptance of conventions, rituals, and mentors.

5. Young Adulthood: Communal Covenants
  (Trust of self with life companions)
The young adult makes permanent promises to self-others-God in the public life covenants—marital covenant, parental commitment, vocational choice, community inclusion.

6. Adulthood: Vocational Covenants
  (Trust of traveler with co-travelers)
The adult affirms and reaffirms the creative and re-creative promises of life—to re-create marriage, renegotiate community, reassess career, readjust parenting, and rediscover goals, values, and hopes.

7. Maturity: Integrity Covenants
  (Trust of life, death, and wisdom)
The mature adult sums up life in the integrative promises of life review—to disengage from the life project, to discover wisdom, to be reconciled with life and death.

---

exchange of values, creation of values, and increase of values for both the individual and the community. The character and quality of the life lived is shaped by the patterning of covenants made with self and other.

The dangers of mismanaging covenants lie in overcommitment, under-commitment, miscommitment, or cheating on commitment. Human beings are covenanting beings who live by the promises made and kept as well as by those betrayed or failed. The possibility of honoring covenants with integrity or of falling short of the promises made is present in every person and thus in every community.

Both community and individual contain polar possibilities and conflic-tual tendencies toward both good and evil, viewed philosophically; to-ward right and wrong, viewed morally; toward sin and wholeness, viewed theologically; toward health and unhealth, viewed psychologi-cally; toward constructivity and destructivity, viewed relationally; to-ward life and death, viewed existentially. All these are present in our origins, in our environment, in our unconscious as well as conscious experience. The pastoral counselor as a representative of community sees person and community as two aspects of a common reality.

Summary

The intercultural pastoral counselor, aware of both individuality and solidarity in her or his own personhood, is sensitive to the great variation of understandings of personal, familial, tribal, and national identity.

Identity may be located in tribal solidarity, in social community, in village locality, or in individual egocentricity. Healthful adjustment of the person to the context can only be defined within that setting. The balance of independence, dependence, and interdependence varies in the definitions of appropriate maturity held by the various cultures. The balance of responsibility—internal or external—and of control—within or without—shapes the personalities of people and of the groups they form. Authentic humanness lies in balance, not in exaggeration of either of these polarities.

The pastoral counselor is guided in the treatment of persons in their pain by a theology of humanness that begins with the individual-in-community as the primary unit of all study and therapy. Humans are covenanting beings, and their lives are created by the covenants they make—with themselves, their significant others, their surrounding com-munity, and their Creator.

4

Inner Controls, Outer Controls, Balanced Controls

A Theology of Grace

"But what if, contrary to what is now so generally assumed, shame is natural, in the sense of being an original feature of human existence? What if it is shamelessness that is unnatural, in the sense of having to be acquired?"

—*Walter Berns, 1971*

"Shame is our ineffaceable recollection of our estrangement from the origin; it is grief for this estrangement, and the powerless longing to return to unity with the origin; shame is more original than remorse."

—*Dietrich Bonhoeffer, 1965*

"IS THAT SO?"
A JAPANESE ZEN TALE

The Zen master Hakuin was praised by his neighbors as one living a pure life.

A beautiful Japanese girl whose parents owned a food store lived near him. Suddenly, without any warning, her parents discovered she was with child. This made her parents angry. She would not confess who the man was but after much harassment at last named Hakuin. In great anger the parents went to the master and accused him of the indiscretion.

"Is that so?" was all he would say.

After the child was born it was brought to Hakuin. By this time he had lost his reputation, which did not trouble him, but he took very good care of the child. He obtained milk from his neighbors and everything else the little one needed.

A year later the child's mother could stand it no longer. She told her parents the truth—that the real father of the child was a young man who worked in the fish market. The parents of the girl at once went to Hakuin to ask his forgiveness, to apologize at length, and to get the child back again.

Hakuin was willing. In yielding the child, all he said was, "Is that so?" (Reps 1961:22)

"The laboratory technician was ill, the surgery schedule was full, and lab studies were absolutely essential," reports a European physician in an Indian hospital. "So I sent a servant to the technician's house to fetch the keys, but he refused. Angered by this noncooperation of a colleague, I walked to his house, demanded the keys, went to the lab, ran the tests myself, then promptly forgot the whole affair.

"In the weeks that followed, strained relationships between myself and the laboratory chief became more and more obvious. Only then did I begin to realize what an affront my confrontation had been. By sending a servant to make my demands I had violated social etiquette, by angrily demanding the key I had preempted his responsibility for his work and role, by doing it all publicly I had caused him to lose face in front of the whole staff. In Western fashion, I confronted him and asked if there was a problem. He assured me all was well, so I assumed it would all be forgotten, but our relationship, in spite of my attempts to make amends by showing respect thereafter, was never the same."

Routine interpersonal behavior in one culture can be ruthless behavior in another. Responsibility focused on tasks and work to be done, as for the doctor, is vastly different from responsibility attached to role and position. Guilt for an inappropriate act is focused on that specific transaction, while shame from a loss of face is a more total, more inclusively relational, and more enduring emotion.

The contrast between traditional and nontraditional cultures has been analyzed across various polarities that stress different aspects: formal vs. informal, restrictive vs. elaborate cultures, outer responsibility vs. inner responsibility, individualism vs. sociocentric personality structure, and shame controls vs. guilt controls. All are aspective perspectives on the same phenomena. In dealing with the emotive element of shame and control in this chapter, we are not seeking to elevate it as a more crucial factor than the others, but to explore it as a significant, even central issue in pastoral counseling and psychotherapy.

Both guilt and shame are largely avoided in Western writing in the latter half of the twentieth century. When references do occur, they tend to label both emotions as repressive forces to be exorcised from the individual in the pursuit of liberation. Oppressive guilt and alienating shame are indeed debilitating forces to be confronted and released, but the constructive and instructive powers of both emotions are largely overlooked. In cross-cultural work, such evasion of these central human emotions becomes impossible.

In this chapter we will be arguing for a new organization of theory and therapy in working cross-culturally with controls—controls within and without the person. Briefly, the argument will maintain:

1. Anxiety, shame, and guilt are the natural, normal, and universal sequence of controls in human personality in every culture.

2. There are no "shame cultures" or "guilt cultures" per se, but a culture may stress one of the three control patterns more than the others.

3. All three processes occur in each person, group, and culture but to varying degrees and with differing configurations.

4. Although these are sequential in development, there is no basis for an evolutionary hierarchy suggesting superior or inferior cultural development for one predominant control vis-à-vis another.

5. The cultural oppression that has come from using a Kantian hierarchy of moral values to judge one culture as incompletely "socialized" or another as "superior in moral conscience formation" is not supported by actual cases or observations.

6. The negative valuation given to shame by Western theorists, therapists, and theologians betrays a bias (whether evolutionary, hierarchical, or philosophical) which both blinds one to the wisdom of other cultures and blocks one's own potential growth.

7. A full acceptance of, integration of, and reconciliation of the polar elements in anxiety, in shame, in guilt can draw on the healing strengths within all these emotions as well as release blocks to liberation and growth in persons and in groups.

8. Anxiety, shame, and guilt all contribute to and find resolution in authentic forgiveness and the experience of grace.

Pastoral counseling and psychotherapy, among all the helping professions, see anxiety as rooted in our human finitude, shame as a gift to our relatedness, and guilt as essential to our moral and volitional existence. Theologically rooted therapy does not deny or avoid the functions of these impulse-control emotions but, rather, understands them as central to our co-responsibility as persons created to live in community.

Pastoral theology, because of its appreciation of the whole human organism, can see both poles of each human emotion as valuable and even essential to our full humanness.

The Negation of Shame

Contemporary Western psychology is almost uniformly negative in both defining and evaluating the emotion of shame. A recent exception is pastoral psychotherapist Carl Schneider, who has examined both sides of shame and challenged this united front.

> Shame and the sense of shame is a devalued dimension of human experience. In contradistinction to the ethical stance adopted by many popular contemporary thinkers, we need to attend to shame, not to dismiss it as a mechanism that is crippling or inhibiting, but rather to suggest that a sensitivity to the sense of shame will result in a richer understanding of what it means to be fully human. (Schneider 1977:ix)

The rejection of shame by Western thinkers and writers is rooted in a faith commitment to individual moral autonomy. Following the Enlightenment, rational models of human experience and evolutionary views of human intellectual development combined to devalue shame and seek to remove it from human experience. In the past two centuries, Thomas Burgess (1839), Charles Darwin (1872), Friedrich Nietzsche (1880s), Vladimir Soloviev (1898), and Havelock Ellis (1899) all wrote incisively on the nature of shame, but in this century, among first-rank thinkers, only Jean-Paul Sartre has explored it positively and in depth (Schneider 1977:6).

Although contemporary scholars such as Erik Erikson, R. D. Laing, and Gerhart Piers have contributed to our understanding of shame, in this century the majority of treatments have considered it a childishly immature, even infantile emotion to be overcome on the way to maturity. A chorus of voices of popular forms of psychology urges an indiscriminate divesting of both shame and guilt in the search for liberation and the discovery of human potential. Among the most creative theoreticians of the new therapies, one looks in vain for a Westerner who understands and utilizes the positive elements in shame.

Gestalt therapy, as defined by its foremost thinker, Frederick Perls, identifies shame as the subversive fifth column within the psyche. "Shame and embarrassment are Quislings of the organism. . . . As the Quislings identify themselves with the enemy and not with their own people, so shame, embarrassment, self-consciousness, and fear restrict the individual's expressions. Expressions change into repressions" (Perls 1969:178).

Bioenergetic therapy, with its reverence for bodily experience and expression of emotional energies, somehow sees shame only as a negative energy to be discharged. "Shame, a derivative of the consciousness of inferiority, robs an individual of dignity, of self-respect, and of the feeling of being equal to (as good as) others" (Lowen 1975:197).

Among the leaders of the human potentials movement, Schutz offers representative opinion. "How is joy attained? A large part of the effort, unfortunately, must go into undoing. Guilt, shame, embarrassment, or fear of punishment, failure, success, retribution—all must be overcome. Obstacles to release must be surmounted. Destructive and blocking behavior, thoughts, and feelings must be altered" (Schutz 1967:20).

The negative definition and evaluation of shame is also virtually unanimous among Western theologians and missionaries, as exemplified by a major paper given at the 1982 Hayama Missionary Seminar in Japan, which concludes:

> Shame always stands between people and pushes them apart. It never draws people together. It makes for concealment, not disclosure of self. It leads to lies, anger, and avoidance . . . it is the mark of slavery to the opinions and attitudes of others, not of autonomy and inwardly responsibly-formed value judgments. It never leads, therefore, to confession and reconciliation. It leads to concealment and avoidance, and therefore to the perpetuation of the situation that caused the shame. It turns people into enemies. It never

makes them into friends. It makes for distrust, not trust; self-defense, not affirmation of the other. Pride, and its reverse side, shame, is the original sin. (MacLeod 1982:12)

In contrast to this total rejection of shame, guilt is presented as a potentially good and redemptive force rooted in responsibility and leading to repentance and growth.

> The main distinguishing feature between shame and guilt feelings, therefore, is that the former incorporate no feelings of responsibility, while the latter must. Guilt is the feeling of pain associated with having been remiss in the fulfillment of one's responsibility. This betokens a stage of human development far in advance of mere shame feelings. In fact it is the characteristic of persons who have entered into the level of being truly human. People incapable of guilt feelings are inhuman. (MacLeod 1982:14)

The view that shame is a "less than fully human" emotion follows the Western bias that sees guilt as a superior motivation because it rises later in the childhood development process. However, we do not devalue attachment, love, trust, or will, which all arise earlier or at the same time as shame. The reasons for viewing this particular feeling judgmentally in Western thought suggest a cultural bias, a bias that is a direct descendant of Enlightenment thought and the individualism, privatism, rationalism, and egocentrism it has offered us.

It is puzzling that we can see the positive and negative sides of anxiety, of fear, of trust, of guilt, and of will but are insistently blind to the two poles of shame. We deny its constructive creative side of discretion and exaggerate the destructive potential of its negative, alienating side. Shame is bipolar; it both separates and presses for reunion; it is an impulse to conceal and a yearning to be accepted; it is responsibility to others and personal recognition of a need to respond in more acceptable ways.

The Two Faces of Shame

The English language has only one word for shame. Indo-European languages commonly have two or more (Greek and Latin each have five; German and French, two). Oriental languages are also more rich (Japanese, Chinese, Thai, Malay, Javanese, Tamil, and Hindi all have more than one word for this complex emotion). In English, shame is synonymous with being ashamed, with disgrace; to express the positive side of shame one must speak of "a proper sense of shame."

The positive side—shame as discretion—can be observed in three forms. (1) As an emotion rooted in the physiology of human beings, evidenced by the spontaneous blush of modesty or at even the thought of intense embarrassment; shame is as intimately related to the blushing reflex as anger is to autonomic arousal, or anxiety to shortness of breath and narrowing of the chest. (2) As a disposition toward choosing socially desirable or acceptable behavior; shame is a habitual tendency, a settled disposition to act in certain ways and according to certain principles. (3)

As an ethical inclination characterized by modesty, moderation, or temperance. "The connection between shame and virtue is even more clearly established when we note that cultures regularly give shamelessness a negative connotation. The concept of shamelessness suggests that the lack of a proper sense of shame is a moral deficiency and that the possession of a sense of shame is a moral obligation" (Schneider 1977:19; note Table 4-1).

The negative side—shame as disgrace—is a painful experience of the disintegration of one's world. It has the instant effect of disrupting one's social relations, disorienting one's whole world and one's place in it, and creating disgust with one's behavior and one's self. As an emotion, it is a feeling of humiliating exposure; as a situation, it is a position of loss of face, respect, and inclusion; as an internal fragmentation, it is being confronted with painful self-consciousness and condemned before or by

---

Table 4-1. Shame

Shame as Discretion *(Before the act)*	*Shame as Disgrace* *(After the act)*
Discretion shame is a complex of emotional, volitional, and dispositional factors.	Disgrace shame is the painful experience of disruption, disorientation, disgust, and the disintegration of one's world.
As an emotion, it can produce a blush in contemplation of a dishonoring choice.	As an emotion, it is a feeling of being exposed, humiliated, despised, totally rejected, and dishonored.
As a motivation, it can evoke choices that have moral character, ethical direction, and recognition of obligation.	As a situation, it is being in a position of loss of face, loss of respect, and loss of inclusion by significant others.
As a disposition, it becomes a virtue, a settled habitual tendency to act according to certain principles.	As fragmentation, it is being suddenly confronted with painful self-consciousness; the self is disclosed to the self; the shame is not just for the act done but for what the self is. Thus it is a total emotion, a rejection of the whole self.
Shamelessness, in almost all cultures, is seen as a negative quality. A lack of a proper sense of shame is a moral deficiency; the possession of a proper sense of shame is a moral obligation.	Shame has the potential of being a totally negative experience of alienation from the self and from others. But shame is intrinsically both positive and negative, essentially ambivalent. The alienation experienced is from a relationship deeply desired. The underlying dynamic is acceptance, affection, and positive valuation deeply needed from other persons and the society.

(Schneider 1977:19–26)

the ego ideal, the internal image of the ideal self. Note its many varieties (Table 4-2).

The intensity of the shame experience is captured in Kurt Riezler's description of being shamed (1951:202):

> Your image of yourself is broken. You are confronted with your own meanness. You despise yourself. You will hate the one who puts you to shame. This hate is the most bitter of all, the most difficult to heal. It has the longest memory. Shame burns. Perhaps decades later you will suddenly remember and blush.

As the Chinese proverb says, "A murder may be forgiven, an affront never."

The impact of shame as disgrace is like a tidal wave of emotion. Although it is outer-directed, shame also seems to break upon one from without, as Helen Lynd comments (1958:32):

> Shame involves a quality of the unexpected: if in any way we feel it coming we are powerless to avert it. Whatever part voluntary action may have in the experience of shame is swallowed up in the sense of something that overwhelms us from without and "takes us" unawares. We are taken by

Table 4-2. Varieties of Shame	
Innocent shame	Shame felt when one's character is slandered without justification
Guilty shame	Shame felt before others when one violates an ethical norm
Social shame	Embarrassment felt when one makes a social blunder or error
Familial shame	Disgrace from the behavior of another family member
Handicap shame	Embarrassment over some bodily defect or physical imperfection
Discrimination shame	Downgrading of persons treated as socially, racially, ethically, religiously, or vocationally inferior
Modesty shame	Shame related to sexual, social, or dress norms and proscribed behavior
Inadequacy shame	Feelings of inadequacy and inferiority from passivity, repeated failure, or abuse
Public shame	Open ridicule in the community as punishment or group pathology
Anticipated shame	The fear of exposure for any planned or desired behavior

(Adapted from Noble 1975:4–6)

surprise, caught off guard, or off base, caught unawares, made a fool of. It is as if we were suddenly invaded from the rear where we cannot see, are unprotected, and can be overpowered.

Shame is both positive and negative, both the capacity for discretion and, when indiscreet, the consequent disgrace. This polar emotion offers the possibilities of keen sensitivity to others and intense pain before others. Both sides of shame are essential parts of humanness.

The feeling of shame reveals its hopeful core, its underlying positive valuation. If all self-respect is lost, the feeling of failure or betrayal does not arouse shame but self-contempt. Shame reveals how deeply the person cares. Paul Pruyser expresses it succinctly: "Shame has the seeds of betterment in it. . . . It is future-directed and lives from hope" (Pruyser 1968:323). As Schneider concludes, "If one stands judged and inadequate before one's better self, one still possesses that better self; while shame may separate the self from the other, it also points to a deeper connection. *In shame, the object one is alienated from, one also loves still*" (Schneider 1977:28).

If one feels solely rejection or contempt for oneself, then the emotional response is not shame but disgust. To be ashamed of oneself, one must maintain a deep level of positive feelings about oneself. In contempt, the object, be it self or another, is rejected, but in shame there is a longing for relationship, a grieving for what has been lost, a yearning for contact to be restored. "The underlying dynamic of shame, then, is a positive valuation" (Schneider 1977:27).

Shame, as Eastern psychologists have tried to tell us, is an intrinsic and essentially healthful part of our humanness, both in its discretion and in the pain of disgrace. We can learn from its sensitivity to delicate human relationships and profit from its alertness to failures anticipated or failures suffered. Shame is not the undeniable sign of immaturity or inferiority in the person or the group. It is a communally oriented, socially responsive concern for relationship, a caring for harmony, a hope for trust maintained or restored.

British existential psychoanalyst Ronald Laing describes a clinical case history (1961:138–139) in which a person is transformed by allowing herself to experience the buried "cleansing shame."

> A successful professional painter was very slick at lifelike portraiture but could not bring herself to do abstracts. She remembered she used to make black messy drawings when she was a young child. Her mother, a painter herself of insistently sweet flower arrangements and such like, valued "free expression." She never told her daughter not to make messes, but always told her, "No, that's not you." She felt empty, ashamed, and angry. She subsequently learnt to paint and draw what she was told was "her." When she remembered the full force of her feelings about those early drawings, which she had lost touch with without completely forgetting, she returned to her black messes after over thirty years. Only when she did could she fully realize how empty and twisted all her life had been. She felt what she called a "cleansing shame" at betraying her own truest feelings. She contrasted this clean shame, and in the strongest terms, with the "shameful

emptiness" she had felt when she had been told that these messy drawings were not really her.

This case illustrates both the positive aspect of existential shame—shame at failing to express and experience the possible, the potential within—and conventional shame, which was repressive and robbed the artist of self-respect. The "shameful emptiness" she recalled when forced to disown her experience of reality was a destructive introjection, which, when discharged, allowed her to recover a deeper, more essential sense of shame, a shame at her "doubt" of her own perception of the world and her right to see what she saw. The power of "cleansing shame" transformed the frozen character structures providing the needed discretion to discern her own authentic direction toward new healing and integration.

Shame Cultures or Guilt Cultures?

The typology of societies as shame or guilt cultures was set forth first and most clearly by Ruth Benedict in *Patterns of Culture* (1934), in which she proposed that each society is directed by an organizing principle that arises from the basic aspects of human personality. This principle was referred to as the "mainspring," "the pattern," or, most frequently, the "ethos." With the publication of *The Chrysanthemum and the Sword* (1946) she drew on Margaret Mead's work, which characterized the Western cultural character as guilt-oriented, and contrasted it with the Japanese culture, terming it shame-oriented.

> A society that inculcates absolute standards of morality and relies on developing a conscience is a guilt culture by definition. True shame cultures rely on external sanctions for good behavior, not, as true guilt cultures do, on an internalized conviction of sin. Shame is a reaction to other people's criticism. A man is shamed either by being openly ridiculed and rejected or by fantasying to himself that he has been made ridiculous. In either case it is a potent sanction. But it requires an audience or at least a fantasy of an audience. Guilt does not. In a nation where honor means living up to one's own picture of oneself, one may suffer from guilt though no one knows of the misdeed, and a feeling of guilt may actually be relieved by confessing the sin. (Benedict 1946:222–223)

This clear-cut distinction between outer-directed cultures as controlled primarily by shame and inner-directed cultures shaped by guilt gained wide popularity among both Eastern and Western thinkers, including Japanese reviewers, for the first decade after its publication. Then its weaknesses as a typology began to emerge.

Benedict's work, brilliant and successful as it was, suffered from the focus, typical of all "national character" studies, on one primary trait as typifying the whole. The Japanese obligational structure of vertical loyalties, with its intricate system of outer-directed motivations and rewards, is even more complex and varied today than in the nineteenth century (the period most similar to Benedict's characterization). It is a pattern that is, today, beyond any one description of temperament or group personality. Later studies by persons in many cultures—in Japan, China, India, the Philippines, and Thailand, to begin the list—indicate that a parallel constellation of psychological traits occurs in all human beings, but the configuration in each group or culture may be unique to that body. Francis Hsu, in holding that "our most important environment is the social environment," goes on to conclude that patterns of affects do exist in various environments, in fact, "the basic pattern of affect of each society is likely to persist, in some cases, over thousands of years" (Hsu 1978:156–157).

Some writers, following Benedict's typology, have suggested that the internalization of norms is the key phenomenon that is present in certain types of societies and absent from others. Those with norm internalization are termed "guilt cultures," since cultural conformity is motivated by rules, values, and norms controlling from within through guilt. Those that do not induce the internalization of norms are termed "shame cultures," since the members of the society conform to cultural norms only when fellow members are present to shame them. A guilt culture functions by intrinsic controls, a shame culture by extrinsic controls.

The theory—parsimonious, clear, attractive to many—does not stand up to deeper examination. Norms exist in the institutions, laws, and structures of all societies and within the persons who make up those societies. We may observe with Spiro that in any society there may be some who have internalized few norms (psychopaths), and many who have not internalized some of the norms, but in all societies most individuals learn, accept, and use the norms and feel moral anxiety should they desire to violate them (Spiro 1961:118).

A more satisfactory explanation is that persons in a society may be more oriented by shame or more directed by guilt, but both are present to some degree in the culture and its people.

To call a society a "shame culture" or a "guilt culture" reduces the complex patterns of affect to a single emotional control pattern. Subsequent research confirms the hypothesis that anxiety, shame, and guilt are a universal developmental sequence, although they occur in varying measures and are expressed in diverse cultural patterns. The emotional dimension is only part process of the control patterns, along with the perception of responsibility as being in the self or in the situation, or the sense of agency may be internal to the person or external in the environment; thus a multidimensional systems model is necessary to understand the configuration of controls, emotions, and responsibilities whether in the person, the group, or in the culture.

When we speak of a group that is more anxiety-controlled, or tends toward a greater shame orientation, or is predominantly guilt focused, this is no longer to imply that the one process is exclusively present. Rather it is to examine part process in an integrative system of controls, while noting that one particular part may play a decisive role in that culture's socialization of the person and the social process in community.

Piers and Singer (1953:53), after laying the concepts of pure "shame or guilt cultures" to rest, still comment on the way in which either emotion may exert a significant influence on a culture.

> Both shame and guilt are highly important mechanisms to ensure socialization of the individual. Guilt transfers the demands of society through the early primitive parental images. Social conformity achieved through guilt will be essentially one of *submission*. Shame can be brought to the individual more readily in the process of comparing and competing with the peers (siblings, schoolmates, gang, professional group, social class, etc.). Social conformity achieved through shame will be essentially one of *identification*. One might, therefore, easily expect to find various cultures characterized and differentiated according to the prevalent use of either shame- or guilt-inducing sanctions to ensure social integration.

Francis Hsu (1949:231) suggests that the key element is not shame and guilt but rather the uses of suppression and repression as restraints in socializing persons into cultural conformity. Shame is a byproduct of suppression, guilt a byproduct of repression.

> Every society is bound to impose some restraint on its members, whether in the earlier years of the individual or later. Since no individual is fully conscious of all the restraints of his society that are applicable to him and since repression usually begins as suppression, it is evident that, in the normal course of events, the individual in every society is subject to some forces of suppression and some of repression. However some cultures employ more suppression for a similar purpose. In a culture which emphasizes suppression as a mechanism of socialization, external controls will be more important to the individual than internal controls. In a culture which emphasizes repression as the mechanism of socialization, internal controls will be more important than external controls. In the former the basic pattern of life tends to be situation-centered. In the latter the basic pattern of life tends to be individual-centered.

Repression is used to signify "the exclusion of painful and unpleasant material from consciousness and from motor expression," so repressed material is buried in the unconscious. Suppression is the restraint from certain actions because of external circumstances—the thought of such actions, however, not being excluded from consciousness. Suppression thus evokes shame, repression provokes guilt.

Not only shame and guilt but also anxiety, the precursor to both, function as controls in every society. Where one becomes the dominant process, it will shape the patterns of social restraints and cultural characteristics. In Table 4-3 the three emotions are compared and contrasted, with both their negative and positive contributions sketched.

Nigerian psychiatrist T. A. Lambo, past deputy secretary of the World Health Organization, Geneva, writes of the pervasive anxiety of African cultures:

> African culture manifests an intensely realized perception of supernatural presence but with a kind of adolescent impetuousness and a fatuous, almost fanatical, faith in the magic of certain symbols to produce certain results . . . thus especially conducive to states of morbid fear and anxiety. Rituals,

Table 4-3. Comparison of Anxiety, Shame, and Guilt

Anxiety	*Shame*	*Guilt*
Anxiety is a loss of calm before a perceived threat.	Shame is a loss of face before significant persons.	Guilt is loss of integrity before one's own conscience.
Anxiety is feared vulnerability before dangers real or fantasized.	Shame is failure before one's ideal or exposure before an audience.	Guilt is condemnation before an inner parent or judge.
Anxiety is arousal before environmental demands.	Shame is embarrassment before social demands.	Guilt is pain under moral demands.
Anxiety is a primal emotion: feelings of powerlessness, fear of powers, dread of loss of being.	Shame is a total emotion: fearing rejection as a person, exclusion from community, or withdrawal of love.	Guilt is a specific emotion: fearing judgment of behavior, correction of acts, or withdrawal of trust.
Anxiety is paralyzing fear, dismay, panic; the impulse is to freeze, to flee, or to fight.	Shame is humiliating exposure, dishonor, self-negation; the impulse is to hide, to cover, to deny.	Guilt is humbling disclosure, discomfort, regretted acts; the impulse is to justify, rationalize, excuse.
Positive Power	*Positive Power*	*Positive Power*
Anxiety energizes, alerts perception, heightens awareness, mobilizes defenses.	Shame is discretion motivating choices, energizing "honor," a disposition to virtue.	Guilt is direction demanding the better, pointing to values, an urge for integrity.
Negative Power	*Negative Power*	*Negative Power*
Anxiety distracts attention, disrupts discrimination, reduces impulse control, overloads cognition.	Shame is disgrace disrupting social life, disorienting the self, dishonoring before others.	Guilt is pain suffering internal division, resenting failure, destroying inner peace.
Resolution	*Resolution*	*Resolution*
Anxiety must be released by reframing, discharged by ventilation, dissipated by action. It is being secure.	Shame leads to earning place, recovering face, regaining honor. It is being accepted.	Guilt leads to exercising responsibility, expressing regrets, acting repentantly. It is being forgiven.

involving sacrifice that may connote life-taking (actual or symbolic), are a logical outcome. "Malignant anxiety," an abnormal psychosocial condition, has developed under the impact of social and emotional difficulties encountered in personalities psychologically ill-equipped to meet them. (Lambo 1964:444)

Malignant anxiety, as a peculiarly African culture-bound illness, is an accumulation of hostility that is not converted into depression or psycho-neurotic or psychosomatic symptoms, as is common in cultures more shaped by shame and guilt formations. Instead, the mounting anxiety may erupt in destructive acts against self, others, or both.

In a culture using anxiety controls predominantly, the characteristic patterns of fear of "powers" and respect for animistic, theistic, or sociopolitical forces direct the emotional mood of the society. The anxiety in the face of these "powers" and the rituals of empowerment and protection shape the ways shame and guilt will appear.

The resultant traditions and structures that emerge center in the safety, security, and survival of the group. Anxiety structures emerge in custom and ritual, mythology and religion, tribal values and tribal law. Describing this survival motive in an Indonesian village, theologian Marianne Katoppo writes (1981:45,47):

> In the rural areas people still live very much by the *adat. Adat* is the tradition, customs, and culture of each tribe or ethnic group. Originally this adat law was intended to maintain cosmic balance, thus preserving the tribe from all evil. As long as one observed the proper rites and lived in the prescribed way of the ancestors, one—and thus the tribe—would be safe. In such a traditional society, it is the tribe, not the person, who is important. Marriage is entered into for the preservation of the tribe, not for the personal gratification of those concerned. . . . The people often do not perceive how the *adat,* originally conceived of to preserve the community from evil, has in itself become evil. Instead of protecting people, it oppresses them.

In a culture shaped predominantly by shame controls, the expectations, sanctions, and restraints of the significant others in a person's world become the agents of behavior control. The shame incorporates the basic anxiety and shapes the guilt through the promises of acceptance or the threats of rejection. "Shame operates best in communities in which there is face-to-face interaction between all members and in which the miscreant can neither hide his deeds nor escape their consequences; it is thus the means par excellence of social control in small towns and primitive societies" (Murphy 1979:137).

In a culture controlled predominantly by guilt, controls are expected to be internal, within the conscience. The guilt is focused on the violation of specific prescribed behaviors, and the anxiety and shame tend to be repressed or denied and the energies redirected.

The variations of intensity in the three successive stages may be visualized by bell curves, as in Figure 4-1. One developmental pattern shows the central tendency skewed toward the anxiety stage, the second shows normal distribution, and the third is skewed toward the guilt stage. Persons in all three patterns exist in every cultural group, but the central tendency of a group may be seen in the culture's values, mores, rules, relationships, conflict negotiation styles, arts, and literature. The impact of a culture can be seen in the way the balance within the person tends to parallel that of the group. Each shapes and is shaped by the other.

When a culture uses anxiety as the primary means of inhibiting undesirable behavior and ensuring the choice of socially desirable options,

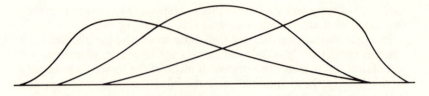

Anxiety	*Shame*	*Guilt*
(Global controls)	(External controls)	(Internal controls)
Increased stress on the first stage, from the culture's "power" orientation, animistic fear traditions, and uses of anxiety in child rearing	Increased stress on the second stage from the culture's "social" orientation, outer direction, and uses of shaming in child rearing	High stress on the third stage from the cultural practice of internal controls, internalized individualistic direction, and use of guilt induction in child training

Figure 4-1. Comparison of three basic loci of control.

shame will still be present in the social process, along with a lesser degree of guilt in internal reflection on failures and rejections or in deciding future alternatives.

Where social controls of inclusion or exclusion provide the dominant inhibition and direction of behavior, the anxiety is absorbed into and utilized by the shame process as a primal source of energy. Guilt exists in internal self-judgment or moral choice, but as a secondary process, with shame being the effective coin of social transactions.

When guilt is the society's normal process of shaping and directing its members' behavior, both anxiety and shame remain more primitive and diffuse, with the investment of social expectations and the threat of failure or loss operating in largely unconscious levels beneath the individual conscience process. Thus we speak of a dominant emotional process operating in the flow of conscious experience, and the parallel processes being largely unconscious but still powerful influences within the personality. Figure 4-2 illustrates the conscious/unconscious dominance of a particular emotional process as compared with the other more repressed and less developed impulse control emotions.

An intriguing example of this conscious/unconscious distinction comes from Japanese studies, which indicates that any characterization of the Japanese culture as a shame culture is not adequate. Both shame and guilt are present in clearly visible forms. The strong achievement drive so often noted among the Japanese is not to be understood simply as a shame-oriented concern with community standards but is also linked with a deep undercurrent of guilt. This guilt is not, as in the West, grounded in a complex of universal absolutes and supernatural sanctions,

Unconscious   *Conscious*

A tribal society of animistic or cosmic fear traditions.

"Powers" and "power" structures are the dominant control; guilt and shame are largely unconscious; anxiety offers energies for inhibition of undesirable behavior and direction toward desired ends.

An outer-directed society of strongly socialized sanctions for inclusion and exclusion.

Shame characterizes the major energies of inhibition and discretion, with controls being predominantly external; anxiety and guilt exist although working in largely unconscious ways.

An inner-directed society of strongly individualized and internalized controls.

Guilt characterizes the major psychic structure of a conscience functioning as "parent judge," with shame and anxiety largely repressed and unconscious.

Unconscious   *Conscious*

**Figure 4-2. The distinction between conscious
and unconscious controls.**

but is instead derived from the system of loyalties that cements the structure of their traditional society. The substratum of guilt among Japanese is not visible to outside observation because of (1) profoundly hidden obligations in familial relationships, the community networks, and the national loyalty of the Japanese vs. the non-Japanese and (2) because the conscious cultural emphasis on external shame sanctions disguises the underlying feelings of guilt, which, severely repressed, are not obvious to most persons themselves (Norbeck and DeVos 1972:32).

> In Western eyes, the Japanese sense of guilt appears to be rather sluggish.
> . . . Where the Westerner tends to think of the sense of guilt as an inner

problem for the individual, the Japanese has no such idea. . . . What is characteristic about the Japanese sense of guilt, though, is that it shows itself most sharply when the individual suspects that his action will result in betraying the group to which he belongs. (Doi 1973:49)

Guilt, in this form, rises from a deep-lying sense of betrayal—the individual betrays the trust of members of his or her own group. The sense of guilt is a function of interpersonal relations, not primarily of intrapersonal dynamics. The sense of guilt commences with a sense of betrayal and ends in an apology; it originates in the self and is directed outward in apology, whereas shame originates in the eyes of the observing world and is directed inward toward the self (Doi 1973:53).

In the Japanese society, shame is the overt social control process, guilt the covert. The motivations of the society may rise from these deeper levels, while the everyday interpersonal relationships are more shaped by the visible external controls.

In Western culture, guilt is the overt process, shame the covert. The person is aware of guilt feelings following wrongdoing, while shame is largely unconscious. (This is not to deny the major levels of guilt that may function in the largely unconscious levels of the personality; see Figure 4:2.) When anxiety and shame are the more covert processes, they tend to be converted into secondary emotions such as anger, resentment, or grief, which only succeeds in concealing them from the self even more effectively.

The Developmental Sequence

Developmental theories each have their own claim to uniqueness, as well as clear similarities. Unquestionably, the most common opinion about the emerging psyche is the sequence of the three primary control emotions. Anxiety intimidates, shame suppresses, guilt obligates. The three rise in serial progression, although the length of each emotion's ascendancy and the intensity of its influence vary significantly from culture to culture. The account given by analytic, behavioral, social learning, structural, and humanistic psychologists utilizes contrasting language and concepts, but fear, shame, and guilt remain as the three basic emotions in every analysis of developing controls.

Among the most integrative accounts of the developmental life cycle is the work of Erik Erikson, offering a psychological-social-biological-spiritual analysis of eight stages of life. Erikson views development as a multidimensional process of biological and psychological drives pressing from within, socializing forces containing and directing from without, and cultural, ritual, and spiritual capacities being opened before the person. In an instinctual-conflictual approach, he sees the child as moved by conflicting drives toward both attachment and separation and therefore seeking a resolution of the appropriate polar tensions that arise in each stage. Both the positive and the negative poles must be present before the integrative "virtue" emerges. Thus both trust and mistrust are necessary for the virtue *hope* to be born; unless there is tension between the urge for autonomy and the doubt of one's ability to risk or the shame from having overstepped one's bounds, the virtue *will* is not created and the child may be willful or will-less rather than willing; if there is no tension between the excitement of initiative in creative playing, risking, and experimenting and the limits of the emerging conscience experienced as guilt, there will be no sense of the virtue *purpose.*

Figure 4-3 diagrams this polar tension and its optimal resolution throughout the life cycle. The length of each stage and the degree of stress placed upon it by the socialization process of the particular family and the supporting group vary widely from one situation or culture to another. The influences in this formation go beyond the obvious elements of the child-rearing practices to the cultural practices and values that form the matrix for parents, the family system, and the emotional field of the supporting community. The family, the social context, and the underlying values shaping both are a cluster of interacting forces that work together in the personality formation of each member of the community.

Erikson has stressed the fact that to discover the personal-social-cultural "meaning" of an event in an individual's life (a crisis, an action, an association, a dream), it must be studied with reference to four "coordinates": (1) the contemporary stage of life of the individual, (2) his or her life history (psychosexual and psychosocial), (3) the contemporary stage of the sociocultural unit of which he or she is a part, and (4) the history of the sociocultural unit (Erikson 1963:247–263; 1964:111–157).

> As we face cultural and historical relativity, let me assert here only one point which in all the years of work with our scheme has not been weakened: while the exact *age* of onset and the *length* of any stage of development as well as the *intensity* of the conflict experienced may all vary dramatically from one culture to another and from one individual to another, the *order* and *sequence* of these stages remains fixed; for they are intrinsically related both to physiological stages and to the basic requirements of any social order.
>
> By the same token, while I have selected my terms with some care in regard to their translatability, I welcome any suggestions for more applicable ones in specific contexts, as long as their interrelatedness and the inner order of the whole scheme is safeguarded. (Erikson 1979a:26)

In a society in which the child is trained by a large number of persons —mother, father, aunts, uncles, grandparents in an extended family— or in which the parenting figures discipline the child predominantly by threats of rejection or punishment from many other persons—"What will others think of, say about, do to such a bad child?"—it is more likely that an outer-directed personality will emerge. The child is unlikely to introject the parents as internal control structures, since impulse control is achieved through an increased sensitivity to the expectations of others. The child feels the threat of the withdrawal of love, of being cut off from the important persons in the family world, and of falling short of the

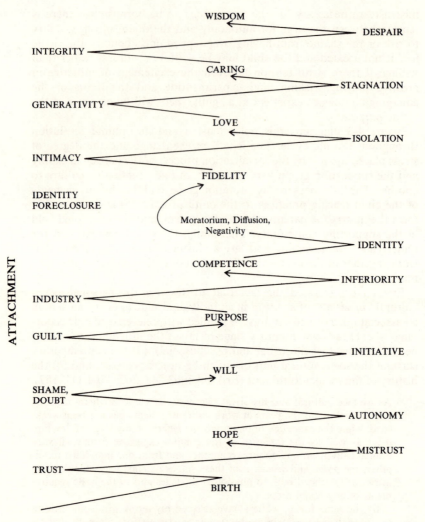

Figure 4-3. Erikson's vision of the dialectic of growth.

ideal self being created within—a good girl or boy who is always loved, accepted, included (Spiro 1961:119).

As a shame orientation forms, the child comes to fear the anger of others at any misbehavior and the shame that would ensue. The fear of offending others, either deliberately or unwittingly, internalizes the sanctions, the "should nots" and "ought nots," as negative injunctions from the ideal self. One should not act shamefully or let oneself be shamed. One ought not offend others, or let oneself be alienated from others. Secondarily, shame defines the positive goals desired—the safety of belonging, the security of being accepted fully by others. Shame as discretion protects the person from the feared pain of shame as disgrace (Eberhard 1967:2).

> The Indian culture is to a great extent a shame-prone culture. The ability to feel guilt is not completely absent, but Indian people are likely to experience shame more than guilt when they violate a moral value. It is not merely the presence of shame or guilt in a culture but the dominance of one of them which makes a culture either a shame- or a guilt-prone culture. The ability to feel either shame or guilt depends on a complex interaction between personality and culture. (Pitamber 1982:6)

Socialization within the joint family system leads to the construction of the superego from the supervision of a complex network of significant adults rather than from two parental figures. Not only the parents but other members of the joint family and the community family come to have parental status, and all these become significant for the person. The child is under constant observation, supervision, and control. External authority is always present in every sphere of life. The need for internalizing what is reliably constant in the context is thus very low. The lack of separation, distance, or privacy creates no opportunity for the construction of a conscience, but the group ego ideal is assimilated in both the actuality of daily interaction and the high value placed on acceptance, conformity, and belonging. Values are relational, not objective and intrinsic.

> In a shame-culture, approval of "parents" is more important than the actual performance of a deed. Approval of deeds by parents is interpreted as approval of the self. Therefore a deed does not have any value in itself, except through the approval of self. (Pitamber 1982:7–8)

Socialization in the joint family–communal family tends to create a familial identity, not a personal identity. When one identifies with the collective rather than with particular persons, one does not individuate a distinct identity; one incorporates a corporate identity.

"Individuation depends on internalizing and identifying not with a group but with particular persons" (Bettelheim 1973:315). Corporate self depends on the experience of solidarity.

Conformity in cooperative affiliation is the positive pole of the person with familial-communal identity. The group ego ideal has become the guiding superego function of each member. In positive spirals of communal solidarity, this is productive of harmonious and unified relationships. In negative spirals, it can escalate rapidly to uncontrollable violence.

> Shame is not aroused in a person if he [she] feels that his [her] acts have been approved by those considered significant. When a person performs any act in the interest of the community, he [she] is not concerned about the wrongness or rightness of the acts, but only with the approval of the self. . . . If a shame-prone person commits violence which is considered valid (in the community of significant people) then such a person has no reason to feel shame. (Pitamber 1982:10)

Mob violence or religious violence can explode with great power, even in a normally cooperative and affiliative group. The intense revenge of Hindus against Sikhs following the assassination of Indira Gandhi and the attacks on the Harijans by upper-caste groups exemplify the uncontrolled, concerted violence possible when the group mind turns toward retaliation or territorial protection.

In a society in which the child is trained by a very few persons—the parents in a nuclear family—these agents of socialization administer punishments and embody the values being enforced. The child then internalizes the society's norms and introjects the parents to form the internal punishing or rewarding structure we call "conscience." The outer direction of shame now yields to inner directions from these newly forming control structures. The child experiences guilt before the internal "parent" and feels self-punishment when falling short of these expectations, whether or not the actual parents know of the misbehavior. The guilt is an internal sense of self-punishment that occurs in response to an act of wrongdoing, usually followed by a sense of remorse and regret.

By the age of five or six, the child is expected to police his or her own behavior. The child is now not only responsible for personal behavior but also responsible for how others behave or feel toward him or her. The child now feels guilty about an act of wrongdoing even if there is no external observer, no one to condemn the action. The judge is now internalized. The one who administers punishment is within, ever-present. And this agent of punishment has been absolutized. Right is right because it is absolutely, unchangeably, and divinely determined as right. And wrong is wrong, in an undeniable, unavoidable, unchangeable sense. The parent within represents the parent without who is the representative of the absolute values that hold all things in the universe together.

Anxiety, shame, and guilt, the three primary control emotions, rise sequentially and then mature throughout the later stages of the life cycle. Just as we can trace the serial progression from infantile undifferentiated anxieties to the global fears of childhood to the egocentric anxieties of youth and to the adult fears that finally emerge in both constructive and destructive forms, so we can note infantile shame with its global self-judgments, youthful shame with its totalism in negating the self as evil and worthless, and adult shame, which is more focused, specific, and proportional. Each emotion has its own maturational patterns that are age appropriate and stage distinguishable.

Cultural expectations may elaborate or inhibit the development of a full range of emotions. For example, in Western societies, where shame is devalued and anxiety repressed, the development of adult shame responses rarely occurs. When shame is felt, it is not as an adult embarrassment before peers and a loss of face in community but as an intensely regressive experience, a return to the global self-negation of early childhood. The totalism of the language, the ultimate judgments, the association of shame with depressive helpless and hopeless feelings all indicate an absence of a more mature and useful form of shame. So painful is this regressive shame that it is frequently hidden under a facade of shamelessness.

In traditional societies, the elaborated forms of social control continue the development of shame into adult forms of social responsibility, mutual preservation of honor in rituals and responses of face-saving behavior, and concern for maintaining one's place in community. Here shame is not the total, ultimate, global emotion of early childhood but the functional, responsible, outer-directed protection of one's own social persona and the careful integration of one's own needs, drives, and goals with those of a community of peers.

The Westerner, with arrested development of shame emotions and increased reliance upon internalized and individualistic guilt functions, views the shame controls of traditional societies with an unconscious bias. The projection of judgments from one's own inferior function—shame, in this case—onto another in whom the function is superiorly developed blocks both perception of the other's world and appreciation of its usefulness and power. In return, the Westerner appears brash and inconsiderate or rude and insensitive to those whose other-directed shame functions are more highly developed. Again, the projection of the inferior function makes understanding difficult. When acting predominantly by guilt controls—which are focused on the behavior in question rather than the person in context—the traditional person feels shameless, irresponsible, egocentric, so these judgments are projected onto inner-directed persons in the assumption that authentic caring is impossible among individualists.

Because each person's sense of shame and honor is rooted so deeply in the social expectations of the native culture, it is almost impossible to escape the "we-they" judgments that spring up from these deeply ingrained values. Such values can feed prejudices, biases, or routinely accepted stereotypes.

For example, "many Japanese and Koreans retain negative stereotypes of each other. Koreans often regard the Japanese penchant for politeness, propriety, and group loyalty as an indication of duplicity, arrogance, and narrow-mindedness. The Japanese regard the Korean tendency for spontaneity, frankness, and individuality as a sign they are impulsive, crude, and stubborn" (Han Sung-Joo 1984:14). The discovery that what is a shame to me is of no consequence to another comes as a shock to many. Later they may learn that those behaviors which are not just an issue of etiquette but are a point of honor to another are sometimes merely a matter of taste or preference to me. The content of shame and guilt feelings may vary widely, but the process, the impact, the pain are truly human. In suffering, we are so much alike that in the experience of pain we can meet human to human.

Shame, Guilt, and "Face"

"Face" is not simply a matter of public image, it is the collateral of the speculator, it is the social capital that serves to provide credit and confidence with others. One's "face" is one's fortune.

"Face" may be viewed as "positive face" (the desire to be understood, ratified, liked, admired) and "negative face" (the desire not to have one's action frustrated and to be free from imposition). Acts that threaten face must be reduced either through "positive politeness," directed to the person's positive face, or "negative politeness." Each of these includes a variety of strategies. Positive politeness is practiced by using group language to claim in-group membership, or by claiming agreement or avoiding disagreement, or by joking. Negative politeness is done by hedging, being indirect, avoiding all pressure (Brown and Levinson 1978:307–309).

Brown and Levinson claim that the seriousness of a face-threatening act is a complex function of three variables: distance, power, and rating of the imposition. Positive-politeness cultures have few serious face-threatening acts (impositions are seen as small, social distance permits easygoing interactions, relative power is never very great). This would include the United States, certain New Guinea cultures, and the Mbuti pygmies. Negative-politeness cultures include the Japanese, the British, and the Brahmians of India. (Face can be seriously threatened in most interactions, social closeness requires formal interactions, and great differentials of power exaggerate threat.)

"Face" refers to "personal integrity, good character, and the confidence of society and of oneself in one's ability to play one's social role" (Hu Hsien-chin 1944:44). "Losing face" results from falling short of the expectations set for one's role, or violating rules of conduct, or breaking the customary standards of community life. The person who loses face is punished by ridicule, contempt, or social exclusion. The judgment and even the ostracism not only are directed toward the offender but also reflect on the family and in some settings even on the ancestors.

Receiving help is always a painful process. To receive help, the person must confront the sense of powerlessness, failure, or betrayal that has precipitated a crisis and face it in the presence of another person. To receive help one must entrust the self to another, for the moment: give up one's way of being alone with a problem and share it with another. It is risking the known for an unknown that may be no better. It is giving up what is painful, yet familiar, for something that feels equally painful and is threateningly strange. Central to this struggle, in every culture, is the fear of stigma, of judgment, and of loss of face.

In traditional cultures around the world, the concern for family pride makes the acceptance of counseling an unattractive option. The family must not lose face under any circumstances, and all other considerations must find their second or third place. "Dirty clothes are washed within the family" is a Haitian proverb that is paralleled by wisdom from many other cultures. In the Chinese family, the central issue on maintaining face is not personal, it is familial. To discuss personal, marital, or parent-child problems outside the family causes parents, spouse, and other family members to lose face. Thus the family boundary, which in the West is called "a rubber wall" when it becomes nonpermeable and binding, is a castle wall in sociocentric cultures, which prize family identity rather than personal identity.

The loss of face, with intense feelings of shame before the family that shares the pain as well as the larger society that observes it, is a severe loss, as Indian pastoral counselor B. J. Prashantham notes (1983:44):

> Among the various types of losses—death, separation, divorce, desertion, loss of finances, limbs, or sight—one must include loss of face. This refers to loss of self-respect in one's own sight or in the sight of the community. This can be a powerfully painful experience, sometimes more painful than some of the other losses mentioned, resulting even in suicide.

The concept of "face," "saving face" or "losing face," is often described as an Asian preoccupation or social obsession. In actuality it is a universal concern of human beings, who live not only by their self-esteem but by esteem reflected from the faces of others.

To people in the West, the long delay for negotiations over the shape of the conference table for the 1972 Paris peace talks between Vietnam and the United States was an example of "Oriental face-saving." But a similar problem occurred in the Congress of Vienna in 1815, when discussion of peace was delayed until the five Western monarchs worked out a strategy of entering the conference room simultaneously; and at the Potsdam Conference of 1945, the conference began at last when Churchill, Stalin, and Truman could enter at the same moment through three separate doors (Hsu 1970:xiv).

The saving of face occurs in ritualized or unintentional forms in every culture, but in outer-directed cultures it is developed with a delicate and intricate finesse. As Michael Bond describes it (1978:7), "A reciprocal conspiracy of face-saving is a mutually beneficial regulator in social interaction."

"Face" for the Thai is a personal esteem to be protected; for the Chinese it is the family's name that is to be preserved against all shame; for the tribesman of Kalimantan or Borneo it is the tribal face to be preserved. But in each, the maintaining of face is the maintaining of worth, of dignity, of social esteem.

Face-saving is a mutual process of maintaining dignity for all parties involved in a transaction. Thus in conflict situations a third-party mediator is frequently necessary to save face for both the protagonist and the antagonist. And in alienated relationships, a mediator can diffuse anger, clarify perceptions, negotiate demands, and effect reconciliation while protecting the esteem of each.

Shame and Healing

Feelings of shame have both internal and external origins. One feels shame before the ego ideal as well as before the community's ideals. Internally, it is rooted in the internalization of values in the emerging ego. The images of "good me" vs. "bad me" are early developments in the second year of life. These rudimentary forms of self-image mark the beginning of what will become the ego ideal. As values of respect, worth, acceptance, and perfection form, the person becomes capable of internal shame. To fall short of one's ideal or to betray one's image before self or before others is intolerable.

> If the person falls notably short of these values the ego ideal produces a specific anxiety with a unique emotional tone: a feeling of shame. It's intrapsychic message is: "You are unworthy!" It describes a unique situation: "I have not reached the goal—I have forsaken my own heroes—I have failed." The sting in feelings of shame is a fear of contempt, exposure, and eventual abandonment. Hence the language of shame: "I could sink through the ground for shame." (Pruyser 1968:310)

Shame, with its ideal demands from within and social demands from without, produces an impulse to hide, flee, avoid, deny. One feels stuck, on the spot, blamed and rejected. A total rejection of the self may occur, especially before one's own self as the ideal image crumbles. The loss of face before others, the loss of honor in the group, the loss of worth before the self all create intense inner pain.

One could indeed, as is said, die for shame. Among Australian aborigines, the priest may, with great ceremony, pick up a charred bone from a heap of animal carcasses burned in a ritual bonfire and point the bone toward a member of the tribe. This ritual marking as "one who must die" evokes a psychosocial death. Within twenty-four hours the person dies without any other act against him or her (Cannon 1957:182).

How does one restore feelings of worth or regain a sense of acceptability to others after an experience of intense shame? Does one atone for shame by earning acceptance through outstanding behavior? So it is said in Chinese proverbs and practical wisdom. Or does one need to make expiation by some sacrifice to honor? So it is exacted in some Arab groups in response to shame; so it is acted out in self-punishment or self-destruction in Japanese culture. Is penance at all possible, or must one silently bear the embarrassment and work toward slowly proving oneself by acting better in all future instances? It is this necessity of earning reacceptance, of deserving renewed respect, that gives shame its power to evoke improvement. It goads one toward the good enshrined in the ego ideal, and toward what is prized by the group whose esteem is so crucial to being a human among humans. "Shame has the seeds of betterment in it, and it may spur one on to love the example all the more and demonstrate one's intentions in changed behavior. It is future directed and lives from hope" (Pruyser 1968:323).

Figure 4-4 offers a four-variable grid to visualize this interplay between internal and external sources and the positive and negative forces present in the experience of shame.

In response to shame feelings, the counselor's unconditional acceptance offers an undergirding esteem where there has been a severe loss of self-worth. This floor of grace reaffirms the basic trust that is the primal layer of personality formation. Only when one has gone beneath the shame to this elemental trust is hope stimulated and assimilation of the shame possible.

In shame, one feels the implosion of the rejecting condemning world. The massive introjection of self-depreciation must be drained off and the positive thrust of the shame process directed toward recovery and healing.

As the healing proceeds, a reclaiming of ego, ego ideal, ego-in-relationship, and ego esteem takes place. Most frequently this requires (1) the recognition of the ego ideals, (2) the reclaiming of the values prized, (3) grieving for their loss or betrayal, (4) reaffirmation of ideals as goals to be sought rather than judgments to be dreaded, (5) the examination of values betrayed before others, and (6) recommitment of self toward regaining respect.

In this process, the pain of disgrace is reframed and the elements of discretion claimed and directed toward the future. The possibilities of

	EGO IDEAL	SOCIAL CONTEXT
DISCRETION	Discretionary values are incorporated as parental ideals and are internalized in early childhood. This ideal prompts, guides, limits, and corrects planned behavior.	Discretionary values are present in the social context and are enforced by conditional acceptance, inclusion, and respect. They serve as a spur to conform to expectations.
DISGRACE	Disgrace is felt internally as one falls short of the ego ideal, so no audience is required for the experience of shame.	Disgrace occurs as one feels exposed, humiliated, rejected as a total person. It is experienced as a loss of face, loss of respect, loss of status.
GOALS OF THERAPY	Internal adjustment, integration, reframing, reconciliation with the ego ideal.	Social acceptance, inclusion in relationship, regaining of face before significant persons.

Figure 4-4. Forces present in the experience of shame.

recovering hope and regaining a sense of worth begin the reduction of shame and the return to open relationship.

Guilt and Healing

In guilt formation, the person has internalized the trial process of Western law. Defender, defendant, judge and jury, victim and villain are all within the self. It is I who bring my protesting self before the bar of conscience. I set forth the evidence against myself. I call upon myself to defend my actions. I am my own prosecutor and defense attorney. I am the judge who hears the case, and I summon my own internal community to act as jury. Both sides appeal to the value systems that are in tension within me. Since all decisions affirm one value at the cost of negating another, both value structures now judge one another. My judging self has summoned me to accountability before my cherished values. I cannot be a person of internal well-being, within Western culture, without this judicial review of my choices and actions. This trial calls me to discriminate between good choices and bad decisions, to discern new directions more consistent with my values, to grieve appropriately for negated values and their consequences, and finally to organize, correct, and implement my values in the future (Oden 1969:42–43).

Guilt is a complex of feelings. It has been variously differentiated as true and false guilt, normal and neurotic guilt, moral and dispositional guilt. The dysfunctional pole of guilt has also been called "unreal guilt," "infantile guilt," "destructive guilt," and "endogenous guilt." The functional elements of guilt respond to the moral values of the self and the culture, to the social customs, conventions, and rituals, and to the inner values of fulfilling one's existence. These may be designated moral guilt, existential guilt, and social guilt. Figure 4-5 provides a framework for conceptualizing the forms of guilt on the polarities of objective and subjective, intrinsic and appraised.

Guilt, although a universal human capacity, takes very different forms in various cultures. Consider these illustrative contrasts.

In Western societies with understandings of moral values as universals, moral guilt has an absolute transcendent referrent. In contrast, the locus of guilt in Japanese society is in the tight nexus of the family and is most clearly typified by the mother-child obligational system.

In Eastern societies, the functions of social guilt are much more elaborate. Conventions carrying the power of tradition and the sanctions of religious beliefs evoke guilt in situations of violation of social solidarity. In contrast, Western societies are characterized by unconventional nonconformist behavior.

In Western societies, the intrapunitive processes turn dispositional guilt into depression, while in many African, Indian, and Chinese settings the outer-directed processes so sharply reduce the degree of pseudo guilt felt that in many settings it is virtually absent.

Because the dominant varieties of guilt vary across cultures, the counselor will need to be sensitive to the moral-ethical style of the con-

OBJECTIVE

INTRINSIC

APPRAISED

Moral guilt

. . . arises from violation of moral, ethical, or contractual standards that exist external to the person in the historical experience of the culture, the transcendent will of God, in understandings of. universal good.

Moral guilt is realistic, objective, refers to specific acts or events, has a quality of proportion, can be assuaged by restitution or reconciliation.

Social guilt

. . . arises from failure to conform to conventional standards, social rituals, cultural norms.

Social guilt arises from disobeying convention (the deep human patterns of maintaining sameness and security) or breaking rituals (the deep cultural symbols of the group). Frequently it rises from overritualized, overconventionalized contexts, which become oppressive or stifling.

Existential guilt

. . . arises from a sense of failed potentialities, or falling short of the possibilities of life.

Existential guilt arises as one becomes aware of denying potential, betraying privilege, squandering opportunity or what is given in one's origin or core.

Existential guilt alerts one to unlived life, unexplored self, unclaimed relationships with others, unexperienced community.

Pseudo guilt

. . . arises from anxiety and shame stimulated by deep inner conflicts, unaware binds, or in Western culture may be a dispositional response to endogenous biochemical imbalances.

False guilt arises as a fantasized process seeking resolution or release through self-negation, recrimination, strategies for expiation or projection, undoing, reversal, blaming, and other strategies of defense.

Pseudo guilt has no reality proportions, cannot be restituted, resolved, released. The denied or displaced drives or the personality disorder rooted in early developmental periods constantly energize it from unconscious pain. Its primary source may be physical rather than psychic, biochemical rather than developmental.

SUBJECTIVE

**Figure 4-5. A framework for conceptualizing
the forms of guilt.**

text (chapter 9) and of the characteristic patterns of psychopathology (chapter 10) when teasing out the source, structure, and goal of the guilt feelings being experienced. Guilt is the experience of demands being turned upon the self. These demands may come from the conscience as it mediates moral values from the society or from the inner self. Tracking down the demands and teasing out their compound interrelationships with each other are necessary for effective resolution.

Only intense shame or an acute anxiety attack is as agonizing as acute guilt. Since guilt is such a powerful feeling, it incites the person to do something quickly in order to get rid of its pain. The three most common reactions to acute guilt are intrapunitive, extrapunitive, and impunitive defenses.

1. *Intrapunitive Defense.* We may accept responsibility for the wrong-doing and feel pain as we punish ourselves for the choice made or the action taken. We may condemn ourselves, apologize, seek to make it up to the victims (whether real or imagined), or even seek some way of being punished. When the individual feels hopeless or helpless to change or act in restitution, the intrapunitive response increases guilt in a negative spiral of compounding recriminations.

2. *Extrapunitive Defense.* We may direct the guilt away from ourselves and seek others who are responsible and blameworthy. "Displacement" of the punitive behavior onto an external target through "projection" can discharge much of the guilt as anger or resentment. This makes change in the self or the situation dependent upon change in the other person or circumstance blamed and, although it may offer a feeling of power from the anger, tends to be powerless.

3. *Impunitive Defense.* We may justify the guilt-producing actions or seek to rationalize the serious nature of what we have done. The behavior is justified as appropriate to the provocation, or inevitable in relation to the circumstances, or a means validated by the end in view. This leads to the substitution of a situational, utilitarian, or pragmatic set of values for the more absolute or deontological (from the Greek *deontis,* meaning necessary as values given in the structure of the universe).

Healthy responses to these three guilt vectors are to release and discharge the guilt either (1) by behaving in conformity to the conscience —that is, submitting to the intrapunitive demands and obeying their values by taking the consequent actions to change and comply—or (2) by examining the internalized values to sort out which are authentically moral, existential, or validly social. This may lead to modification of the moral understandings, reduction of the existential aspirations, or contention with the social expectations. Where neurotic pretensions are uncovered, these must be confronted and canceled.

We need not assume that all guilt is a reflection of ultimate and absolute values which transcend and command the person, or that guilt is primarily a feeling response to expectations and demands that are relative introjections of our cultural conditioning. Both are part process of the conscience.

A Theology of Grace

The biblical story opens with the human experiences of anxiety, shame, and guilt. Placed in an anxiety context of taboos with life-and-death sanctions, the man and the woman dare not transgress the divine prohibitions. Naked yet unashamed, they live in a paradise of innocence until willful disobedience disrupts all.

Anxiety triggers flight; shame reveals nakedness. The two persons experience the anxiety surrounding seeing and being seen, knowing evil and being known by it, acting willfully and being exposed in it—these are components of shame.

And guilt follows. A vengeful punitive yet protective angel is internalized to become the guardian of moral choices. To disregard this guardian evokes guilt. The angel, like the conscience, resists our slipping back into the innocent garden of denial ("nothing matters, it's only play, no one sees, no one knows, all is acceptable") and urges us forward toward maturation, adaptation, and the resolution of pain through new obedience.

Even more central to the story is the presence of grace. Created in divine similarity—in the image and likeness of the Creator—humans are invited into relationship with their Maker. Given both privilege and responsibility, they are pursued when they choose concealment, encountered in their flight, confronted with options for a new future, and promised hope and steadfast love. Throughout the biblical accounts, human shame and guilt occur in this context of grace offered as steadfast love. All human activity, whether honorable or shameful, responsible or guilty, occurs in this context of the unchanging steadfast love of the Creator which constantly draws all creatures toward wholeness and healing.

Grace offers the support that allows trust to replace anxiety, acceptance to restore honor where we were shamed, and forgiveness to resolve guilt.

Shame and Guilt in Scripture

The Old Testament is rich in references to shame. There are over 150 occurrences of shame and its derivative words. However, guilt and guiltiness occur rarely in the Old Testament. Exemplary passages are Hosea 4:6–7; Jeremiah 3:24–25; Ezra 9:6–7; or the sharp contrast between Psalm 31, with its pure expression of shame, and Psalm 32, with its focused expression of guilt and yearning for forgiveness. The word "shame" occurs eight times more often than guilt in the total scriptures.

In the New Testament, shame is used less frequently than guilt, and concern for the sense of shame seems almost missing. The lack of shame among early Christians is shown in their desacralization of holy places, their demystification of ritual, the bold claiming of intimacy with God, and the broad inclusion of people from all races, ranks, and levels in a community of grace.

The few references to shame in the New Testament are matched by relatively few to guilt. The focus is not on subjective feelings but on celebration of objective events of God's acting in incarnation, presence, acceptance, forgiveness, and liberation of humankind. Paul's treatment of guilt in the letter to the Romans (Rom. 1–3) centers on the facts of human guilt rather than on feelings of self-recrimination, on standing fast in the new freedom (Rom. 5–8) rather than exploring the old bondage.

In the New Testament, grace is the undergirding reality beneath all human pain. This grace speaks to shame and its doubts of self-worth as well as to guilt and its judgment of behavior and intention. Both judgment and grace exist together as two elements of the same reality. Both are presented throughout the biblical record, but in the New Testament the overwhelming emphasis is on grace.

Paul uses the word "grace" frequently to designate the new reality that Christ has disclosed to us. Grace is divine acceptance, given out of God's steadfast love for humankind. It heals human brokenness, draws people from evil toward good. This unconditional love called grace is a gift, gratuitous, unmerited, an acceptance that cannot be earned or achieved. Whether one's theology views grace as "the appraisal of humans as worthful" or "the bestowal of worth on humans," the grace is unmerited and the worth unearned.

Whether one's theology has stressed the anxiety-punishment-release motif of grace or the shame-alienation-reconciliation model or the guilt-condemnation-forgiveness pattern, grace offers acceptance, inclusion, forgiveness as gift.

Grace and Worth

The basic affirmation of personal worth and being that occurs in Christian and Jewish monotheism is grounded in a certain understanding of the relationship between God and human beings called grace. This relationship is rooted in the creation of human beings, but it is more than the esteem a creator might have toward the object of creation, more than the familial relationship of being created in the divine image and partaking in the divine nature, more than the essential givens of our humanness.

The thoroughgoing assurance of God's affirmation of our worth comes through an all-inclusive love called grace. Grace is the acceptance and affirmation of the person before and independent of any action a person can take in the world. Grace affirms that each human being is irreducibly valuable—nothing done or not done can increase or decrease the worth given in the love of God.

"Grace is assured in the covenant God makes with humanity, which is God's all-inclusive, even pre-temporal *yes* to humanity" (Outka 1972: 242).

It is possible for humans to refuse the call of God toward wholeness, to choose to live outside the healing relationships of mutual love, but even this rejection takes place within the context of grace. The divine *yes* is a constant invitation to the renewal of life and to the recovery of integrity. God is for us. This most elemental of convictions of Judaism and Christianity undergirds all healing and liberation.

Grounded in Grace

All therapeutic intervention into human pain is grounded in grace, whether it is named or unnamed. The diagram of relationships in Figure 4-6 shows the deeper significance that undergirds and validates all caring and acceptance.

The caring of a counselor for the counselee offers unconditional positive regard, which accepts the other where he or she has felt unacceptable. This acceptance takes place in the human context of transferent relationships; so that the counselor comes to represent—in fact, to take the emotional place of—the parents, the family, and other significant persons in the counselee's childhood and development. This is possible

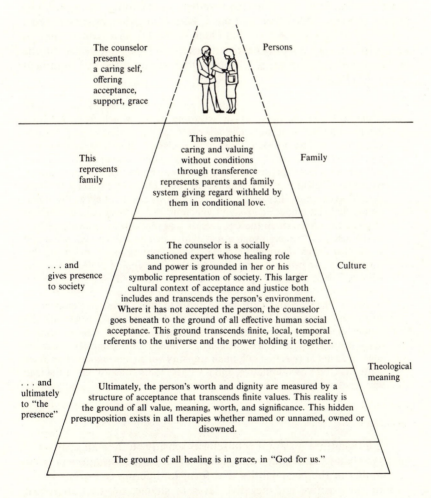

The counselor presents a caring self, offering acceptance, support, grace — Persons

This represents family — This empathic caring and valuing without conditions through transference represents parents and family system giving regard withheld by them in conditional love. — Family

. . . and gives presence to society — The counselor is a socially sanctioned expert whose healing role and power is grounded in her or his symbolic representation of society. This larger cultural context of acceptance and justice both includes and transcends the person's environment. Where it has not accepted the person, the counselor goes beneath to the ground of all effective human social acceptance. This ground transcends finite, local, temporal referents to the universe and the power holding it together. — Culture

. . . and ultimately to "the presence" — Ultimately, the person's worth and dignity are measured by a structure of acceptance that transcends finite values. This reality is the ground of all value, meaning, worth, and significance. This hidden presupposition exists in all therapies whether named or unnamed, owned or disowned. — Theological meaning

The ground of all healing is in grace, in "God for us."

Figure 4-6. Diagram of counseling relationships.

because of a unique role: the counselor is a culturally recognized expert whose healing power is invested by the society. As a symbolic representative of society, the counselor offers care to the injured, acceptance to the rejected, support to the weak, direction to the confused, correction to the distorted. As spokesperson for the deeper cultural realities, the therapist embodies the concern for humanness that the society has been incapable of offering to the person. Where the community has failed to nurture the growth and welfare of the person, the counselor goes beneath these injustices to recover the ground of justice and grace that is the basis of all communal coexistence and communion. Ultimately, the worth of this person, family, and group is based on a structure of acceptance and dignity that transcends the finite boundaries of each culture. This transcendent reality is the ground of all value, worth, and significance. It is the grace that holds the universe together. In extending this grace, one is truly present to the other, and one is embodying the presence of God.

Both Browning (1966:153) and Oden (1966:21) have argued that all authentic presence not only bears witness to but is possible *because of* the essential undergirding grace of God. Oden summarizes this argument concisely (1974:45–46):

> The freedom to engage in the frame of reference of another is only possible if one exists in the midst of an accepting reality which frees one from defensive self-righteousness. *For how can I enter your frame of reference or language or culture unless I understand myself to be understandable to and understood by a larger process of empathetic understanding which embraces us both?* This larger process of empathetic understanding is the unacknowledged ontological presupposition of all these forms of empathy at work, regardless of where they occur. The kerygma speaks precisely at this point, saying that this empathic love and unconditional positive regard, which is implicitly assumed in all these processes, has made itself known explicitly in the history of Jesus in such a way that it can be known and celebrated in all other forms of human knowing. Thus all our means of employing this empathetic love become an implicit doxology, a hymn of praise to the One who has made himself known as sharing in our condition, providing an overarching frame of orientation for all of our empathetic extensions and concerns. The Christian faith has no desire to limit or derogate humanistic empathetic processes. It only wants to celebrate its good news that the ground of all unconditional positive regard in all these processes is revealed in the history of Israel and in the Christ. Therefore, Christian proclamation is not a denial or rejection of human empathy but an affirmation of its inner center as God's own initiative, and a witness to its constitution in the One who gives us life.

Summary

The intercultural pastoral counselor is sensitive to human controls—anxiety, shame, and guilt—and aware of the wide variation in their functioning in the personalities that form in differing contexts.

Both the positive and negative faces of shame, the excitation and fragmentation of anxiety, the directive and the punitive functions of guilt are necessary to the full functioning of the personality. Cultures cannot be typed as shame or guilt cultures, since all three functions are present in all. However, the balance and character of control functions are culturally conditioned by developmental processes, shaped by social expectations, and expressed according to the culture's mores and customs.

The pastoral counselor as a moral theologian is concerned both for the balancing of internal control structures and the contents of anxiety, shame, and guilt.

5

Values, Worldviews, and Pastoral Counseling

A Theology of Value

"From the day we are born we are invited into a remarkable learning process. Life calls us to be valuing beings and ushers us into the pursuit of multiple goods. Parents, peers, pedagogues, and pundits all point out potential goals, values, goods, and ideals to be incorporated into the growing self. Acculturation is an extended learning process in which one weighs, sorts out, and organizes various values and goals into some self-shaped, internalized whole."

—Thomas Oden, 1969

THE VALUE OF SIMPLICITY
A CHINESE FOLKTALE

As Tzu-Gung was traveling through the regions north of the river Han he saw an old man working in his vegetable garden. He had dug a deep well and an irrigation ditch. The man would descend the circular steps into the well, fetch up a vessel of water in his arms, and pour it out into the ditch. While his efforts were tremendous, the results were meager.

Tzu-Gung said, "There is a way whereby you can fill a hundred ditches and irrigate a hundred gardens in one day, and whereby you can do much with little effort. Would you not like to hear of it?"

The gardener paused in his work, looked at him, and said, "And what would that be?"

Tzu-Gung replied, "You take a long wooden lever weighted at the back and light in the front, and hang a bucket from the end of the lever. In this way you can bring up water so quickly that it just gushes out. This is called a draw well."

Then anger rose up in the old man's face, and he said, "I have heard my teacher say that whoever uses machines does all his work like a machine. He who does his work like a machine grows a heart like a machine, and he who carries the heart of a machine in his breast loses his simplicity. He who has lost his simplicity becomes unsure in the strivings of his soul. Uncertainty in the strivings of the soul creates conflict and dissension within one's very nature as a human being. To endanger one's humanness is something which does not agree with honest sense. It is not that I do not know of such things; I am ashamed to use them." (Heisenberg 1958:20)

At the center of all truly human existence there are values. Humans are evaluating beings. To exist is to choose.

Values may be thought of as the central organizing principles of a society. The cultural heritage acquired in growing up to be human is clustered around a central set of values that make a people's behavior meaningful, give direction to each member's life, and connect the persons in society to each other.

Values are the broad principles (guides to behavior) assumed by each culture, transmitted from generation to generation, and operative in the daily life of its members. These values are moral (what is just), ideal (what is admirable), aesthetic (what is beautiful), political (what is socially possible), affective (what is held dear), and so on. These values provide patterns for living, criteria for decision making, and units of measurement for evaluating oneself and others.

"Humans are valuing beings," wrote Gestalt psychologist Wolfgang Köhler.

> The human mind is not the domain of indifferent facts. Intrinsic demands, ideas of fittingness, conceptions of wrongness occur in an ordering of the contents of perception and memory. We give the name *value* to this common trait of intrinsic requiredness or wrongness, and *insight* to the awareness of such intellectual, moral, or aesthetic value. We can then say that value and corresponding insight constitute the very essence of human mental life. (Köhler 1938:31)

Values are the core motivations of the human person. Every human acquires preferences, then assimilates understandings of the required, the necessary, the admirable, and finally the prudent and the possible. Behavior gradually becomes organized, controlled, and directed by these values or, more often, by the dominant one of the conflicting values learned in the family, community, and society of origin.

In this chapter we shall examine the nature of values, how they differ and agree from culture to culture, and what their function is in cross-cultural pastoral counseling and psychotherapy. We will explore the wisdom of alternative value systems, the means of affirming one's own values without being encapsulated by them, and the freedom to appreciate other values without a value-free relativism. As particular cases, we will examine the Indian values of hierarchy and the Chinese values of filial piety.

The Nature of Values

What is a value? Among the range of definitions, here is what is most frequently used in the field of psychology and counseling:

A value is a conception, explicit or implicit, distinctive of an individual or characteristic of a group, of the desirable which influences the selection from available modes, means, and ends of action. A value is a formulation of the desirable, the "ought" and "should" standards which influence action. (Kluckhohn and Murray 1948:59)

Charles Morris, in his classic work *Varieties of Human Value* (1956: 10–12), postulated three different uses of the term "value." *Operative values* refer to the "actual direction of preferential behavior toward one kind of object rather than another." These are the values that function in shaping decisions and directing actions. *Conceived values* refer to the "preferential behavior directed by an anticipation or foresight of the outcome of such behavior. An alcoholic may believe that it is better to not drink, a drug addict may be utterly convinced that it is better to not use drugs." These values are held but not followed. *Object values* refer to values that are preferable if the holder of the value is to achieve certain ends or objectives. In warfare, for example, the aggressive behaviors may not be preferred in fact (operative values) or be symbolically desired (conceived values) but are followed because they are directed toward desired ends (object values). These three uses of the term "value" are not mutually exclusive, but they can be clearly distinguished.

Do values exist apart from the valuer? Are there objective values, or are they all subjective? The controversy about the existence of objective values independent of circumstance and conditions vis-à-vis relative values dependent upon time, place, and relationship cuts across great disciplines of thought—anthropology, sociology, theology, economics, and jurisprudence.

Objective values are values that exist independent of the valuer's appraisal. They are the "preferable" rather than the "preferred." Rauwolfia and digitalis, as herbs, contained intrinsic medicinal value long before being recognized as such. The medical substance possessed the same healing effectiveness apart from human appraisal. It was an objective value by virtue of its intrinsic properties, whether valued by a user or not. The objective value of physical properties—mineral, vegetable, or animal —are assumed in all scientific research. But the existence of objective values in the nonphysical or metaphysical areas is a source of ongoing controversy. Are justice, harmony, and equality objectively valuable or only of worth because they are so appraised by valuing persons? Are certain things intrinsically preferable or only extrinsically preferred? Is an object invested with value by being valued or does it have value whether prized or ignored? (Biestek 1967:32).

Subjective values are ascribed values; they are the preferred rather than the preferable. As taste is individual and idiosyncratic and thus cannot be ranked in order, so valuing is essentially subjective, arbitrary, and ultimately relative. The only standard of consistency or measure of priority becomes the social consensus of the dominant society, culture, or group. A Rembrandt painting may be highly prized by connoisseur and common viewer alike until it is identified as a copy and its value vanishes. Subjective consensus may bestow worth, but objective validation of its historical lack of authenticity can destroy the worth when subjective and objective valuations conflict. The difficulty of defining which cultural, individual, or universal values are essentially relative and subjective and which are fundamentally human, intrinsically necessary, and unconditionally "good" has caused many philosophers, ethicists, and social scientists to move to a value-free universe and relativistic criteria. The more typical pattern of contemporary reasoning about values locates the worth in the person(s) and group(s) who evaluate.

The philosopher Spinoza expressed the view of ascribed value most succinctly by saying, "In no case do we strive for, wish for, long for or desire anything because we deem it to be good, but on the other hand we deem a thing to be good because we strive for it, wish for it, long for it or desire it" (*Ethics III*, Prop. 9).

Values are most commonly seen in the field of psychology as attributes of the person valuing who perceives worth in the person, object, or relationship viewed. This is a permanent or semipermanent valuation, not just a transient preference, since values are not indicated by a single response to a particular situation but by the integrative responses to what a person judges to be a class of recurring situations.

Levels of Evaluation

Three kinds of components combine in characterizing levels of values: (1) There is a cognitive component, described variously as belief, opinion, cognition, or conceptualization; (2) there is a normative component, a prescriptive or proscriptive aspect of "oughtness"; and (3) there is a preferential component, which is of two types, emotional and intellectual. The emotional preference is an affective tie to a situation, behavior, belief, or relationship; the intellectual preference is based rather on logical inference or rational judgment. Different personalities place widely varying weights on these components, so that one person's values may be rooted in deep affect, another in detached judgment, and a third in an integration of both thought and feeling and so on and on (Keats 1981:69).

What we call "values" is a high level of abstraction, which summarizes preferences into a value construct. These constructs may be also organized into value systems, which cluster and rank values according to inclusiveness, importance, and ultimacy.

To visualize the various kinds of thought, a pyramid of abstractions, as in Figure 5-1, is useful. The rush of stimuli a person perceives are grouped into elemental categories in order to facilitate labeling with words, to give names to experiences and perceptions. These elemental groupings are viewed not just as facts; meanings are ascribed to them that are composed of feelings as well as ideas, affective energies as well as cognitive judgments. This is the first level of conscious valuing experience, and it emerges from the application of values to the incoming data.

From these categories, concepts and theories are constructed, and, out of all this organization of experience, values arise.

The values in turn are used in each of the preceding levels, just as the theories constructed may facilitate new perceptions or selectively screen out other stimuli. Thus the higher abstractions shape the more concrete processes, and new data entering at the level of concrete observation may invalidate or corroborate the more abstract conclusions. The most functional thought processes alternate between the concrete and the abstract in rhythmic movement. We reach out to meet the environment and then withdraw attention to reflect on its meaning. Meeting and meaning are the two poles of authentic contact with the world. When one meets the world of stimuli, the mind is overwhelmed with "meeting"; when one is preoccupied with meanings, the world is blocked out or distorted by the preoccupation with evaluations. The free rhythm of contact-withdrawal-contact-withdrawal allows perception and valuation constantly to correct and enrich each other.

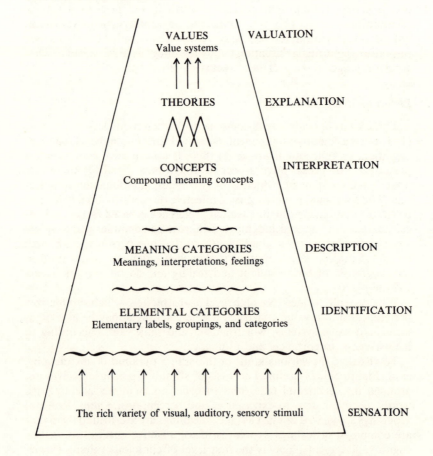

Figure 5-1. A pyramid of concepts, constructs, and values.

Universality of Values

Two central questions emerge in all reflection on values, the questions of universality and relativity. Are there any universal values? Is there any hierarchy of values? Are there absolute values?

The questions may be applied to each specific culture as well as to all cultures. Are there human qualities, behaviors, or relationships highly regarded in many or in all cultures? For example, examine this cluster of values.

> A good man was, and is,
> one who respects the old people,
> is brave and demonstrates fortitude,
> conforms to the obligations of the kinship system,
> is devoted to village cooperation and unity,
> is generous, gives away property in public,
> gets along well with others,
> and avoids overt expressions of aggression in relationships.

This is the value system of an American Indian tribe, the Mandan-Hidatsa, as recorded by Edward Bruner. In his study of cultural transmission and cultural change, he found that the values showed "remarkable persistence, even though there was vast change in the larger units of social organization, in the economy, and in most of the religious-ceremonial system" (Bruner 1961:192). These values persist over time within the cultural group. Now we might ask, What elements are shared with all other groups?

Tentatively, because the variations in societies are both subtle and great, we can assert several quite general universals which appear in the above case.

First, the preservation and continuity of human society is a universal value. Each cultural group values its own continuity. For this to be possible, each group has a preference not only for survival but also for safety and security.

Second, the need for safety and security is demonstrated as a universal in societies either as (1) a strong preference for peace, (2) a preoccupation with defense, or (3) an ambivalence between the means for and pathways to maintaining security. From this some infer a universal reverence for life—selective life in some societies, all life in others.

Third, the respect for and conformity within social relationships with fellow human beings is a universal value. Every society values relationships and defines some system of order—familial, generational, kinship, or communal order.

These three values, universal in character, occur alongside of the cultural values expressed clearly in the example: altruistic generosity, filial piety, courage, endurance, obligational duty, cooperation, harmony and unity, and nonaggressive affinity. Many of these are shared with a large number of traditional societies, yet the means of expressing them, the pathways and patterns of their occurrence, and the varieties of goals for these values make them a study of both similarities and contrasts.

Accepting the reality of cultural relativity frees us to perceive inter-pathically and enter other cultures authentically. Yet this is not synonymous with a relativity of values. No valuing person can escape making judgments about the values either of self or other. A value cannot be accepted and condoned simply by reason of its existence. This is the naturalistic fallacy, which is circular and ultimately meaningless. Relativity is the initial step toward clear perception, but it is not the end of authentic encounter, reflection, and understanding. The valuing person prizes pluralism and supports the right of alternate value systems to exist, yet the very act of valuing recognizes that both the preferred and the preferable are being discerned.

The relativist-absolutist controversy was present at the birth of Western philosophy. In response to the Athenian Sophists—relativists—Plato argued that although different societies adopt different values, this does not in and of itself show that they are right in doing so or that one society's values may not be preferable to another's. Regardless of what some societies choose, some things ought to be valued, others not, because there are eternal forms of goodness, truth, and beauty that do not change. Plato's was the first recorded absolutist position, which held that certain absolute moral values are always and will always be binding on all people whether recognized by them or not. The debate between the two poles has continued to this present day, with the Western world divided among Marx, a relativist, Mill, a utilitarian absolutist believing that the promotion of happiness is the supreme moral consideration, and Kant, who held that justice is the supreme categorical imperative by which all values must be judged and ordered.

Variety in Central Values

The values a culture comes to rank most highly in its hierarchy of values will affect its structures from the individual personality to the corporate political process. Comparing values between cultures is difficult, because some concepts do not have parallel forms in neighboring cultures. For example, the Greek virtue of "a voluntary willingness to yield to the welfare needs of significant others" has no exact parallel in many other cultures.

The Greeks used the word *philotimos* to characterize people. A person is *philotimos* to the extent to which he or she is willing to make sacrifices for friends or other members of the family. For example, for a man to delay his marriage until his sisters have married and been provided with a proper dowry is a normal expectation among traditional rural Greeks. A person who does so is praised as more *philotimos* than one who does not. This variable can be expressed in English by some kind of lengthy explanation, but no other group has an exactly comparable value. Thus a cross-cultural comparison is not possible unless it is made at some higher level of abstraction that contains a common dimension (Triandis and Vassiliou 1967:38).

Values may contrast sharply in adjoining cultures, as is seen in sharp relief in the case of two neighboring peoples in Nigeria. Comparing the Yoruba and the Hausa, LeVine writes (1973:26–27):

> A most obvious difference had to do with sociability. The Yoruba engaged in a great deal of jovial public conversation with many different persons, often accompanied by laughter and other indications of friendliness. The Hausa, though also sociable, were much more restrained in their expressions of friendly interest. . . . The Yoruba sociologist, Fadipe, wrote: "The Yoruba is gregarious and sociable . . . more of an extrovert than an introvert. The self-contained, self-reliant person who can keep his mental and physical suffering to himself so that others may not express their sympathy for him is regarded as churlish and one to be feared."
>
> In contrast, the Hausa value highly the personal quality called *fara's* . . . which has the connotation of a calm, stoical pleasantness no matter what the stress or provocation, and they admire the quality termed *fillanci* and *filako,* which connote reticence, the denial of one's own needs in public, and the ability to endure severe pain without complaint.
>
> These differences in the normative ideals of sociability and sharing one's suffering with others seemed to be widely realized in . . . actual behavior. . . . Physicians and nurses in the local hospital reported that Yoruba women cried out and moaned freely during childbirth, while Hausa women hardly ever made any sound even during difficult deliveries. Here is evidence that conformity with their respective cultural ideals is achieved even during the pain and stress of this universal biological event. This is programmed into personality functioning, determining emotional response to pain.

These neighboring peoples present two diametrically opposed patterns of behavior. Each group has its own consistent patterns of expectations and rewards its members for fulfilling its injunctions. The members have internalized these expectations and fulfill them as their own guides for living. Group values and individual values are congruent. The Hausa's stiff upper lip is the converse of the Yoruba's freedom of expressing feelings. Living in the same country breeds both misunderstandings and the superficial understandings facilitated by stereotypes such as "emotional, just like a Yoruba" or "cold as a Hausa."

In a 1972 study of twenty values as ranked by various cultures East and West, these findings emerged as most significantly different.

In parts of India status and glory were valued most, while wealth was not valued because it was associated with arrogance and fear of thieves. Neither courage nor power was viewed as highly desirable values.

The Greeks were unique in valuing punishment, which they associated with justice, power, and reasonableness, while all other cultures studied gave punishment a very low value.

The Japanese prized serenity and aesthetic satisfaction and disvalued ignorance, deviation, and loneliness.

Americans rated love and friendship as their most important life concerns. They ranked health as fifth, in contrast to Koreans, who ranked these same values 12th, 14th, and 19th.

Work, as a value, was regarded as a good thing in moderately difficult environments where economic development was rapid, but it was rated lower in both easy and difficult environments (Triandis and others 1972: 20).

When a society prizes "doing" rather than "being," the culture will be shaped by activism and a preference for invention, technology, progress, success, and production. The Chinese peasant, as described in the classic folktale that opens this chapter, epitomizes the perspective of "being" as more to be valued than "doing." The contrasts in views of nature, time, and human relationships shown in Table 5-1 offer Papajohn and Spiegel's concise key to five central dimensions of values that vary significantly among cultures.

Amerindian and Anglo Values

No two cultural groups could differ more widely in value systems than Amerindians and white Americans—Anglos. Anglos have little awareness of their own value systems. Acting nonreflectively from their habitual perspectives, they do not recognize the fundamentally different ways of perceiving the world that shape divergent life-styles. Whites rarely use the phrase "value system," but it appears constantly in Indian conversations. The contrast in primary ways of seeing, thinking, and being is clear to Indians, but, because Anglos do not listen, value, and respect Indian culture, Indians are judged instead of understood, condemned instead of being respected. They are constantly evaluated by white values, without the recognition that these may not be relevant criteria for considering the behavior in question. See Case Study: Worldview Contrasts.

The contrasting values in Table 5-2 gathered by Edwin Richardson show the polar apposition of the two cultures. There are many more contrasts in value systems, such as Amerindian patience and American impatience, indifference to hardship vs. the compulsion to elimate pain, and a gentle acceptance of time as opposed to the compulsion to not waste time and to stay busy while watching the clock.

The Amerindian value system is ethically responsible to its own principles, consistent with its commitment to corporate solidarity, coherent as a way of valuing nature, self, and others.

A Minniconju Sioux Indian at the Cheyenne River Eagle Butte Indian Reservation had just received a large sum of money and was thinking of a way of celebrating his good fortune when he saw a big truck loaded with beer. With a great sense of humor, he bought the entire load from the trucker, lock, stock, and barrel, and had him deliver it to the reservation that evening to share with the entire tribe. The resulting party cost him his entire cash allotment, enriched the trucker, and delighted the entire community with his generosity and playfulness (Richardson 1981:228).

This "irresponsible mismanagement of money," as whites would judge it, does not show "white common sense," but to the Indian it represents a choice of happiness (playful sharing with others) and an expression of generous giving and celebration with the entire tribe. It had a distinct purpose congruent with the culture's positive valuation of one who

Table 5-1. Value Orientation Modalities and Preferences: An Interpretive Key

Modalities	Value Orientation Preferences		
Activity	*Doing:* Emphasis is on activity measurable by standards conceived as external to the acting individual; i.e., achievement (American core culture).	*Being:* Emphasis is on activity expressing what is conceived as given in the human personality; i.e., the spontaneous expression of impulses and desires (Mexican rural society).	*Being-in-becoming:* Emphasis is on the kind of activity that has as its goal the development of all aspects of the self as an integrated whole (Classical Greek society, Yoga, Gestalt psychology).
Relations	*Individualism:* Individual goals are preferred to group goals; relations are based on individual autonomy; reciprocal roles are based on recognition of the independence of interrelating members (American core culture).	*Collaterality:* Individual goals are subordinated to group goals; relations are based on goals of the laterally extended group; reciprocal roles are based on a horizontal, egalitarian dimension (Italian extended family).	*Lineality:* Group goals are preferred to individual goals; relations on a vertical dimension are hierarchically ordered; reciprocal roles are based on a dominance-submission mode of interrelation (British upper classes).
Time	*Future:* The temporal focus is based on the future; emphasis is on planning for change at points in time extending away from present to future (American core culture).	*Present:* The temporal focus is based on the present; the past gets little attention; the future is seen as unpredictable (Italian and Latin American societies).	*Past:* The temporal focus is based on the past; tradition is of central importance (Traditional Chinese society).
Man-nature	*Master-over-nature:* Man is expected to overcome the natural forces and harness them to his purpose (American emphasis on technology to solve all problems).	*Subjugation-to-nature:* Man can do little to counteract the forces of nature to which he is subjugated (Spanish rural society).	*Harmony-with-nature:* Man's sense of wholeness is based on continual communion with nature and with the supernatural (Japanese and Navaho Indian societies).
Human nature	*Evil:* Man is born with a propensity to do evil. Little can be done to change this state, so the only hope is for control of evil propensities (Puerto Rican culture).	*Mixed:* Man has natural propensities for both good and evil behavior. *Neutral:* Man is innately neither good nor bad. He is shaped by the environment he is exposed to (American core culture).	*Good:* Man is innately disposed to good behavior. Society, the environment, etc., corrupt him (Neo-Freudians).

(From J. Papajohn and J. Spiegel, *Transactions in Families*. Copyright © 1975 Jossey-Bass, Inc., San Francisco, CA. Reprinted by permission.)

CASE STUDY: Worldview Contrasts (United States)

Ann Blackthorn is referred to the pastoral counselor by her section leader at the factory where she has been employed for three months under its affirmative action fair-hiring practice. An American Indian, Ann works well and has many friendships among co-workers but comes under criticism by her supervisor because of absenteeism and frequent lateness. She explains her absences as family responsibility for aging parents, excuses her lateness as "things she had to do before work." The supervisor reports that her lateness is often caused by doing favors for co-workers. She lends money readily, offers the use of her car, and generally allows others to "take advantage of her."

The therapist recommends that she join an assertiveness training group to learn to be less "passive," to learn to set clear limits, to assert her rights, to develop her ability to say "no."

Ann's behavior in the group is "withdrawn," she does not self-disclose, and she drops out after other members confront her on her lack of involvement. When the counselor seeks to contact her the following week, he discovers that she has quit work and returned to the reservation.

Counselor's (and group's) central values	*Counselee's central values*
Doing—worth in achievement	Being—worth in existence
Individualism—asserting rights	Collateral relationships—mutuality
Mastery over nature—profit motive	Harmony with nature—sharing
Future value orientation	*Present value orientation*
This orientation seeks goals through action, change, self-realization, and fulfillment of future potentials and goals.	This orientation seeks selfhood in relationships with significant others, harmony with the life situation, and acceptance of the present and its possibilities.

places the community above self, gives gifts in joyful abandon, and celebrates solidarity. If Western education teaches this man to be "better at managing money," it will be destroying other values that are even more central to his community.

An intriguing illustration of "pastoral intervention" is told by Richardson to illustrate the contrast in values, assumptions, and ways of expressing them between American and Amerindian. An Indian had been fattening his dog, much as white people prepare cattle for market. To the Indian people the Tatonka (buffalo) and the Shunka (dog) are holy animals, and to eat their meat gives special powers. This Indian had killed his dog, gutted it, and built a fire to singe the hair—like we singe the feathers of poultry. A priest, seeing this Indian, presumptuously assumed that the dog had been diseased and that the Indian was attempting to cremate it, so the priest took over and "helped" the Indian burn up the dog. The passive Indian, made to feel ashamed of his "primitive values" by the culture of whites, watched indifferently as his dog was burned to ashes. The priest was new to the reservation and did not know that the Indian was a medicine man who was preparing this dog meat for a holy meeting, and the medicine man did not want to embarrass him (Richardson 1981:228).

American or Anglo core values are the exact converse of most Amerindian priorities. The most central value is the contrast between communal solidarity with the tribal group and individualistic self-reliance.

The one fundamental core value of American people, concludes Francis Hsu, is self-reliance. The most persistent psychological evidence is the fear of dependence. Catalogs of American values become recognizable as authentically American as they relate to the core of self-reliance: "achievement," "success," "activity," "equality," "individual personality," and "freedom" as well as racism, group superiority, acquisitiveness, and external conformity. Contradictory as some of these values are, all are expressive of the American commitment to self-reliance (Hsu 1972: 248).

Self-reliance as a cultural value is basically the same as the continental value of individualism that is the parent value, but it carries the self-interest element even farther. Where qualified individualism with a qualified equality is central to European political, social, and familial institutions, Americans have insisted on an unlimited self-reliance and an unlimited equality. This equality is more often a conceived (idealized) value than an operative (actual) one, since in practice some people "are much more equal than others." Yet equal opportunity to be self-reliant is militantly defended, as are the virtues of the ideal society in which "every individual is his or her own master, in control of his or her own destiny, and will advance or regress in society only according to his or her own efforts" (Hsu 1972:250).

No individual can be as self-reliant as the American ideal prescribes. We humans are interdependent upon our fellow human beings intellectually, emotionally, socially, economically, and technologically. We may have differing degrees of awareness of our need for others, but only in denial can one say that he or she needs no one. Yet the goal of adjustment, and the process of psychotherapy in American culture, is largely to eliminate dependency and inculcate self-reliance.

Self-reliance is an operative value as well as a conceived value in the American culture. In its positive expression it appears in the emphasis placed on freedom, on equality in economic and political life, on hard work and achievement, and on individual capacity to be responsible, moral, and social; negatively, it emerges in egocentrism, racial superiority, situational ethics, and bigotry.

Table 5-2. Differences in Amerindian and Anglo Values

Indians	*Anglos*
1. Happiness is paramount. Be able to laugh at misery; life is to be enjoyed.	1. Success is the goal, generally involving status, security, wealth, and proficiency.
2. Share: everything belongs to others, just as Mother Earth belongs to *all* people.	2. Get your own things. It's better to own an outhouse rather than share a mansion.
3. Put tribe and extended family first, before self.	3. "Look out for Number One."
4. Humble—causing Indians to be passive-aggressive, gentle head hangers, and very modest.	4. Compete. "If you don't toot your own horn, who will?"
5. Honor your elders; they have wisdom.	5. The future lies with the youth.
6. Learn through legends; remember the great stories of the past, that's where the knowledge comes from.	6. Learning is found in school; get all the schooling you possibly can because it can't be taken away.
7. Look backward to tradition; the old ways are the best ways, they have been proved.	7. Look to the future to things new; "Tie Your Wagon to a Star and Keep Climbing Up and Up."
8. Work for a purpose; once you have enough, quit and enjoy life, even if for just a day.	8. Work for retirement; plan your future and stick to a job, even if you don't like it.
9. Be carefree; time is only relative. Work long hours if happy. Don't worry over time, "I'll get there eventually."	9. Be structured and aware of time. "Don't put off until tomorrow what you have to do today." Don't procrastinate.
10. Be discreet, especially in dating. Be cautious with a low-key profile.	10. Flout an openness. "What you see is what you get."
11. Religion is the universe.	11. Religion is individualistic.
12. Orient yourself to the land.	12. Orient yourself to a house, a job.
13. Be a good listener; it is better if you use your ears and listen well.	13. Look people in the eye; don't be afraid to establish eye contact.
14. Be as free as the wind.	14. Don't rock the boat.
15. Cherish your memory; remember the days of your youth.	15. Don't live in the past, look ahead. Live in the here-and-now.
16. Live with your hands; manual activity is sacred. "Scratch an Indian and you'll find an artist."	16. Live with your mind, think intelligently. Show the teacher how well you know the answers to questions. Be good at books.
17. Don't criticize your people.	17. A critic is a good analyst.
18. Don't show pain; be glad to make flesh sacrifices to the Spirits.	18. Don't be tortured; don't be some kind of a masochistic nut.
19. Cherish your own language and speak it when possible.	19. You're in America; speak English.

Indians (*contd.*)	*Anglos* (*contd.*)
20. Live like the animals; they are your brothers and sisters.	20. "What are you, some kind of an animal? A pig or a jackass?"
21. Children are a gift of the Great Spirit to be shared with others.	21. "I'll discipline my own children; don't tell me how to raise my kids!"
22. Consider the relative nature of a crime, the personality of the individual, and the conditions. "The home wasn't any good anyway."	22. The law is the law! "To steal one penny is as bad as to steal ten thousand. Stealing is stealing! We can't be making exceptions."
23. Leave things natural, as they were meant to be.	23. "You should have seen it when God had it all alone!"
24. Dance is an expression of religion.	24. Dance is an expression of pleasure.
25. There are no boundaries; it all belongs to the Great Spirit. "Why should I fence a yard?"	25. Everything has a limit; there must be privacy. "Fence in your yard and keep them off the grass!"
26. Few rules are best. The rules should be loosely written and flexible.	26. Have a rule for every contingency. "Write your ideas in detail."
27. Be intuitive.	27. Empiricism leads to the truth.
28. Mystical experience is reality.	28. Be scientific.
29. Be simple; eat things raw and natural. Remember your brother the fox and live wisely.	29. Be sophisticated; eat gourmet foods, well prepared and seasoned. Be a connoisseur of many things.
30. Judge things for yourself.	30. Have instruments judge for you.
31. Medicine should be natural herbs, a gift of Mother Earth.	31. Synthetic medicines are best. "You can make anything in today's laboratories."
32. The dirt of Mother Earth on a wound is not harmful but helpful.	32. Things must be sterile and clean, not dirty and unsanitary.
33. Natives are used to small things, and they enjoy fine detail.	33.Bigness has become a way of life with the white society.
34. Travel light, get along without.	34. Have everything at your disposal.
35. Accept others; even the drinking problem of another Indian.	35. Persuade and proselytize—be an evangelist/missionary.
36. The price is of no concern.	36. "You only get what you pay for."
37. Enjoy simplifying problems.	37. "Nothing in this world is simple."

(After E. Richardson in D.W. Sue, ed., *Counseling the Culturally Different*, Copyright © 1981 John Wiley & Sons. Reprinted by permission of John Wiley & Sons, Inc.)

Hierarchy or Equality?

The value of equality is to Western societies what hierarchy is to the East. To those committed to egalitarian structures, hierarchical patterns seem intolerable, unjustifiable, and untenable, but in Eastern societies, such as India, Indonesia, or China, the principle of hierarchy, and the virtue of respect of the superior by the inferior, is the organizing dynamic of social relationships.

"The Hindu social order," wrote American sociologist Kingsley Davis (1949:170), "is the most thoroughgoing attempt known in human history to introduce absolute inequality as the guiding principle in social relations."

Some sociologists offer critiques that are wholly negative, seeing no strengths in vertical orientations in traditional societies. "In the caste system," says anthropologist Gerald Berreman (1972:385), "birth deals out a life sentence to each member of a caste. For the lower-caste person, that sentence is a life of disprivileges of all sorts."

French social anthropologist Louis Dumont, in his book *Homo Hierarchicus,* accuses such critics as being sociocentric; that is, perceiving and judging from the viewpoint of one's own society. In contrast to Western competitive society with its alienating forces of ambition, individualism, and worth by achievement, the caste system involves a "holism" that is oriented toward the welfare of all. Although all castes do not receive equal rewards, they do receive returns proportional to what they contribute, as judged by the underlying values of the caste system. Thus, Dumont concludes, although all castes are not equally rewarded, all are integrated into the system. By Hindu ideals, all are cared for, and the system exists for the benefit of all (Dumont 1970:107).

Dumont's argument sounds not only foreign but heretical to egalitarian Westerners. The central values of the American society, for example, assume equal opportunities in education, occupation, home location, upward mobility, and achievement of success and place a high value on individual fulfillment. Such values are fostered within a context of an expanding economy in an affluent environment and with the wide range of possibilities of the industrial and technological revolution. The caste system exists in a vastly different economic and political context, as well as for a highly compressed population in limited land space.

The contrast of vertical vs. horizontal relational views is seen in Figure 5-2. The ranking of groups, the contrasts in status, and the differences in privilege are all fixed as constants, as is the person's station in life.

There are three elements to the maintenance of the caste system: hereditary specialization, hierarchy, and repulsion. *Hereditary specialization* refers to the fact that the son of a blacksmith will be a blacksmith just as the son of a warrior will be a warrior. Professions become the obligatory monopoly of families, and to perform them is not merely a right but a duty imposed by birth upon the children. *Hierarchy* refers to unequally divided right, to the fact that such prerogatives as dress, ornaments, wealth, and tax that are the birthright of one are denied to

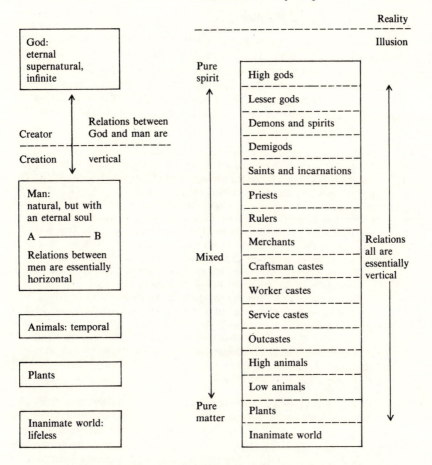

American Concept of Life

God:
eternal
supernatural,
infinite

Creator | Relations between
God and man are
Creation | vertical

Man:
natural, but with
an eternal soul

A ———— B

Relations between
men are essentially
horizontal

Animals: temporal

Plants

Inanimate world:
lifeless

Indian Concept of Life

Brahman: the only reality,
unknowable to the passing world

Reality
Illusion

Pure
spirit

High gods

Lesser gods

Demons and spirits

Demigods

Saints and incarnations

Priests

Rulers

Merchants

Mixed

Craftsman castes

Worker castes

Service castes

Outcastes

High animals

Low animals

Pure
matter

Plants

Inanimate world

Relations
all are
essentially
vertical

Figure 5-2. Comparison of American and Indian views of life.

(Hiebert 1976:36)

another, and that personal status for life is determined by the rank of the group to which one belongs. *Repulsion* refers to the fact that the different groups within the society repel each other rather than attract. Each draws toward itself and makes every effort to prevent its members from contracting alliances or entering relationships with neighboring groups (Hsu 1963:128).

Repulsion is carried out in the rituals of purity and impurity, which limit and control interactions. The castes are ranked according to the interactions among them, and rituals for maintaining the clarity and purity of all boundaries guarantee the attraction within groups and the repulsion between.

Rank, Status, Social Position

Hierarchy as a value is expressed in some cultures through daily utilization of status and rank as a means of identification and definition of one's place in interpersonal relationships. Rank is present in all communications. Special pronouns are required for superiors, equals, inferiors, intimates, and strangers. When speaking Japanese, one must bear in mind the relationships of rank and intimacy in every conversation. Nakane notes:

> Without consciousness of ranking, life could not be carried on smoothly in Japan, for rank is the social norm on which Japanese life is based. In a traditional Japanese house the arrangement of a room manifests this gradation of rank and clearly prescribes the ranking differences which are to be observed by those who use it. The highest seat is always at the centre backed by the *tokonoma* (alcove), where a painted scroll is hung and flowers are arranged; the lowest seat is near the entrance to the room. This arrangement never allows two or more individuals to be placed as equals. Whatever the nature of the gathering, those present will eventually establish a satisfactory order among themselves, after each of them has shown the necessary preliminaries of the etiquette of self-effacement. . . .
>
> Since ranking order appears so regularly in such essential aspects of daily life, the Japanese cannot help but be made extremely conscious of it. In fact, this consciousness is so strong that official rank is easily extended into private life. A superior in one's place of work is always one's superior wherever he is met, at a restaurant, at home, in the street. When wives meet, they, too, will behave towards each other in accordance with the ranks of their husbands. (Nakane 1970:31–32)

The Western view is of persons possessing role rather than rank. All societies see persons as holding place in the social structure, but the nature of place ascribed or achieved contrasts from culture to culture.

Every person is an officeholder of a kind, since each occupies an office in life that carries certain rights and responsibilities. Every society sorts and classifies people according to its dominant values. Ralph Linton, in *The Study of Man* (1936), offered the widely used systematic theory for describing this place in the social order each occupies with the following typology: "Status" refers to a position or office within a social system. It does not focus on rank or prestige but, in a neutral sense, on the niche in life a person fills. "Role" is used to denote the behavior expected of a person in a particular status. Role, with its dramatic connotation of actions and lines in a play, suggests the part a person acts (Murphy 1979:41).

A professor has, for example, a specific status in Western society. There are specific educational requirements, certification of institutions, and a series of duties. The setting (a school), the schedule (catalog and syllabus), and the occasion (class and office) all structure how the work of teaching will be done. This codified set of responsibilities and rights form the role. The role includes teaching, research in preparation, disciplining, communicating, evaluating, and certifying. Each professor is unique and yet within the boundaries of institutional and communal sanctions. Radical departure leads to eccentricity, deviancy, and possible censure or loss of status through violation of role.

Statuses bestowed at birth are "ascribed statuses"; those attained or earned are called "achieved statuses." Ascribed statuses are unavoidable —sex, family, caste, kin—although the role can be altered to some degree in mobile social systems.

In traditional societies the ascribed status is relatively fixed and only rarely altered. In a hierarchical society such as Japan, rank is given both by ascription and achievement. Once received, it is regarded as decisive in all areas of social functioning.

Think of the 620 million people of India divided into thousands of mutually exclusive micro-communities, each person belonging to only one. The relationships between members of these communities is highly personal, virtually all face-to-face. Members consider each other as kinspersons, since they are related closely or distantly by blood or marriage. Each micro-community is an oversized kinship group; it has its own special skill, so it is a work group; its own gods, so it is a religious congregation; its own judicial councils, so it is a self-governing community; its own social life, so it is a group intensely and intimately interested and involved in the lives of its members. The castes have a solidity that has no counterpart in the Western world.

Contrasting Worldviews

The concept of "worldview" is an essentially visual, spatial image, as Ong has noted (1969:635):

> However we break it down or specify it, the term "world view" suggests some sort of major unifying perception, and it presents the unification as taking place in a visual field. "View" implies sight, directly and analogously. The concept is of a piece with many other spatially grounded metaphors we commonly avail ourselves of in treating perception and understanding: "areas" of study; "fields" of investigation, "levels" of abstractions, "fronts" of knowledge, "waves" of interest, "movements" of ideas and so on indefinitely.

The contrast of worldviews summarized by Paul Hiebert in Table 5-3 pairs the values of Indian thought with contrasting Western orientations. The differences are rooted in primal ways of perceiving reality and in basic assumptions about existence, frequently revealing converse epistemologies.

The cross-cultural pastoral therapist with theological and philosophical tools must of necessity encounter these differences at a greater depth than members of related helping professions. This places greater demands on the therapist's interpathic skills, cultural awareness, and inte-

Table 5-3. Contrasting Worldviews

American Worldview	Indian Worldview
EMPIRICISM. The physical world is real, orderly. It can be tested, measured, controlled. Material things are worthy goals of human striving.	SUBJECTIVISM *(maya)*. The natural world has no ultimate reality. It is a transitory ever-changing creation of our minds.
Absolutes. In the real world functional absolutes exist. There is a categorical difference between the natural world and our dreams and fantasies.	*Relativism.* There are no absolutes, no sharp distinctions between fact and fantasy, myth and reality, dreams and daily life.
Naturalism. There is a sharp distinction between natural and supernatural worlds. We live in a natural world of objective events.	*Supernaturalism.* There is no sharp distinction between natural and supernatural. Gods and spirits are as real as natural objects.
Linear time. Time is linear, sequential, and never repeated. Past, present, and future extend in a uniform scale.	*Cyclic time.* Time is a continual rerun of events and persons. The universe and all beings repeat in cyclical epochs.
Order and immutability. The world is consistent, orderly, and predictable according to natural law.	*Mutability and unpredictability.* Things are not what they appear to be. The beggar may be a king, the lion a demon.
Knowledge. The human mind by rational process can discover the order of the universe and control it. Knowledge has high value.	*Wisdom.* The goal of life is wisdom, an intuitive understanding of reality. Wisdom is an inner light.
CATEGORIZED WORLD. The world can be classified into distinct categories. The sciences provide elaborate and particularistic categories.	UNIFIED WORLD. All things manifest one spirit. Life is stratified in many levels, yet it is one; many castes yet all are one.
Equality. Within each category there is equality, autonomy, opportunity. Since all people are within the human category, they are to be equal, free, voluntary.	*Hierarchy.* All is organized by hierarchy. Gods, religions, persons, animals, and nature are all ranked in fixed hierarchies of values.
Individualism. The individuality and worth of each person is taken for granted. Rights, freedom, self-reliance, and fulfillment are valued.	*Interdependence.* Specialization and interdependence link diversity and cooperation in society and family.
Competition. In an individualistic world all forms of life compete for resources and dominance.	*Patron-client relationships.* Some people are born to greater rights and responsibilities, others to service. Hereditary patron-client relationships unite hierarchy and interdependence.

NATURAL MANAGEMENT. By their knowledge of natural and moral laws people control their destiny.

COSMIC LAW *(karma)*. In an organic harmonious universe all is governed by the law of karma—destiny.

Science and technology. These shape all education, industry, research, and daily life.

Pilgrimage (samsara). One's life condition is determined by actions in previous lives.

Uniform morality and justice. Society is based on self-evident principles of love, equality, respect for rights of others, and justice for all.

Relative morality. Right and wrong depend on one's place in the universal and social order. Actions are not right or wrong but fitting or not fitting.

Mission. Those who have knowledge, whether scientific or religious, have a moral obligation to share it.

Tolerance and inclusivism. Cultural pluralism and ethnic relativism are inclusive, accepting diversity with no urge toward conformity.

EXPANDING GOOD. The world of good is expanding, new frontiers are always opening, new opportunities are always available for those who seek them.

LIMITED GOOD. There is a limited amount of wealth, land, power, status, love. It cannot be increased, so ambition is a threat to others.

Achievement orientation. Personal achievement, not illustrious background, is the measure of worth and position; work, effort, achievement are intrinsic goods.

Ascription orientation. Security and meaning are found in belonging, not in material things acquired. Relationships are the measure of status and power.

Associational groups. Groups outside the family are based on voluntary association and contractual relationships. Status rises by joining new groups.

Castes (jati). Membership in primary groups is by birth. Variation is permitted, but defying rules can lead to ostracism.

Success and progress. The ability to produce results, to make profits, to achieve status and demonstrate superiority are the goals of life.

Release (moksha). Not self-realization but release, not achievement and success but detachment and wisdom are the goals of life.

(Adapted from Hiebert 1976:359–362)

gration of theory and theology. Yet it also opens greater possibilities for authentic understanding and depth encounter in the therapeutic or supervisory hour.

> In Japan once rank is established on the basis of seniority, it is applied to all circumstances, and to a great extent controls social life and individual activity. Seniority and merit are the principal criteria for the establishment of a social order; every society employs these criteria, although the weight given to each may differ according to social circumstances. In the West merit is given considerable importance, while in Japan the balance goes the other way. (Nakane 1970:29)

This superior-inferior differentiation serves functions of maintaining vertical status positions, thus sustaining the heritage of obligational relationships consistent with historic cultural values. Social relationships are nonsymmetrical with a constant awareness of rank, of superordinate and subordinate.

Filial Piety, the Vertical Virtue

In traditional societies the central value, or the vertical virtue, is hierarchical respect and obedience. Although it bears different names and varied forms in each culture, its obligational generational character is consistently central.

The Chinese traditional virtue of five-dimensional filial piety—parent, sibling, sovereign, spouse, friend—provides an excellent case for examination of such a cultural structuring. Filial piety is the basic moral principle of both ethics and politics in China. Family life is the environment in which filial piety is first learned and practiced; government is the sphere in which the political realization of filial piety takes place. The character for filial piety, *hsiao,* is made up of two radicals: an old man and a child. The fundamental image is that of a son bearing up and supporting his father. The central characteristic is faithful obedience of inferiors toward superiors; that is, the son to the father, younger brothers to the older, wife to the husband (Ng 1982:16–17).

But the focus is on the parent-child relation. As the closing lines of *The Classic of Filial Piety* phrase it, the services of love and reverence to parents when alive, and those of grief and sorrow to them when dead —these completely discharge the fundamental duty of life (see Case Study: A Marital Puzzle).

Disobedience to one's parents is considered the most heinous crime. As the Chinese proverb states, "Under heaven, no parent is ever wrong," although the Book of Rites or *Li Chi* states, "When his parents are in error, the son must remonstrate with them with respect and gentleness."

The Classic of Filial Piety was written shortly after the time of Confucius, about the fifth century B.C., but filial piety was already over a thousand years old. This obedience to elders in their lifetime, and veneration of their spirits after death, has been the central duty of a fourth of the world's population for over four thousand years. Duties to parents

CASE STUDY: A Marital Puzzle (Hong Kong)

Husband and wife, 31 and 29, have two daughters, 5 and 3. The problem is an impending separation. The wife is fed up with her husband's work patterns, her tensions with his family, and her sense of rejection as an outsider and plans to leave Hong Kong, taking her daughters back to her home community in the United States.

H and W met when both were students at the University of California. He is Cantonese, she a second-generation Chinese American. She is acculturated to American expressiveness, open warmth, immediate confrontation; he to traditional concern for respect, dignity, emotional restraint, and filial piety.

Their return to Hong Kong heightened these differences. He returned to the family business, where he worked a sixty-hour week with intense loyalty to his father, who had made his education possible. When W objected to H's absence, particularly from the children, he spoke of the obligation a son feels to parents, of owing all work possible to the family enterprise.

W discovered she was responsible for all decisions surrounding parenting, without the support of either her husband or her in-laws. Her mother-in-law, deeply disappointed at the birth of daughters and their decision to limit their family to two children, refused to visit. Since W did not speak Cantonese, she felt outside all important family discussions and community life.

W appealed to their shared Christian faith, to the need to leave parents and cleave to his wife, to his responsibility to obey God, not his father, when choices came in conflict. H saw his loyalty as eldest son as non-negotiable but felt torn between his wife's demands and his Christian faith, with its stress on freely chosen commitments, and the unquestionable patterns of filial piety; between the tension of his personal identity as a Christian and his cultural identity within the extended family. Her final decision to leave Hong Kong only polarized the differences further.

---

are continuous, never-ending, alive or dead. The stream of tradition flows on from generation to generation. When asked by Tseng Tsu, "Is filial piety the highest of all the virtues possessed by a great sage?" Confucius replied, "There is nothing so great in the world as man, and there is nothing so great in man as filial piety" (Ng 1982:18).

Filial piety and fraternal submission are seen as the essential root of the five classic virtues: *hsiao; jen,* benevolence and love of all human beings; *li,* propriety and attendance to ritual, ceremony, and courtesy; *yi,* righteousness and virtuous obedience to communal values; and *cheng,* harmony of life with nature, heaven, and humanity. Figure 5-3 lists the five in their classic sequence, but the second is clearly central, the crucial value on which all the others depend.

There is an absolute obedience demanded by classic filial piety. Within the family there is the obligation to remonstrate gently with a parent who

1. Jen (仁) Benevolence

A sympathetic heart. Love of all human beings, respect for and prizing of true humanity. This love of others is rooted in love of parents, in filial piety.

2. Hsiao (孝) Filial piety

The fountain of all good conduct is filial obedience. The five central relationships are between sovereign and subject, father and son, husband and wife, elder and younger brother, and friend and friend. "Filial piety and fraternal submission, are they not the root of all benevolent actions?" (Analects I.2)

3. Yi (義) Righteousness

Virtuous obedience to communal values expressed in reciprocity, concern for others' welfare, and honoring of the five relationships. Righteousness is the outworking of benevolence shown in true filial piety.

4. Li (礼) Propriety

Attendance to ritual, ceremony, and courtesy, a sense of respect, honor, and emotional balance. Propriety is the social behavior of righteousness.

5. Cheng (諧) Harmony

Harmony of life with nature, heaven, and humanity keeps all in balance, expressing benevolence in the five relationships through righteous action, in ritual propriety.

Figure 5-3. The five classic Chinese virtues.

is in error, but there is nothing in the Confucian position to justify such defense before a sovereign. The note sent by the censor Tso Kuang-tou to his sons just before he was tortured to death by the emperor on a trumped-up charge in A.D. 1625 is a psychologically revealing testimony to the power of this unswerving vertical obedience:

> At this moment my pain and distress are extreme; I can no longer even walk a step. In the middle of the night the pain gets still worse. If I want water to drink, none is at hand. Death! Death! Only thus can I make recompense to the Emperor and to the two imperial ancestors. . . . All sorts of punishments I have willingly endured. Since I have already argued at the risk of my life, why need I shrink from running against the spear and dying? My body belongs to my ruler-father. I am lucky I shall not die in the arms of my wife and children; for I have found the proper place to die! I only regret

that this blood-filled heart has not been able to make recompense to my ruler, and that my aged parents cannot once again see my face. This will be my remorse in Hades! . . . My misery is extreme; my pain is extreme. Why do I live on? Why do I cling to life? Death! Only thus can I make recompense to the Emperor and to the two imperial ancestors in Heaven.

The heroic quality of unwavering loyalty reveals the strength and endurance of a four-thousand-year-old tradition that empowered a great civilization. The Confucian phrasing of the relationships in Tso's speech reveals his total loyalty, which extends back through parents to previous ancestors and reaches down through the sons to future generations.

Filial Piety vs. Neighbor Love

Filial piety is as central to Chinese ethics as neighbor love is to Western Judeo-Christian thought.

Filial piety is the fundamental and central characteristic of Chinese ethical thought, much as charity has been in the Christian tradition. Filial piety is not mere dutifulness to one's parents, but rather it constitutes an integral approach to what it means to be human. The external practices of filial piety are only the natural consequence of a personal self-identity in which the self is viewed, not as an isolated ultimate human unit, but rather as a member of a family and ultimately a member of a clan of people, a being whose existence is based on the existence of others. Thus filial piety for the Chinese is the only correct orientation to one's existence, an existence which overcomes ego-centrism with a living realization that one's being is not a self-enclosed unit, but something inherited, passed on from one's parents. (Lian 1981:38)

There are voices in classic Chinese thought that call for a broadened neighbor love rather than the vertical obligations of familial lines. The philosopher Mo Tzu (fifth century B.C.) taught that unconditional love or filial piety ought to be equally extended to all humankind and not reserved in a special degree for parents or family relations. Confucianists thought the Mo Tzuists contrary to both human nature and Chinese family ethics, and the Confucianist view of particular rather than universal love prevailed. The two are not opposed in Confucian thought. Universal love is seen as a natural result of profound filial piety. The vertical virtue, when obeyed, energizes all others.

"Western philosophers," comments Hsieh Yu-wei, "generally appeal to reason, to conscience, to sympathy, or to the idealism of universal love of mankind in order to discover or expound the source of morality. All these are important, of course, in the exploration of this ethical domain. And yet, without filial piety as their mainstay, all go adrift in confusion or are limited in their development and application" (Hsieh Yu-wei 1962:415–416).

Mencius, in the *Doctrine of the Mean,* points out that "the ways of the superior man may be compared to what takes place in traveling, when to go a distance we must first traverse the space that is near; and in ascending a height, we must begin from the lower ground" (Mencius XV). For this reason, Mo Tzu's "principle of all-embracing love" or Jesus' teaching of unlimited universal love has not been readily acceptable to the Chinese, who focus on the practical, the immediate, the first familial steps. This does not oppose universal love, it begins from the filial and then step by step expands to the larger realm.

The Power of the Vertical Vision

The power of this vertical vision shapes not only personal, familial, communal, religious, and political life, it is the center of philosophical ethical and theological thought emerging from the Chinese tradition. Such central issues as the nature of love (vertical benevolence is its highest form rather than the equal regard of the West), the process of forgiveness (vertical generosity and gracious mercy is its essential nature rather than mutual reciprocal acceptance), and the understanding of authority, power, justice, equality, freedom, responsibility, and all other virtues begin with this central vertical virtue.

The Communist revolution in 1949 and the Cultural Revolution that followed three decades later demanded that sons denounce fathers and that families discard the ancestral tablets, worship rituals, and husband-wife patterns which had been inviolate for millennia. The public denunciations of family members, the demand for auto critiques read to the community, did great violence to familial, social, and communal patterns, repressing them for two generations of Chinese. Yet tradition returns with power as the controls are being gradually withdrawn.

The power of communism to substitute economic, equalitarian, utilitarian, and produce-oriented values in a traditional culture such as the Chinese is an astounding historical fact. Its challenge to the forms of vertical structure and its ability to utilize them in creating a new society of intense loyalties can be seen as a synthesis of East and West, a blend of Maoism and Marxism. As Robert Bellah notes (1970:165):

> In its origin Communism can be understood only in relation to the Christian symbolizations which preceded it, and its appeal in various Western countries has been partly conditioned by the variety of Christianity prevailing in them. I would suggest that Chinese Communism must be understood in terms of the particular background of Confucian symbolization. It has apparently succeeded in tapping at last the age-long repressed aggression of sons against fathers as is indicated by the symbolic denunciation of the father which forms the high point of Chinese Communist "re-education." But it could do so only by bringing in a basic reference point which transcends the given social and familial order. The capacity of Communism to do this derives in part from its own Christian lineage. And so Christianity, in parody form at least, has come closer in the last fifteen years to the missionaries' dream of "total evangelization" than in the whole preceding century of effort. The subtle dialectic between surviving elements of the Confucian tradition and Crypto-Christian Communism helps to explain the dynamism of current Chinese society.

Values in Pastoral Psychotherapy

That all pastoral psychotherapy is value-based and value-directed, not value-free, is true by its very definition of the identity of the pastoral counselor. But assumed values must be brought to full awareness, assessed, and often redirected.

Pastoral psychotherapy, as practiced in almost all cultures, promotes the values of clear thinking, openness to feelings, responsible choosing, effective communicating, and courageous acting. There are basic values implicit in each of these values that may be assumed without question.

If we reward clear and critical thinking, we are valuing rationality. But this may be incongruent with a culture's core values.

If we support openness to feelings, we are valuing intuition and emotion. But which feelings, in a setting where face is primary?

If we invite moral reasoning, we are valuing equality and justice. But a culture may prize harmony and unity more than these.

If we suggest freedom of choice, we are valuing autonomy and independence. But dependence and solidarity may be core values.

If we reinforce divergent perceiving and thinking, we are valuing creativity. But repetition and conformity may be preferred.

If we advocate conflict mediation, we are valuing mutuality and equality. But conflict suppression may be the cultural norm.

Psychotherapy cannot be value-free, because values are implicit in all preferences made and explicit in the process utilized. In this chapter we have invited the testing and experiencing of alternative value systems. The effective therapist can enter alternate world views interpathically and perceive as well as feel the consequences of the view upon the person or group's life situation.

The task of the pastoral counselor within each culture is twofold. First, the pastoral counselor's task is to examine the value structures of that culture and to challenge the inconsistencies of practice and confront the injustices perpetrated. Since the therapist is in contact with marginal persons and is intervening in the pain of the troubled and oppressed, she or he cannot avoid caring, speaking, and acting in behalf of neglected or betrayed values. The second task is to reflect on what values and universal, ultimate concerns must command our allegiance and to practice these in the therapeutic process, call for them in the community, and work for their presence in the nation.

As a case in point, let us examine the oft-stated public values of the American people. The classic American values are: belief in the equality of all as a fact and as a right (yet prejudice, discrimination, and bigotry are still powerful forces); freedom of the individual in ideal and in reality (yet power differentials and discrepancies in opportunity exist, particularly for some minority and marginal persons); democracy as participative government with local involvement of every citizen (yet marginal and minority groups have often been excluded); religious freedom and pluralism on issues of faith (yet religious practice has tended to move toward an innocuous civil religion); success by achievement, acquisition, and material comfort (yet this has become the prerogative of the white middle-class majority); scientific methodology and secular rationality (yet there is often a resurgence of emotive, cultic, faddish, or popular infatuations); and moral orientation toward responsible ethical commitments to human rights (yet there is consistent national support of totalitarian states who support our economic, industrial, or military objectives).

The therapist functioning from the cultural matrix of American life must be aware of the contradictions between the stated and practiced value systems, as must every counselor with his or her native culture. The task becomes more complex and more imperative within a pluralistic culture. One must discern between legitimate variety in values and the failure to pursue and fulfill central values that are essential to the societies' vision of life and destiny. As John Gardner pointedly notes:

> In a pluralistic society the consensus must necessarily be at what one might call a middle level of values. Obviously it cannot deal with the surface trivialities of manners and daily customs; neither can it sound the depths.
>
> . . .
>
> To force consensus in the depths of belief would be intolerable. To remain preoccupied with the whitecaps on the surface would be meaningless. So pluralistic society wisely seeks to establish its consensus in the middle depths. . . .
> The fact that we are not always faithful to these shared values does not indicate confusion or a failure of the consensus. *We know the values to which we are being unfaithful.* One might ask, "What difference does it make that we agree on our values if we aren't faithful to them?" The answer is that if one is concerned about therapy, it always makes a difference what the patient is suffering from. This society is suffering not from confusion but from infidelity. (Gardner 1964:117–118)

The prophetic task, which is a part of the pastoral therapist's calling, is to differentiate between plurality, which is to be prized and protected, and moral infidelity, which is to be confronted and corrected by all involved. It is the ongoing task of the pastoral counselor to aid in the recovery of essential values, review their appropriateness in the light of other groups' values, compare them with universal values revealed in history and in theology, and continue to correct short-term and penultimate values by what is eternal and ultimate in character.

A Theology of Value

In the fields of theology and philosophy, three central concerns are metaphysics, epistemology, and values. *Metaphysics* seeks to know the ultimate nature of reality and to arrange the whole of reality into an all-inclusive system. *Epistemology* as a theory of knowledge attempts to know how far we, as knowing beings, are capable of knowing the truth. *Values* investigate the processes and content of evaluation; that is, the processes that precede, accompany, or direct all human behavior. "I think, I theorize, I evaluate, therefore I am."

Values, as life-meaning, ethics and aesthetics, may be examined on multiple levels: personal consciousness as conscience; social constructs as folkways and mores; laws that determine organization, integration, structure, stability, and productivity of a social group; and cultural values, the cultural goods that are prized and followed in life.

Cultural values emerge from seven central needs of humans and human society.

1. Economic goods, which realize the economic value called *utility.*

2. Ideological goods, which realize the theoretical value called *truth.*

3. Political goods, which realize the power value called *dominance* or *governance.*

4. Solidarity goods, which realize the social value called *fidelity* or *loyalty.*

5. Ethical goods, which realize the ethical value called *morality.*

6. Aesthetic goods, which realize the aesthetic value called *beauty.*

7. Religious goods, which realize faith values called the *sacred* or the *holy.*

All institutions express all seven values. Religion, when alive, is economically concerned, theologically clear, politically responsible and prophetic, socially uniting, ethically compelling, aesthetically reverent and celebrative, and religiously sacred. The same clustering of values is true in each area. Political institutions have economic, moral, aesthetic, solidaric, religious, and theoretical aspects.

Cultural goods express and seek to realize the value system of the culture in an ongoing, evolving, dynamic process. As they are united into cultural value clusters, these compound cultural goods may be homogeneous in some societies but are heterogeneous in most. Societies, as well as persons and groups, are conflicted, troubled, and ambivalent.

An effective theological perspective integrates the economic, ideological, political, social, moral, aesthetic, and religious concerns of humans into an integrated worldview. Value theory plays a crucial role in such a comprehensive theological stance, as it does in the definition of ethical positions. The language of faith and the thought forms of theology are enriched by the study of values and the human process of valuing. However, to reduce the language of theology to the language of value is as serious an error as to ignore the study of values in doing theology. All speech about God or about values is interrelated; indeed, God and value are interdependent concepts and neither can be intelligibly discussed apart from the other.

Three basic theological perspectives on values are: (1) as objective entities: values have intrinsic worth by nature of their very being; (2) as subjective entities: values have extrinsic worth as others appraise them as valuable; and (3) as relational entities: there is no such thing as a value in and of itself; values exist only in the context of relations between and among beings.

The three perspectives would affirm that "love of neighbor" is (1) a value in and of itself, (2) a value as it is so prized by persons; and (3) a relationship of valuing of others that provides the context for values to arise.

To illustrate more definitively, the three options may be distinguished by comparing them with the attributes of color, position, and preference. One might say a Royal Poinciana tree is (1) flaming red, (2) south of me, (3) beautiful. All these attributes are relative. Red, although generally considered an intrinsic attribute, present in the nature of the flowering tree, depends on light, on time of day, and on the observer's eyes being color-sensitive. South is a given direction, but the particular tree may be north of you while south of me, so its position is relative to the observer. Beauty is relative to the taste and preference of the observer (Grant 1984:35).

Value is like the directional attribute. It has a transcendent referent —north is physically, consensually a given point, yet all references to it are relative to the position of the person making the judgment. Value is rooted in both a transcendent center of value and a relational center between the value and the valued.

Value is thoroughly relational in character, argues Richard Niebuhr (1963:107). There is no such thing as value in and of itself; value exists only in the context of relations between and among beings. Value arises in, but is not reducible to, such relations, since value is not a relation but arises in the relations of one being to another.

Yet value also possesses an objective relation, in that another observer can confirm the relation. To say "the tree is north of me" can be confirmed by another in a way that neither the degree of redness nor the quality of beauty can. Values possess this quality of objectivity, "in the sense that value relations are understood to be independent of the feelings of an observer but not in the sense that value is itself an objective kind of reality" (Niebuhr 1963:108).

The Center of Value

All valuing is relative to some center—the ego for an egocentric valuer, humankind for the humanitarian, the family or tribe for the tribal person, God for the theist. Thus every value system is constructed around some being, group, or thing that is accepted as the center of value. "The center of value" for every person is functionally that person's "god." One's life may be organized around one center of value, God, or around multiple centers, many gods, which order and rule life.

This center—or these centers—of value may take the forms of polytheism, henotheism, or radical monotheism. Niebuhr offers a model for conceptualizing these various definitions of God by pointing out that these types of faith logically rest on four possible combinations of two polar continua: the one and the many, and finite to infinite (Figure 5-4). This model sets the various value centers and types into the human faiths of polytheism, henotheism, and radical monotheism. Polytheism is essentially conflicted. With no organizing unifying center, values are in constant competition and contradiction. Henotheism does not resolve this conflict, it broadens it from an intrapersonal to an interpersonal conflict. Now each person defends his or her competing god or center of values. Henotheism recognizes the need for a single center of value but chooses a finite, temporal center, which cannot guarantee meaning to life or call forth the ultimate loyalty of faith (Grant 1984:50–53).

Value judgments cannot be avoided; they must be made in life. Each person selects one value relationship as the core value that is definitive in decision. Whether something is good, needed, or desirable is determined by a relationship that is taken as a center of value. For the patriot, what is chosen is what is esteemed good for the country; for the egotist, what is good for the self; for the loyal executive, what is good for the company; for the military officer, what is good for the army; for the humanist, what is good for humanity; for the total churchman, what is good for the denomination.

In each situation, one relation is taken as definitive in decision making. In choosing such a center of value as the final criterion in decision making, that relationship is properly termed "god." As this center is chosen as the starting point for values, for decision making, and for judgment, it is treated as though it were ultimate even though it is a finite entity or relationship (Grant 1984:128).

INFINITE

Infinite and one	*Infinite and many*
"radical monotheism"	(logically inconceivable in Western thought)
The one center of value is the critical principle, the organizing center, the supreme value unifying all other values	Present in animism, spiritism, and folk religions
Finite and one	*Finite and many*
"henotheism"	"polytheism"
One god is the center of value, yet that god is one finite reality among others	Multiple value centers with no unifying inclusive center of value
Nationalism, naturalism, and humanism are all henotheistic elevations of one finite center of values	No unity is possible with plural gods: utilitarianism and hedonism are polytheistic, as are animism, spiritism, and folk religions

ONE — MANY

FINITE

Figure 5-4. The four possible centers of value, after Niebuhr.

(Grant 1984:51)

Summary

The intercultural pastoral counselor has a highly developed sensitivity to values: their nature, universality, variety, and power in directing life. Objective values—the preferable—and subjective values—the preferred —differ significantly between cultures, but universal values do exist. Among these are survival, safety, security, and social solidarity.

Every culture is shaped by selected core values. These vary sharply between cultures. Cases in point are the contrast between hierarchy and equality as valued in traditional and modern cultures respectively. The vertical vision of unchanging status and rank is a significantly different value from horizontal egalitarian views, which provide mobility and the promise of achieving a marked change in status.

The pastoral counselor is especially sensitive to central values since all work is grounded in a theology of value. Further, the pastoral therapist recognizes that all human valuing is relative to a center that functions as or points to the supreme good, or God. In crossing over, the intercultural person becomes more aware of essential values and more committed to the central value that shapes culture, family, and person.

6

Family, Family Theory, and Therapy Across Cultures

A Theology of the Family

*"Happy families are all alike,
but an unhappy family is unhappy in its own way."*

—*Leo Tolstoy, 1887*

*Untrue. Unhappy families are remarkably similar.
But happy families develop in a rich variety of ways.*

THE FOOLISH OLD MAN WHO REMOVED MOUNTAINS
CHINESE FABLE

Long long ago in northern China there lived an old man who became known as the foolish old man of North Mountain. His house faced south, and beyond his doorway stood two great peaks, Tai Hang and Wangwu, obstructing the way, blocking the view, and hiding the setting of the sun in winter.

The mountains must be removed, he one day resolved, and he called his four sons. With hoe in hand they began to dig up these mountains with great determination. Another graybeard, known as the wise old man, came by, stood and watched them digging furiously, and said derisively, "How silly of you to do this! It is quite impossible for you five men to dig up these two huge mountains and carry them away."

The foolish old man replied, "You see but five men, but I have committed my whole family. We are all there is now, but when I die my sons will carry on. When they die, there will be my grandsons to carry on, and so on to infinity. High as they are, the mountains cannot grow any higher, and with every bit we dig they will be that much lower. Why can't we clear them away?" And having refuted the wise old man's wrong view, he returned to his digging.

—*Mao Zedong*

"Family" occurs in such a diversity of forms that it is difficult to claim "family" as universal. Yet all people live in relational networks.

"The family," as a concept, has little meaning in many parts of the third world. There is not even a word for "family" in some parts of Latin America and Africa. In Botswana the nearest equivalent word is *lolwapa*, which means "compound," the place in which people live. The family as the social ideal, the basic unit of society in the West, emerged with the creation of the middle class and its mobile nuclear family with division of labor between husband and wife. Before that, for the majority of society there was the clan, the tribe, the community, the dwelling unit.

Families are survival units for most people in the nonindustrial world. The family is created—with a variety of relationships—to get people through the year. Cooperative economics can be a far more binding tie than love.

> Love is not something the poor seek. It creeps up on them unawares. Does a mother dare love her child when she knows the chances of its dying before the year is out are two to one? Does a man look for a wife to love and cherish —or just a woman with a strong back and shoulders to weed his fields and carry his water? If there is simply time for eyes to meet in an understanding smile, who could ask for more? (Taylor 1982:9)

In this chapter we will examine marriage, the nuclear family, and the extended family from the viewpoint of family systems theory and therapy in a cross-cultural pastoral perspective. Marriage, in most therapeutic approaches, is viewed as the central relationship that influences effective parental, filial, and sibling relationships throughout the extended system (although it is secondary to vertical relationships in many groups).

With recognition of the almost infinite variations of human "family relations," we shall begin with the essential male-female coalition of marriage and then move to the family. Western families will be contrasted with Indian family patterns and then with other cultures, to illuminate the task of doing pastoral family therapy in differing contexts.

Marriage Across Cultures

Marriage expresses the rich diversity of humanity. Each culture defines marriage uniquely. Each person experiences the marriage of origin and the marriage of procreation in a way distinct from all others.

Viewed across cultures, marriage may be political, economic, romantic, religious, reverent, impulsive, civil, legal, common law, heterosexual, homosexual, monogamous, polygamous, incestuous, endogamous, exogamous, trial, serial, experimental, and so forth. In all times and places, people have explored the possibilities of marriage and its potential variations. Yet commonalities do exist to provide a starting point for the examination of this most basic human institution.

The characteristics of marriage that appear most nearly universal are permanence, fidelity, and need fulfillment. The ways in which each of these qualities is expressed in differing cultures is a study of variations on a common theme.

Marriages, for all their fascinating breadth in both form and content, are intended to endure. Such durability demands fidelity between the partners. This may be predominantly a fidelity of sexuality, or economics, or social face, or personal emotional support, or love, or some or all of the above. The goal of this enduring and faithful commitment is the fulfillment of certain core needs of both parties. In some cultures, marriage is expected to fulfill virtually all basic human needs; in others, the expectations are much more modest. No one relationship can fulfill all the needs of a person. Expecting one person to provide so much is asking the impossible from marriage, so the stress on the contemporary nuclear family and on marriage as the central coalition is increasingly heavy.

In their book *Marriage: East and West* (1960:294–296), the Maces found the most striking difference in the area of expectations. In the East, expectations of marriage are relatively low; consequently, they are fairly easily fulfilled, and contentment usually results. In the West, by contrast, expectations are so high that in most cases they can't reasonably be met, so some degree of disillusionment is almost inevitable.

Marriage is defined in the social sciences as a communally recognized and normatively prescribed relationship between at least two persons that designates economic and sexual rights and duties owed each to the other or others and that provides the primary means in a society by which offspring are recognized as legitimate and accorded the full birth status rights common to normal members of their society or social situation.

But any definition is subject to exceptions and alterations in any particular society. The description of general cross-cultural characteristics is often more useful than any rigid definition. Vivelo (1978:170) suggests four such characteristics:

1. Viewed cross-culturally, marriage is frequently a relationship between groups rather than just a relationship between two individuals. As a contract between corporate groups, the arrangement does not necessarily end with the death, withdrawal, or divorce of either partner. There are ongoing relationships, duties, and obligations and in some societies a subsequent marriage (levirate or sororal).

2. Marriage is not only a sexual relationship, it is a form of exchange involving the transfer of rights and obligations between the contracting parties. These may be economic (bride wealth payment or dowry, shared finances between the two parties) or political (as an alliance between families).

3. All societies have restrictions, taboos, and exogamous and endogamous boundaries. No society allows indiscriminate marriage or mating.

4. Comparatively few societies limit their members to one spouse. In many if not most societies, it is desirable to have more than one.

To illustrate these four points, the following case is apropos.

A young woman from one of the northern Hagen, New Guinea, tribes was caught in conflict between her husband's family and her family of origin. Her kin were dissatisfied with the bride wealth received and, in hopes of finding better elsewhere, asked her to leave her new husband. She refused, protesting that this would make her name bad and since they had accepted the bride wealth they should now be content. Her husband's relatives were full of praise for her desire to stay. She had proved herself a good wife indeed. "She has come inside us," they said. She had truly joined her husband's clan. In this society, a woman is expected to remain a member of both groups, to stay "in between" as an intermediary between families (Strathern 1972:vii).

All processes of propositional definition tend to view relationships in a unidimensional and reductionist fashion. A systems approach examines marriage and the nuclear, joint, and extended family network organismically as a living dynamic whole.

The Systems Perspective

The most inclusive means of examining the nature, function, and health of families arises from the systems perspective, which views the configuration of the family gestalt, whether nuclear, extended, joint, or the emerging serial polygamy of the West, in active dynamic concepts.

It is helpful to have a clear concept of "system" before applying it to the family. Otherwise the concept "system" may take on a mechanical cause-and-effect content rather than the dynamic interrelated interdependent function necessary to systems thinking. The clearest way to define this process is to show the connectedness of four key concepts: element, structure, process, system.

Elements are simply things—material things, conceptual ideas, logical propositions, mathematical data, or social roles. Unconnected elements form only a data pool, or what physicists call a "heap," without structure.

Structure is a pattern of elements—an organized configuration of elements related meaningfully to each other. The parts of a watch lying on the table comprise a heap; assembled, they become the structure of a watch. Skeleton, nerves, muscles, circulation, organs, and skin are all anatomical structures but not a human being. What is missing is the process, life.

Process is a pattern of events—an order of movement, change, and growth in sequence and repeated occurrence, not random but with regularity. Combining process and structure produces system.

System is a structure in process; that is, a pattern of elements undergoing patterned events. The human person is a set of elements undergoing multiple processes in cyclical patterns as a coherent system. Thus a system is a structure of elements related by various processes that are all interrelated and interdependent.

Systems may be closed to the outside environment or open, thus possessing nonpermeable or permeable boundaries. They maintain themselves in constancy over time through equilibrium, which may be fixed or fluid and dynamic. Systems both change and stay the same in a moving equilibrium, in the way that a growing child is still recognizable yet very different (Scherer and others 1975:260–262).

Applied to the concept of family, systems theory offers a powerful way of perceiving, understanding, and intervening when this is appropriate.

To examine the family, we may take as elements the roles of father, mother, son, daughter, brother, and sister, found in a particular pattern or structure—the nuclear conjugal family, the extended three-tier family, or the lateral joint family—which relate in regular patterns of events that comprise the family system. This system has its boundaries, closed or open, its possessed subsystems—mother/child, brother/sister, etc.—and its ongoing equilibrium.

The Family as a System

The family is best understood as a living system, composed of members who do not function independently of one another but as a unified whole. The parts are connected by a central sense of oneness. This oneness can be a healthy balancing of affectionate connectedness and respectful separateness, or it can be an unhealthy "stuck togetherness" at one pole or an emotionally distant abandonment at the other extreme. Either pole—the emotional glob that forms when the family fuses or the cold isolation when it freezes—is destructive to the members.

From the various approaches to applying family systems theory, we shall select the pioneer work of Murray Bowen (1978). His formulation of eight interlocking concepts of family functioning provides a basis for exploring how families grow or stagnate in any culture. The strength of Bowen's model for cross-cultural work rises from its firm biological base, its clear interpersonal stance, and its sociocultural orientation.

The biological model of anxiety management recognizes that all organisms can reasonably adapt to anxiety for brief periods, but when the anxiety becomes chronic, the normal safety valves begin to fail and tension rises throughout the system. This tension overload often results in symptom formation in the family, dysfunctions in relationships, and illness in members. How the family handles anxiety and chronic tension will determine whether symptoms, dysfunctions, or illness emerge or whether the family will remain free by adjusting to circumstances or taking clearer positions toward each other.

The interpersonal stance sees balanced, open, rational, feelingful one-to-one relationships as the basic building block of healthful family systems. When dialogue and dyadic resolution of differences fail, a third person is drawn in (triangled) or the whole system becomes dysfunctional.

The sociocultural orientation of family systems theory recognizes that the family system is a subsystem of the community, the community is a subsystem of the society, the society of the national culture, and the culture of humanity. All these interrelate; each sets the emotional, rational, relational, and moral tone for all others because all are interdependent, and change in any one affects the whole.

The eight interlocking concepts of family systems theory (Figure 6-1) serve to connect and clarify how the family functions to manage anxiety on the individual, dyadic, and systemic levels.

1. *Differentiation of self.* A person without a "self" shares the common self of the family "group self," or ego mass. As people differentiate into distinct persons, two dimensions of differentiation occur: *differentiation within,* which separates emotional reacting from rational responding to life and others, and *differentiation between,* which provides the necessary separation between persons in the family matrix so that each can think, choose, and act as a centered person rather than react as a non-self, expressing only the thoughts, values, feelings, and opinions of the system.

Differentiation refers to the complexity of a system's structure. A less differentiated system is in a relatively homogeneous structural state, a

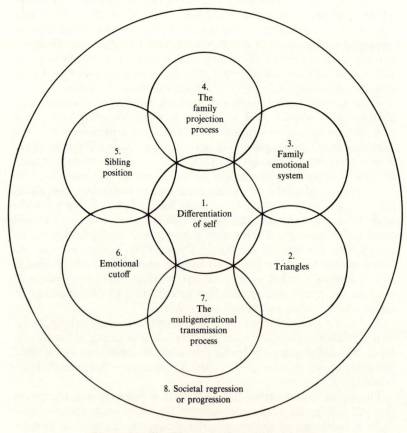

**Figure 6-1. The Bowen family systems theory
of eight interlocking concepts.**

differentiated system is a relatively heterogeneous state. The more differentiated, the more specialized it becomes in separating parts of the system to perform various functions. In the person, the more differentiated, the more discrete are the psychological functions; that is, feeling is distinct from perceiving, thinking from acting, volition from attraction. With an increase in separation there is a concomitant increase in integration or else it would simply be fragmentation, not differentiation.

The degree of differentiation is conceptualized as a continuum (see Figure 6-2). At a low level one is totally relationship-oriented, devoting enormous amounts of energy to seeking approval and demanding validation by others. Since they are dominated by emotionality they cannot separate fact from feeling.

People at moderate levels of differentiation can begin to distinguish between thought and feeling. Even though they are still ruled by the emotional system, they are more flexible and experience a limited sense of self. Relationships are still very important, but they cannot be truly close without an increase in anxiety, and so they react with distance and alienation. Much time is spent excusing or accusing others or swinging between conflict and closeness.

People with good differentiation are capable of clear thought and rich feeling, with neither overpowering the other. They interact freely without fear of being either absorbed or abandoned. They maintain close contact with all the significant people in their system but without being flooded by others' anxiety or fleeing into distance to manage stressful times.

In times of stress, any individual may regress to a less differentiated position. The lower one is on the scale, the longer it takes to recover and the more chronic the anxiety; the more differentiated person experiences temporary symptoms or dysfunction in times of stress.

The crucial insight for understanding differentiation is that it is always balanced between union and separation. Differentiation is not radical independence but centered responsive interdependence. Figure 6-2 indicates this theoretical centering between the two poles, but cultures vary on the degree of dependence or independence appropriate to the particular context. The Western nuclear family (C), when congruent with its social context, is centered at four, toward independence. Thus the optimum balance between union and separation in the forming of a self is relative to the cultural understanding of personhood.

2. Triangles. A family is made up of a complex network of triangles. Some are flexible, some rigid; some are central, others marginal; some benign, others malignant. In Western cultures, triangles are viewed with mistrust. Healthful functional relationships are person-to-person with the character of dialogue; conflicts are managed and resolved between the two; clear open communication of thoughts and feelings allows rational discussion as well as emotional investment. However, as tension increases beyond the ability of either person's management skills, a third person is "triangled" to reduce the anxiety. In healthful relationships the

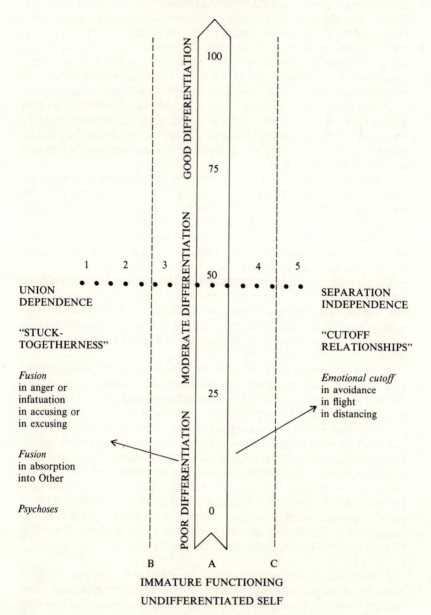

Figure 6-2. Differentiation as a continuum.

A is the theoretical balance for optimal functioning;

B is the traditional joint family;

C is the Western nuclear family.

third person is intentionally chosen for special skills and neutrality, but in less differentiated systems, a vulnerable person who is more susceptible to emotional pain is more likely to be triangled and impaired by the binding situation of "emotional mediation." Triangulation often leaves the third party disabled long after the triangle has dissolved. When a triangle is overloaded, others in the family system get drawn in as a network of interlocking triangles, which may reach into the extended family or the community resources—neighborhood, church, police, helping professionals.

Western styles of conflict resolution value one-to-one direct address, confrontation, self-disclosure, negotiation, and resolution. The movement to triangular processes is seen as a sign of high anxiety or inadequate skills in one or both parties. In the other two thirds of the world, conflicts are immediately referred to a third party—an older, wiser, neutral, skilled family member or a trusted person from the community. Triangulation serves to save face for both parties and to reduce shaming in the system. Healthful triangulation uses a disengaged, nonemotional third party; unhealthful processes draw in persons who are emotionally entangled and likely to be impaired by the process. In cross-cultural work, the crucial issue is not the presence or absence of triangles but their health or unhealth, and the goal of therapy is not inevitably to return the resolution to the two parties in conflict but to facilitate healthful triangular resolution. Triangular patterns cannot be isolated from their cultural context, nor can they be judged as universally troubled or dysfunctional. Triangles take their meaning from the cultural context, not from the number of persons involved. A triangular relationship is disruptive in a Western nuclear family, where a strong marital dyad is crucial. But in an Indian joint family, for example, conflict is resolved in multiple triangles; the marital dyad is rarely the strongest relationship, so it is frequently triangled in benign ways.

3. *Family Emotional System.* Every family develops its own patterns for managing anxiety. Individuals choose mates with levels of differentiation similar to their own; in fact, the choice is made unconsciously by the emotional field of each person's family of origin.

There are three basic patterns for channeling anxiety in nuclear families: one can focus it in the marriage, in one of the partners, or in a child. This results in either marital conflict, dysfunction in one spouse, or impairment of one or more of the children.

When anxiety gets focused on the marriage relationship, the two persons become dependent on each other but act independent. Tension becomes chronic, with high negative and positive feelings, so the two alternate between conflict and closeness in a continuous cycle.

When anxiety is focused on one partner, that person adapts to absorb most of the undifferentiation of both and a symptom forms and may endure for decades.

When anxiety is denied by both parents and hidden behind a united front, it is usually deferred to the child. Denial is the perfect context for a "family projection process," which we will examine as the next concept.

In traditional joint families, anxiety may be located between the wife and the mother-in-law. In India, the special relationship of daughter-in-law as responsible for the household while being supervised by the mother-in-law often makes this the hot side of the most active triangle in the family. In China, the father-son relationship, with its high demands and hierarchical control patterns, may be the central axis of tension. Thus the joint or extended family provides additional loci and foci for anxiety within its emotional system. We shall examine these key coalitions later in the chapter.

4. *The Family Projection Process.* This fourth concept deals with the way parental tensions and immaturity are projected or trickle down to the children. It is present in all families but in widely differing degrees. The classic pattern is the mother-child overinvolvement with a distant and uninvolved husband. The mother's anxieties are displaced into the child through an invisible umbilical cord. The father may either support this symbiotic relationship or withdraw. In the first instance the two partners are "together" in their concern for the impaired child; in the second the father abandons the family and the tensions are invested in the mother-child attachment.

The "problem" child who is most attached to the fusing parent—mother or father—is typically the lowest in family differentiation, displaying the least amount of independent functioning and autonomous reasoning. An oldest, only, or youngest child, any child with a birth defect, or one born in a time of high family anxiety is most likely to be triangled.

This process is visible cross-culturally. In some cultures the tradition names the oldest son automatically, but if the parent is a younger child he or she may have a preference for the child of his or her own birth position. We shall return to this in the next concept.

5. *Sibling Position.* The fifth concept is the rank order of children in the family. One would expect the order to follow the chronological birth order, but it rarely does. The child with the lowest level of self is ranked number one, the next is number two, and so on. The child with the greatest sense of self is the last one in the ranking. On the basis of levels of differentiation, one can predict patterns of dysfunction in the family and in the generations preceding and to follow.

Cross-culturally, sibling positions are often invested with duty, obligation, power, privilege, and pain. Discovering the meanings within the culture, the function within the family, and its special impact on the persons in question can open new understandings of the particular family's process.

6. *Emotional Cutoff.* In early life, all humans are emotionally connected to parents and family of origin in symbiotic fusion. As we grow, we individuate, but at greatly varying rates from family to family, person to person, and culture to culture. The way in which a person resolves this union with others has a lifelong effect on the person's inner management of feelings and outer handling of relationships. The greater the level of unconscious, automatic, reactive connectedness, the more likely a person is to repeat such involuntary fusion in other relationships.

In an emotional cutoff, the person either uses physical distance—moving hundreds or thousands of miles away—or emotional distance—by isolating from all family feeling—or a combination of the two. The degree of cutoff indicates the depth of fusion. Growth happens as a person can stay in meaningful feelingful contact to these significant others, while functioning maturely, responsibly, and responsively, without either fleeing into distance or slipping back into a dysfunctional oneness.

The balance point of individuation varies from culture to culture (see Figure 6-2). Individuality and individualism are two different concepts. Individualism is most frequently gained in the West by means of a marked degree of emotional cutoff. Individuality emerges through authentic differentiation. Its appropriate cultural center point between union and separation is culturally relative within a latitude of much greater or much less connectedness. The key to effective mental health is in the congruence with the cultural context. Within each culture, connectedness beyond this cultural mean produces the familiar "stuck togetherness" of an "emotional glob," and exaggerated distance from the mean produces emotional cutoffs.

7. *The Multigenerational Transmission Process.* No symptom is ever just one generation deep. A minimum of three generations is involved in any personal problem—self, the parents one is reacting or responding to, and the grandparents, who are the repetition or reverse of the parents' emotional style. In fact, one can trace the evolution of pronounced patterns in a family kinship system for up to ten generations. The more differentiated and healthy the family process, the more variation there will be in persons and generations; the less differentiated, the more pronounced will be the fixed patterns, the repetitious scripting of lives, and the clear transmission of pain and impairment from generation to generation.

Western families often experience problems in tracing more than three or four generations because of high mobility and the great amount of emotional cutoffs. A Chinese friend of mine from Guangzhou has full family data for thirty-six generations—over one thousand years. The recognition of good and evil following and flowing from generation to generation is present and powerful in all cultures.

8. *Societal Regression or Progression.* The family is a subsystem of the surrounding society, and family and society share common processes and operate using similar principles. Chronic anxiety is present in both families and societies, and both react or respond in a similar way according to their levels of differentiation.

The more undifferentiated a family or society, the more likely it is to seek short-term solutions to chronic serious and pervasive problems. Although these solutions may relieve the anxiety of the moment, they depend on the affective climate rather than the principled commitment and internalized values of a people. Societal maturation increases as both leadership and people are able to participate, by whatever means their political system utilizes, in long-range, thoughtful, intentional planning that includes both remediation and development.

The rise and fall of societies and cultures in cyclical movement is observed by sociologists, historians, and philosophers who attempt to understand the dynamics of the paranoia that affects nations such as the United States and Russia in the latter half of the twentieth century and sweeps smaller nations into the emotional field of their chronic outer-directed anxiety. As a consequence, for example, the nations of sub-Saharan Africa spend a major part of their gross national product purchasing armaments from the superpowers while famine rages across their lands unchecked.

The social solidarity of Chinese family-community-national identity allows for sweeping changes in economics, work, production and consumption, reproduction, and religion as the total is controlled within traditional hierarchical patterns. The higher degree of undifferentiation allows for the toleration of and participation in such destructive periods of great human suffering as the Cultural Revolution of the seventies and in the constructive periods of higher personal dignity, freedom, and productivity of the eighties. Within the societal regression to collective violation of basic human rights—essential differentiation—the family suffers internal compression and its own pathology and health is altered. With the return of greater differentiation in the social order, the context of familial life becomes more life enhancing and growth promoting.

The higher degree of societal undifferentiation in a traditional culture such as India offers immediate solutions to the need for cohesion in a setting with twelve major languages and two hundred dialects symbolizing the tribal, political, and religious differences that create deep divisions in the national spirit, but the dysfunctions are inevitable concomitants. The tragic social homicide of thousands of Sikhs following the assassination of Indira Gandhi reveals the degree of corporate ego mass demanding revenge on the corporate personality of the other group with no consideration of personal claims to justice.

The Indian Family System

To contrast Western applications of family systems theory with that of a traditional society, we will examine the Indian family from the perspectives of systems theory. For the sake of economy we shall refer to the Indian family as a designation of a style present among the highly diverse, linguistically, historically, and ethnically discrete groups of the Indian subcontinent.

It is helpful, at the outset, to reflect on Sudhir Kakar's description of person-family-society in Indian life (1978:124).

> Implicit in the organization of Indian society, in which each individual is part of a complex, hierarchically ordered, and above all stable network of relationships throughout the course of his life, is a psychological model of man that emphasizes human dependence and vulnerability to feelings of estrangement and helplessness. The core of emotional life is anxiety and suffering, *dukha* as the Buddhists would call it. Thus Hindu social organization accentuates the continued existence of the child in the adult and elaborates the caretaking function of society to protect and provide for the security of its individual members. We might also view traditional Indian society as a therapeutic model of social organization in that it attempts to alleviate *dukha* by addressing itself to deep needs for connection and relationship to other human beings in an enduring and trustworthy fashion and for ongoing mentorship, guidance, and help in getting through life and integrating current experience with whatever has gone before and with an anticipated future.

In Western theories of family dynamics, the basic unit of analysis is the individual. The family is understood essentially as a contractual social group, composed archetypically of two adults, each with a self-defined identity, who have entered into a relationship that involves the procreation of other persons who are viewed as individuals from birth and actively invited to individuate as rapidly as the developing cognitive structures allow. From a traditional Indian perspective, the Western family is a social group that is "a kind of 'roof organization' constructed on top of the primary 'pillars' of individuals which are conceived of as separate entities right from the start or at least from the age of a few months, when a primary empathy between mother and child is supposed to give way to an awareness of one's individual existence" (Hoch 1966: 62).

In contrast to this interpersonal contract view of the family as a "roof organization," the traditional cultures of the world see the family as a "root organism," with a basic foundational oneness out of which persons emerge into an individuated consciousness at widely varied life stages (see Figure 6-3). In India, the caste system provides a secure social order for groups, and the four *asramas*, or life stages, offer levels of personal achievement for those who grow toward personal responsibility and individual self-understanding; however, such growth is not the norm of human maturation. Life in symbiotic union with a family identity provides safety and structured stability for persons with no need for the development of "individuated ego boundaries," as an isolated individual identity is described in the West.

It is not uncommon for family members, who often (and significantly) accompany the patient for a first interview, to complain about the patient's *autonomy* as one of the symptoms of his or her disorder. Thus the father and elder sister of a twenty-eight-year-old engineer who had a

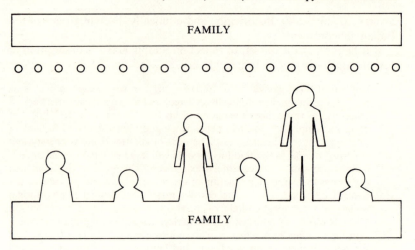

Figure 6-3. Two views of the family.

(Above) The family as a "roof organization" made up of individual "I"s connected by contract and covenant. It is understood by examining the dynamic interaction between separate entities. *(Below)* The family as a "root organism" from which persons emerge in varying degrees of individuality and individual consciousness. It is understood as a symbiotic unity functioning out of a primary oneness.

(Adapted from Hoch 1966:63)

psychotic episode described their understanding of his central problem as one of "unnatural" autonomy: "He is very stubborn in pursuing what he wants without taking our wishes into account. He thinks he knows what is best for him and does not listen to us. He thinks his own life and career more important than the concerns of the rest of the family" (Kakar 1984:9).

When a person, through social tragedy such as war, famine, or epidemic, is thrust out of this symbiotic family identity, emotional imbalance or mental illness often results. The necessity to act as an individual before one is capable of such agency can cause high anxiety, depression, hysteria or possession (the outer-directed form of hysteria), and psychosis. The movement of families with symbiotic systems to urban settings that fracture the monolithic solidarity of group identity into personally defined and privately determined pieces places intense stress on members who have only the joint family model to offer one another in a nuclear family situation, or only symbiotic empathic self-understandings in an individualistic competitive open society.

The traditional form of family in India is composed of three tiers of persons either in hierarchical arrangement or in lateral sibling patterns.

> We can call a household a nuclear family if it is composed of a group of parents and their unmarried children, or of a husband, wife, and unmarried

daughter not related to the other kin through or by property or income or the rights and obligations pertaining to them. We call that household a joint family which has a greater generation depth (i.e., three or more) than the nuclear family and the members of which are related to one another by property, income, and mutual rights and obligations. The members may be related colaterally or lineally. (Desai 1956:147)

The traditional Indian joint family functions as a closed family system within a nonpermeable boundary. It is characterized by many significant transactions within the family, but few personal transactions outside the family. The family meets the world with the united front of an integrated unit. Such a family in Western society is diagnosed as an undifferentiated family ego mass with unhealthy fusion and loss of personal identity in the absorbing and oppressive family system. Extrafamilial exchanges of an emotional or intense relational nature are conducted by the entire family from within its "rubber wall." The family wall is much stronger than the individual boundaries of the persons within (Hoch 1966:64; see Figure 6-4, top).

Western families tend to be open systems with permeable boundaries (Figure 6-4, bottom). The persons within the family, with clearly defined ego boundaries, carry out transactions with the outside world on their own initiative and in pursuit of their own interests. There are few transactions by the family as a unified group, since each person is encouraged to think, speak, and act individually. Relationships of members may be more intense and satisfying with persons outside the family than with others within the family. Such a family in Indian society would be diagnosed as anomic, fragmented, exaggeratedly individualistic, and likely to produce unhealthy, alienated personalities.

Ego boundaries, essential and necessary in a setting where persons must have individual identities to interact harmoniously, are unnecessary character armor in a sociocentric society. In familial identity, the experiences, frustrations, and anxieties that appear in one family member are the common property of all. Whatever passes through the consciousness of one—information, emotion, success, or loss—is highly likely to permeate the whole family atmosphere. Family superstitions, taboos, ceremonies, rules, and rituals all are used to ward off any external forces, any hostile invasion, any unexplained misfortune.

A central characteristic of the Indian family is a powerful relational magnetism that draws each member into the family self. The individual self is derived from the familial self. "Separation and individuation of the self simply do not take place in the Indian child and later adult personality as it does in the West" (Ramanujam 1978:35).

Socialization in the joint family gives little importance to "I, me, and mine" and much to "we, us, and our." High sensitivity to others' wishes, expectations, and feelings is demanded. The ideal of maturity is continuous and satisfying dependency relationships throughout life.

Cohesion and dependency are the most significant diagnostic measures in Indian family theory. The family typology scale (Table 6-1) measures the range of closeness and distance from the fused altruistic type and the

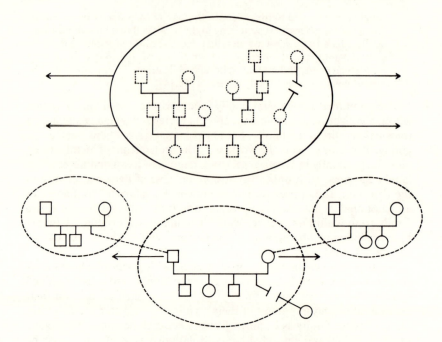

Figure 6-4. Two views of family boundary.

(Above) The traditional Indian family has a strong nonpermeable family boundary. Family members have indistinct ego boundaries. Transactions with the
outside world are carried on by the family as a whole. *(Below)* The Western
nuclear family is an aggregate of individual egos each differentiated from the
family ego mass. The boundary is permeable, permitting active two-way exchange and extrafamily loyalties with the outside world.

(Hoch 1966:63)

enmeshed egoistic type through the normal cohesive family to the fragmented anomic family. The accent is on mutual dependency in interdependent transactions.

When a person is separated from the family matrix by educational,
economic, or political change a variety of responses is possible. First, the
person may seek to reproduce the family of origin by reconstituting it
from peers, teachers, or associates found in the new situation, transfer-
ring the old psychic dependency to the new cluster of persons, who
themselves do not know the roles that are projected on them. Second,
the person may withdraw into a defensive posture, which surrounds the
self with a reactive, protective, neurotic armor. Third, the person may
be overwhelmed by the external world, the weak ego boundaries may
rupture, and psychosis may result. Or, fourth, the person may grow in
self-definition, identity formation, and individuation. These options are
parallel to the identity crisis of persons in every culture. Erik Erikson
observes similar resolutions in identity formation as persons either (1)

foreclose on the identity dictated by the family of origin or (2) postpone identity formation by taking a moratorium or (3) experiencing a loss of self in identity confusion or diffusion or (4) achieving an identity through crisis and integration. Life outside the joint family ego mass demands either rapid growth to a new individuality or regression into defensive structures.

The entire joint family feels the shock wave throughout the system when one member begins a determined move toward a more individualistic position. Individual interests will no longer coincide with the common interests of the family. As the overlap in worldview or life goals decreases, the anxiety level in the family rises. The remaining family members may attempt to fill the void created by the person's departure by drawing together more closely to fill the breach. In a nuclear family, the

---

Table 6-1. Scale of Family Types

---

1. *Normal Cohesive.* These families adhere to institutional means to achieve culturally prescribed goals, follow the set patterns of behavior based on the normative standards of the contemporary social system, and are held together by mutual attraction and work for the common objectives of the family. In the normal cohesive type the family strives to attain the real self by accepting the normative system of the society in totality.

2. *Egoistic.* These families are so bound by traditions that they are oversensitive to any sort of threat to the "family image" and attach prime importance to the "social prestige" of the family. The family as a social system becomes excessively independent of and impervious to influences from the society. Cordiality at the interpersonal level is maintained largely for the maintenance of the family image. In the egoistic type the family as a whole works for family self without any consideration of the actual normative patterns of society.

3. *Altruistic.* These families are characterized by extreme cohesiveness and too much "we" feeling. The members have high mutual trust and firm interpersonal commitment. The atmosphere is saturated with emotional warmth. The members are prone to immaturity and dependency with the result that self-reliance, self-help, and self-sufficiency are poorly developed. Solidarity and mutual help dominate the transactions in these families to such an extent that they lead to pathological dependency in some members. In the altruistic type the entire family works for the social self, forgetting the real and family self.

4. *Anomic.* In these families individual members have their own way of life, style of interaction, and personal convictions, which are often idiosyncratic. They are highly individualistic and do not bother about the other members and are rarely influenced by them. There is hardly any discussion and no common way adopted to achieve the family goals. In extreme examples, except for living under one common roof, the family members have nothing in common. In the anomic type of family individual self is given the highest importance by the family as such.

(Channabasavanna and Bhatti n.d.:154)

lonely partner may invest the emotional energy previously exchanged with the symbiotic spouse into an intensified parent-child relationship. If this becomes an enveloping dependence that absorbs the child into the parents' needs for a common family world, it stifles growth as a person.

The breakdown of the joint family ego leaves the person who is pushed out alone into the world extremely vulnerable and exposed. The previously outer-directed personality now feels overwhelmed by the confusion of messages coming through the dependent empathic processes learned in a safe controlling family environment. The personality may feel flooded by external controls, "possessed," or persecuted by a hostile world. For the person left behind in a changing family situation and trying to communicate with persons who are becoming individualistically inner-controlled and internally responsible for their lives, the situation becomes crazy-making. There is a constant encounter with a strange new set of values through the individualistic free-thinking of the other persons. So the abandoned member of the old joint family that the empathic communion once enjoyed now meets a foreign impenetrable surface. Spouses find they cannot reach, influence, or control the other in the same intuitive way. It is common to measure the degree of the other person's "love" by how anxious he or she becomes in response to the partner's anxiety. "Love" is the ability to control another's emotions. As the other becomes inner-directed, the emotions become less available to manipulation, the thoughts move into foreign worlds, the personality takes on an unknown character. The member of the old joint family process seeks in vain for signs of authentic interest, affection, and loyalty. When these are not forthcoming, jealousy and fantasies of the other's being seduced, bewitched, or possessed may arise. In advanced stages the person may feel poisoned, contaminated, persecuted, or oppressed by the influx of alien ideas and attitudes into what was once a homogeneous family unit.

As the larger joint family matrix is breaking up from movement from the rural village to the urban setting, from economic pressures to seek employment by movement into new areas, and from the impact of Western ideas through education and cultural change through technological revolutions, the nuclear families that are emerging are qualitatively different. (1) The emotional intensity and familial symbiosis cannot be maintained on the smaller scale of the conjugal group. (2) In the nuclear family, individuals must accept responsibility *for* self and *with* others instead of the previous responsibility of all to and for each other. (3) In the new family, each person is accountable for his or her own relationships with the outside world rather than speaking for the whole family or being protected in and represented by the family ego mass. (4) The criteria for decision making now become the goals and values of the person rather than the corporate family goals. (5) Parents must adjust to horizontal ties between spouses becoming more powerful than vertical ties between generations. (6) The coalition between marital partners must become more pronounced than the parent-child coalitions for the nuclear family to sustain itself healthfully, whereas in the joint family the diffuse system of obligations and relational ties permitted father-son or mother-son relationships to be the central axis of affectional bonds.

The stress of such changes may bring greater evidences of mental disturbance to the surface, which previously were absorbed into the family's extended structures. As Hoch concludes in her comments on change in India (1966:94):

> In the old joint family, much of the tolerance, peace, and harmony that may have reigned was bought at the expense of stunting of personalities and suppression of personal emotions. But if the expression of such individualized tendencies was not acceptable openly, the old social order at least had its more or less recognized "sick-roles" for its members. The beliefs that various types of mental illness were due to possession by ghosts, to magic, to the evil eye of neighbors, to poisoning or various mistakes in diet, etc., provided a convenient alibi for a person whose suppressed emotions had to find an outlet in hysterical demonstrations, compulsive rites, paranoid delusions, psychotic outbursts, or chronic hypochondriac invalidism.
>
> The corresponding therapeutic practices, even if they brought no cure or even relief, at least gave everyone the satisfaction that something had been invested or even sacrificed, and, no doubt, the frustrated family member, who had assumed or been forced into the role of the mental patient, "got something out of it."

Systems and Kinship Structures

Family systems vary in both form and content. This becomes clearly visible, for example, in examining the dominant relationship in the family (form) and its meaning (content). Francis Hsu has noted that the major cultural traditions have each stressed a different "dominant dyad" or central relationship. Hsu has theorized (1972:414) that

> kinship structure describes the formal patterns of arrangement—rules of descent, residence, inheritance, joint or nuclear family, and so forth—while kinship content refers to the characteristics that govern the intensity, tenacity, or quality of interaction among persons related through familial lines. It crystallizes itself into such values as individualism and self-reliance, romantic love in marriage, emphasis on youth or on the importance of ancestors.

The dominant or governing dyad is the most emphasized relationship in the family system. It may be father-son, husband-wife, mother-son, or brother-brother (Figure 6-5). No family system gives equal prominence to all potential dyads, and the elevated dyad tends to reduce or eliminate other dyads in the group. Nuclear families stress the marital dyad, extended families the parent-child. The four basic patterns, or forms, and their content are:

1. Mutual dependence among members of kin and community that is rooted in emphasis on the father-son axis at the expense of all other relationships. (This includes the majority of Oriental peoples—Chinese,

TYPE A

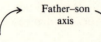

Father–son
axis

Elaboration of   Inclusiveness
ancestor cult   and continuity

Mutual
dependence

Majority of Oriental peoples
(Chinese, Japanese, Koreans,
Siamese) but not the
major inhabitants of India—
Hindus and Muslims.

(Patrilineal, patrilocal, and
patriarchal)

TYPE B

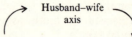

Husband–wife
axis

Individualism   Exclusiveness
and self-reliance   and discontinuity

Independence
of children

Western peoples—European in origin—
and all European peoples throughout
world.

(Patrilineal, patrilocal or neolocal, only nominally patriarchal)

TYPE C

Mother–son
axis

Longing for   Some
continuity   exclusiveness
of one-sided or   and
all-embracing   discontinuity
dependency
relationship

One-sided dependence
upon an all-answering
figure.

Hindus, and many Muslims of
Indian subcontinent.

(Patrilineal, patrilocal, and
generally patriarchal)

TYPE D

Brother–brother
axis

Ancestors and   Horizontal
gods, useful   orientation—
for present   vertical
claims;   dissociation
great importance   (inclusive but
of personal   discontinuous);
                        each generation
                        loyal but not to
                        previous
                        generation
                        of brothers

Brotherhood of man
but also unreliability
of men because of
competition.

Majority of Africans south of
Sahara.

(Patrilineal, patrilocal, and
patriarchal)

Figure 6-5. Four types of dominant dyads.

Japanese, Koreans, Siamese—but excludes the major groups inhabiting India, both Hindus and Muslims. It tends to be patrilineal, patrilocal, and patriarchal.)

The father-son relationship is elevated; all others are subordinated to it. This provides total inclusiveness and solidarity as well as the necessary continuity. The obligations are mutual, with the son owing the father all services desired, unquestioned obedience, extreme respect, and complete support; the father owes the son marital arrangements, protection, and inheritance. The vertical solidarity extends into the ancestor cults, which are invariably characterized by positive protection beliefs. (In no Oriental society do people pray for forgiveness to the ancestral spirits during emergencies or natural disasters, as is the practice in African ancestor cults.)

These societies tend to be hierarchical, conservative, and polytheistic, with low motivation to change since the strength of the way of life lies in its permanent solidarity between the living, the dead, and the unborn. Compartmentalized sexuality is seen as functional but not central to life.

2. Self-reliance on the part of the individual that is rooted in the supremacy of the husband-wife axis at the expense of all other relationships. (This includes Western peoples who are European in origin and all European peoples throughout the world. It tends to be patrilineal, patrilocal, or neolocal and only nominally patriarchal.)

The husband-wife relationship is elevated; all others are subordinated to it or patterned after it. This creates relationships of exclusiveness and discontinuity, since each husband-wife relationship ends when one dies. It is exclusive because the dyad is complete in itself and is intolerant of intrusion by a third party. Other family relationships are reduced to more or less levels of friendship.

These societies tend to be individualistic and self-reliant, stressing God-given uniqueness, freedom, rights, equality, and self-reliance. This encourages creativity as well as alienation, change, and revolution. Repressed sexuality drives art, religion, and culture.

3. Supernatural reliance, which is found where the mother-son axis tends to have more primary importance over other relationships. (This includes Hindus and many Muslims of the Indian subcontinent. It is patrilineal, patrilocal, and generally patriarchal.)

The most important structure is the mother-son relationship, which is inclusive but discontinuous, since the son cannot become a mother. It is more one-sidedly dependent, with the son remaining in symbiotic connectedness longer than in other cultures.

The mother-son relationship is the central axis of the family. The husband-wife coalition is secondary and in the joint family may be no stronger than the other adult relationships. "Those who strive for separation and individuation try to break away from the family of orientation, often it is the father who helps the son to do so, but it is not acceptable to the mother because she needs him more than the husband" (Channabasavanna and Bhatti n.d.:150).

This produces a strong climate of dependence in the family and in the realm of supernatural beliefs. There is little or no individualism, strong mutual dependence, the welcoming of the feminine in divinity and in the daily life of humanity, and a diffused sexuality leavening art, religion, and culture.

4. A degree of mutual dependence together with the emphasis on brother-brother axis and practically no worship of the ancestors. (This includes the majority of Africans south of the Sahara.)

The brother-brother relationship is elevated. It is seen as inclusive, but it is also discontinuous because there are multiple brothers and those of one generation have no intrinsic relation with the preceding. It is inherently competitive, because brothers are more equal. Ancestral worship is not an expression of solidarity, as in Asia, because the dead are feared, propitiated, and seen as causes of epidemics, accidents, and disasters. The brotherhood rites affirm fraternal solidarity but also signal the realities of intense sibling rivalries, which appear in intertribal tensions (Hsu 1972:400–450).

These are not intended as empirically supported conclusions but as heuristic explorations. They are of interest to family systems as they typify the power axis of the ideal family inherent in the core values of the society. The therapist working with a nuclear family may work at strengthening the boundary around the marital dyad and reduce the triangling with either a parent or a child. But in an extended family such elevation of the marital dyad threatens the traditional continuity across generations and competes with more primary dyads of father-son or mother-son.

The families based on intergenerational centrality and continuity will have contrasting boundaries and authority patterns when compared with those based on husband-wife centrality.

In the extended family we can expect (1) a greater division of labor along gender lines, (2) lower demands on the spouse for intimacy and need satisfaction, (3) fewer joint marital decisions and less conflict, (4) authority located in the dominant dyad rather than the marital pair, (5) more complementarity in marriages, and (6) mediation of difficulties by significant persons within the family system.

In the nuclear family we are more likely to find (1) a voluntary romantic marriage with its fragile affectional ties, (2) the marital boundary closely guarded to maintain its exclusive integrity, (3) authority shared by the dominant dyad and dependent on their reaching consensus rather than in fulfilling tradition, (4) the dyad leaning toward symmetrical or parallel relationship, with power shared in quid pro quo negotiations, and (5) confusion about vertical obligations to parents and to offspring that creates tension in relationship.

In the brother-brother family network the horizontal relationships take precedence over all other dyads. The Mexican "amigo system" provides lifelong friendships, which offer patronage connections and economic loyalties as well as friendship affiliation. These triangles, viewed in common therapeutic parlance, are dysfunctional and disruptive of family solidarity, but in a context where peer relationships are primary the triangles may serve functions of continuity, economic solidity, and community solidarity and do not promote marital discord.

Family triangles serve very different functions in various contexts. The presence of a competitive triangle in one family may be destructive of marital exclusiveness and solidarity; in another cultural context it may have the reverse function. The pastoral therapist must be aware of the contrasting cultural dynamics within marriages of several cultures in order to be sensitive to the deeper dynamics of the family being interviewed. The meanings of all events lie in the context, the configuration of relationships, rather than in propositions extracted from one or even more cultures.

Multigenerational Obligations

In systems theory we speak of multigenerational transmission of traits occurring in the family's unconscious processes. In traditional culture this process is both hidden and revealed by continuing communication with and worship of the preceding generations.

Indian family theorists tend to play down the transmission hypothesis as a Western phenomenon, exaggerated by having only one or two models in the isolation of the nuclear family.

> The proponents of the "transmission hypothesis" believe that parents having marital breakup fail to give an adequate role model and socialization of their children is always faulty. But in Indian culture, an individual is always guided by group decisions. He [she] is born in a group, grows in a group, and matures in a group. Throughout life he [she] is a member of a group and has a strong group affiliation and commitment. Hence, it is the group which is responsible for the marriage and not the individual. (Bhatti and Channabasavanna 1979:80)

However, the presence of multigenerational influence patterns is underlined in religious, social, anthropological, and psychiatric studies. The tight connection visible within the Western parent-child relationship is not as visible, as Bhatti maintains, but the broader connections throughout the joint family network are even more elaborate and entangling than in the West.

A joint family is united by common ancestry and property. To the property they owe protection, care, and reverent tilling or use; to the ancestors they owe dutiful obedience to tradition and the rituals of worship. These twin aspects weld the family into unified solidarity.

In India, veneration of ancestors and prayers offered in behalf of these ancestors, or *pitris,* who are living under King Yama, the god of death, is an obligational debt that unites the family and demands its procreation and continuance. The Hindu way of life demands three most important steps for every individual—to marry, to have sons, and to worship the family spirits. The obligation to produce a son is intensified "because one's son by offering ancestor-worship after one's death, and to one's ancestors, would help them in their spiritual march. Indeed the word *putra,* meaning 'son,' comes from *put,* meaning hell, as 'one who saves the father from going to hell' " (Kapadia 1966:167). Even better than a son is having a son's son, since it is only a great-grandfather who can enter the world of the sun. In some areas a daughter's son or grandson can fulfill these duties; in the absence of offspring, a son may be adopted. "Although the rite is evil and religious, its real goal is spiritual, that the adopted son may perform the ceremonial rites of the *shraddhas* to find a place for the father and grandfathers in the sun's world. Without descendants to do worship, salvation and peace of one's ancestors is not possible" (Taylor 1966:16–17).

In China, the most vital religious element in family life was the worship of ancestors. Ancestor worship was a central force for the integration and perpetuation of the family as a basic unit of Chinese society, since it united the family present with the family past, giving departed predecessors a continuing role among the living generation. The ancestral altar in the main room of the house, with the wooden spirit tablets, each representing a dead ancestor, the ever-burning lamp, and the ceremonies performed for them, all symbolized that the ancestors continue to oversee conduct and participate in the family struggles (Yang 1961: 29–30).

Ancestor worship dealt with the grief threatening the psychic integrity of the corporate personality of the family by affirming both immortality and the ongoing presence of the person in the family life process. The mortuary rites functioned to confirm family solidarity as well as to facilitate the comfort and happiness of the dead during the passage to the other world—to notify the proper governing authority of the underworld, to perform ceremonies to help the dead person pass through the various bridges and the ten courts of judgments, and to protect the living from the dead. The daily, periodic, and festival sacrifices in the home and the sacrifices at the ancestral temple demonstrated that people are truly filial. Filial piety is the central virtue of the Chinese family. Thus the ancestor cult, with the power of filial and familial obligations, cemented an extended family into a well-organized kinship structure and guaranteed its stability.

In Africa, ancestors play an important part in religion as they are vested with mystical power and retain a jural role in the world of the living, particularly in the lives of their descendants. "Indeed, African kin groups are often described as communities of both the living and the dead. Ancestors are regarded as ambivalent, at best capricious" (Brain 1973:122).

The benevolence of ancestors can be generally ensured through the practices of propitiation and sacrifice, although punishment may be incurred by any neglect of such ceremonial obligations. The living members of the tribe relate to the dead ancestors through the elders of the clan who are the closest genealogical and chronological link to the ancestors being honored. African writer W. E. Abraham explains:

> In what is called ancestor worship, ancestors are invoked to give succor to their family descendants. A great deal of respect is shown to them on such occasions. The basis of the respect is two-fold, first that the ancestors are our predecessors, our elders, and for this reason alone command our respect; and second that in their spiritual state they note more than we can, being in unhindered touch with the essence of things. The rites of ancestor worship are not rites of worship, but methods of communication. (Abraham 1966:63)

This link of communication and ritual political authority between the living elders and the ancestors endows the elders with a qualitatively superior kind of authority and power that is unavailable to a leader, except through ancestral solidarity.

Thus the family system in traditional form is many layers deep in the transmission of traits through the family unconscious, and it is also reinforced by conscious loyalties, conscious reaffirmation of obligations, and conscious commitment to the replication of essential values that will ensure the family's solidarity, prosperity, and continuity. The three-tiered family living together in extended form is a visible expression of the multi-tiered family functioning through them. The ancestors are not dead; they are alive and functioning well within the family ego mass, embodying and ensuring customs and rituals, values and viewpoints.

Modernization, urbanization, and the technological revolution accelerate change, facilitate mobility, and dictate new life patterns that are breaking up the multi-tiered family solidarity, but as many pastoral counselors note, this drives it farther into the family and personal unconscious, where it is less accessible to reflection or introspection, and cuts the person off from the setting, the joint family members, and the cultural context that could help in discharging anxieties, clarifying confusion, and choosing new direction during times of family transition.

From Joint to Nuclear Family

The increasing acceptance of the fundamental individual rights of the human person and the essential equality of women and men in society are calling for a repatterning of traditional joint families in virtually all societies (see Table 6-2). "The family as an institution and system of human life cannot withhold itself from the processes of equalization, diversification, imposition, and liberation which operate in both the Third World countries and those more highly industrialized" (Lenero-Otero 1977:6).

In India, R. W. Taylor comments (1966:7):

> The Western ideas which have most directly influenced our understanding of family relationships can be summarily stated. (1) Respect for human personality. (2) Different understanding of sex relations and the concept of romantic love. (3) The weakening of traditionally accepted religious sanctions by the general trend towards secularism. (4) The current view that the criterion of social values was utility and that social institutions and even

**Table 6-2. Distinctions Between Family Structures
of Less and Highly Developed Nations**

Less Developed Nations	*Highly Developed Nations*
The family is likely to be joint, extended, or three-tiered.	The nuclear family is the dominant pattern.
Households tend to be in rural agricultural areas.	Dwelling units are more frequently urban.
The family provides its own social controls and enforces behavioral norms.	External agencies and institutions enforce laws, regulations, standards.
Families tend to be patriarchal and patrilocal.	Families tend toward equalitarian styles.
The family or kinship group takes precedence over the individual. Dependence is valued.	Individualism and independence are encouraged; each seeks personal fulfillment.
Religion and religious beliefs play a major part in the daily lives of family members. Family participates as a unit.	Secular institutions compete with religious ones for devotion and commitment. Religion is an occasional experience, not a way of life.
The family fulfills multiple social functions, as economic base and work unit. It is the primary context for socialization, education, health needs, and religious training.	Major societal functions are delegated to several different social institutions. The economic, educational, political, and health care systems are all extrafamilial.
Education has a low value because it does not contribute immediately to the family.	Education is a prerequisite for social and economic success.
Elders are respected and revered for their wisdom and experience.	Old people are no longer needed, respected, or cared for by the family.
A rigid castelike social structure precludes upward mobility. The person is born to a fixed station in life.	A class system exists but there is opportunity for upper or lower mobility.
Mate selection is often arranged by parents.	Emphasis is on romantic love, personal selection of mate.
Monogamy is the dominant marital form, although polygamy occurs in some societies.	Serial monogamy is the dominant form in every highly developed nation.
Sex is performed primarily for procreation rather than pleasure. Little birth control.	Sex is eroticized, procreation often avoided. Birth control generally used.
The divorce rate is low.	The divorce rate is high.

(Adapted from Das and Bardis 1978:viii–ix)

individuals should be judged in terms of their contribution to human welfare.

In his major work on modernization theory, William J. Goode argued that change in family patterns is not a simple effect of one cause, industrialization. Ideological changes precede, facilitate, and in turn are intensified and spread by the industrialization-urbanization shifts in a society.

Family systems, social systems, economic systems, and political systems are all interdependent part processes of the human system. Hypotheses that see the family system as dependent and industrial development as determinative are simplistic. All parts of the larger system are affected by changing social and personal ideologies and values—ideologies such as economic progress, individual success and fulfillment, egalitarianism in opportunity, and the movement from the extended to the nuclear family. The "world revolution" toward industrialization and urbanization is producing a homogenization of family patterns as the diverse types of extended family forms converge toward some type of conjugal family system (Goode 1963:18).

These ideological changes in both Western and "non-Western" societies, Goode argues, are clustered into three main shifts, which aim directly or indirectly at ending the dominance of the extended family system over the conjugal family, over women, and over youth. These ideologies are:

1. The ideology of economic progress and technological development places stress on the society's industrial growth and change and relegates tradition, custom, and the authority of the status quo to a lower level of importance.

2. The ideology of the conjugal or nuclear family asserts the worth of the individual over the lineage, and personal welfare over family continuity.

3. The ideology of egalitarianism between the sexes places emphasis on the uniqueness of each individual within the family, with lesser importance given to sex status and seniority, so sexism and age inequalities of families are reduced, undermining two traditional patterns of subordination: female by male, the young by the old.

All three ideologies minimize the traditions of societies and assert the equality of the individual over class, caste, sex, or religious barriers.

> The ideology of the conjugal family proclaims the right of the individual to choose his or her own spouse, place to live, and even which kin obligations to accept, as against the acceptance of others' decisions. It asserts the worth of the *individual* as against the inherited elements of wealth or ethnic group. The *individual* is to be evaluated, not his lineage. A strong theme of "democracy" runs through this ideology. It encourages love, which in every major civilization has been given a prominent place in fantasy, poetry, art, and legend as a wonderful, perhaps even exalted, experience, even when its reality was guarded against. Finally it asserts that if one's family life is unpleasant, one has the right to change it. (Goode 1963:19)

The great power of these ideologies to effect sweeping change in virtually all cultures emerges from two dimensions of functional fit. The first fit is with the desire of the individual to maximize his or her need for equality and individualism and the type of family that will satisfy those needs; the second fit is with the needs of an industrial social order for mobile, unrestricted, self-sufficient, psychologically independent family units. (See Case Study: Family Revolution.)

The massive amount of comparative data that Goode gathered cross-culturally from the West, Arabic Islam, sub-Saharan Africa, India, China, and Japan indicate that all family systems examined are moving toward some form of a nuclear family system. These trends show three characteristics:

CASE STUDY: Family Revolution (Africa)

Kigoma is a successful coffee grower on the slopes of Mt. Kenya. British colonists discovered the rich soils and the constant climates of high altitudes in the tropics produced tea and coffee of high quality. Kigoma worked as a foreman until independence; then he was able to buy land and begin a coffee operation. Kigoma married three wives who gave him twenty-six children. The wives do not speak Swahili (the trade language) or English, although Kigoma speaks both. Each has her own house, kitchen, and garden. Their focus of interest is on the children, not on self-fulfillment. Kigoma travels frequently to Nairobi and Mombasa and has been to England and Holland as well.

Kigoma is convinced of the value of education for both his daughters and sons. Several have bachelor's degrees; others are students in India, England and the United States. The graduates are employed in government, education, and mechanical engineering. The children who are married are monogamous and practice family planning. They live in urban areas and are free to visit the home farm. This is significant: daughters who marry are not expected to return to their home areas, since traditional marriage is patrilocal. The educated children are all independent but show great respect for the father when in his company.

The eldest son has immigrated to New York, married an American black, and is in business. The father expects him to return and lead the family coffee farm, but life in the Kenyan highlands would appear impossible, especially to an American wife.

In one generation, the family patterns have changed dramatically: rural to urban, patriarchal to egalitarian, patrilocal to neolocal, familial production unit to individual jobs, no formal education to college degrees, respect for age to impatience with "old ideas," polygamy to monogamy, mobility of husband to mobility of both spouses, authority of elders to individual thinking.

(Litwiller 1985)

First, free choice in mate selection. In extended family systems, the arranged marriage asserted the continuing familial control over the future generational development of the extended kinship system. Such arrangements, including dowry and bride-price, are disappearing.

Second, emphasis on individual welfare as opposed to family continuity. The authority of parents over children, husbands over wives, and one generation over the next is diminishing. Greater sexual equality is manifest in the patterns of legal changes in inheritance, divorce, and sexual discrimination and in the weakening of class, caste, kinship, and sexual barriers.

Third, greater emphasis on the conjugal role relationship. Spouses are moving increasingly toward independent households (neolocal vs. patrilocal or matrilocal) and toward bilineal descent systems (affection and choice more powerful than obligation).

Goode's work articulated the common assumptions of much Western thought: civilizations are evolving toward modernity, superiority is exemplified in Western culture, tradition and modernity are mutually exclusive systems and one must replace the other, individualism is the innate nature and destiny of humans, and progress is an essential good. Further research presented evidence contrary to the assertion of a worldwide trend toward nuclear families. Not only was Goode's own work influenced by his strong commitment to a view of the evolutionary superiority of the Western model, he considered the shifts he observed to be the hope of a new day.

> I welcome the great change now taking place. . . . I see in it the hope of a greater freedom: from the domination of elders, from caste and racial restriction, from rigidities. Freedom is *for* something as well: the unleashing of personal potentials, the right to love, to equality within the family, to the establishment of a new marriage when the old has failed. I see the world revolution in family patterns as part of a still more important revolution that is sweeping the world in our time, the aspiration on the part of billions of people to have the right for the first time to choose for themselves. (Goode 1963:380)

This view of traditional societies as rigid, oppressive, and static is not supported by other research into how such societies function. Traditional societies are not static but dynamic. Traditionalism, which glorifies old patterns, can stifle adaptation and healthful functional accommodation to economic, technological, and ecological realities. But tradition without traditionalism is a rich and resilient cultural resource for the ongoing life of a community or a whole culture.

Family patterns throughout the world are showing a resilient ability to maintain their variation. In Singapore, the breakdown of extended families through the construction of public housing with small flats is being surmounted by the housing authorities' move toward the grouping of extended family units in adjoining apartments to regain the strengths of the family clan. In India, families are increasingly living in nuclear family units, but culturally there are few or no nuclear families. The social network of the joint family with its complex of roles and status positions and its shared parenting functions by multiple adults produces multidimensional dependent interpersonal relationships. The overall social network for Indians is virtually the same, whether they live in a nuclear family unit or in a large joint family complex.

Changes in Chinese Patterns

The traditional Chinese family was a corporate unity with little and often no individual autonomy.

> Nor does Confucianism have a place for individualistic concepts of the person. There are no individuals as such—only family members whose roles change through the life cycle. At no time is the person regarded as separate from his family and social roles, and maturation is a deepening of understanding of one's place in a system; that is, in a social unit which is, again, part of yet a larger social unit. One's ultimate duty, as well as one's ultimate psychological security, is to be found in family or group continuity, not in the continuity of the self. (DeVos 1980:121)

The Chinese family has undergone great change from this traditional homogeneous patriarchal form to its present modern style. Present patterns of living are so radically altered from those of the past that the changes since the 1950 marriage law must be described as revolutionary.

The two models shown in Table 6-3 present the ideal types of the old traditional family and the new modern Chinese family. Just as exceptions existed in the traditional period—the large extended family was found largely among the wealthy gentry classes—so there is wide variation in the present time, but the median families, even the majority of families, approximate the pattern shown in the contemporary column. The greatest change has been in the liberation of women through the guarantee of equal rights, dignity, and freedom of choice to enter or to end a marriage.

Among Chinese families in Indonesia, Hong Kong, Singapore, and the many other countries where they are scattered, significant changes are unfolding. Observing the changes among Singapore Chinese, Stephen Tan writes:

> The traditional "extended" or "joint" family where several generations—children, parents and grandparents, and other relatives—lived together has been almost broken down and replaced by the nuclear family, which consists of only parents and their children. The social repercussions of this structural change in the family and social relations system are multifarious and monumental.
>
> First, the role of the individual in the nuclear family is more specific and less complicated. The individual feels that he or she has more freedom, more independence, and more self-orientation. The change simultaneously imposes on the individual greater strains, emotional tensions, and frustration engendered by the uncertainties and insecurity of life in a completely strange and new community. Second, children undergo a transformation. Depending more and more on formal school education, they are exposed,

Table 6-3. Distinctions Between Old and New Chinese Families

The Traditional Chinese Family	The Contemporary Chinese Family
Members are related by blood and marriage; they have a common budget and common property.	The nation becomes a "big socialist family" with "revolutionary ties."
Family interests and goals come before the individual or the nation.	The interest of the party and nation come before family or individual.
The ideal form is the large extended family.	The ideal form is the small nuclear family.
Family is formed by arranged marriage, child betrothal, early marriage; romantic love is disfavored.	Family is formed through freedom of marital choice; marriage is delayed, based on common revolutionary pursuits.
Horoscopes and socioeconomic backgrounds are matched.	Compatibility of personalities and ideological stands is sought.
Internal structure of the family is patriarchal, patrilineal, and patrilocal, with generational hierarchy, subjugation of women, and the authority of the clan.	Internal structure of the family is democratic, equalitarian, bilateral in lineage, and neolocal; exalts youth over age, protects sexual equality; clan has no authority over family or person.
Procreation is most important function, because continuity of family line is a primary value.	Social service and personal participation is most important. Continuity is not valued, birth control advocated.
Worship of ancestors in filial piety is a continuing duty.	Secular family values have replaced ancestor rites.
Family is the primary unit of economic production. Cooperation is all-important.	Family is part of larger economic structures, little cooperation required.
Status is ascribed in family.	Status is achieved individually.
Family socializes and educates children.	State shares socialization and education.
Family is center of social and cultural life.	Individual social and cultural life is outside family.
Family relationships: father-son is central, husband-wife is primarily institutional, and parent-child is basically authority and obedience; mother-in-law and daughter-in-law relationship is difficult.	Family relationships: husband-wife is central, husband-wife is basically companionship, parent-child is seen as comradeship; relationships between in-laws are harmonious.
Remarriage of divorced or widowed is disfavored.	There is freedom of divorce and remarriage.
Concubinage and prostitution are accepted.	Monogamy is practiced, prostitution prohibited.

(Adapted from Wong 1978:273–274)

perhaps prematurely, to extra-family influence so that parents cease to be their children's reference group at a very early stage of personality development. Third, social structure changes in the family system cause social alienation and isolation of the nuclear family. Contact with parents decreases, care for the elderly is relegated to the state. Fourth, divorce rates and juvenile delinquency increase. (Tan 1978:75)

These changes in family style, although not as consistent and concerted as Goode hypothesized, do show a significant movement toward monogamous marriage and nuclear family clusters rather than the extended or joint patterns of the past.

After examining the changes in the Asian family—including Thai, Afghan, Pakistani, Iranian, Chinese, Korean, Filipino, and Japanese family systems, as reviewed by sociologists from each country—Das and Bardis (1979:419) conclude:

> We can summarize the general trends that have resulted and will continue to emerge as industrialization, urbanization, and modernization proceed . . . trends toward a greater degree of: (1) equalitarian family relations, with less sexual segregation and limited subjugation of women to an inferior status; (2) emphasis on individualism and independence; (3) greater differentiation and specialized functioning of social institutions; (4) life in an urban setting; (5) birth control and family planning; (6) social mobility; (7) marital disruption and divorce; (8) neglect and improper care for the elderly; (9) formal education for children; and (10) governmental influence on family activities.

Traditional marriage is giving way to intentional companionate marriage. The contrast between the two (as described by Figure 6-6) places the person at the center rather than the family; affectional needs preempt generational obligations. Thus what was optional has become central and vice versa as partners take into their hands the control that once belonged to the community and extended family.

The pastoral family therapist is thus in need of a coherent theology and a consistent value base in the midst of a myriad of relational forms. (See Case Study: Under a Spell.)

Theology, Marriage, and Family

Since marriage and family are such varied human structures, any theology of marriage and the family must address a world of institutions. From the monogamous to the polygamous, the indissoluble to the terminable, the forms of marriage are richly diverse. Polygynous societies in Africa and polyandrous societies in the Himalayas have their own ethics and mores. Nuclear families in the West and joint, three-tiered, and extended families in the East have their own traditions and values.

African pastoral theologian Masamba Ma Mpolo (1982:19) sees the central theological issue as content and meaning, not form. "To say this or that family structure is the only one God approves does not have strong biblical grounds. Nor is it rooted in human experience. There is no single family arrangement advocated in the Bible—what is important is the quality of relationships between people."

As a theological case, we may ask, What is a consistent pastoral attitude toward polygamous marriages? Such marriages are not loose multiple associations but stable parallel unions contracted under communal law, recognized as marriage by the society, entered with lifelong intentions, and providing a permanent context for offspring.

The four positions most frequently taken by pastoral counselors are (Hastings 1973:73):

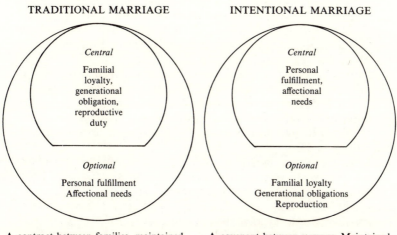

TRADITIONAL MARRIAGE

Central

Familial loyalty, generational obligation, reproductive duty

Optional

Personal fulfillment
Affectional needs

INTENTIONAL MARRIAGE

Central

Personal fulfillment, affectional needs

Optional

Familial loyalty
Generational obligations
Reproduction

TRADITIONAL MARRIAGE	INTENTIONAL MARRIAGE
A contract between families, maintained by communal cohesion.	A covenant between persons, Maintained by internal cohesion.
Tasks and roles clearly defined	Tasks and roles negotiated and shared

Male—Female

Insemination	Pregnancy
Provision	Homemaking
Authority	Submission
Public world	Parenting

No socially fixed roles
Mutual intimacy and sexuality
Shared career and homemaking
Mutual decision and problem solving
Mutual communal life and parenting.

The community defines and shapes the meaning of its marriages.

The partners control the meaning of the marital exchange.

Meaning is dependent on the goals of both partners and of the community.

Meaning is dependent on mutuality of intention and reciprocity of persons.

Divorce is seen as a rending of both marital unity and communal solidarity and granted only because of serious abuse.

Divorce by mutual consent is regarded as more human than divorce granted because of serious emotional injury.

**Figure 6-6. The contrast of traditional marriage
and intentional companionate marriage.**

CASE STUDY: Under a Spell (Singapore)

Stephen Wee and Ting Jin have been married for four years. The problem is her constant fear of being bewitched by some evil power. Ting Jin, 24, from a very traditional Chinese family, has a strict Chinese education. Nominally Protestant, she is married to Stephen Wee, 25, an executive with an international organization. He is a second son of a family of six whose Chinese dialect is different from his wife's. He is Roman Catholic, educated in English in a Catholic school.

Stephen courted Ting Jin in Western style. She was happy with his friends, although quiet, both from temperament and because of her limited English, which was the common language for the many backgrounds. Two years after marriage their only child, a daughter, was born. Bitterly disappointed at not having a son, Ting Jin was ill for some weeks and became convinced that someone had put a spell on her, prevented her from conceiving a son, and now was persecuting her. After several months she accepted her daughter but now became overprotective and refused to leave her in the care of an amah and return to work. With the coming of the baby, Ting Jin became more withdrawn, showing less interest in Stephen's friends or family, although she blossomed during extended visits to her own family of origin.

After four years of marriage, Stephen became attracted to a fellow worker, a twenty-year-old woman with an English education. Their lunchtime friendship had only progressed to the point of light physical intimacies. Both felt intense guilt over erotic feelings toward each other. Stephen feared his wife's jealousy and anger. "She would take a chopper to me," he said. "She would never forgive me if she knew of my feelings." Nevertheless he continued to seek out the co-worker because "she is so open, talks so freely, and is interested in all that concerns me." Ting Jin's withdrawn state, her constant conviction of being persecuted by a spell, her limited English all distanced the two, driving him closer to the other woman. Male colleagues assured him that a girlfriend on the side was perfectly normal in Singapore. But his guilt, his thoughts of being shamed before his wife and family, and the dominating force of his wife's fears of being persecuted kept both immobilized.

(Adapted from Leslie 1979:20)

> *Note:* The conflict of multiple cultures in Singapore, the impact of rapid urban Westernization, the persistence of beliefs in spirits and charms mixing with Christian faith, the contrast between Christian views on fidelity and the double standard of the Chinese "straights" culture, the cultural demand for a male heir, and the failure of the central wife/mother-in-law coalition all contribute to the situation.

1. Polygamy is unacceptable. It is simply a sin comparable to adultery.

2. Polygamy is an inferior form of marriage, not sinful where it is the custom but always unacceptable for Christians.

3. Polygamy is a form of marriage less satisfactory than monogamy and one that cannot do justice to the full spirit of Christian marriage, but in certain circumstances individual Christians can still put up with it, as they put up with slavery, dictatorial government, and much else. Existing multiple marriages can be accepted while monogamous change is invited.

4. Polygamy is one form of marriage, monogamy another. Each has its advantages and disadvantages; they are appropriate to different types of society. It is not the task of the church to make any absolute judgment between them.

A pastoral theology cannot address this issue from clear biblical directives, since none exist. Rather, it must be based on biblical values, their trajectory toward exclusive mutuality, and their service toward the expression of full humanness. The pastoral counselor who begins with theological values of justice based on equality, fidelity defined by covenant, and intimacy expressed in loving encounter must face the issues of form and content. Does the pastoral counselor facilitate persons acting in a more loving way within the accepted structures of the particular society? Or does effective pastoral care require a critique or rejection of some structures and the innovation of others?

The 1973 Archbishops' report *Christian Marriage in Africa* concluded:

> There are natural structures (i.e., patterns of life and organization fully accepted and justified within a given society) which seem more or less tolerable with Christian insight, while there are others which seem (or should seem) quite intolerable, at least for those who have even a slight opportunity to alter them. The church is finally committed to something in each approach. It cannot opt out of the existing world, nor alter fundamental social patterns in a day, and it should think very hard before claiming that some accepted practice is quite impossible for a new Christian (though doubtless there are such practices: for example, the exposure of infants). At the same time it is to be expected that in one way or another Christianity should challenge every side of society; it is, or should be, a structurally revolutionary force. (Hastings 1973:62)

A Theology of Marriage

The teachings of Jesus offer two basic principles that can revolutionize marital relationships of every culture.

1. Marriage creates a unity that takes precedence over previous parental, familial, or obligational bonds. Marriage "from the beginning" as Jesus asserts (Mark 10:6) is for both procreation and for the unity of man and woman. He bases his theology of marriage and family on one of the oldest human documents. "A man leaves his father and his mother and cleaves to his wife, and they become one flesh" (Gen. 2:24). The unity

of husband and wife is seen as stronger than—superior to—the unity of blood and kinship.

2. Marriage initiates a reciprocity of fidelity and responsibility. The Old Testament views marriage as a covenant promise demanding fidelity of the wife; the New Testament stresses reciprocity in a world with an absence of such reciprocity. Its contemporary societies did not admit that a husband could commit adultery against the wife, but Jesus makes no difference between the two (Mark 10:11–12). The teachings of the epistles recognize equality in both rights and duties, require reciprocity in love and responsibility, and recommend mutual service and submission (1 Cor. 7:3–4, 33–34; Eph. 5:21). Although Paul made cultural adaptations in structural inequality for wives as he also did for slaves, the principle of male-female equivalence is stated in uncompromising equality (compare 1 Cor. 11:1–3 and Eph. 5:23–24 with Gal. 3:28).

Thus two approaches exist side by side: principled commitment to equality, and reciprocity and situational adaptation to cultural possibilities. The tension between a clear affirmation of what should be—the prescriptive—and what can be—the situational—is present in the earliest disciple's practice, although absent in the forthright ethical teachings of Jesus.

Theologically, marriage exists as a conjunction of three fundamental values: (1) The personal dimension creates a flesh that takes precedence over previous ties of kinship or obligations to family of origin, (2) the covenantal dimension of marriage is a mutual reciprocal relationship of permanence and exclusiveness; and (3) the public dimension of marriage makes it a unique ceremony—sacred in religious communities, mystic in animistic groups, socially or civilly celebrated in others, and sacramental in faith communities. Thus if two persons willingly and knowingly enter a recognized form of marriage contextually consistent with their society, the counselor also recognizes the two as married. Elements of the personal, covenantal, and public dimensions exist, although the full extensions of these dimensions to primary unity, permanent exclusiveness, and communal actualization may not.

Marriage is an institution created for humanity, not the reverse. Marriage is a servant of justice, fidelity, and love, not a tyrannical system that absolutizes finite covenants between fallible humans. Christian marriage proclaims values, serves human need, and unites in fellowship. Thus it participates in kerygma, diakonia, and koinonia of the church.

A Theology of Family

A review of the family throughout history and across cultures reveals broad diversity and rich complexity in both form and function. This variation is equally present in biblical history and teaching. The constant adaptation and evolution of the family over time as well as the wide variety and diversity across cultures make it both impractical and impossible to seek a single pattern that can be normative for all periods or peoples. Biblical and theological studies that seek to offer a single model for families violate the rich diversity present in two thousand years of biblical history. A theology of the family that seeks to deal inclusively with the biblical diversity is best expressed in paradoxical truth rather than in propositional truth.

The values of the individual and of the group both exist in every family unit. The needs for independence and interdependence, the goals of conformity or diversity, the responsibility to both the previous generation and the present one—these are universal issues that families must balance in ways satisfactory to their context and culture.

The many contrasts in family form exemplify the exaggeration of one pole of these paradoxical dimensions of life. Individuals may be elevated over the group, or independence may be stressed beyond interdependence. Family values are paradoxical rather than polar because each of these opposing values is incomplete without the other. One pole may be visible and pronounced, the other unconscious and virtually invisible. Or both may be fully present in a culture as competing, contrasting, or fully complementary values. Here are seven such paradoxes.

1. *Individual vs. group.* The person is the highest unit of value in the universe. Each family member is an end in himself or herself. *Yet* no one is human alone; personhood and family-group-community membership are indivisible.

The pastoral therapist responds to each person as irreducibly valuable, worthy of respect, essentially precious. *But* the therapist sees the person as indelibly imprinted by and undeniably rooted in the family of origin. The dual commitment to work for the integrity of both the person and the group, the individual and the family, is an expression of a theology that takes personhood and peoplehood as equally important expressions of humanness.

2. *Independence vs. interdependence.* The family creates, nurtures, and trains persons to become autonomous, to decide responsibly, to act independently, to stand alone. *Yet* the family directs its members toward interdependence with each other, toward being responsible with one another, toward accountability with significant others.

The pastoral therapist invites individuation and growth in uniqueness, diversity, and autonomy. *But* the therapist knows that therapy is a socializing process that teaches persons to live effectively with their network of relationships, to conform appropriately to the shared values of family and community, and to join in working toward the goals of their significant group. The final goal of all independence is interdependence with others. Autonomy and solidarity complete and nourish each other.

3. *Inner-directed security vs. outer-directed service.* The family exists to nurture its members, to reproduce itself, to provide security and guidance to the following generation, support and care to the preceding. *Yet* the family is a force for social change, a unit for service to others, a group for social, economic, and political action in the community.

The pastoral therapist recognizes the balance necessary between inner direction in providing safety and security and outer direction that gives meaning, task, and project. A healthy family maintains this bidirectional movement because love is seeing others' safety, security, and satisfaction as equally important as your own, and meaning is received from finding a cause larger, broader, and worthy of investing the self. The pastoral therapist, as a representative of the faith community, is uniquely situated to assist the family in finding its balance of centrifugal and centripetal forces.

4. *Love vs. justice.* The family offers unconditional acceptance to its members, totally apart from their performance or appearance. *Yet* the family's integrity is evidenced by its fairness; its wholeness is maintained by its sense of justice.

The pastoral therapist embodies both love and justice. Pastoral theology affirms that love and justice are elemental to all healing, just as grace and judgment unite in salvation. The gift of unconditional acceptance invites the family to care for one another with unlimited positive loyalty while working for equal justice for all members. The practice of forgiveness unites prizing of the other person with a diligent struggling with repentance to work out integrity that resolves past injustice, restores trust in the present, and reopens the future.

5. *Horizontal vs. vertical.* The horizontal relationship between husband and wife is the central crucial structure in a family. *Yet* the vertical relationship to the preceding and following generation are primary obligations.

Pastoral family therapy must vary widely on the balance between horizontal and vertical obligations as it seeks to be contextually congruent. Hierarchical cultures place a higher stress on vertical obligations, often to the minimizing or ignoring of the horizontal. Family therapy thus seeks to strengthen the marital coalition without evoking irresolvable conflicts in the joint or extended family. In contrast, Western families may be emotionally cut off from the family of origin and so place exaggerated demands on the horizontal relationship. Reopening and restructuring relationships with vertical layers of the family may ameliorate the tensions and evoke health in the nuclear family.

6. *Private and personal vs. public and communal.* The marital covenant and the family rules are intimate, personal, and private matters belonging to the partners and the parent-child cluster. *Yet* the marriage contract is a public event, and the family patterns of conduct are communal responsibilities that exist within the matrix of larger networks of people.

The pastoral therapist, by nature of role and position on the faith community boundary, is a specialist in guarding what is confidential and private as well as in clarifying what is public and communal. The pastoral counselor has what is essential to every therapeutic process but is frequently lacking—a community of caring persons to surround, support, and sustain both the healing process and the healing persons involved.

7. *Biological family vs. spiritual family.* The biological family is the central concern and primary responsibility of all family members. *Yet*

the spiritual family or faith community is the ultimate human concern and thus transcends all finite or temporal obligations.

The pastoral therapist takes the family more seriously than any other perspective because of the sacramental nature of marriage, the sacredness of birth, life, and death, and the reverence for familial bonds and boundaries. *Yet* the theologically grounded therapist sees beyond the representative—the family—to that which is being represented—the family of God uniting humans as sisters and brothers around the divine Parent. Neither can be sacrificed easily for the other, yet the ultimate concerns of faith are able to transcend, clarify, and correct the injustices and ingrown bondages of family practices; simultaneously, the integrity of love and truth in the family can correct religious values that sacralize what is fallible, eternalize what is temporal, and absolutize what is finite.

A pastoral theology that recognizes the paradox present in each polarity of family relationships will neither draw sharp boundaries nor seek definitive moral guidelines. Rather it will seek the center, clarify the central commitments, and make firm the values that can direct family living, changing, and healing.

Summary

The intercultural pastoral counselor works with essential human groups—family, marriage, kinship—as well as individuals. A systems perspective on the family offers a useful language for understanding family dynamics and intervening in family dysfunction. The contrasts and similarities between families in the East and the West illuminate the need for understanding family process from within the culture and by its own roles, myths, and values. Families exhibit great differences in form across cultures but also fascinating similarities in relationship, needs, and emotional content. The cultural shifts in form (movement toward nuclear family units) and content (change from traditional to intentional marriage) are occurring in most cultures.

The pastoral counselor as a family therapist must function with a flexible psychological theory and an inclusive theology that addresses the great breadth of paradox in family systems while maintaining faithfulness to the central values and commitments of living in relationships of integrity.

7

Women and Men
in Cross-Cultural Therapy

A Theology of Liberation

"Women are subjugated by four thick ropes. A man in China is usually subjected to the domination of three systems of authority: political authority, clan authority, and religious authority. As for women, in addition to being dominated by these three systems, they are also dominated by the men. But women hold up half the sky."

—Mao Zedong, 1940

"Women live in such a different economic, cultural, and social world from men that their reactions cannot be understood from a master model developed in male society."

—Berit As, 1981

THE LION AND THE SNAKE
AFRICAN FOLKTALE

The lion and the snake were fighting. The snake escaped the lion's claws before the lion could kill it, and fled to a man's house. The snake begged the man to hide it because the lion was pursuing it. The man hid the snake in his cupboard and the lion never found it, although he searched the house.

When the lion had gone, the snake took his leave from the man, saying, "How are good deeds rewarded?" The man said, "Normally good deeds are rewarded with money, but since you have no money you may give me an animal as soon as you have been successful at hunting." The snake said, "But do you not know that snakes reward good with evil? I am going to devour you, man!" The man said, "No, no, that isn't fair. We men always reward good with gratitude and useful goods. Let's ask the bee first." The bee said, "I never get any gratitude. Man just takes my honey after having smoked me out of my own house." The man said, "Let's ask the mango tree." The mango tree said, "I never receive thanks. Man takes my fruits, and when I bear no more, he cuts me down and throws me into his fire." The man said, "Let's ask the coconut palm." The coconut palm said, "It is true, good is rewarded with evil. Man takes my nuts, taps my sap, and to cap it all, he cuts off my leaves for his roof."

The snake said to the man, "You see, now I will eat you." The man said, "Wait till I have said good-bye to my wife." The snake agreed, and they went to the man's house. The man said, "Dear wife, the snake is going to eat me, good-bye!" The wife said, "Surely, Mr. Snake, you would like some eggs as an *hors d'oeuvre?*" She took a bag of eggs and held it open for the snake. The snake put in his head to take an egg. The woman pulled the string tight and so caught the snake with its head in the bag. Then she took a knife and cut its throat, saving her husband's life. But the husband divorced her, for men reward the good women do them with evil.

An old Chinese proverb expresses the adaptability required of women in centuries of Eastern marriages, marriage being the one option open to women for centuries: "If a woman marries a chicken, she should act like a chicken; If she marries a dog, she should act like a dog."

The Chinese ancients said, "A woman follows her father before marriage, her husband after marriage, and her son after her husband's death." The Hindu scriptures say the same thing except for substituting "is protected by" for "follows," and they conclude, "A woman is never fit to depend upon herself."

Yet in spite of this formal inequality, there is the paradoxical recognition that the mother may have great power in both cultures. One Hindu sacred book said:

> The teacher is ten times more venerable than a tutor,
> A father is a hundred times more than the teacher,
> A mother is a thousand times more than the father
> Because she bears you in her womb and rears you to adulthood.

The contradictions of the Indian culture and the radical inconsistencies of the Chinese are duplicated throughout the world. The content of male-female roles varies, but the injustices of the forms of relationship are a constant. Women are venerated and violated, exalted and exploited, admired and abused.

The paradoxical and the contradictory are characteristic of woman's situation as it has been since time immemorial. But with the resurgence of feminism the ignored and denied are becoming visible.

We speak of the cultural oppression of women in the way Paulo Freire (1970:40) has defined the oppression of persons by situations and structures.

> Any situation in which "A" objectively exploits "B" or hinders [the] pursuit of self-affirmation as a responsible person is one of oppression. Such a situation in itself constitutes violence, even when sweetened by false gener-

osity, because it interferes with [a person's] ontological and historical vocation to be more fully human.

The daily lives of most women in Western and non-Western countries vary not in kind but in degree. In some countries there are statutes barring sex discrimination, or legislation on equal rights, yet everywhere stereotypical views based on traditional norms and historic patriarchal values prevail. The movement from feudal to modern societies has been partial even for the most "modern."

A society is modern when it "is successful in removing social and structural constraints and in establishing appropriate compensatory mechanisms so that all individuals, regardless of their categorical membership such as age, sex, race, religion, ethnic origin, or social class, can have equal access to a wide range of options in all sectors" (Safilos-Rothschild 1970:17). By such definition, no society has achieved the justice envisioned by modernity.

> In Yugoslavia, for example, archaic and traditional social customs persist despite the legal emancipation of and the granting of political rights to women. Similarly, in Algeria, an advanced socialist ideology calls upon women to work alongside men as equals but is countered by Islamic cultural traditions, which uphold a highly secluded role for women. Government-financed day-care centers, anti–job discrimination statutes exist in countries where the majority of people still feel that woman's primary fulfillment is as wife and mother. (Iglitzin and Ross 1976:xvii)

Male-dominated institutions based on male-oriented values have endured through the centuries, profoundly rooted in the socialization patterns of childhood, the rites of passage of adolescence, and the sanctions, rewards, and punishments of the whole culture. These values form a set of attitudes that constitute the patriarchal belief system. Lynne Iglitzin offers a model of the sex-role stereotyping of females that is inherent in all patriarchal systems. A society is patriarchal, according to this model, when most of its members hold the following beliefs:

1. The sexual division of labor reflects natural differences between men and women. The functional role of serving and helping, whether in the home or in the job market, is best suited to the female personality; therefore, traditional "women's work" occupations, such as teacher, secretary, and nurse, reflect the female affinity for nurturant roles.

2. A woman's identity comes through her relationship with men. She is sister, daughter, wife, and mother; she may be sex object or helpmate but always her identity is contingent upon some male in her life; women without a significant male relationship deviate from the norm.

3. Women achieve their highest fulfillment as wives and mothers. No matter what outside job or career she may undertake, a woman is first a wife and mother; within the family, the man remains the prime breadwinner, assuming major responsibility for the family.

4. Women are childlike. Women cannot achieve fully independent status unaided; they need paternal protection from the rigors of the

world and this can be provided by some male relationship; women who are alone, by choice or by circumstance, are deviant.

5. Women are apolitical. If given the choice, women prefer the private sphere of home and hearth and are content to leave business and politics to men. (Iglitzin and Ross 1976:15)

The patriarchal gestalt, which has been one of the most widespread and long-lasting cultural universals, is composed of four interlocking premises or justifications: biological, cultural, economic, and religious. *Biological:* the greater physical strength of the male was taken as a pattern of nature for defining the nature of roles. *Cultural:* the cultural patterns of aggression, domination, procreation, and spouse and child protection have universally, with only a few exceptions, formed patriarchal families and societies. *Economic:* the movement from communal to private property and the changes in production and distribution of goods have been largely male dominated or directed. *Religious:* virtually all religions have been cited as establishing, certifying, and regulating male superiority, dominance, or privilege. The confluence of all four premises has provided until recently an unquestioned position for domination of half the world's people by the other half.

The major world religions have, in practice, agreed on the subordination of the female. Judaism saw woman as instrumental and largely responsible for the fall of man, a view perpetuated by Christianity and Islam. The Hindu *Laws of Manu* established inferiority and dependence for Indian women. A Confucian marriage manual instructs: "The five worst infirmities that afflict the female are indocility, discontent, slander, jealousy, and silliness. Such is the stupidity of her character that it is incumbent upon her, in every particular, to distrust herself and to obey her husband" (Croll 1978:12–13).

So the Muslim purdah of veiled seclusion, the crippling binding of the feet in Chinese religion, and the Indian burning of widows only begins the long listing of extreme measures for the subordination and oppression of women. The patriarchal polities and male-oriented doctrines of virtually all religions have both sanctified and sacralized the practices established by economic, political, and social structures. Against this interlocking system of controls, any changes initiated by women proved powerless to evoke more than individual exceptions for gifted or token persons. For the masses of females, it has been subordination as usual.

The literatures of the great traditions—anthropology, sociology, medicine, philosophy, history, psychology, theology, economics, politics—have invariably presented part process as the whole. The ruler is studied, not the ruled; the winning general, not the defeated; the physician's role rather than the patient's; the parents' child-rearing behavior, not the child's response. And the most monumental omission of all—of half the human experience—is that of women. Thus data on roles, power, influence, development, and personality of women are missing from the records of virtually all societies.

Patriarchal societies produced patriarchal histories by patriarchal historians. Patriarchal researchers—in sociology, psychology, anthropology—focused on research among males and extrapolated their findings to include females, refusing to consider that such things as their development, personality organization, relational styles, conflict behaviors, and cultural patterns could differ significantly from those studied and were equally valid and perhaps even more revelatory of the nature of humanness, family, community, and society. (See Figure 7-1.)

Psychotherapy, designed by males from male norms to reach adjustment to male values and male goals, is appropriate for males but can by no means be applied cross-sexually. True, there are universals in cross-sexual therapy just as in cross-cultural therapy. But there are crucial uniquenesses, distinctive and highly significant differences, that alter the process, goals, and outcome of pastoral psychotherapy.

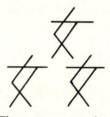

Three women together
means "noisiness" or
"badness."

Woman under a roof
means "peace."

Young woman and man
means "wickedness":
she seduces man.

Woman with child by
her side means "good."

Woman under the ruin
means "death, destruction,
perishing."

Woman combined with
littleness means
"exquisite."

Figure 7-1. Sexism in Chinese ideograms.

Western women deplore the sexual connotations attached to their languages; however, a worse situation exists when values are attached to the language, as in Chinese characters.

(Chung 1981:77)

Learning Sex Roles

When asked how he pursued his discoveries, Albert Einstein once responded, "I challenge a basic assumption." "Barely perceptible beneath the surface of most affirmations about men and women, by both the lay and the learned, lie the same basic assumptions," comments Nancy Reeves (1971:72) as she identifies the three most influential of these:

1. The past is imperative. The whole sweep of the history of women is viewed as static and institutionally determined, with invariable patterns that delineate the fixed contours of female nature.

2. The organism is imperative. The anatomy of the second sex is viewed as a paramount physiological design that determines the absolute range of woman's social function—that is, her destiny.

3. A cultural universe divided by sex is imperative. Psychological traits are viewed as sex-linked certainties, forever separating masculine and feminine roles, talents, and temperaments. The body fixes the limits of the soul. The social distance between the sexes is conceived as an integral part of the human condition.

Cultural conceptions of maleness and femaleness reveal the full range of human variations. No one area of human differences is held more rigidly or evokes greater defensiveness or emotionality than the sexual roles of men and women. The assumptions, beliefs, biases, and myths that cluster around this basic polarity of life are the most rich source of art, literature, and custom and of the most painful, irrational, and indefensible oppression and exploitation.

There are consistent differences in the way many societies discriminate between the sexes in childhood socialization emphases. Barry, Bacon, and Child, in 1967, based their conclusions on data collected from forty-five societies in the Human Relations Area Files at Yale University. Sex differences were observed in every society in nurturance, responsibility, and obedience—with females displaying more of these classes of behavior—and in self-reliance, achievement, and independence—with males displaying more of these (Segall 1979:139). The questions on socialization are puzzling, the answers unknown.

Have all societies observed certain innate, inborn tendencies in males and females and shaped their socialization practices in the rearing of children to reinforce such biologically determined tendencies?

Have all societies developed socialization practices from the obvious anatomical, reproductive, and muscular aptitude differences and from these developed the universal behavioral contrasts?

Have all societies developed socialization practices from biochemical hormonal tendencies—that males are more likely to initiate sex, to express dominance, to be more aggressive; that females are more likely to conform, defer, comply, or submit to an authority figure of either sex but especially the male?

What is clear is that certain differences, such as those already noted, are virtually universal. In the cross-cultural study of male and female children in Okinawa, India, Kenya, Mexico, the Philippines, and the United States, the following pattern emerged. In these six diverse societies, boys generally outscored girls in (1) expressing dominance, (2) responding aggressively to instigation to aggress, (3) manifesting aggression both physically and verbally, and (4) seeking attention (male dependency). Girls showed a superiority in (1) nurturance abilities, but only among 7- to 11-year-olds, and (2) seeking help and seeking or offering physical contact (female forms of dependency). The degree of differences in these traits in some societies—for example, Kenya and America— were smaller or less frequent than in the other societies (Whiting and Edwards 1973:171).

Females and males do indeed have some differing dispositions, but "thanks primarily to cross-cultural research, it is clear that these sex differences are the product of cultural forces, operating through socialization practices and reflective of ecological factors" (Segall 1979:162).

The cross-cultural counselor must have a clear understanding of maleness and femaleness, with as few as possible of the distortions of the sexism present in each culture. The double burden of sexist beliefs and values from multiple cultures may not clarify or reduce the prejudices in the person on the boundaries between cultures; in fact, the second culture's sexism often serves to confirm the commitment to the rightness of the first. The processes of unlearning and relearning that are necessary for growing toward a nonsexist understanding of persons and relationships require intentional investment of the whole self, since the deepest roots are in the counselor's affective feelings rather than in the cognitive belief system.

The research data on the differences between the sexes that are universal or well documented: (1) females have greater verbal ability, first in early childhood, then once more after age ten; (2) males excel in mathematical ability, especially after age twelve, and in visual and spatial ability, particularly in adolescence and adulthood; (3) males are more aggressive; however, how much is physiological as a hormonally based readiness to respond more aggressively and what part is social training is not yet clear.

Women are more affiliative. In every age and virtually all cultures, relationship, bonding, attachment, networks, and groups have always been more characteristic of women than men. Historically, from the "scenes of women in close companionship with each other which abound in Greek vase decorations" to "present-day Chinese women's courtyard communal groups," culturally, from "village women . . . with associations, institutions, and cults, so essential for group solidarity" to Western consciousness-raising groups that nourish participants and stimulate change, networks are ever-present among women (Bernard 1981:41, 43).

Networks, both intentionally and unintentionally, serve as therapeutic and healing contexts for women. The specific needs seen by Western feminist therapies are also the primary goals of these natural groupings:

"to develop self-esteem and a sense of personal power; to take self-responsibility; to become self-nurturant; to face anger; to deal with depression; to learn how to drop covert manipulative behavior; to be serving without being subserviant; to balance independence with interdependence" (Gingrich 1985:5). In more traditional contexts, the goals are for familial or group change, for family pride more than self-esteem, for mutual accountability rather than self-responsibility, for mutual rather than individual nurturance, and to achieve effective interdependence. Networking provides the context for growth, adjustment, support, and healing for most of the world's women.

Differences between the sexes in tactile sensitivity, competitiveness, dominance, compliance, nurturance, timidity, anxiety, activity, courage, and fear are now believed to be largely if not completely culturally conditioned or genetically based rather than sex linked. There is no significant difference in achievement drives, task persistence, or motivational levels. Thus similarity is much more pronounced than differences in basic potential and ability. The wide variations are clearly related to the very different socialization process males and females receive in every known culture. Most attempts to define the differences between the sexes ignore the much wider variations within each sex.

Genetics has not proven useful in tracing the origin of sexual differences. Even aggressiveness as a trait seems more hormonally than genetically related, since very young children are much more similar than dissimilar. Certain biological events that females alone can experience—pregnancy and childbearing—make women's lives profoundly different from those of men.

The most open differences are in life stages and life roles. The stages of development vary between the sexes. Although the early stages are highly similar, the great difference in the value placed on males and females in many cultures affects the degree of recognition of dignity, certification of the woman's worth, and validation of her right to feel, think, and choose. In many traditional societies, all three are extremely low or totally absent for females. From puberty throughout the life cycle, the stages of adult life vary markedly. Each sex is assigned behaviors, values, priorities, activities, and roles throughout the life cycle that significantly shape the personality formation and participation in the family, community, the working world, and society at large.

> Inequality between the sexes is not unidimensional; rather, each sex in any society has primary control over certain activities, and the rewards and power accruing to each sex depend upon the centrality of these activities to the society as a whole. Even in the most male-dominant society, women have clear areas of control within the household and male interference in these areas is censured by both sexes. . . . Even in sexually stratified societies, there are mitigating circumstances that check male dominance and permit women to gain some measure of autonomy. (Schlegel 1977:355)

Consider this Liberian folktale (adapted from Abrahams 1983:148):

A man, a woman, and their child were making a hard journey through the bush. They had nothing to eat with them, and as they traveled they became very hungry.

Suddenly they spied a herd of bush cows grazing in a clearing. The man said to the woman, "You have the power of transforming yourself into whatever you like; change now to a leopard and capture a bush cow so that I may eat and not die."

The woman looked at him significantly and asked, "Do you really mean what you ask, or are you joking?"

"I mean it," said the man, for he was famished.

The woman untied the baby and laid it on the ground. She dropped her loincloth, and hair began growing upon her body, her hands and feet turned into claws. In a few moments, a wild leopard stood before the man, staring at him with fiery eyes. He was frightened nearly to death, and forgetting the baby he clambered up a tree for protection. When the leopard saw that she had the man good and frightened, she ran upon the flock of cattle, captured a young heifer, and dragged it to the foot of the tree. The man, as far up in the branches as he could climb, piteously begged the leopard to transform herself back into a woman.

Slowly the hair receded, the claws disappeared, and at last a woman stood beneath the tree once more. The man was so afraid he would not come down until she had taken up her clothes and tied the baby to her back. Then she said to him, "Never ask a woman to do a man's work again."

Women must care for the house, tend the farm, raise the breadstuffs, even catch the fish, but it is man's work to do the hunting and bring the meat for the family.

A review of the rich anthropological literature on sex differences around the world leads one to conclude with Monroe and Monroe (1975:116) that (1) there are modal sex differences in behavior in every society and (2) every society has some division of labor by sex. These two phenomena, which seem to be interrelated, are universal (or nearly so) and quite consistent in content. For example, food preparation is done predominantly by females in nearly all societies. Child rearing is usually the responsibility of females. Although there are many cross-cultural variations in the content of sexual divisions of labor, there are very few significant reversals of sex-typed tasks (Segall 1979:161).

The explanations for the universality of this labor division are all conjecture: (1) It arises from biological differences—size, strength, child-bearing, and nursing required close-to-home functions, and (2) tasks emerged as a means of socializing children for adult activities, so girls are trained in increased nurturance, obedience, and responsibility, boys in greater assertiveness, achievement, and independence.

> Division of function, however, does not necessarily lead to stratification; rather, it can lead to balanced complementarity. Sexual stratification, then, is not panhuman but rather poses a problem that must be explained, for each society in terms of the forces to which it is responsive, and cross-culturally in terms of variables that exist across societies. It is an enormously complex problem, and a challenging one. (Schlegel 1977:356)

What is clear is that as societies move toward greater technological and industrial development the differences in sexual roles become less and less significant.

Women's Roles—Viewed Across Cultures

The roles played by women and men are both parallel and opposite. Such roles as parent, grandparent, single person, divorced person, child, worker, and friend are common to both sexes, but their social, economic, political, religious, and emotional consequences are extremely different. In classic China, the son was seen as the parent's means to salvation through ancestor worship. He was the bearer of the family line and its continuity in immortality. The daughter was not recorded in the family genealogy by name but marked by *nu,* the symbol for female. She was considered an "outsider" or temporary family member, like "spilled water," since her economic value would go to her husband's family.

The overwhelming evidence of anthropological studies of male and female roles is that virtually no society in the world offers women equal status with men. In some societies women are given considerable social recognition and power, but in no society does their publicly recognized power exceed that of men.

Rafael Patai (1967:16) suggests a tentative working hypothesis that seems well supported by available data: "The greater the distance between the status of the lower and the higher classes, the greater the inequalities between men and women, and vice versa."

Cross-cultural comparisons of women's roles (see Table 7-1) reveal that most stereotypes are unsupported by data collected from multiple cultures. All contemporary societies are to some extent male-dominated, and although the degree and nature of female subordination vary greatly, the asymmetry and injustice are universal facts of human culture.

Sexual roles are shaped not only by tradition but by the economic, agricultural, and technological needs of the society. As these change, there are also alterations in both expectations and possibilities for women and men.

> The needs of a given society can be correlated with the role behaviors of men and women in that society. Societies that put a premium on physical strength tend to make stronger distinctions between the appropriate behavior for men and women. More industrialized societies in which physical strength is less essential show less differentiation in sex roles. As a society moves from more manual labor to technical labor, change in sex roles is accelerated. (Barry and others 1957:332)

> An intriguing case is the Kung people of Africa. For centuries they have lived as nomadic hunters and gatherers, and men and women shared the work of the group on a largely equal basis. The recent shift toward a sedentary village existence has also led to a more specific division of labor between men and women with boys and girls now being trained for different tasks. (Draper 1977)

Table 7-1. Cross-Cultural Comparisons of Women's Roles

Stereotypes	*Cross-Cultural Data*
Women are biologically unable to do certain work.	Sex, reproduction, and child rearing do not preclude women from hard physical labor, complex commercial dealings, or artistic creativity.
Women choose submissive roles and prefer to be dominated.	Women of traditional societies are not acquiescent, subservient, and passive but are active, claim rights, and resent male dominance.
Women possess an esentially maternal instinct, primarily expressed in love for sons rather than daughters.	Women possess capacities for relational, familial, parental commitments. These are human traits, not feminine ones.
Women's lives, roles, and opportunities are circumscribed and limited.	In traditional societies few alternatives are available to either males or females, although women are more contained in the domestic sphere; men hold a more dominant position and have a larger sphere.
Women are universally subordinate to men.	The degree of subordination varies least in small-scale tribal societies, most in complex patrilineal-patrilocal ones.
Women are comparatively powerless.	Women wield a great deal of power. In many societies they constitute a major labor force, exercise full control of domestic resources, provide much of the subsistence, and influence, underwrite, and facilitate the more prestigious activities of their men.

(Adapted from Hammond and Jablow 1976:135)

> The view commonly held, that women have traditionally been oppressed in Third World societies and that "development" is the key to changing their situation, is false. Women's status was good in many (not all) Third World societies in the past, and the structure and ideology of male dominance were introduced as corollaries of colonialism. Furthermore, accumulating evidence shows that although contemporary development may afford political and professional roles for a few token women, given its imperialist context it continues to undermine the status and autonomy of the vast majority. (Leacock 1981:310)

The oppression of women is inextricably bound up with the world system of exploitation. Women bear the heaviest burden of national, economic, class, and religious oppression. They are often told that their own liberation must wait for the attainment of larger goals for the whole society's liberation. But such change is so great that to delay liberation for one half of humanity until improvement has been made for the whole delays justice indefinitely.

Liberation in the Two-Thirds World

The status of women in South and Southeast Asia was higher in earlier times. More highly regarded by society and family, educated before marriage, women married only after physical maturity. In Southeast Asia, women could divorce and remarry and retained rights to property and children (Whyte and Whyte 1982:203).

The Indian woman's position deteriorated until the writing of *The Laws of Manu,* around the second and third centuries B.C., which enshrined the subservient role. Buddhism absorbed this social pattern and carried it to China.

In early China, women also enjoyed a more egalitarian position, but by the time of Confucius it had become a servile dependency. Among the patrilineal majority of Chinese women, there were no rights to land or property, remarriage of widows was forbidden, and a divorcee lost access to her children.

Confucius (c. 551–479 B.C.) and Mencius (c. 372–289 B.C.) were the principal spokesmen of classic times in preserving the traditional superior-inferior relationship between men and women as heaven-ordained. "Man dispenses and woman accepts," said Mencius. Women were to observe the Three Obediences—obedient to the father and elder brother when young, to the husband when married, to the oldest son when widowed—and the Four Virtues—to know and keep her place, to be silent and not bore others, to adorn the self for the pleasure of the male, and to perform household chores with diligence (Lin Siu-Tsung in Iglitzin and Ross 1976:346).

Chinese women, the largest disinherited and oppressed group, made a great leap forward in human dignity and functional equality after 1949. "Women hold up half the sky," Mao observed and moved to give women equal opportunity in the labor forces. Article 53 of China's constitution proclaims: "Women enjoy equal rights with men in all spheres of political, economic, cultural, social, and family life. Men and women enjoy equal pay for equal work."

The liberal 1950 family law, the first law passed by the Communists, provided freedom of choice in marriage, abolished concubinage, and gave women the right to own property, use their own names, and sue for divorce. Abortion has since been legalized and free on demand, women in cities receive a minimum of 56 days paid maternity leave, six months if they sign a pledge to have only one child. Many Chinese women now go to college. One third of all scientists and engineers are women.

However, a confidential study on the status of women and marriage prepared by investigators for the women's federation in 1980 discovered that old patterns persist. In one commune in Shanxi there were 146 girls under the age of five who were betrothed, accounting for 43 percent of their age group. Among those five to ten years old, 81 percent were engaged. In practice, women were more frequently assigned the most backbreaking labor, transplanting rice or picking beans while the men were driving tractors. One sociologist who lived in a North China commune calculated that women did 80 percent of all the field work, pay was less than equal, and job opportunities for women were less than equal (Butterfield 1982:166).

As welcome and surprising as the changes have been, historic patterns bend slowly. China is still a man's world. In many areas, divorce is still considered immoral, more so if the woman requests it. If divorced, she is not to remarry. As the proverb states, "A good horse won't accept two saddles; a good wife doesn't marry twice."

Dimensions of Liberation

Two dimensions of liberation must be considered in any reflection on the movement from oppressive patriarchal to more equal societies: the long-term dimension of the gradual movement of the larger society toward so-called Western values and the immediate dimension of the specific goals of women, which focus more on familial economic advancement than on individual or sexual role change.

First, the long-term cultural change—the continental drift toward Western technological, individual, and social values—also shows a significant trend toward change in women's status and roles. Speaking for those who see the change as an inevitable social transformation, Patai writes (1967:16):

> Whatever the impediments, however great the conservative opposition, the movement for the emancipation of women is not only well under way, it is gathering momentum. In the second half of the twentieth century, no country in the world remains isolated. Changes, whether in technology, industrialization, urbanization, labor relations, political organization, or social structure, bring with them concomitant changes in the position of women. The rate of change differs from country to country, but its general direction is identical everywhere. The women emerge from their purdah, they shed their veils, in some areas decisively and defiantly, in others hesitantly and shamefacedly. The liberation movement begins in the big cities, primarily in the capitals, and spreads from there into the countryside.

The two major forces in the liberation of women are socialism and Westernization. The most rapid and sweeping changes have come from socialist revolutions, but in each of these the equality promised and the reality achieved often do not converge. Socialism, like most utopian theories from Plato to Mao, supports the participation of all citizens through its commitment to an economy of equity rather than efficiency and of shared opportunities rather than competition, which favors the stronger or the less encumbered by household and child-care responsibilities—inevitably males.

In socialist and capitalist nations, women are claiming the freedom to change roles that were once seen as unchangeable. The education of women is the crucial first step. In the twenty-year period of 1960–1980, the number of girls entering school worldwide went from 15 to 75 percent. Literacy provides the power to enter more fully into the economic world, the political arena, and the social world of expanding relationships. Literacy, more than the power of legislation, has influenced the programs of population control. Education is raising the consciousness of women, allowing choice to occur in the most significant area of their lives. Official policies of birth control, which contradict age-old religious and sociocultural traditions, are in themselves enough to create radical change in the life pattern of Indian and Chinese women. This submissive, suppressed creature who dared not speak up in the presence of the dominant males, who was the victim of sexual exploitation and an obligatory annual pregnancy, is now suddenly addressed by society, asked to decide whether a child should be born to her, and invited to feel that in this most vital area of her and her husband's life she is in charge of her own destiny! Never again can a woman who has learned birth-control techniques and acquired the mentality required for their practice be a subservient self (Patai 1967:15).

Second, the immediate and specific goals of women in much of the two-thirds world are focused more on family economics and less on individual advancement or sexually defined liberation. In societies in which familial identity is equally or more important than individual identity, it is no surprise that women are more committed to the liberation of the family from poverty than of themselves and their sisters from sexual oppression.

Asian women see themselves and are seen by their societies as one component of a family, and often of an extended group related by birth and marriage. The concept of individuality, still less individual freedom, is alien. The aspirations of Asian women are directed toward their families; they seek enhanced status for the family and, above all, better family economic well-being: a bigger, better house, more and better land, financial security, freedom from worry. Individual goals are rarely mentioned (Whyte and Whyte 1982:12).

Western feminism is seeking liberation from inequality in all areas: social, economic, political, career, religion, and the arts. Women are claiming freedom from unequally shared family responsibilities in order to have opportunity for creative or professional activities as individuals. Attempts at dialogue with Eastern and two-thirds-world women are frequently the cause of great surprise at the differences between their objectives and those of Western women.

In Asia, the "collective personalities" of men and women shape the ways in which both males and females define their problems and choose the goals desired for their joint liberation.

> Asian women are less inclined to see themselves oppressed as women than oppressed as members of a socioeconomic group. Only in Japan has the women's movement acquired the aspects of confrontation which are familiar in the West. Elsewhere in Asia, where the average standard of living is

far lower than in Japan, the women's movement is submerged in the aim of improving the livelihood of society in general, even though it has been demonstrated that raising the standard of living does not automatically improve the quality of life for women. (Whyte and Whyte 1982:8–9)

This inclusive way of envisioning the changes desired is not only an Asian characteristic, it is true throughout developing countries. The boundaries of oppression look different to a woman in Latin America or sub-Saharan Africa than to one in Europe or America.

"For most Third World women, class barriers are equally if not more important obstacles to genuine equality than sexual oppression" (Safa 1977:22). The changes desired by many of the women of the two-thirds world are more basic than individual esteem. They want the larger changes that will increase their options and permit new beginnings. A woman who drops the veil of purdah in order to take her place beside the men of her society can find such a place only in a setting that is, at least in part, Westernized. In a traditional African or Asian socioeconomic structure there is no place for women except their age-old custom-determined roles. Traditional society, in Asia and Africa, closely defines the roles open to men and women. To break out of circumscribed roles is to break out of the cultural framework. If a girl from a traditional Japanese or Philippine village wants something more than age-old local options, she must leave the village, because no alternative way of life exists for her to adopt. In the city, Westernization has invaded, and "modern" occupations and roles are available. Every step women take in the direction of emancipation, of equal rights and other improvements in their position, inevitably leads to departure from the traditional culture. In this sense, all women who fight for emancipation fight for modernism and Westernism (Patai 1967:17).

The movement from traditional to Western values is clearly seen in the change from polygamy toward monogamous marriage. The changes in marriage patterns show a significant trend. In Turkey and Tunisia, polygamy is officially outlawed. In Syria, Lebanon, Egypt, Jordan, and Iran it remains legal but has almost completely disappeared from the upper and middle sectors of society. In Pakistan, modern-minded women are countering the centuries-old opinion of Muslim religio-legal experts and declaring that the true intent of the Koranic passage upon which the legality of polygamy had been based for thirteen centuries is to prohibit plural marriages. In Muslim Indonesia, the complaint of women is much more cautious. They criticize those men who, in disobedience to Koranic law, marry two or more wives than they can support. In non-Muslim Asia the changes have varied in impact. India has outlawed polygamy and child marriage, but the extent of obedience to the law is unknown. In Burma, polygamy is still legal but rarely practiced. If practiced, the husband must maintain a separate home for each wife. In China as we have seen, concubinage, the traditional form of polygamy, has been abolished, and men and women are now equal before the law (Patai 1967:14).

A common assumption among Westerners is that Westernization and liberation are not only synonymous but that they both lead to much more desirable states of individuation and growth.

In fact, sociocultural and economic change often worsens rather than improves the position of women. Bourguignon (1980:10) raises some of the crucial questions that the pastoral counselor must consider in a situation of rapid socioeconomic and cultural change.

> How is the position of women altered? Is it improved, or, to the contrary, is it worsened? Is change stressful and disorientating or, primarily, liberating? Is it more stressful for women than for men, or vice versa? How are the relations between men and women affected? Is the distribution of authority, power, and prestige changed? Is the quality of interpersonal and familial relations altered? Culture change is likely to involve modifications in a whole series of aspects of life, of which economic changes are likely to represent only one segment, albeit often the most visible. We observe contact with other groups, or at least their products, awareness of other worlds and of alternatives, some degree of Western education, and a change in levels of aspiration. Often, but not always, men are more rapidly and intensively exposed to changes than women. When this happens discrepancies may develop between their perceptions, their expectations, and their values. Their total behavioral environments may be so modified that, in effect, men and women cease to live in a shared world, and a degree of alienation may result. In this country, we have heard a great deal about a "generation gap." One might well speak, in some instances, of a "gap" between the sexes, with regard to their cultural worlds.

The easy assumption that women's status improves with modernization, Westernization, and greater societal complexity is a sophisticated version of the classic imperialism. It begins with the supposition that all two-thirds-world women are downtrodden and any movement toward similarity with Western patterns is certain to be liberating. In many cases this has been shown to be true, but in many others the outcome is only more complex, not healthier, better, or more fulfilling.

In examining the impact of change on women in West Africa and the non-Hispanic Caribbean, Sidney Mintz studied how growth in the economy reduces or destroys the trading activities of women who operate as entrepreneurs with great economic skill and complete independence. These women traders tend to use their profits for the education of their children, particularly daughters, leading to jobs as teachers, nurses, and social welfare workers, but these are less independent, less enterprising, less risk-taking than those of the mother. Mintz (1971:267–268) then asks rhetorically:

> Who is more modern, more western, more developed: a barefoot and illiterate Yoruba market woman who daily risks her security and her capital in vigorous competition with others like herself; or a Smith College graduate who spends her days ferrying her husband to the Westport railroad station and her children to ballet classes? If the answer is that at least the Smith girl is literate and wears shoes, one may wonder whether one brand of anthropology has not been hoisted by its own petard.

Confronting Sexism in Counseling Therapy

The attempt to encounter each person as a fully human being with few sexual biases is the goal of effective counseling in the Western world and, increasingly, in the two-thirds world as well. In the second world, laws enforcing equality of opportunity, employment, and privilege have made first strides toward equality in practice in socialist states. In the first world, in spite of great change and the impact of feminism, the democratic process resists the constitutional action necessary to legislate change. Thus the context is ambivalent about these values in every culture as modernity and tradition compete for primacy.

> There does not yet exist any truly feminist psychoanalysis or therapy. The existing schools, basically, have analyzed psychic development within patriarchy and created therapies that reinforce male domination. Critical psychologists have got only far enough to reveal the male ideological character of these descriptions of psychic phenomena as a reflection of male power relations over women. But we have barely begun to uncover what is concealed under these male projections. . . . What women might be like, how we would symbolize the polarities of self and other, thinking and feeling, activity and receptivity outside these traditions of male domination is something that we cannot know until a nonsexist society is created where women are recognized as full human persons with a right to develop their potency not only for others, but for their own self-fulfillment. (Ruether 1975:159)

The immediate attempt to eliminate all sex-biased values of one's culture from the relationships of the counselee is neither fully possible nor desirable. To live within the culture is to continue struggling with its strengths and weaknesses, its oppression and its freedom. The fantasy of a value-free position offers little to either therapist or client. It is far more useful to discuss and explore values with the counselee rather than to attempt to breathe and speak and live in a value-free vacuum. Sexual justice is not value-free, it is value-committed to the maximum justice possible for each person, and is flexible, malleable, and equitable (Rawlings and Carter 1977).

The questions of *what* steps toward liberation the counselee can make and *how* to encourage her to take them are perplexing issues in therapy. "What" and "how" in the implementing of values held by the therapist, the person in therapy, or both is a central issue in all psychotherapy, but particularly important when the external context is a greater contributing force to the person's pain than are the internal conflicts. (See case study: Shanti—Cyclic Abuse.) Collier (1982:8) summarizes the questions that therapists face.

> What should therapists do in the face of the barriers society places to women's full development? Should they attack them? Should they play "neutral," going along with them to a certain extent? Should they manipulate them? Should they knowingly or unknowingly cooperate with barriers which keep women from receiving their fair share of money, power, status, knowledge, or opportunity? These barriers may be less dominating than

they were a decade ago, but they still manifest themselves in such areas as the limitation of job opportunities, the timing of a woman's career development, family systems which strongly discourage a woman's freedom, exclusion from the decision-making nucleus within an organization, the devaluation of a woman's accomplishments in favor of encouraging her as nurturer or office mother, or (perhaps most damaging of all) a woman's sense of powerlessness at the relatively poor pay and status which women's occupations are likely to produce. Which of these matters is or is not a matter of concern to a mental health professional? How much of it should therapists confront or ignore?

CASE STUDY: Shanti—Cyclic Abuse (India)

"The day I finally went to the women's center to see a pastoral counselor took great courage. It is hard to admit that one has been beaten by her husband, not once but over and over again."

Married eleven years, both Shanti and Raj were cut off from their families by the "love marriage." The lack of support from the joint family, the tensions with both sets of parents, the difficulty Raj had in keeping a job all increased the strain in the marriage. The birth of a first child only added to the responsibilities. Soon after, Raj began a cyclical brooding, explosive rage, wife abuse, contrition, then a return to brooding. Shanti, repeatedly disappointed, allowed herself to be talked into accepting promises of change, covering for his public abuse and explaining her injuries as accidents. The alienation from both families severed the traditional means of help through members of the joint family. Her attempts to talk with friends only triggered further rage.

When the abuse began to include the second child, four-year-old Usha, Shanti at last went for counseling. The pastoral counselor arranged for residence for Shanti and the children at the women's center operated by the church in this major Indian city. With a male co-therapist, the counselor was able to have two sessions with Raj and one joint session. No basis for renegotiating the marriage could be established. Shamed by exposure but owning no shame for his behavior, Raj exhibited explosive anger in both sessions.

A joint meeting with Shanti's older brother, the clan leader, opened conversation, and the family was able to purchase a flat from her share of inheritance funds and to help find an opening at her previous work as a secretary. Reconnected with the joint family, Shanti found the normal support processes of her childhood community assisted her and her children in the stress of the separation.

Pastoral counselor's comment: Shanti's case is exceptional rather than typical of Indian wives who suffer spouse abuse. The wife (1) rarely has an available counselor, (2) has no financial resources to find alternate lodging except to move back to the joint family, (3) has little skill training for finding employment, (4) receives strong pressure from the family to stay in the marriage, (5) is blamed by the family for choosing the marriage and for causing the abuse, (6) may suffer increased abuse for having opened the problem to anyone outside the family, (7) fears death by "accidental fire" from the husband in one of his episodes, and (8) may assume that violence is an unavoidable part of marriage.

Three different approaches to therapy focus on equivalent justice for males and females: nonsexist therapy, androgynous therapy, and feminist therapy.

Nonsexist therapy, in Western society, has as its goal the ability of the client to claim freedom, responsibility, and equality as an individual within the larger society. It sees the intrapsychic causes of a person's problems as—in most cases—less influential than the sex-role expectations and the society's patterns of discrimination against and limitations upon women. The anxiety, guilt, and depression resulting from feeling powerless or from defying the social expectations are relieved by encouraging the individual's right to define her own way of being and living differently in a varied society.

In the two-thirds world, solutions to sexual oppression do not come by claiming the option of individualism, which already exists in the social order. In settings where persons—male or female—develop not a personal identity but a family identity, the therapeutic mode that is more effective is relational, familial, and group change process. The focus of the therapy is not on creating an autonomous, independent woman capable of defining her existence apart from the social group, but rather on facilitating change and growth within the family and the social system. The goal is a more equal interdependence, not an individualized independence.

The basic assumptions of nonsexist therapy as set forth by Rawlings and Carter (1977:51–54) focus on a recognition of one's cultural biases, a respect for variation and differences, and an openness to view sex-role reversals as an issue of personal preference rather than a pathological violation of the society's norms. These basic assumptions are summarized as follows:

1. The therapist should be highly aware of his or her own values, especially as they relate to expectations for "males" and "females." Since the evidence shows that most therapists are subject to the same biases as are the rest of the culture, this is already a professional requirement that most are unable to meet without special training.

2. Differences from the norm in sex-role behavior are seen as normal and appropriate. Choices should be made on the basis of what will work best, not on what should or should not be.

3. The dominance of biology in determining sex differences is rejected, though it is usually seen as a factor.

4. Behaviorally, reversals in sex-role predispositions are not seen as pathological, and the desired outcome for all clients is the ability to choose adaptively.

5. Females and males are viewed primarily as individuals. Females, for instance, are seen as capable of the same autonomy and assertiveness as males, and males of the same expressiveness and tenderness as females.

6. The therapist avoids using the power inherent in her or his position to reinforce or punish behavior that appears to be decidedly masculine or feminine.

7. Test instruments that contain sex bias are avoided.

8. Diagnosis does not depend on a client's "failure" to achieve behavior in accord with her or his culturally prescribed sex role.

9. Therapist and client work cooperatively to achieve the values and choices appropriate for this person in this situation regardless of gender. Sex-role transcendence is the goal.

These assumptions bear the cultural stamp of Western individualism and must be translated, adapted, and redirected by persons in corporate social settings, but the commitment to change toward equal justice and mutual responsibility in decisions remains the central directing force.

Androgynous therapy sees the primary goal of human growth as the development in each person of those characteristics that society has polarized as male and female and located in the separate sexes. The whole person, androgynous therapists teach, embodies both assertiveness and affiliativeness, both strength and tenderness, both confrontation and support, both competitiveness and cooperation, both rationality and intuition, both thought and feeling. These polar traits, often split and assigned to either maleness or femaleness, are both necessary for health and wholeness in each human. Authentic humanness transcends such divisions of the self and expresses the full range of responses to others and to life.

Androgyny has a long history and a wide cultural base. It is found in Plato, Tao, Gnosticism, Tibetan Tantra, Kundalini Yoga, alchemy, astrology, and the Kabbalah and in Freud and Jung. Some scholars insist that it is found in the first words of the Bible: "God created male and female in his own image"—that is, the image of an androgyne.

Central to the thought of Carl Jung, the androgynous view of humanness is based on the assumption that every individual, though socialized to exaggerate those behaviors routinely ascribed to her or his gender, also possesses a cross-sexual pole of the personality that is necessarily repressed into the unconscious. Here it is united with the archetype of masculinity—the animus—or of femininity—the anima—to become the inner cross-sexual voice of the unconscious. The woman, then, taught to fear her own "masculinity," must become attentive to her animus and incorporate its strength into her conscious awareness and her lived experience if she is to achieve wholeness. It is not perfection but completeness that is the goal of growth, and from this completeness rises a balanced wholeness of sexuality and an androgynous gender identity.

Some cultures polarize "masculinity" and "femininity" sharply, with rigid definition and maintenance of roles. Others allow the person to fulfill various roles in different life stages. Still others are complementary in flexible and interchangeable functions in various domains of life—family, marketplace, field work, social and religious life. Androgyny is a more natural development in some cultures and a violation of deeply held taboos in others.

The androgynous therapist invites the counselee to recognize, approve, develop, and express the full range of behaviors in relationships and to appreciate them richly within the self. This goal of inner wholeness and completeness hides a strong Western individualistic premise, as Pedersen notes (1981:326). "One example of the self-contained, individualistic perspective might be establishing the androgynous individual as an ideal type, as a sign of good health where each individual is self-contained and self-sufficient."

In the Western social context, androgyny as self-contained individualism and morality as independence or transcendence from collective loyalties are often related to high self-esteem and personal success. But serious doubts remain whether a society can manage its complex problems of energy, population growth, and social welfare programs, for example, when all is based on an individualistic and atomistic outlook. Human welfare must be based not on detachment from others, or on self-containment, but on a profound commitment to social interest, solidarity, and moral responsibility.

Androgynous views based on more collective understandings of humanness are possible within the original Jungian framework. It is not the theory of individual psychology itself but the cultural developments and applications of it within Western society that exaggerate its tendencies toward self-sufficiency as a measure of full humanness. Our future, not just in psychology but also in economics and politics, depends on our ability to go beyond individualistic assumptions and on our willingness to learn from cultures that stress relational perspectives as primary criteria of mental health, personal adjustment, and sexual wholeness.

Feminist therapy begins from the conviction that females and males are culturally, not biologically, determined and are environmentally, not internally, disposed toward illness or pathology. Men and women should seek and possess equal opportunity for personal fulfillment, economic well-being, institutional influence, and political power. All relationships between individuals should be egalitarian; the counselor–client relationship is a model of this egalitarian dignity, and this is itself a social and political statement.

Janet Radcliffe Richards (1980:1) offers a philosophic base for feminism: "Feminism has a strong fundamental case, what I mean is that there are excellent reasons for thinking that *women suffer from systematic social injustice because of their sex.* . . . This proposition is the essence of feminism and anyone who accepts it may be counted as a feminist."

Feminism is not solely a concern for women's problems, it is a commitment to justice for all. "Feminism is not concerned with *a group of people it wants to benefit,* but with a *type of injustice it wants to eliminate*" (Radcliffe Richards 1980:5).

The basic assumptions of feminist therapy are:

1. The inferior status of women is due to their having less economic and political power than men.

2. Though the circumstances in which a woman exercises power will vary according to her economic and social class, neither of these affects her individual value to the same extent as her gender.

3. The main source of a woman's problems is likely to be social and external, not personal or internal, but focusing on the external as a source of problems does *not* relieve the individual of responsibility for her choices. On the contrary, the individual can change both herself and the external world.

4. Friendship, love, pairings, and marriage should be based on equality of personal power.

5. Other women are not the enemy, nor are men. Both are victims of sex-role socialization. Social change is an important goal for the individual, who should concentrate on choosing behaviors that are appropriate rather than sex-role stereotypical.

6. Economic and psychological autonomy are both important goals for women. (Rawlings and Carter 1977:37)

Feminist approaches require a new theory base, new understandings of personality, and new insight into the nature of women, because all old approaches are based on male observations, male models, and primarily male-based research. "Feminism is truly a venture into a *terra incognita.* It must not only seek the reshaping of social relations for a humanized world. It must simultaneously create the therapy for a new selfhood of women and men appropriate to a humanized world" (Ruether 1975: 159).

The therapeutic process of feminist therapy reveals the clarity with which the approach defines the person as a sociocultural rather than a biological or genetically determined being. This allows for its cross-cultural use in confronting personal, familial, economic, and political injustices in any society. The major differences among the three approaches is that androgyny tends to look inward for integration, resolution of conflicts, balancing of polarities, and clarification of individual identity before reaching out to confront or contradict the environment. Nonsexist therapy emphasizes the need for all human beings to be able to actualize personal health, economic well-being, and familial and communal solidarity regardless of gender. Feminist therapy seeks to actively combat sex-role stereotyping and oppression by utilizing the political and philosophical values of the women's movement.

"It is not useful to argue about which approach is better," Collier suggests. "The issue, rather, is which approach is more appropriate for the client." She recommends the nonsexist approach for the woman with more traditional values, to whom feminism is threatening, and feminist approaches for the woman who finds cultural restrictions binding; best of all is to use all approaches at different times with the same counselee, the basic idea being to begin with where the person is in her total situation—personal, familial, cultural, economic, or political—and help her move to whatever more freeing and healthful place is possible.

Many counselors in various countries experience difficulty with the strong value system required of a feminist therapist and of the exclusivism it demands. Many feminist theorists maintain that no male can satisfactorily undertake feminist therapy (Chesler 1972:65,247). Others, such as Collier, believe that although only feminist therapy can meet certain needs in particular situations, other therapies are necessary in others, and that any therapist, male or female, can and should use enough of the ideas and information of feminism to be useful to the person. "One does not have to be a committed feminist to use the information and attitudes common to feminist therapy" (Collier 1982: 38).

All three approaches recognize that the problems of a female counselee are only partly within her and are more significantly rooted in the injustice of preceding generations and the present situation. Nonsexist therapy sees woman's development and behavior as determined more by her being human than by being female, and it sees her goals as human objectives rather than sex-related ones. Feminist therapy agrees in principle but sees female goals as primary and necessary before one can claim fully human goals. The issue is one of degree, not difference, since feminists·tend to invest the environment with most responsibility and see the woman as reactive rather than a responsive participant. Both encourage her to define herself and choose her goals, set her boundaries, discern her values. Feminist therapy more accurately pinpoints the source of women's problems, since the research of the last half of the twentieth century has outlined the difficulties unique to women of this century. All women in therapy and all therapists working with women must use the information and knowledge of women's position and the impact it has on them, on marriage, society, children, career, and their larger world values.

All human therapy seeks to alleviate personal distress, reduce interpersonal difficulties, and remove growth-blocking factors so that the person or family can live together more effectively. All therapy that seeks justice for both sexes needs the contribution of all three approaches we have examined. To achieve a sexually just therapy, one needs the insight, information, and values of feminism, the commitment to be nonsexist in all male–female relationships, and the internal balance of traits and affects that makes one fully alive in maleness, femaleness, and humanness.

Can only women counsel women, or men understand men? The opening assumption that people of the same sex have had the same experiences, felt similar pain, and identify more deeply is both true and false. It is true in those rare cases of shared experience and insight, but it is false for at least three reasons.

1. The female bond of solidarity is no easier to create than any other human bond. Male affinities are not simpler to establish. All require voluntary empathy and interpathy.

2. The "natural" understandings of each other possess no special virtue. In fact, they are as problematic as they are advantageous, and no more likely to point out what is essentially responsible and causative of the pain experienced. Clear, tested, reflective insight and experience from a person of same or different gender is far more important than simple identification.

3. Identification frequently hinders growth, because sympathy based on similarities reinforces pain by joining the other rather than transcending and inviting transcendence.

The crucial elements seem to be not same sex but clear consciousness of the life situation of the other, a capacity to discern factors internal and external to the person, sensitivity to another's life experience, and an understanding of its dynamics.

Only the therapist who has a profound sensitivity to the differences in the life cycle, life roles, and life possibilities of male and female within his or her culture of origin and in the culture of the client dare enter into a therapy contract. To enter into cross-cultural and cross-sexual therapy at the same time is to attempt the transcendence of two great divides in one transaction. The likelihood of both cultural and sexual oppression taking place is increased geometrically. Only he or she who has become at home on the boundary of cultures and at peace with the maleness and femaleness within each person is able to be interpathic with those who are other than the self.

A Theology of Liberation

All theology should focus toward salvation from what oppresses, binds, and enslaves. Theology and liberation are inseparable. Just as grace and judgment are necessary to salvation, and caring and confronting to growth, so justice and equal acceptance lead to liberation.

Throughout the third world (third meaning the neutral third party), or the two-thirds world, as it is often called here, the exciting edge of theology is focused on issues of justice in the tradition of the prophetic from Amos, Hosea, Isaiah, Joel, and Jeremiah to Mary and Jesus. Minjung theology in Korea, the rice roots theology of Thailand, the theology of the womb from Taiwan, and the liberation theologians of Indonesia, India, Africa, and Latin America all focus on the proclamation of justice to the oppressed.

Feminist theology has common roots with many types of so-called third world liberation theologies. In speaking of themselves as an oppressed world majority, some women have adopted the term "fourth world." "We identify with all women of all races, classes, and countries all over the world. The female culture is the Fourth World" (Burris 1972:118).

The goal of women throughout the two-thirds world is more frequently familial and communal rather than personal liberation. In cultures where individualism is seen as irresponsible or pathological autonomy, the collective personality seeks justice and liberation for the group, not the isolated self. At a world conference of women, Olivia Nyembezi Makuna expressed this clearly in a prayer.

> And this talk of liberation, Lord, is confusing because it means different things to different people. For me and my people in southern Africa, it means to be human for a dehumanized people—not that I don't want women's liberation, but that I am not yet human. For my friend from England it means to be more than just a wife and mother. For the Palestinian refugee it means having a place to call home. (Quoted in Herzel 1981:79)

Just as exploitation is present in every culture and countenanced by those in power, so inequalities between classes, castes, races, and ethnic groups have been supported by all organized religions. But all this is dwarfed by the culturally universal subjugation of women. In all their diversity, the major religions of the world—Christianity (950 million), Islam (500 million), Hinduism (520 million), Buddhism (250 million), and Judaism (14 million)—are united by a common theme. This theme is male domination of women through patriarchal systems. If one is to understand the impact of religion upon women through the centuries, one must feel the weight of the centuries of both benevolent and malevolent oppression done in the name of God.

Liberation theologies are lifting several central themes that challenge the exploitation of man by man and of woman by man. The three most crucial of these are (1) conscientization, which focuses on the achieving and internalizing of the conviction of personal worth and dignity; (2) cooperation in the overcoming of social contradictions and in uniting to build a community of caring for all persons; and (3) humanization, which honors the longing of oppressed peoples to be whole, self-determining, and self-sustaining beings.

The Nature of Woman

Human nature as a theological inquiry has traditionally been called "the nature of man." Inadvertently, the title was more accurate than the theologians knew. The definitions of the nature of man elevated traits, values, and behaviors that were culturally attached to the male gender.

The nature of woman, often largely unstated, was composed of culturally conditioned myths, stereotypes, and generalizations about the opposite of man. The definition of woman from biology ("anatomy is destiny") and man from spirit and intellect was only one of the many rationalizations for maintaining the oppressed state of women. Consider this parable:

> The scene of the parable is the church of Santa Lucia in Nagasaki. A young boy is found exhausted at the entrance and cared for by the Bateren (Fathers). They love him for his piety, his sweet countenance, and for his voice, pure as that of a girl. About the time Lorenzo (for that was the name they gave him) comes of age, the rumor spreads that the daughter of an old

parasol-maker in the neighborhood—also a Christian—has fallen in love with him. Questioned, Lorenzo denies the fact. Somewhat later, a love letter from the girl is found in the convent garden. "I never talked with her," Lorenzo maintains. Time passes. One day, the girl confesses that she is pregnant with Lorenzo's child. Lorenzo is expelled from the community and reduced to beggary. In due time a girl is born to the parasol-maker's daughter.

Fire breaks out in Nagasaki, and the parasol-maker's house is enveloped in flames. Only Lorenzo dares to rush in and save the baby. From the billowing fire he emerges, his clothes aflame, and thrusts the unhurt child into its mother's arms. As he collapses, crushed by burning timbers, the young mother kneels before a priest, confessing: "This baby girl is not the child of Lorenzo. . . . I loved Lorenzo. But he, having deep faith in God, did not return my love. Hence, I started hating him and lied about the father of the child. Yet his noble mind refused to scorn me for my sin. He risked his life to rescue my baby from the inferno of the flames. For his mercy and his solicitude, I adore him as Jesus Christ come back to earth."

"Martyr, martyr," cries the crowd as Lorenzo breathes his last. Only then does his burnt and torn clothing reveal that Lorenzo was a girl. (Akutagawa 1952:72)

Alongside the exploitive reality, an idealized fantasy of the nature of woman was constructed in each society in ways complementary to the prevailing image of man. Any definitions of the nature of humanness must be equally true for both man and woman, so definitional inequality is as nonhuman as it is inhumane to either sex.

> There is no one definition of what it means to be human. Each subculture, each ideology, each religion explains the reality of human nature in its own way. Yet it is clear that to be human involves: first, the ability to participate in understanding and shaping the world in which a person lives; second, being accepted as a subject and not as a thing or object of someone else's manipulation. The gospel has much to say about the image of humanity in Jesus Christ, and new theological interpretation of the meaning of incarnation is needed as we respond to the thirst for humanization in our day. (Russell 1973:4–5)

Several revolutionary truths are slowly breaking through in the theological and psychological world of thought.

First, woman is no longer to be seen as she has been, as the "other," the antithesis against whom one defines authentic (inevitably male) selfhood. Essential humanness is defined by woman as well as by man from the first word of definition, the first elements of theory construction, the first concepts of human personality and development.

Second, language can no longer be twisted, as in many cultures it has been, to "include" women in terms that denote males. Masculine nouns and pronouns, adjectives and adverbs are exclusive, not inclusive, are subliminally biased, not sex fair, are presumptuous and arrogant, not interchangeable.

Third, service can no longer be defined, as it traditionally has been, with vertical implications of superior and inferior, or rendered with attitudes of subjugation from either above or beneath. As Jean Baker

Miller writes, "One of the major issues before us as a human community is the question of how to create a way of life that includes serving others without being subservient. How are we to incorporate this *necessity* into everyone's development and outlook?" (Miller 1976:71).

The view of certain persons as inherently inferior, servile, carnal, or less human than others created both a symbol system and a social system in which people could be easily pigeonholed as slaves and masters, ruled and rulers, subjugated and privileged.

Human Liberation

Central principles for human liberation are shared by all peoples, all genders, all cultures. Equality, mutuality, and integrity are underlying values for full humanness, but their meaning varies in each context. These principles are (1) *the value of equality* (women and men are equally fully human, equally deserving of positive regard), (2) *the value of mutuality* (human persons are relational beings who are fully alive in reciprocal exchange), and (3) *the value of integrity* (men and women are responsible persons capable of thinking their own thoughts, feeling feelings, choosing options). The ways in which these principles are expressed are culturally defined, but the trajectory in every culture is from limited equality, mutuality, and integrity toward whatever maximum of these values is possible.

> Feminists quite obviously are not the only persons who have come to convictions about the principles of equality and mutuality. Yet for feminists the content of these principles is not simply equatable with every other articulation of them. . . . No tradition or movement has adequately addressed the situation of women. This is not just a failure of extension. Rather, it represents a fundamental need for deeper analyses of the concepts of human life, concepts of the human self, categories of human relation. . . . Feminism assumes ground-breaking work on questions of human dignity and models of human relationships. (Farley 1985:45)

A clear exploration of social, anthropological, psychological, and theological theory reveals the basic inequalities, limited mutuality, and partial integrity assumed of half the human race. "Equal regard for persons as persons" was excellent moral theory, but in practice women were assumed as second among equals, just as "equal protection under the law" in all cultures has been less than equal. Even equality and mutuality in marriage more often emerged as complementary relationships in which one is dependent upon the other.

An equitable share in the resources, privileges, and services necessary to life is the basic right of all human persons. An authentic mutuality allows persons to know and be known, to hear and be heard, to love and be loved, to fully participate in the give-and-take of relationship. An integrity of thinking, feeling, choosing, and changing is at the very center of humanness.

Theologian Letty Russell (1979:18) uses the concept of partnership to define the relationship that typifies true equality, mutuality, and integrity.

> *Partnership may be described as a new focus of relationship in which there is continuing commitment and common struggle in interaction with a wider community context.* Partnership is always growing and dying, for it is a human interrelationship that is never static. . . . Partnership defined in a static image would no longer be able to provide clues to the organic, living, and risky nature of that which we seek not only to describe but also to live.

Facilitating mutual partnership between the sexes, a primary objective of pastoral counseling, is an exercise in the art of the possible. One teaches the principles of full mutuality, equality, and integrity and models these attributes in all therapeutic, social, and private relationships, while recognizing that the change process in each culture operates at a different speed and unfolds in differing ways.

Mutual partnership requires four basic characteristics that connect persons with positive regard yet maintain their separate dignity through mutual respect. These are (1) *consciousness* of the inequalities assumed and injustices overlooked; (2) *commitment* to cooperative sharing of responsibilities, resources, and privileges; (3) *collaboration* in working out patterns of justice and equality even in a social context of injustice and inequality; and (4) *community,* as a network of relationships, structures, and groups for both support and correction. Only as consciousness is increased, commitment deepened, collaboration pursued, and community enriched can effective mutual partnership be envisioned and the first steps be made toward experiencing it in relationships.

The pastoral counselor who sees each person as an end, not a means, resists the use or abuse of any other human. The embeddedness of injustices to women in virtually all cultures makes it very difficult for counselors, male or female, to be aware of the ways they are affected by dehumanizing forces. The counselor, the counselee, and the process itself are all shaped by assumptions about genders and their cultural meanings, sexuality and its impact on development, sex roles and what is possible for each person.

The goal of all truly human pastoral therapy is the transformation of sex roles for the liberation of both males and females. However, the educational and therapeutic processes of altering sexual roles in both Eastern and Western cultures stimulate defensiveness and opposition from males within all traditional heritages. Inevitably there is immediate denial that women have limited or no opportunities for change, growth, self-expression, and realization and immediate reference to those who have achieved equality or prominence within the system as it is.

Theologian Elisabeth Schüssler Fiorenza describes this "acceptable equality" (1975:31).

> Women in our [Western] culture are either denigrated and infantilized or idealized and put on a pedestal, but they are not allowed to be independent and free human persons. They do not live their own lives, but are taught to live vicariously through those of husband and children. They do not

exercise their own power but manipulate men's power. . . . Thus women evidence the typical personality traits of oppressed people who have internalized the images and notions of the oppressor.

As women who are at work in most present systems recognize from daily experience, the freedom fully to be themselves, express their gifts, and offer their leadership is still limited by those who define the rules of the game. "To get ahead in a patriarchal society, woman is expected to become a man, i.e., to cease being the threatening other. In politics—whether church or state—we will often find that the few women who 'reach the top' have often become so 'man-ly' that they do the woman's cause far more harm than good" (Katoppo 1981:7).

The antagonism of men to the liberation of women comes because they fail to perceive that it is also human liberation. As men assume that *man* is the *norm*, says Katoppo, they presume that woman, being the deviation, is not human. What is most needed is the right for both women and men to celebrate their otherness, not the threatening other as adversaries, or the less-than-human other as a deviation, or the subordinate other of the servant or sexual object, but as the fully other who gives meaning to the life of each sex, since meaning comes in the discovery of, respect for, and prizing of what is truly other.

> All good counseling is consciousness raising, that is, helping a counselee to discover and nurture her or his full and unique humanness. Any theory or method of counseling is ethical and effective in nurturing individual and collective wholeness if it views every individual first as a person rather than first as a woman or a man. We have for centuries made the mistake of equating *femaleness* and *maleness,* which are biological terms, with femininity and masculinity, which are cultural terms. (C. Clinebell 1976:4)

As males and females seek to enhance their differences rather than to diminish them by forcing conformity, the full potentials of community get expressed. It is not by becoming androgynously redundant that we create the most richly creative society, but as we are excited and enriched by our differences. Androgynous wholeness is not to be synonymous with becoming identical, but of doubling the possibilities of human variety; nor is it aimed toward the creation of more resistant individualism, expressed in isolated independence, but toward more resilient personalities connected in interdependence.

Summary

The intercultural pastoral counselor is aware of the inequities of gender roles, sensitive to the exploitation and abuse of women historically, traditionally, and universally, and committed to work for any increase in justice that is possible.

In the light of cross-cultural data on women's roles, sexual stereotypes, myths, and values must be challenged, the processes of learning and maintaining sex roles altered, and the consciousness of both males and females raised to allow for new flexibility and creativity in human relationships.

Liberation has significantly different meanings in various cultures. In more sociocentric and familial-identified cultures it takes corporate rather than gender-related directions, but in all cases the needs of women are among the most crucial and show the greatest disparity.

Various approaches to a more sexually just therapy may be used as appropriate to the particular culture or individual's needs.

The pastoral counselor, as a theologian, is by definition committed to the liberation of all humans, and especially of women. This calls for a clear redefinition of views of the nature of women, a new vision of partnership, and a firm commitment to achieving justice and equity for all who suffer oppression.

8

Ethical and Moral Issues in Counseling Across Cultures

A Theology of Moral Character

"To build a moral community is to contribute to health. To help establish the value framework for right action is to contribute indirectly to health. To minimize value confusion, to clarify the objects and values worthy of people's loyalty, is to contribute to their emotional and mental well-being. . . . Healthy action and moral action are not necessarily synonymous. . . . Healthy action has to do with the capacity to act without conflict. Moral action has to do with the intention to act responsibly so that the consequences of one's action contribute to the enrichment of values for oneself and the wider community."

—Don S. Browning, 1976

THE FOUR GREAT TRUTHS
UIGUR FOLKTALE, CHINA

One day a poor porter sat in the bazaar with his carrying pole, looking for work. After a long hot day of waiting, a great lord came by and called, "I have bought a case of procelain. To the man who will carry it home for me, I shall give three incontrovertible moral truths. If he can prove any one of them false, I shall then pay him the worth of the porcelain."

No one volunteered for the job. Who were they to dispute with so wise a man over incontrovertible moral truth? The poor man, seeing the day was almost ended and having little to lose, picked up the case with his pole and followed the lord toward his palace.

As they walked, the poor man said, "May I hear the first truth as we walk?"

"Yes," said the lord. "If you do not do to others what you would not want done to yourself, you will injure no one."

The poor man who had often been abused, nodded his head. "Truly an incontrovertible moral truth," he said. "And what is the second?"

"If you live each day as though it were your last, you will not waste one hour of your life."

"True," said the poor man, his back breaking from an hour of carrying the heavy box.

They arrived at the palace, and the lord turned with laughter and said, "Now hear the third incontrovertible truth. If anyone tells you that in this world there is someone more foolish than you for carrying such a heavy burden for nothing but words you cannot eat, for heaven's sake do not believe him."

The poor man heard him thoughtfully, then opened his hand from the carrying pole, and the case crashed to the ground and down the stairs to the street. "Now hear a truth which invalidates all three of yours. 'A wise man who knows the truth but does not practice it is as foolish as one who trusts his porcelain in the hands of a man he has abused.' " (Adapted from Gigliesi 1982:28)

An American high school student who attacks and beheads a young woman from a rival school whom he meets on a walk through the park would be imprisoned by the community as criminally sociopathic or hospitalized as psychotic. A Naga youth returning with a human head from a member of a neighboring village he met in the fields would be celebrated as a successful headhunter.

The moral assessment of human conduct may arrive at diametrically opposite destinations in contrasting cultures. To a Western audience, a sexual liaison between a son and his father's wife is utterly immoral. But to a Tibetan, the sharing of one wife by a father and a son is seen as a perfectly natural arrangement. The content of such moral choices is clearly culturally bound, but the process of making moral choices, setting moral boundaries, and obeying the communal moral code is an essential human behavior.

Ethical concerns are central to humanness. Human existence is moral existence. Moral values, moral choice, and moral responsibility are human universals. The forms are varied; the content is both similar and distinct. There are a few universals, much more that is culturally bound, and a great deal that is peculiar to clans, families, and persons.

It is a central insight of Emile Durkheim (1966:398) that the collective image of humans and human society, in every culture, forms what we can call a field of morality.

> Everything which is a source of solidarity is moral, everything which forces one to take account of others is moral, everything which forces one to regulate conduct through something other than the striving of the ego is moral, and morality is as solid as these ties are numerous and strong.

Morality, in this sense, is fully half of the world of meaning. It is a kind of meaning that designates direction, purpose, and motivation in the connecting and bonding of human cooperation. No one and no group is without an ethic. In every culture there is a sense of "ought."

The network of "oughts" that are formed by the demands of family, friendship groups, faith groups, professional guilds, economic institutions, political structures, and faith communities all interlock to create the moral ethos of the social context in which pastoral ministry takes place. These moral claims become organized into "a subtle web of values, a pattern of rules, principles, stories, maxims, expectations, rewards, legitimations, and punishments that constitute the operating norms of a community woven into the very structures of society and giving that society a peculiar moral identity" (Stackhouse 1978:327).

Within each culture, life is shaped by the ethos in which persons are formed and where they rooted their sense of identity. Yet this moral ground is not stable and without contradiction. Every ethos is a field of competing and conflicting claims. Each community offers its own formulation of what the central value or organizing principle shall be.

The ethic practiced is rooted in the values prized and the basic worldview assumed, as Geertz has clearly illustrated (1973:130).

> The sort of counterpoint between style of life and fundamental reality which the sacred symbols formulate varies from culture to culture. For the Navaho, an ethic prizing calm deliberateness, untiring persistence, and dignified caution complements an image of nature as tremendously powerful, mechanically regular, and highly dangerous. For the French, a logical legalism is a response to the notion that reality is rationally structured, that first principles are clear, precise, and unalterable and so need only to be discerned, memorized, and deductively applied to concrete cases. For the Hindus, a transcendental moral determinism, in which one's social and spiritual status in a future incarnation is an automatic outcome of the nature of one's action in the present, is completed by a ritualistic duty-ethic bound to caste. In itself, either side, the normative or the metaphysical, is arbitrary, but taken together they form a Gestalt with a peculiar kind of inevitability; a French ethic in a Navaho world or a Hindu one in a French world would seem only quixotic, for it would lack the air of naturalness and simple factuality which it has in its own context. It is this air of the factual, of describing, after all, the genuinely reasonable way to live which, given the facts of life, is the primary source of such an ethic's authoritativeness. What all sacred symbols assert is that the good for man is to live realistically; where they differ is in the vision of reality they construct.

The ultimate value selected by the culture has vast formative power in shaping the moral vision and the ethical system that emerges.

The interpathic pastoral counselor is aware of alternative moral worlds, able to enter them with understanding and emotive involvement, capable of discerning the moral options and the rationale utilized, and free from the need to impose her or his own moral perspective. At the same time, the effective pastoral counselor may be able to stimulate challenge to traditional assumptions and help expand a one-dimensional moral world to embrace a wider vision of ethical accountability and moral discernment. We shall explore such contrasts in moral worlds and the unique vantage point of the theologically trained therapist to enter into ethical dialogue with personal integrity and invite multidimensional integration.

Values, Ethics, and the Moral Universe

There are many values from which to choose one as the ultimate value to order those that follow. Among these are pleasure, freedom, truth, justice, beauty, utility, happiness, and loyalty.

Western thought, from Greek to medieval times, took truth as the ultimate value; since the Enlightment, justice has been more prized as a supreme value, ordering, correcting, or protecting all others. Justice requires two ethics, an ethic of ends and an ethic of means. Ends, as the basis for an ethic, requires the pursuit of just goals. It is primarily value oriented. Means, as an ethical base, involves the recognition of laws, of duties and obligations. It is duty oriented.

Japanese thought has, in classic times, chosen beauty as the ultimate value. In ancient times, there was no category of good and evil, but of beauty and ugliness. Health, life, and beauty were esteemed more than anything else, and disease, death, and ugliness were despised. Morality was aesthetic, and the ethic required purity of mind, refinement of tastes, harmony of individuals, mutual love. It was more fundamental not to stain one's name than not to shame it, so it was not a shame culture but a purity culture, a culture of impunity. The ethic that emerged was neither an ends nor a means morality but a morality of harmony, whose basic principle is sympathy and whose virtues are love, mercy, kindness, benevolence, and so forth. One can find such a morality also in Buddhist, Hindu, Confucian, and Christian—as well as classic Shinto—ethics. This aesthetic point of view recognizes the value of both personality and society. The value of the individual is not dissolved into that of the group or vice versa, as in the West. In sympathy we become one, "But this does not mean that we lose our individualities. We are not melted into simple oneness. I am I, you are you. In this sense, individuals do exist in the East. 'One in manyness, many in oneness' is the fundamental principle of Japanese ethics and metaphysics" (Masaaki 1967:258).

Indian thought has traditionally postulated truth as the supreme value. In classical Indian thought, truth was the core of *dharma* (*dharma* is conceived in three ways: ontologically as the foundation of all morality —truth; deontologically as the rules and codes of right conduct, duty, and law; and teleologically as the mode of moral reasoning—righteousness as a regulating principle).

Gandhi, who titled his autobiography *My Experiments with Truth,* claimed truth as the main motivation of life. Truth is the substance of morality, morality is the basis of all things, so truth is existence or being while untruth is virtually nonexistence or non-being. "God is truth," he posited in his early years; in later life he reversed it, saying, "Truth is God," meaning that truth is not only epistemological as known reality, it is ontological as ultimate reality. He named his nonviolent movement *satyagraha,* which means persistence or steadfastness in truth (Das 1979:58).

Three Ethical Orders

Examining ethical thought across cultures, we can identify three dominant ways of arguing moral issues. Some appeal primarily to categories of "right," some to "good," and some to "fit." Any holistic ethic must contain all three, but each ethic tends to choose one as the fundamental principle and the others as corollary means of decision making. (See Case Study: An Ethical Dilemma.)

An ethic of "right or wrong" answers the question "What shall I do?" by turning to laws, principles, and rules that are regarded as universally valid. This approach, the deontological, seeks to answer the moral query by asking, first of all, "What is the law and what is the first law of my life?"

An ethic of "good or evil" answers the question "What shall I do?" by looking toward goals, ideals, ends. It raises the prior question of "What is my ideal, or telos?" This stance, the teleological, seeks to answer the moral question by looking toward intended outcomes and the production of the greatest good for the greatest number of people.

An ethic of "fitting or not fitting" responds to the ethical question by first inquiring, "What is going on?" It takes the immediate situation very

CASE STUDY: An Ethical Dilemma (India)

The railway train from Samastipur to Banmankhi had just entered the bridge across a deep river basin when the engineer saw a man driving two animals ahead on the bridge, apparently unaware of the train bearing down on him. The engineer needed to make a split-second decision about attempting to save the pedestrian by braking the train on a high trestle.

The driver applied the emergency brake and the train jackknifed, seven of the nine cars tumbling into the swirling waters below. With several hundred persons packed in each car, the loss of life was over a thousand, including the pedestrian and his animals.

When the engineer reported to his superiors, he was urged to identify external causes for the accident—a storm, a broken rail. But his Christian ethic against telling an untruth demanded that he accept full responsibility for his decision and go to prison.

Note: The interface between a deontological ethic and an ethic of fit reveals weaknesses of both. For the system, the options are to externalize responsibility and thus excuse or to penalize and avenge retributively. For the engineer, the absolute values immobilized him from permitting one death to avoid the sacrifice of a thousand, a decision more common to teleological thought.

seriously. An action is morally fitting when it is taken in conscious response to a particular and concrete situation.

> The differences among the three approaches may be indicated by the terms the *good,* the *right,* and the *fitting;* for teleology is concerned always with the highest good to which it subordinates the right; consistent deontology is concerned with the right, no matter what may happen to our goods; but for the ethics of responsibility the *fitting* action, the one that fits into a total interaction as response and as anticipation of further response, is alone conducive to the good and alone is right. (H. R. Niebuhr 1963:60–61)

These three approaches, present in varying degrees in most systems, seem to occur in particular patterns in various cultures. Table 8-1 contrasts the three ethical patterns, their foci strengths and weaknesses, and notes in which cultures each appears to be ascendant.

> The three "great surviving cultural traditions," i.e., the Western, the Chinese, and the Indian, can be explained—although only partly and roughly —in terms of the three ethical models. The exclusive approach to reality of the Western people, the "either-or" approach, is closer to the ethics of "right and wrong." The inclusive approach to reality of the Chinese people, namely the "both-and" approach, is more compatible with the ethics of "good and evil." Finally, the "neither-nor" approach of the Indians is more suitable to the ethics of "fit and unfit." (Darmaputera 1982:415)

All three ethical views are, of course, present in all three worldviews, but the ordering of the three varies not only in ideal types but in broader patterns of cultural development.

> Ethics, in every society and culture, must have all three elements to be whole. And, in fact, all the profound ethics of the world's great religions touch on all these matters in one way or another. Indeed, in Christianity we hold that God's law, God's purpose, and God's love for the human situation are the foundation of all ethics and that by grace these cohere perfectly in God's holiness. Under conditions of human sin, however, we have only relative approximations to that integration. Thus we are constantly caught between the tensions and contradictions between human rights, human goods, and human sensitivity to concrete situations. (Stackhouse 1978:330)

Each ethical perspective differs in its prescriptive patterns and in its view of what is necessary for intensifying moral responsibility or growth in the society. The cure for any loss of moral values is in strengthening the teaching of rules—a consciousness of sin—or in increasing the attraction of ideals, goals, and ends—the lure of the possible—or in clearer analysis of contexts and better discernment of relevant and cogent actions.

In applying these three ethical visions to the Indian experience, Stackhouse notes (1978:335):

> Indian concepts of the right are more closely tied to concepts of the fitting than is the case in the West. The classic concepts of *dharma* contain a notion of universal right, but each communal group and each individual is

Table 8-1. Comparison of Three Ethics

An Ethic of Right and Wrong	An Ethic of Good and Evil	An Ethic of Fit or Unfit
Deontology—rooted in the essential nature of moral existence.	*Teleology*—pointed toward the valued good.	*Contextual*—oriented by situational good.
Focus on rules, universals, principles, and categorical laws.	Focus on goals, ideals, purposes, and ends that are desired or desirable.	Focus on what is fitting in responsibility to the context and situation.
States what *acts* are required, forbidden, or permitted in human relations.	States what *ends* are envisioned—perfection, justice, maturity, *moksha* (release from birth and death cycle).	Sees the *context* as crucial, the appropriateness of the act or end to the situation.
Articulates the basic principles, values, and warrants for ethical conversation.	Accents the potential present in a concrete situation to attain the desired objectives.	Focuses on aesthetics of ethical action—what produces harmony, simplicity, consistency, beauty, virtue.
Criteria are rational: clarity and universal applicability.	Criteria are consistency of means and ends to achieve the latter.	Criteria deal with the "right," the "good," and the "possible."
Example: The Ten Commandments.	*Example:* The kingdom of God, as present and future goal.	*Example:* Responsibility as the "ability to respond" to the ethical dilemma.
"By the very constitution of human existence, it is universally right to be truthful, just, loyal. It is wrong to lie, to cheat, to steal, to betray."	The subjective type focuses on the striving to be honest, authentic, genuine in moral acting. The objective type focuses not on intentions but on actual consequences.	The conservative versions may rely on tradition, social custom, manners, morals, etiquette that fit group ethos like a round cork in a round bottle.
When exaggerated, it may lead to *legalism* with oppressive systems of rational rules and binding laws. When ignored, it leads to antinomianism and anarchy.	When exaggerated, it tends toward utilitarianism or even hedonism. May blur the sense of consistent or universal "goods"—i.e., what is "right"—and so rule out other forms of moral sensitivity.	When used exclusively, ethic becomes highly situational, feeling-oriented, subjective, or leads to conformity with what fits social expectations, group ethos, peer demands.
Predominant in most Western thought.	Predominant in Chinese ethical systems.	Predominant in Indian, Indonesian, and African systems.

(Adapted from Stackhouse 1978:328–330)

thought to have a particular *dharma,* fitting for that entity alone. The rational calculation of the good, and of the means to good ends, is more developed in the West, whereas the spiritual vision of the end purposes of life are more pronounced in India. In the West, at present, there is a loss of a profound sense of the ultimate purpose or ends of life coupled with a rather frantic and active establishment of proximate goals and a pragmatic attitude towards the development of means to fulfill them.

An Ethic of "Fit"

An ethic of fit is not to be construed as utilitarian self-interest, since it may be situational out of altruistic concern and compassion.

> Hindu ethics is not absolutist and unbending, but is reflective and contextual in its approach to ethical problems. To safeguard this situationalism from degenerating into privatism, the scriptures make it plain that exceptions are only to be made for the sake of others, not for one's own private advantage. (Crawford 1974:223)

Traditional Indonesian ethics, much like its Indian heritage, is an ethic of fit. The group solidarity, communal consensus, and neither-nor positions on differences all contribute to this strong preference for contextual ethics.

> In an ethical construct where the ideas of fit *(cocok),* feeling and intuition *(rasa),* and appropriateness *(pantes)* are dominant, the questions of "right" and the questions of "good" are understandably subordinated to the understanding of what is "fit." What is "right" and what is "good" are determined by the situation. (Darmaputera 1982:424)

The concern for harmony and the ethic of "fit" blend into one another, since in the Javanese worldview all things are in fixed place in a totalistic, monistic, hierarchical unity. As Darmaputera concludes (1982:216):

> Harmony of the universe is thus preserved by strict observance of fixed norms according to status and place in the order. This consequently implies moral pluralism or ethical relativism. There is no one objective and absolute norm of what is good and what is evil, right or wrong, fitting or unfitting. Everything depends on the place and rank of the actor. What is right for a king is not necessarily right for a commoner to do. There is no Truth but truths. What is right, good, and fitting is what is appropriate *(pantes)* with regard to the actor's status. Failure to fulfill one's obligation is not guilt or evil, but shame. Something has to be done or is to be avoided not because it is right or wrong, but because it is *pantes* or shameful *(ngisin-isini).*

This internalized value pairs notions of a worldview with instructions on personal conduct. Persons within the community are to conform by fitting in, and to practice an ethic of "fit" in situational responses to circumstances and to others.

> Between ethos and worldview, between the approved style of life and the assumed structure of reality, there is conceived to be a simple and fundamental congruence such that they complete one another and lend one another meaning. In Java, for example, this view is summed up in a concept

one hears continuously invoked, that of *tjotjog*. *Tjotjog* means to fit, as a key does in a lock, as an efficacious medicine does to a disease, as a solution does an arithmetical problem, as a man does with the woman he marries (if he does not, they will divorce). If your opinion agrees with mine we *tjotjog;* if the meaning of my name fits my character (and if it brings me luck), it is said to be *tjotjog*. Tasty food, correct theories, good manners, comfortable surroundings, gratifying outcomes all *tjotjog*. In the broadest and most abstract sense, two items *tjotjog* when their coincidence forms a coherent pattern which gives to each a significance and a value it does not in itself have. . . . The notion that life takes on its true import when human actions are tuned to cosmic conditions is widespread. (Geertz 1973:129)

The Javanese world is totalistic and monistic. The whole universe is seen as a totality in which all things are interdependent. All things visible and invisible, past, present, and future are parts, aspects, and emanations of one single wholeness called "God." All things come from and return to the one. This monistic universe is manifest in dualisms that fit each other ranked in hierarchies that fit together. So the equally balanced forces of left and right, sea and land, below and above, earth and heaven, internal and external live in tension and balance. The cosmos is elaborately ranked and ordered, with everything fulfilling a fixed place and status (Darmaputera 1982:212–215).

When order means fitting into hierarchy, then equality makes no sense, discussion of individual rights seems absurd, and real political participation is irrelevant. Change is viewed as a disturbance to the established order. All must be kept in balance. Each must be in the assigned place, fulfilling an assigned role and obeying predetermined rules and norms.

This outer-directed ethic, shaped by external controls and followed in external responsibility, leaves little to the person (not the "individual") to decide. The moral task is to fit the context, to behave fittingly, to remain fit to participate fully in the life of the community.

> The moral autonomy of the individual is considered as minimal. The individual person is considered "morally weak, with strong tendencies to follow drives and emotions, and should be controlled by fellow members who judge the person's behavior and eventually exercise pressure to make him or her conform." (Mulder 1978:46)

A man and a woman left alone in a room are assumed guilty of sexual indiscretion, so society seeks to shield itself from the passions of the individual. Yet within this social ethic of "fit," an altruistic morality is present in various religious groups such as the Javanese Kebatman mystics, who have condensed all ethics to the formula: "Not to be self-interested; to be active in the world; to beautify the world."

These three principles function as "fitting" responsibility. "Sacrificing self-interest" is discarding ambition, defeating passions, to achieve a quiet heart, wisdom, and harmonious conformity. "Active practice of good deeds" is to occur within one's station in life, accepting it as one's karma, or given role. "Adorning the world" is serving others freely, but not with the intent of changing the world, since one accepts the world hierarchy as given (Mulder 1978:38).

These values of hierarchy, conformity, and harmony combined with acceptance of one's ascribed or inherited status create a moral system perfectly suited to the small village or subsociety where direct social control can be exercised. People "know" each other thoroughly and can maintain a "fitting" system through the sanctions of mutual obligations and expectations. When persons move from village to city, the loss of the familiar and controlling context creates a vacuum, leaving them susceptible to a morality of what is "handiest" or vulnerable to mob emotion in times of social stress.

The Hindu ethic of "fit" is a systematic progression from the objective level—social ethics—to the subjective level—personal ethics—to the supraethical level—the ultimate end which is the life absolute and transcendental.

Objective ethics, the first stage of Hindu *dharma,* presents morality by social codes demanding external conformity. Psychologically, this is the stage of socialization and introjection. Conscience is understood as the interiorized voice of the group, and its power is the fear of punishment for duties undone. This is a "must consciousness" of conformity to external controls.

Subjective ethics, the second stage, moves from the "must consciousness" of conformity to the "ought consciousness" of inner direction. This transformation, arising from deepened self-awareness, concern for inner purity, and acting from free will, represents the movement from duty to external sanctions to free response from internal sanctions. Duties are driven by fears and prohibitions, but virtues arise from self-respect and chosen preferences. Duty is tribalistic, virtue is individualistic. Objective ethics springs from duty with an element of coercion, subjective ethics springs from virtue produced by love.

Transcendental ethics, the third stage, is a post-ethical plane of being. Ethics is only significant as long as one finds the world divided and in conflict; but the breakthrough to a higher plane of supramundane unity frees one to transcend all empirical contradictions—cold and heat, pleasure and pain, praise and blame, good and evil, right and wrong (Crawford 1974:223–229).

Moksha, "release," is a path for renouncing the world and attaining eternal salvation. In the quest for *moksha* one seeks hibernation by detaching from worldly goals, pleasures, and physical desires and gains freedom from passion, and especially the assertion of the ego.

The achievement of *moksha* ethics is not antinomian. Rather, love and compassion to all creatures are the spontaneous products of wisdom. Since the divine is seen in all things, one does not become otherworldly but takes social responsibilities all the more seriously.

If we define ethics as involving intention, will, freedom, the relation of one individual to another, we are imposing a Western concept on India. Admittedly, Hinduism has little or no ethics in this sense. But if ethics involves a set standard of behavior, based on duty, social custom, religious faith in *karma,* then Hinduism puts a high premium on moral conduct.

Hinduism has no concern for others as others, as individuals deserving separate treatment, but it does have concern for others as members of the group or as part of universal Reality. (Panikkar 1965:27–28)

The confusion that occurs along the boundary between an ethics of "right" and an ethics of "fit" emerges from a North American pastor's story in a Haitian setting. (See Case Study: Promises, Promises). Two contrasting ethics are at work. For the pastor the process of reasoning is: (1) I am lending the school bike, which is for school functions, so he must honor the institution's rules. (2) He gave his word of honor, which cannot be broken with impunity: truth is truth, integrity is integrity, right is clearly right. (3) He is a member of the same faith group and duty bound to be responsible; he will only break the agreement if it is an authentic life-and-death emergency.

For an ethic of fit, the criteria are equally clear. (1) A person's needs are more important than an institution's needs since institutions exist to serve persons. (2) My wedding is a once-in-a-lifetime occasion, but the class takes place every week. (3) If I am late I will be shamed before the whole community; if I do not return the bike I am shamed only before the pastor. (4) If I arrive on the cycle I am admired by all my friends; the pleasure is much greater than the difficulty of explaining later. (5)

CASE STUDY: Promises, Promises (Haiti)

Two hours before my weekly motorcycle trip to teach an extension class, a friend appeared at my door asking to borrow my motorcycle to travel to his wedding, thirty miles distant. He needed the cycle immediately. He had no other means of travel. He would be late if I did not help. If the cycle were not back in two hours I would have no way to meet my class. So I struck a compromise, on his word of honor as a fellow Christian and member of the same church. He would take the bike and a rider halfway, catch a ride with his brother, and the rider would return it in time for my travel to the class.

I waited the rest of the day, but the bike was not returned until late that night. Later the groom explained, "Pastor, I needed the bike, so I had to go all the way with it." I was puzzled at his willingness to break his word of honor with no regret after he had given me all the reassurance possible that he would keep his promise.

I discussed the situation with a Haitian pastor, who did not wait for the end of the story. "I know how it ends. He didn't send the bike back. You should have known that he wouldn't keep his word on a thing like that."

(Myers 1983)

Besides, the issue is not if but when I return the bike, and time is not a fixed unbreakable thing; time is people, time is relationships, time is for meeting each other's needs.

An Ethic of the "Good"

Traditional Chinese ethics have focused on the teleological, on the ends in view. This ethical position is powerful in its definition of what is normative, but without the internalization of "rightness and wrongness" that creates the depth constructs of guilt in deontologically oriented ethics.

The classic Chinese approach begins not from the "is" but from the "ought." John Keynes, an economist (1981:34–35), writes of the distinction between positive science and normative science. Positive science "is a body of systemized knowledge concerning what is; a normative science is a body of systemized knowledge discussing criteria of what ought to be."

In his analysis of pastoral care among the Chinese community of Singapore, Stephen Tan (1978:18) observes the dominance of normative processes.

> In the Chinese cultural tradition, it is always important for those who know a problem, whether objective or subjective, to make a normative judgment, to distinguish what is good and what is bad, and to tell people what ought to be done and what should not be done. If the scholar who knows the issue well remains independent of normative judgment, who else will be more competent to make normative judgment?

The goal-oriented ethic of the Chinese culture both permitted and supported a cultural revolution, with its transformation of a feudal to a collective society. As Mao Zedong wrote in 1940; "The aim of all our effort is the building of a new society and a new nation of the Chinese people. In such a new society and a new nation, there will be not only a new political organization and new economy, but a new culture as well" (Mao in Brandt and others 1952).

The means of collectivization might be measured in the deaths reported of millions of landlords and intellectuals, and millions placed in labor camps: revolutionary violence to replace or redress the old systemic violence. Revolution is—with the exception of Gandhi—invariably teleological, and the sweeping changes of the Cultural Revolution suggest a responsivity to such goal-oriented moral thought in the Chinese people.

The morality that has subsequently emerged is also markedly teleological. The central assumptions are framed in social and national goals, focused on the survival and growth of the nation: subordinate the personal to the communal; utilize communal and personal scrutiny of the individual to actualize harmonious sociality; displace "law" with ideology to deal with social needs above all others; center morality in the community rather than in the person (Spae 1976:162).

In concluding their study of morality in Theravada Buddhism, Little and Twiss (1978:236) note that the ethical processes, both intrapersonal and interpersonal are exclusively teleological. "Theravada Buddhism manifests a teleological bias with respect to practical justification. The *effects* or *consequences* of attitudes and acts determine practical goodness and badness, rightness and wrongness. We have encountered no evidence of deontological reasoning."

In this end-directed morality the goals are set in polarities. Moral actions—the good—produce capacity to trust, integrity, no distinction of class barriers, cooperation, confidence in leaders, enhanced self-respect, and fulfillment of individual potentialities within communal fulfillment. Immoral actions—the evil—produce inability to trust, duplicity, class distinction, noncooperative attitudes, exploitation of others, low self-respect, and dwarfed individual capacities.

The ethics of right, good, and fit, viewed psychologically, are suggestive of the three developmental controls. The ethic of right has occurred in cultures predominantly concerned with issues of guilt and forgiveness surrounding transgression. The inexorable conscience of Western peoples is rooted in the deontological finality of right and wrong as givens in existence. The ethic of the good has shaped cultures where shame is the ascendant control process. Shame, arising from a falling short of the ideal self, failing the goal, betraying the end espoused by one's community, is the inevitable effect of transgression of behavior codes or boundaries. The ethic of fit brings together anxiety about exclusion, inclusion, shame at reproach, and guilt from failure of responsibility, but the element of anxiety appears as the predominant control.

The three aspects of ethics, like the three varieties of control, all occur in every person or culture, but in parallel fashion we may argue that one tends to be the ordering process for the others in the constellation.

Cross-Cultural Moral Development

The most thorough cross-cultural research based on empirical methodology has come from the work of Jean Piaget. This is of particular import on the study of moral reasoning, because the most significant stream of research on moral development stems from his empirical research into structural epistemology. Piaget's great contribution is in the formulation of sequentially emerging but often parallel stages of functioning.

A stage is a broad period of development with certain distinct characteristics. Stages frequently overlap in the person's development, and one stage is not necessarily exclusively present in any given time after the acquisition of more than the first. Stages frequently overlap; they may run parallel; they vary in duration from person to person and may survive into adulthood as enduring levels or styles of moral behavior.

Piaget (1932:26–29) observed that (1) the child's understanding of rules seems to progress through three stages of increasing complexity, (2) these understandings are related to the development of cognitive structures, and (3) each stage facilitates the ability to enter into different kinds of interpersonal relationships, so that (4) each stage is characterized by a different understanding of the nature of authority.

The first stage, *the egocentric,* is marked by an absence of rules. Those rules encountered are seen as interesting events but not as obligatory realities. The functional sanctions are immediate anticipations of pleasure or pain. This is the morality of egocentrism.

The second stage, *the transcendental or heteronomous,* emerges with the advent of concrete thought ability. Rules are now seen as sacred and untouchable. They are concrete, objective realities in the environment that must be accepted and obeyed because they come as commands from authoritative persons. As these are internalized, the authority no longer need be present. The concept grasped is that moral rules have no real significance except to compel conformity to the letter, not the spirit, of the law. This is the morality of restraint.

The third stage, *the formal,* arises with the capacity for reciprocity and social give-and-take. The social-relational nature of moral rules becomes a functional understanding. Rules are not imposed from authorities above but serve as ways of resolving group difficulties by means of social contract. Flexibility and adaptability are now possible. The difference between the concrete and the formal is so great that Piaget calls them two moralities. The morality of restraint is heteronomous, authoritarian, external, unchangeable. The morality of cooperation is egalitarian, democratic, based on collaboration and mutual respect. Within the third stage, there are two substages: "reciprocity," which retains the legalism of the preceding stage in a rigid egalitarianism, and "equity," which gives consideration to the unique factors in each situation, informing reciprocity with altruism to produce a creative, flexible, pliable concern for others.

Following Piaget's theory and research, Kohlberg (1969) reasons that just as cognitive development has a normal developmental course, so moral reasoning can be traced through a natural universal pattern of increasing maturity. The more mature can be considered a better or more desirable form than earlier ways of moral thinking.

The implications of Kohlberg's theory are fascinating to social scientists and educators. If people move in the same direction in moral development, perhaps we can expect universal similarities to exist underneath the behavioral differences. In a world where persons are universally maturing toward principled moral reasoning, perhaps differences can be surpassed and universal codes of right and wrong emerged. World law might emerge from effective education and eventual thoughtful negotiation. If moral systems can be evaluated by levels of maturity, then objective standards of good could be developed for human societies or for a universal society. If objective morality can be defined, then moral values are not relative to culture, time, and place as many contemporary theorists believe.

Kohlberg's findings, in longitudinal studies of males in several cultures, indicated the sequence of three levels of moral development—

preconventional, conventional, and postconventional—that parallel Piaget's work. The six stages within these are (1) punishment and obedience orientation, (2) instrumental hedonism, (3) good-boy nice-girl conformity, (4) law-and-order orientation, (5) social contract or legalistic principled orientation, and (6) orientation to universal ethical principles.

Research findings by a variety of scholars supporting Kohlberg's sequence of growth in moral reasoning among Western males offer significant support. There is a progression of moral reasoning abilities from early childhood to late adolescence (Kohlberg and Kramer 1969; Kuhn and others 1977; Rest and others 1974). These changes are associated with beliefs about law and order, rules, and justice (Tapp and Kohlberg 1971). Children are able to comprehend reasoning only one level above their current stage (Turiel 1966).

Political ideologies were found to parallel moral reasoning in research among students and faculty at eight major universities. Preconventional levels favored radical political action and even violence, conventional levels were politically conservative, and postconventional levels were political liberals. Natural science faculty and administrators tended to be conventional-conservative, social science and humanities postconventional and liberal (Fontana and Noel 1973).

Cross-cultural studies in Africa and Asia suggest that people in different cultures do undergo similar changes in the development of moral thought; however, cultures differ in the level of maturity achieved (Kohlberg and Turiel 1971; White and others 1978). Adults in preliterate cultures tend to prefer solutions that match the preconventional and early conventional stages. In the Bahamas, researchers had difficulty finding adults beyond stage 3 moral reasoning (White 1975), as contrasted with adults in more technically advanced cultures, who prefer "morally advanced" options. Kohlberg hypothesizes that preliterate preferences for concrete thought are due to little use of written language, so they stabilize at earlier stages. In technologically advanced societies, written language, abstract symbolic thought, and rapid change facilitate growth in reasoning to more "mature levels."

The assumption of a universal ethic based on research using Western males as the primary index for maturity is more suggestive of an ethical imperialism than of a universal ethic.

> It is dangerous business to posit a hierarchy of moral dispositions when that hierarchy allows the highly educated adult male a disproportionate likelihood of being on top. In effect, Kohlberg's theory places men of western society in a position of moral superiority. By implication, others are placed in inferior positions—a point of view that may have unfortunate consequences. (Gergen and Gergen 1981:229)

Research on Western women's decisions about abortion indicated that decisions were based not on abstract principles but on a sense of responsibility toward the significant people in their lives. This would fall in Kohlberg's stage 3, but it may be a higher moral process if viewed on a continuum that values responsibility and integrity of relationship rather than rights and principles (Gilligan 1982:62–63).

The first three stages in Kohlberg's sequence closely parallel the fear, hedonism, and conformity motivations of Piaget's research and are empirically supportable. The final three move from legalism to utilitarianism to Kantian universal categorical imperatives. The close parallel to Western deontological and teleological ethics and the presence of Kantian structures in both Piaget's and Kohlberg's work suggest the Western philosophical values implicit in research design and methodology.

The focus on abstract principles is rooted in a Western Newtonian view of a static and stable world in which propositions, laws, and abstract rules of morality are assumed. Many social scientists suggest that dialectic thinking is able to deal with change and complexity in a way that principled thinking cannot. In moral reasoning, the principle is not the end of ethical thought but the beginning. The opposing values that are in conflict in most ethical decisions are given full weight and respected even as one searches for a synthesis. Research on moral choice shows that dialectical thought increases with age, education, and practice of moral reflection. Perhaps it is a higher level of reasoning than Kohlberg's Kantian vision of universal principles (Basseches 1981:227).

The distinction between moral reasoning and moral behavior allows one to rate high in moral reasoning but low in actual moral behavior. Do the stages thus have discriminant validity and predictive utility?

The "progress" from the legality of stage 4 via the utilitarianism of stage 5 reaches the universal imperatives of a Kantian stage 6, with the central principle being justice. Are not other central themes equally acceptable as the pinnacle of principled behavior? Among the classic virtues—love, justice, prudence, temperance, and courage—only one has been appointed supreme. The Christian ethicist may see "the love of God and humanity" or the profound delight in "knowing and doing God's will" in a balanced commitment to all the virtues as an equally valid expression of voluntary, autonomous, principled behavior. Japanese ethics may choose beauty; Indonesian, harmony; Chinese, utility; African, solidarity; and so forth.

The preference for cognitive psychology rather than the affective (which deals with feelings and emotions) and the conative (which deals with active doing and striving) leaves Kant's account of moral development much too formal. Passions for justice, sympathy for humanity, and concern for mutuality contain emotion, intention, and intuition as well as cognition in the full agency of the moral person. These may well be the roots of moral life. Faith development affirms that love of God and love of humanity are inseparable and intensify one another, achieving actualization when localized in a living interacting community.

Cognitive approaches to moral development offer only one layer of the moral process. Ethicist Ralph Potter (1969:23–24) offers a conceptual schema for visualizing the interpenetration of faith and moral development. In the making of any moral decision, four analytically separable but intermeshed factors come into play.

1. *The empirical, factual definition of the situation or dilemma.* This includes the range of available alternative actions and assumptions about their probable consequences.

2. *The mode of ethical reasoning to be employed.* The kinds of moral logic the agent brings to the weighing of all relevant moral considerations. Kohlberg's stages are focused here on the structural characteristics of the various modes of ethical reasoning.

3. *The affirmations of loyalty.* Consciously or unconsciously, we choose the primary object of concern. We create expressive symbols that represent a center of value, locus of commitment, or source of identity. It makes a difference whether they are dedicated to a nation, an ideology, a church, "humanity," an ideal community, or some other object of loyalty.

4. *The theological beliefs or assumptions.* These include theological beliefs concerning God, humanity, and human destiny and anthropological assumptions concerning the range of human freedom and human power to predict and control historical events.

Any satisfactory view of moral development must invite the interpenetration of these four factors. Cognitive, affective, volitional, and conative elements are all inseparable parts of truly moral being and behaving.

These critiques all serve to question whether the sequence of stages of moral thought is an adequate measure of moral reasoning, either cross-culturally or within a given culture.

Simply because empirical research indicates that Kohlberg's sixth stage of moral reasoning is an end result of a sequential, irreversible, cross-cultural sequence of human development, it is not proven that justice should be the supreme universal value. Physical disintegration and death are also sequential, finally irreversible, and cross-cultural, but that does not mean we should encourage the process. Kohlberg has demonstrated that if we provide certain conditions for people (e.g., moral reasoning at one level beyond their own), they will grow in certain predictable directions. Physical educators tell us that given the right conditions for children, almost everyone could run a five-minute mile. Behaviorists have demonstrated that, with the right reinforcement, pigeons play Ping-Pong. This does not mean necessarily that all pigeons should play Ping-Pong or that all people run a five-minute mile or reason morally. These are value choices that cannot be proven, ranked, or imposed (Kirschenbaum 1977:14).

Ethics as Storytelling and Story Living

Ethical thinking, in all cultures, seems to spring more immediately and cogently from stories than from moral dictums or principles. Vision emerges from the stories heard, the dramas experienced, the life-story events observed rather than from rationales or theories held by persons or groups.

Proverbs and stories are indirect and impersonal means of engaging in deep discussions. Among traditional peoples, face and feelings are guarded closely, so direct questions and confrontations are not useful. Stories, myths, and proverbs allow issues on fundamental problems of social relations, authority and obedience, and ethics of choice in difficult situations to surface.

> Virtue, in the context of African storytelling, resides both in the ability to argue eloquently and in the ability to demonstrate a command of tradition . . . it is the flow of discussion that counts, not the finding of a solution. Through argument, the customary practices of the community are rehearsed and celebrated. . . . Many of the moral stories and dilemma tales alike focus on aspects of living "correctly" within the family. (Abrahams 1983:108)

African moral teaching is offered by the Hausa dilemma tale, as in the following example (adapted from Abrahams 1983:117–118). The ethical issues that rise along the boundary of self-realization vs. communal obligation and the contrast of vertical obligations to preceding generations vs. horizontal commitments all are highlighted in situations of authentic conflict.

> There was once a poor man who had no work but to catch ground squirrels. Taking his son to work with him one day, he bid him watch at the hole while he dug from the other entrance, but the squirrel escaped the son's stick and made off. So the father struck the son and left him lying senseless.
>
> Later that evening, a wealthy Arab merchant passed by, picked up the boy, brought him to his senses, washed away the ants from his eyes and nose, and dressed him in rich garments. Since he had no son he made him his own.
>
> Now in this area, the sons of rich merchants competed on the racetrack, so the Arab gave the boy a priceless horse with rich trappings and said, "Whatever the other riders do—you do it too." So he rode with the rich merchants' sons, but great arguments broke out as to whose son he truly was.
>
> So the other fathers, to test if he was truly born to wealth, told their sons, "Tomorrow, give away your horses; then we shall see if he has the generosity which demonstrates true wealth." When the boys gave away their horses, the Arab boy did the same. The next day, the fathers told them to draw the sword and cut down the horse at the end of the gallop. And all did so. Indeed, the Arab's new son left the saddle and trappings as well.
>
> Time passed and the Muslim festival came. And the young man rode in the procession in great finery. And it came to pass that the squirrel digger came to town and joined the crowd. When he saw his son he cried, "Hey, get down from that horse, you rascal, it is not your father's. Look at your brothers. One has killed nine squirrels, another ten. And you are lazy and idle." And the Arab said, "Quiet, keep it to yourself, I will settle with you."
>
> In the evening, the Arab saddled three horses, and all three rode out into the bush. Suddenly he produced a sword and gave it to the boy, saying, "Now! Either me or your father—cut down one of us!"
>
> Which shall he kill—the Arab who had given him so much, or his own father, who had struck him unconscious and left him to die because of a ground squirrel?

Storytelling, in African traditional cultures, facilitates the discussion and discernment of an "ethics of fit." The fit must be with the present participants and with the ancestors, "the living dead." The wisdom of stories from the past, freshly interpreted and applied to the present, maintains the fit with all levels of the society—past, present, and future. Such a fit is better expressed in metaphor than by proposition. In all cultures, metaphors are the root of ethical choice and action. The stories told, the character being formed in the teller and the hearers, and the community that owns the storytelling process are all interrelated and indivisible.

To introduce a young person to moral life and to develop authentic character is a group task, a communal process carried out through corporate storytelling. The stories heard at the parent's knee or by the tribal campfire can unite descriptive, prescriptive, and relational ethics into a believable pattern for moral choice.

> The metaphors that determine our vision must form a coherent story if our lives are to have duration and unity. Such stories create the context of meaning for the concrete moral rules and principles to which we adhere. There is no principled way to separate the "religious" from the "moral" in such stories. (Hauerwas 1974:3)

Metaphors and stories suggest how we should perceive ourselves, our peers, our world. Stories, the preferred way of thinking of most humans, provide narrative connections and explanations that provide coherent meaning for our lives. As James Olney writes (1972:30–31):

> Metaphors are something known and of our making, or at least of our choosing, that we put to stand for, and so to help us understanding something unknown and not of our making. . . . In other words, the meaning emerges with our perception of a pattern, and there can obviously be no pattern in chronologically or geographically discrete items and elements. We must connect one thing with another and finally assume the whole design of which the element is only a part. Metaphor supplies such a connection. Metaphor is essentially a way of knowing. To a wholly new sensational or emotional experience, one can give sufficient organization only by relating it to the already known, only by perceiving a relation between this experience and another experience already placed, ordered, and incorporated.

The essential metaphors of our lives are assimilated early and lie buried deeply, often within the unconscious. The earliest perceptions of self, significant others, and the environment are images, not propositional sentences, and are evoked in particular moments as emotive flashbacks, metaphorical condensations of vivid life experiences, feeling-toned pictures of that person's inner reality.

The human brain simultaneously carries on two complementary processes of thought, what some psychological research terms right- and left-brain functions. The "left brain" performs rational, analytical, linear functions and the "right brain" metaphorical, synthesizing, affective, and holistic functions. People communicate with two contrasting languages

—precise, logical, rational left-brain discourse and metaphorical, figurative, pictorial right-brain speech. The most important function of right-brain thought is to synthesize each person's life experience into a metaphor or portrait that provides a "holistic world image" unique to that person. This world image is utilized to interpret the world and make sense of outer realities (Watzlawick 1978). As psychologist Robert Samples concludes (1976:19):

> When an idea comes into the metaphoric mind, a sudden rush of relationships flashes into being, and the original thought expands rapidly outward into a network of new holistic perceptions. The role of metaphoric thinking is to invent, to create, and to challenge conformity by extending what is known into new meadows of knowing.

The metaphors, images, and stories of morality—those surrounding shame, guilt, duty, obligation, privilege, reward, debt, gift, failure, success, obedience, rebellion, autonomy, conformity, selfishness, and sacrifice, to begin a partial listing—these can evoke powerful images, affective moods, and feeling-colored attitudinal sets. Stories connect these mood images into moral montages of memories, learnings, warnings, and injunctions.

In therapy or growth, people change only when the essential metaphors that direct their emotional, relational, and moral life come to awareness and are reframed or replaced by new, more inclusive, or more liberating metaphors. Our stories shape our life, and only new stories or old stories renewed can reshape our living.

> Ethical statements are intelligibly interpretable at all only if their implicit "stories" are explicated. The need for stories then lies precisely in the fact that policy-statements are about intentions to act in certain ways, and action is inconceivable apart from stories. It is stories that display how the concepts "action, person, will, heart, inner and outer" are used. The precise meaning of and hence the difference between Confucian policy-statements and Christian policy-statements are entirely a function of their differing stories. (Langford and Poteat 1968:217)

Our ethical behavior and reasoning are guided by the stories we tell and retell to instruct ourselves in seeing clearly what is and what ought to be.

The Buddhist, remembering the story of self-sacrifice of the *bodhisattva* sacrificing his own body to provide food for the starving tigress and her cubs, sees the metaphor for compassion. The ideal of Mahayana Buddhist spirituality is formed by the belief that the *bodhisattva* does not enter *nirvana,* leaving the rest of us behind to struggle on alone with our human fate, but continually reenters time and history to assist others in achieving their redemption. A Christian may find the metaphor, which offers human life for animal life, less compelling than the belief that ensues. Yet the Christian's commitment to self-sacrifice in agape love rises from the story of God becoming human and sacrificing the self in compassion for humans in parallel metaphor.

The Confucian metaphors, the Zen koans, the Jewish Wisdom stories, the tribal narratives of Indonesia, the African epics all instruct their ethics and reinstruct the participant in situations requiring response. It is the metaphor, not the moral injunction or aphorism, that has power to direct behavior, particularly for the three fourths of the world's population who think, with rare exception, in stories and images rather than in linear sequential reasoning.

An ethical example from a Western Christian would clarify this process of reasoning by moral metaphor. A person may live in such mutuality that he or she exemplifies the rule to treat others justly, serve their needs sacrificially, and love others as the self. But if asked for the central maxim of this principled behavior, the person would reply with a story —Christ's story of the final judgment and the call to treat all humans as if they were sisters and brothers of Christ (Matt. 25). It is clear that this person's behavior is the fulfillment of many ethical rules, but his or her self-understanding rises from a story, a metaphor, an internal image. In fact, it has a more comprehensive power than even a network of interlocking propositions, because the person can look, through this commanding story-vision, at others as actually the sisters and brothers of Christ (Hauerwas 1974:73).

Personal identity is formed from the cluster of significant stories that define an I and a me. Families exist in meaningful connection by virtue of their shared history—the sequence of stories. Clans, tribes, ethnic groups, nations require their stories and their history as the primary means of self-definition. And the moral processes of a people rise from the ethical import of participating in "our story."

> To be moral persons is to allow stories to be told through us so that our manifold activities gain a coherence that allows us to claim them for our own. The significance of stories is the significance of character for the moral life, as our experience itself, if it is to be coherent, is but an incipient story. Our character is constituted by the rules, metaphors, and stories that are combined to give a design or unity to the variety of things we must and must not do in our lives. Therefore it is crucial to our moral life to allow the metaphors that make up our vision to check and balance each other in terms of their appropriateness for the various demands of our life and the overall life plan that we live. (Hauerwas 1974:74–75)

In focusing on the narrative nature and the metaphoric roots of our ethics, we dare not deny that moral reasoning is also a significant forming and norming element. Thus we shall proceed to examine moral development in cross-cultural perspective.

But its role as rational arbiter is a more formal one—providing form while story and metaphor, compassion and commitment are the moral content. Both are necessary for a living ethic.

> Even though moral principles are not sufficient in themselves for our moral existence, neither are stories sufficient if they do not generate principles that are morally significant. Principles without stories are subject to perverse interpretation (i.e., they can be used in immoral stories), but stories without principles will have no way of concretely specifying the actions and prac-

tices consistent with the general orientation expressed by the story. (Hauerwas 1974:89)

A Theology of Moral Character

The central concerns of the discipline of ethics include not only what is right and wrong about human actions and good and bad about their consequences, but also what is moral human character. What are the roots of morally good and bad action?

This third concern is pivotal to much of the pastoral counselor's perceptions, interventions, and therapeutic intentions. Is the human person morally capable or incapable? Is the personality biased toward evil or innately tending toward good?

Four possible views of the moral character of human nature shape how one approaches ethics, moral education, and pastoral counseling. Is human nature essentially good, evil, neutral, or both evil and good?

1. *Human nature is essentially good.* Evil is external in source, not inherent in human nature. It is, in fact, a denial of or a contradiction to human nature. Evil is subhuman, inhumane.

Obviously, people are not universally good, and evil may exceed the good in persons, but such evil originates in the environment, in the destructive socialization of the person, in the contradictions of existence in the world.

In spite of the evil context and the internalization of evil, there remains an inner drive toward the good, an unfolding tendency toward growth. Much of evil is the distortion of these drives—hate is frustrated love, dishonesty is distorted self-protection.

Pastoral counseling or moral guidance, from this perspective, places high confidence in the self-directing wisdom of the human person and little faith in external forces, community supports, or social structures to guide authentic moral behavior.

2. *Human nature is essentially evil.* There is an inherent destructiveness and deceptiveness to the human nature that must be directed by socialization, contained by civilization, transformed by religious experience.

Persons are not totally corrupt or evil, but every faculty, emotion, potentiality is affected by the evil, which turns even the best intentions toward self-interest to the exclusion of social interest. Thus what is appraised as good is covertly evil, or virtue arises from unvirtuous motivations. Moral and ethical values serve to inhibit evil and channel the innate drives toward socially productive and cooperative ends. The intrinsic evil within must be controlled, shaped, reformed by the sanctions of civilization and its socialization.

3. *Human nature is neutral,* neither good nor evil, but capable of becoming either or both. No tendency is innate; rather, the capacity for development in either or both directions is essential to humanness.

The society, the developmental experiences, and the crises of life shape and determine the directions the person will take in moral, social, and personality development. This places great responsibility upon the educational experiences of the person because these write upon a blank slate —*tabula rasa*—the directives for life. Since evil tendencies do not require inhibition, the processes may be direct, positive, educative.

4. *Human nature is essentially both good and evil.* This combines views 1 and 2, seeing both potentialities as essential, innate core qualities in humanness. To be human is to be morally divided, ambiguous, contradictory at the core. Rather than perceiving human beings as good but tainted with evil, or evil but on occasion good, or alternately good or evil, or a blend of good and evil traits or characteristics, this view sees the human being as inevitably mixed in central motivations.

Authentic goodness may in itself be the occasion of evil; love and hate, compassion and apathy are inextricably intermixed. Moral growth occurs as the resources for creativity are enhanced and the capacities for destructive attitudes and acts are controlled or redirected.

Human beings are not morally neutral; they are born with equal tendencies toward both evil and good. In the act of deciding, the human person becomes what he or she wills to become. Evil is experienced before the capacity to choose evil is developed—we are sinned against before we sin—so the tendencies to both good and evil are nourished, modeled, reinforced by the context before they are the content of our thought or choice.

A pastoral theology that takes the whole human experience—both the good and the evil—into serious account must challenge the positive and the neutral theories as optimistic rather than realistic. The view of humans as essentially evil is equally problematic. Its pessimism ignores the healing potential within and the social responsibility between persons. Both good and evil are present in humans and the human community.

The biblical record affirms both original goodness and original sin in the human experience, and the capacity for both good and evil emerges from the core of the human psyche or soul. As Reinhold Niebuhr observes (1964:161), "Christianity measures the status of humans more highly and their virture more severely than any other alternative view."

The Human Condition

Ethical reflection is shaped by one's vision of the human condition. Are humans beings of sufficient freedom, rationality, and responsibility to be truly moral agents? Or are we essentially determined by economic necessity, historical inevitability, or cyclical human destinies?

What is the human condition? Are we masters of life, the only agents who can direct this world and its future? Are we fixed links in the chain of existence, determined by the cycles of fate and destiny? Or are we something more—persons with both evil and good in our roots as well as our acts? These three options have been expressed tersely by ethicist Max Stackhouse (1984:271):

> Is the human condition such that all heaven and earth depends on our human decisions and human actions? If so, humans are and ought to be masters of life. Does what we do determine everything? This is the view predominantly held in [Marxism] and by minorities in all lands.

This perspective is shared by surprising combinations of groups. Not only Marx and Lenin see social forms, meaning, and history determined by willed human actions; those Christians of evangelical perspective who focus primarily on "justification by faith alone" and who hold faith as a blind leap against human reason are standing on the same premise. "When justification by faith (not justification by grace) is central, the human decision to believe, utterly beyond reason or precisely against reason, becomes the determining factor of salvation and meaning within the human heart" (Stackhouse 1984:271). What Marx applies to the society, such Christians focus on the individual, but the central perspective is the same. Humans are called to decide the fate of soul and society by an existential decision and action that are predetermined by either the inexorable logic of human history or by the predestining power of God. This position takes many forms in various cultures where a high premium is placed on human responsibility for the future.

> Or is the human condition such that we always shall be what we are, and cannot be other than what we are? Is it true that the law of the universe is such that each must accept and live out the various eternally recurring stages of life in accord with the natural hierarchical structures of being? Is the primary task to develop our consciousness of who we truly are so that we can more appropriately fit into the divine ecology? (Stackhouse 1984:272)

This is the predominant view of Hinduism, of classic Gnosticism, and of many other religious and cultural groups who call on humans to accept their being, respond to the natural harmonies within the soul and the society, and cultivate the native virtues of human existence. This view sees all humans as having a piece of the universal spiritual reality that requires cultivation. Each person is to be what he or she is, each group to be what they are, and this differs for each and all.

In this vision, one's fate or destiny directs the recurring cycles of individual, familial, and social existence. The wise person finds the appropriate station in life, the place in the order of things, through acceptance of what is and realization of the self that is. This tends to produce a moral passivity and a deferring of ethical responsibility to structures outside the self and is often seen as inexorable and unavoidable.

> Or is it the case that we are sinners—that is, that humanity stands under a power, a purpose, and a moral law that we cannot make or unmake, that we cannot be or actualize in our own existence. If this is the basic human condition, we are called upon to "own"—that is, to accept as guiding for our lives—principles which we do not construct and which we cannot cultivate out of our own resources. We stand in a relationship to an "other" by which we are empowered and called to obedience. We are called to bond ourselves to that which we are not and cannot be, recognizing all other

persons as having a dignity because *the* Other is in relation to them. On the basis of these relationships, clarified by mutual, rational discourse, we find a constitutional basis for respect for all "others," we find a courage to transform "natural" hierarchical relationships of sex and kinship toward a new voluntary mutuality, and we find the will to subordinate the pretentious wills of class, party, and regime to principles of righteousness. (Stackhouse 1984:272)

This view preserves freedom because the freedom is guaranteed by the transcendent point of reference by which persons can be clearly seen and from which people can be liberated from the determinisms of psyche, of family, of culture. It is rational, since it cannot be rationally refuted on the basis of its own presuppositions, as can many alternate views, including Hinduism and Marxism.

This perspective is potentially universal and it is highly practical in guiding a society toward meeting human needs. As Stackhouse concludes (1984:275):

1. A creed which holds that there is a metaphysical reality other than humanity, but which humans can know in some measure, provides a basis for both freedom and rationality; only a metaphysical reality which transcends the accidents, determinations, and subjectivism of a particular culture, history, social arrangement, or group belief can be the basis for reliable cross-cultural judgments, for genuine universality, and for practical implementation of human rights in diverse social contexts.

2. The kind of social group most likely to bring about a concern for human rights in all societies is that kind of group which does not have direct power but which actually and practically bonds people into communities of discourse and solidarity which have no other purpose than the reconciliation of humans to one another throughout the world under a transcendent norm and power. Freedom of religion, in the concrete social sense of the right to organize groups on a voluntary basis around ultimate concerns for the sake of all, is the primary social factor in the historical actualization of human rights.

Western ethics has tended to begin from human points of reference. What is good for human beings? What are right relationships between persons? What is good for human beings and for their world? This human-centered stream of ethics is dominant with both theological and secular ethicists. "Man is the measure of all things," said the Greek philosopher Protagoras. The horizontal elements of ethical decision making proceed without any transcendental referent point. But perhaps the creator, rather than the creatures, should be the measure of all that is.

A theocentric ethic, as James Gustafson argues (1981:88–89), would no longer see the good of humankind as the moral measure of all things. God is the referent point of ethics, and a transcendent point of origin permits a whole new perspective on decisions of what is good or evil, right or wrong.

The universality of God's activity in all humanity is seen by many ethicists as the crucial moral datum, and one must begin from the understanding of God's action rather than examining human capacities. As Lehmann writes of a Koinonia ethics, "What is ethically common to all must be understood not as a proof of a common rational moral nature but as a sign that the humanizing action of God includes all humanity" (Lehmann 1963:153).

We can affirm our human commonalities as an expression of God's Lordship over all, those who know God by name and those who do not.

> The Christian community, then, is not the only one that generates mores —all do. It is not the only community under God's Lordship—all are. It is not the only community that nurtures those bonds which facilitate the realization of universal community—many do, and the church does her share of the fracturing of that community. Yet history, language, symbols, and meanings again and again break the church open to a more universal commonwealth. (Nelson 1971:53)

The pastoral counselor, recognizing that human character is composed of capacities for both good and evil, and seeing the human condition as that of accountable persons under God, finds the moral referent point God, not humanity. In the values that are transcendent to our human relationships and individual experiences, we can find a basis for evaluating history, culture, and human community.

The Pastoral Counselor as Ethicist

No form of counseling or psychotherapy is morally, politically, or culturally neutral. There are values implicit in any approach to giving care, and these become explicit in all acts of care. Just as all care-giving takes place within a particular political and cultural context, it also occurs within a moral context. Any attempt to counsel in a morally neutral frame of reference is in vain because such a choice is selecting a value-free option that is one of a variety of possible moral positions.

Secular as well as religiously committed ethicists have insisted that psychotherapy own and clarify its moral assumptions in responsible fashion. Rather than seeing its role as primarily negating abuses in moralism, it must affirm healthful valuing. As Erich Fromm comments (1947:6):

> While psychoanalysis has tremendously increased our knowledge of man, it has not increased our knowledge of how man ought to live and what he ought to do. Its main function has been that of "debunking," of demonstrating that value judgments and ethical norms are the rationalized expressions of irrational—and often unconscious—desires and fears, and that they therefore have no claim to objective validity.

A quarter century later (1972:6), Fromm returned to this theme with a concern for the recovery of the personal moral center—the soul.

> Psychology has tried to imitate the natural sciences and the experimental methodologies. In this scientific orientation, dimensions such as values,

conscience, and knowledge of good and evil were pushed aside and relegated to philosophy, and declared insignificant for psychology. Psychology thus became a science lacking its main subject matter, the soul.

"There is a moral context to all acts of care," says Browning (1976:11), as a basic hypothesis for looking at the structures of values which surround all counseling and psychotherapy.

> It is important for both the counseling minister and the secular psychotherapist to recognize this truth . . . for the minister because it is a primary task to provide this moral context as a *background* to pastoral care and counseling. . . . For the secular psychotherapist . . . it is becoming increasingly acknowledged that secular therapists assume a moral world that extends beyond the therapeutic situation and provides a moral horizon to the therapy even though it may not be directly invoked by therapists in the process of counseling.

The secular therapist, perceiving her or his role as a social scientist, has largely eliminated moral dialogue from the counseling hour and limited exploration of these issues when they inevitably rise. But as one therapist observes; "Psychotherapy, then, is primarily concerned with a technical goal, the preservation and restoration of mental health; nevertheless its own development leads it, inevitably, to take up the role of moral legislator" (Margolis 1966:175).

In virtually all major forms of both secular psychotherapy and pastoral psychotherapy in the Western world, moral conversation is so rare as to be described as avoided. Having recognized the destructive power of moralism for increasing the repressive forces of the superego and exaggerating the intrapunitive action of the conscience, most caregivers have come to consider the discussion of moral values as irrelevant to the therapeutic task and have dealt solely with their effects on the person's intrapsychic balance. The care with which psychotherapists seek to avoid becoming moralistic with their counselees, or to suggest their own moral values, is seen as a measure of their ability to be effectively neutral in transferent relationships. Effective pastoral counseling and secular psychotherapy both seek to maintain a clear boundary between a moralism that seeks to direct, coerce, or punish by use of evaluation and an authentic moral concern that arises in both counselor and counselee for discovering what is healthful, worthy, moral.

The pastoral counselor has a direct professional responsibility as a minister, and a personal commitment as a woman or man of faith, to help form and maintain the moral values of the community. The secular therapist, although rarely seeing the task as including the shaping of personal and social morality, is increasingly coming to recognize having an implicit part of all therapy and an essential part of all helping relationships.

> Most psychotherapists would like to assume the stance of moral neutrality and leave to the minister, philosopher, or poet the task of projecting society's normative values and standards of conduct. The very nature of psychotherapy, however, makes this difficult. Psychotherapy attempts to help

persons with their pain and suffering. It aspires to help individuals to change the course of their lives and to grow. It frequently holds out images of cure. Insofar as it tries to move people from some state of unhappiness and distress to a new state of happiness or well-being, psychotherapy has native parallels to the dynamics of religion. (Browning 1976:12–13)

We humans are "valuing beings" and we do not live apart from our valuing experience. Values that we fail or neglect or reject have their effects upon our psychic as well as our moral lives. Values that we prize and follow may be conjunctive and integrative or disjunctive and destructive.

It is being recognized increasingly that value conflicts and value ambivalences are themselves a major cause of problems in living and in even the more severe forms of mental illness. One of the strongest assets to good mental health is the existence of a relatively firm and accurate moral universe which gives indices to the good and suggests appropriate actions to reach the good. (Browning 1976:98)

Human change, whether in growth, reconstruction, or healing, must include conversations on values and valuing. The uniqueness of the pastoral counselor is rooted in the valuing community which the counselor represents. "To fulfill the traditional role as a mediator of religiocultural values, the pastoral counselor must be as much a moral philosopher (or moral theologian) as an expert in the diagnosis of emotional and interpersonal dynamics" (Browning 1976:37).

In the counseling process there are multiple moral dimensions occurring.

First, the moral context, for the pastoral counselor, is symbolized by the role and setting in which the counseling occurs. The pastor is a representative of a community of faith; the church is the "holy turf" which represents that community and its accountability before God, the ground of morality. As invitation, the setting frees both to reflect on the moral dimensions of life; as inhibition, the setting may evoke memories, feelings, or fears of the repressive and binding aspects of morality in the counselee's past experiences or present situation.

Second, the moral content that emerges in the counseling process invites exploration. The mutuality of love, the responsibility of relationships, the reciprocity of meeting needs, the justice of distribution of opportunity, the equity of power, the balance of union and separation all have moral as well as functional and relational aspects. Responding to such issues with empathic or interpathic understanding rather than evaluation or moralization invites depth and wholeness to the therapeutic process.

We have learned from modern psychotherapy that we must not moralize, and that we should educe from the troubled person the initiatives and value framework needed to improve that individual. We have learned that lesson well, and it was an important lesson to master. But we now need to rediscover the ancient context in which to place our nonmoralistic attitudes. We need to learn that we can afford the luxury of not moralizing only when we have already developed a relatively firm moral outlook which both the helper and the person being helped can affirm. Only when our pastoral care contains within it dimensions of practical moral inquiry do we earn the right temporarily to relax these moral concerns and concentrate specifically on the emotional difficulties and the unique feelings of the person for whom we care. (Browning 1976:15)

Third, the moral conduct of the therapeutic hour is shaped by the personal modeling of the therapist. The clear respect for the other as an Other, the prizing of the person apart from performance and behavior, the maintaining of boundary lines of responsibility, the affirmation and reverence for the other's sexuality, the high value placed on honesty, the respect for culturally appropriate self-disclosure: these begin the listing of moral values that are embodied by the therapist and reinforce moral growth in the counseling process.

Summary

The intercultural pastoral counselor recognizes the universality and inevitability of moral thought, choice, and behavior in the human community. The constancy of form and the contrasts in content show similarities across cultures and distinct emphases both within and between cultural traditions. Ethics of rule, of goal, and of fit exist in all cultures but with varying configuration and balance.

Moral development shows parallel patterns in cognitive growth during early stages, but later stages are contextually formed. Content and context are as essential to moral process as cognitive capability. Ethics as storytelling and story-living serves an integrative and educative function in many groups.

The pastoral counselor, as ethicist, looks to the moral values of the counselee as well as functioning out of his or her own experience in the resolution of intrapersonal and interpersonal conflicts. Intercultural pastoral counseling is grounded in a view of human nature that recognizes both the good and the evil, the potentials and the limitations of persons, groups, and society. Moral accountability is seen as essential to all human experience and human community.

9

Possession, Shamanism, and Healing Across Cultures

A Theology of the Demonic

"How can I rid myself of a tyrannical ghost, who seems to possess my body and soul? For many days this horrible specter has persecuted me viciously. It has fastened itself on my back and will not let go of me. In the still of the night, he strikes me with terror, the hair on my head stands up, my eyes stand out. He steals the power from my body. Why did this ghost choose me? Is he one of my own family? Or one who was murdered? What may I do to appease him? What can I offer to be set free?"

—*Clay tablet found at Nineveh, 2000 B.C.*

THE MAD MAN
A PERSIAN FOLKTALE

Once there ruled in the distant city of Wirani a king who was both mighty and wise. And he was feared for his might and loved for his wisdom.

Now in the heart of that city was a well, whose water was cool and crystalline, from which all the inhabitants drank, even the king and his courtiers; for there was no other well.

One night when all were asleep, a witch entered the city, and poured seven drops of strange liquid into the well, and said, "From this hour he who drinks this water shall become mad."

Next morning all the inhabitants, save the king and his lord chamberlain, drank from the well and became mad, even as the witch had foretold.

And during that day the people in the narrow streets and in the marketplaces did naught but whisper to one another, "The king is mad. Our king and his lord chamberlain have lost their reason. Surely we cannot be ruled by a mad king. We must dethrone him."

That evening the king ordered a golden goblet to be filled from the well. And when it was brought to him he drank deeply, and gave it to his lord chamberlain to drink.

And there was great rejoicing in that distant city of Wirani,

because its king and its lord chamberlain had regained their reason.
(Gibran 1918)

Disease and healing, mental troubledness and calm, are understood in
vastly different ways when one compares the modern Western worldview
with that of traditional societies.

A few centuries ago, there were more similarities than differences in
the healers, shamans, exorcists, and practitioners of witchcraft, voodoo,
and divining in virtually all cultures.

In modern Western society, the movement from a mythical to a scientific vocabulary has resulted in a major shift in paradigm which has
excluded most middle-zone explanations of troubling life experiences.
Rollo May (1969:124) has noted the benefits and liabilities of this shift.

> It was entirely right that the Enlightenment and Age of Reason, in the flush
> of their success in making all life reasonable, should have thrown this out
> [the belief that we are taken over by little demons flying around equipped
> with horns] and have regarded it as a deteriorated and unproductive ap-
> proach to mental illness. But only during the last couple of decades has it
> been clearly impressed upon us that in discarding the false "demonology"
> we accepted, against our intention, a banality and a shallowness in our
> whole approach to mental disease.

In discarding beliefs in little horned demons, modern Westerners also
lost an awareness of the demonic and, with the disappearance of the
demonic, a sensitivity to both good and evil. The illusion of a value-free
universe beckoned us into a flattened, simplified, and morally neutral
scientism.

But in three fourths of the world, the old model of a multistoried
universe prevails. Above the world of demonstrable, observable, replicable science there are layers of folk religions that explain the "why" of
events and experiences that are seen as random chance in modern Western thought. The two-tiered view of reality, which prized science as the
secular realm of sight, experience, and the natural order and saw religion
as the realm of faith, miracles, and the sacred, left a vacuum between
tiers—an excluded middle zone (see chapter 1, Table 1-3). Science provides theories that order the perception of the universe according to
universal natural laws, and religion is called upon to explain the miraculous, the mystical, the meaning that must be derived from the transcendent. But no place is left for the middle zone of understanding or preventing misfortunes, making sense of illness and congenital defects,
understanding failures in business, crops, marriages, or interpersonal
relationships. Study Figure 9-1. Its two-dimensional model correlates the
seen-unseen on the vertical dimension and the organic-mechanical dimension as two parallel columns. The middle zone is included in different realms in the two approaches, but it is always present in folk religions, while virtually absent in Western religious thought (Hiebert
1982b: 93–94).

These middle-zone issues—life, health, suffering, fortune, safety, suc-

Unseen or supernatural	High religion based on cosmic forces	High religion based on cosmic beings	Other-worldly
Above natural explanation,beyond sense experience, based on indifference or on supernatural experiences.	Kismet, fate, Karma and Brahman, impersonal forces. ———————— *Folk or low religion* Local gods and goddesses, ancestors and ghosts, spirits, demons and evil spirits, dead saints.	Cosmic gods, angels, demons, spirits, of other worlds. *Magic and astrology* mana, astrological forces, charms, amulets, magical rites, evil eye, evil tongue. ———————— *Folk natural science* Interaction of natural objects based on natural forces.	Sees events and entities as occurring in other world(s) or time(s). *This-worldly* Sees entities and events as occurring in this world and universe.
↑ ↓ *Seen or empirical* Directly observable: data based on senses, observation, experimenta- tion.	*Folk social science* Interaction of human beings, possibly animals and plants.		

Organic analogy	*Mechanical analogy*
Based on concepts of relationships between living beings.	Based on concepts of impersonal objects controlled by forces.
Stresses life, personality, rela- tionships, health, disease.	Stresses impersonal mechanistic and deterministic nature of events.
Forces are normal in character.	Forces are normal in character.

Figure 9-1. A framework for analysis of religious systems.

Two dimensions, the seen–unseen and the organic–mechanical, offer analogies for our analysis of religion.

(Hiebert 1982b)

cess in love, status, prosperity, control of weather, healing of disease, death—are all "power" issues. The encounter of these "powers" in a culture's life, myths, and rituals occurs along the interface of religions —folk religions as well as the major world religions.

The African universe, in contrast to the Western two-tiered world-view, offers three tiers (Sow 1980:61,74):

1. The elements of the immediate human microcosmos. This human microcosm includes the intrapersonal and interpersonal conflicts of human beings.

2. The elements of the intermediary, invisible mesocosmos. This middle zone, with its implacable laws and its inevitable fate, is peopled by human doubles and the spirits of ancestors and other spirit powers.

3. The diverse structures encompassing the macrocosmos. This larger universe unites all in a single structured whole.

"In African culture reality lies in the realm of the soul and not in that of internal or external things. Reality lies, not in the relationship between man and things, but in that of men with the spirits" (Lambo 1960). The phenomena of possession, spells, amulets, shaman's incantations, and voodoo rituals are central issues of concern for the pastoral counselor because they deal with what is powerful, what is sacred, what is real to the counselee. To secularize the counselee's problem and seek to provide naturalistic explanations is to miss the central issue of power encounter, faith struggles, and the collision of values, of worldviews, and of ultimate visions of reality. On the other hand, to accept the patterns of magical manipulation of God is to betray the central concepts of faith that empower Christianity and Judaism.

> Magic is based on a mechanistic view—a formula approach to reality that allows humans to control their own destiny. Worship, on the other hand, is rooted in a relational view of life. Worshippers place themselves in the power and mercy of God. The difference is not one of form, but of attitude. In religion we want the will of God, in magic we seek our own wills. (Hiebert 1982b:94)

Anthropologist Bronislaw Malinowski, building on Durkheim and Frazer, developed a distinction between magic and religion that is expressed in a series of contrasts.

Magic is a means to an end; religion, being "a body of self-contained acts" that are "themselves the fulfillment of their purpose," is more of an end. Magic depends on simple circumscribed techniques; religion involves a whole supernatural world of faith, including pantheons of spirits and demons. Magic supplies us "with a number of ready-made ritual acts and beliefs which bridge the dangerous gaps in every important pursuit or critical situation; religious faith establishes, fixes, and enhances all valuable mental attitudes such as reverence for tradition, harmony with environment, courage and confidence in the struggle with difficulties and at the prospect of death" (Malinowski 1948:69–70).

Close examinations of avowedly religious behavior will reveal that it frequently includes instrumental magical elements, and observations of magical practices will show that they frequently include religious beliefs and worldviews and point to an end in themselves.

The pastoral counselor must be aware of the world of magic, of folk religion, of religio-science, and of their presence and impact on all the healing arts of the culture.

In this chapter we shall focus on relationships between pastoral counselors and shamans, healers, and folk practitioners. The occurrences of possession and the practices of exorcism will also be examined. We shall stress the necessity of a pastoral care that is not only accountable to the realities of high religion and responsible to the world of science, but also effectively confronts the middle zone of religious and healing practices.

Shaman, Curer, and Healer

A shaman (the word is Siberian, from the Tungus language) is a charismatic religious leader who claims a direct contact with the supernatural that provides healing, prophetic pronouncements, and social power. The shaman's authority rises from the ability to convince others of this power by doing supernatural acts and speaking messages from spirits, gods, and ancestors. Shamanism is more common in loosely structured societies, which are less developed in organized formal religious institutions. The shaman, fiercely individualistic, is a sharp contrast and often a threat to institutionalized religion (Hiebert 1976:380).

A priest, in contrast, is authoritative not through charisma but through the office held in a religious organization or church. The power to influence or invoke the supernatural resides in the institution, not in the person. The priest is part of a succession of leaders who pass ritual, tradition, office, and authority on from generation to generation.

Shamans are most often "chosen" or "elected" by spirits outside themselves. This usually occurs in the form of an initial possession, followed by a slow recovery. The person is thereafter in contact with a spirit or with supernatural powers and can enter a trance in diagnosis of a disease and in prescription of a cure. Shamans have been variously described by psychological anthropologists as psychotic, hysteric, schizophrenic, obsessive-compulsive, psychopathic, or epileptic. All attempts at general labeling of personality and behavior have been proven contradictory. The following hypothesis seems to be the most accepted.

> In some societies a deep emotional disturbance *may* be a characteristic of shamen and may even be a role requirement; in others, a shaman may undergo an intense emotional experience without having been or becoming emotionally disturbed; in yet other societies there may be a variety of personality types including *some* who may have undergone a neurosis or psychosis but used the process of becoming a shaman as a self-cure, and other shamen who never were even temporarily deranged. (Foster and Anderson 1978:6)

The identical psychological characteristics that make a shaman effective in the culture of origin, may, in a Western person, necessitate treatment or perhaps institutionalization. Strong cases have been made for both the health and unhealth of the shaman's mental state: "The shaman cannot be regarded as abnormal in a psychopathological sense because he/she is well adapted to society and serves a useful function" (Ackerknecht 1971:73); "There is no reason and no excuse for not considering the shaman as a severe neurotic and even as a psychotic" (Devereaux 1956:28).

Murphy, in his studies of the St. Lawrence Island Eskimo, suggests that it is not an issue of normal or abnormal but a matter of degree. The Eskimo use the term *nuthkarihak* for "being crazy," and they apply it only to people who simultaneously manifest three or four aberrant behaviors, such as talking to oneself, screaming at a nonexistent person, believing that a witch has murdered a spouse or child when no one else agrees, believing oneself to be an animal, running away, getting lost, drinking urine, or killing dogs. The term is never used for a single symptom.

In contrast, the ability to see what others do not see, to prophesy and predict, is called "thinness." This is highly valued and is possessed by diviners and especially by the shamans. It is never called "being crazy." The shaman in a curing trance may imitate a dog or talk to the self but will not be considered crazy. "When the shaman is healing, she is out of her mind, but she is not crazy," one informant said. When the behavior is controlled and used for curing, it is regarded as normal; when it is uncontrolled and takes multiple forms, the person is seen as crazy (Murphy 1976:1022).

The "calling" of a traditional healer may come through a rich variety of channels: (1) inheritance of the role from parent or grandparent; (2) appointment by relatives, elders, other healers, or the spirits or gods; (3) apprenticeship by seeking training from a healer, gaining entrance into a cult or guild, or gaining knowledge, rituals, or charms through purchase or theft; (4) a crisis experience of possession, a vision quest, dream, trance, or drug-induced journey; (5) miraculous healing from an illness, injury, accident, lightning, or attack by animal; (6) exceptional gifts such as high intelligence, emotional control, or wise judgment; and (7) disability or deformity such as a physical, psychiatric, or behavioral abnormality. Any one or several of these in combination may certify the person to the self and the community as a healer who can be trusted with illness and cure.

Training for traditional healers may take as long as an eight-year apprenticeship for learning the great volume of songs, herbs, incantations, and treatment lore. Most important, the curer must come to understand, and be able to control the guardian spirit (Torrey 1972:95).

The healer possesses a positive charisma that is trusted by patients with a faith that may induce high suggestibility. The reverse is frequently true for those shamans or witches who are feared for their ability to cause illness or death. These practitioners possess a "negative charisma" in that they are disvalued yet feared, disrespected yet obeyed, in such a way that unusual influence over others exists. The unpredictable is believed to be predictable through such an individual's charismatic powers; the uncontrollable is feared to be within the witch's charismatic control. This confers unlimited power. The witch can, then, not only predict the most crucial and terminal certainty—death—but is also feared and so believed to cause it. The charismatic *via negativa* can by definition not be disproved, nor avoided, nor escaped unless one has a higher power to countermand the threat. The range of shamans runs from totally benevolent, through mixed, to largely malevolent. Within each group there may be multiple shamans who specialize in particular needs of the tribe.

In his work with the Sanuma (Yanoma) of north Brazil, Kenneth Taylor gathered data on five types of Shamanism: (1) Curing shamanism is the most common, used to scare away the offending spirit causing the person's illness and thus to extract or eject the illness from the patient's body. (2) Protective shamanism scares away or diverts the powers of enemy spirits which threaten a village or family. (3) Festival hunting Shamanism prepares for the ritual hunt and the "festival for the dead." This is a group ritual to ensure success. (4) Hunting shamanism is routinely used to protect the hunters from accident or attack and to invoke success spirits. (5) Shamanism to attack enemies sends spirits and evil powers to inflict harm on foes (K. Taylor 1979:206).

Traditional Healers and the Healing Process

The healer believes in the powers she or he commands. This belief in one's own ability or the capacity to summon powers beyond the self can inspire confidence in the person being helped. The methods used to evoke such confidence have often been questioned as dishonest by Western observers, since sleight-of-hand and other feats of legerdemain—stock-in-trade for the art of shamanism—are considered unprofessional conduct in other cultures. From a Philippine psychic surgeon who spills blood from a rubber false thumb, to an Indonesian healer who produces a bit of blood-soaked cotton from his mouth after biting his cheek to draw blood as evidence he has sucked out the pain, to the Californian shaman who produces a bloody quartz crystal from his mouth by the same means to prove a correct diagnosis and successful treatment of an intruded disease object—all these are seeking to evoke belief and trust. Deceit or placebo effect? One healer is a charlatan; another is able to call out intense trust. In evaluating the Iban *manang* of Sarawak, E. F. Torrey (1972:97) comes to a conclusion that probably is correct in similar cases: "My conversations with three of them convinced me that while they are not above trickery, they use it in the belief that they are helping the patient. They have absolutely no doubt that the patient's soul is lost, and they believe that anything which will assist in its retrieval is not dishonest."

Frauds exist in both primitive and technologically advanced societies. Unscrupulous indigenous curers exist who exploit the gullibility of their fellows, but most believe deeply in their power to heal. The healer who can enter a trance state at will does not find it incongruous to believe that his or her soul is traveling in search of a lost or stolen soul to return it to the rightful owner, the ill person. In a world filled with spirits, the shaman who is most skilled at communicating as a medium does not consider such claims at soul travel in space or ocean depths as deceit;

it is simply giving symbols to the spirit realities of the community's worldview, using the spirit realities that are the powers of health and illness, sanity and insanity. To a Westerner demanding evidence, empirical proof, experimental methodology, and the ability to replicate a process in other situations, such healing methodology is fraudulent and false.

Much of the power of the healer is communal power—the power of the group of believers conferred upon the healer as the representative of their belief system. Beliefs, rituals, and healing experiences are culturally congruent without and "ego-syntonic"—acceptable to the ego—within.

> If a Kansas businessman and a youthful Plains Indian questing for a power-giving vision saw the same vision, qualitatively both persons would be equally abnormal. Of the two, however, the Kansas businessman would be quantitatively more abnormal, since in his case the eruption of the primary process and of visual hallucinations would not be supported and facilitated on the ego level by cultural expectations and cultural conditioning. The same considerations are applicable also to suggestibility and hypnosis. When a Plains Indian medicine man told a mortally wounded man to rise and behave as though he were well, his suggestion fell on culturally sensitized ears. It had the full support of cultural conditioning and mobilized important ego mechanisms; hence, the man could and did rise and walk around for days, even though he inevitably died. A similar command given to an Occidental patient would probably not produce comparable results, because of the lack of a cultural reinforcement of the shaman's command.
>
> The effectiveness of a primitive shaman's suggestions and hypnotic interventions thus cannot be doubted. The shaman is, by definition, held capable of performing certain feats. This means that his commands are reinforced by cultural conditioning and are therefore highly effective. Also, the primitive is eager for miracles; his desire is overt and conscious, and above all, extremely ego-syntonic. The desire for miracles is, of course, present also in Occidental man; however, it is often only preconscious or unconscious, and in most cases, is certainly not ego-syntonic. (Devereaux 1966:278–279)

In the aboriginal Apache conceptualization, all disease and misfortune are caused by the actions of affronted "powers," witches and ghosts, and the shaman's power is required to negate those actions. This belief appears to exist in all of today's Apaches on some level of consciousness, despite more than a hundred years of Westernization and the graduation of some individuals from universities.

The Apaches conceptualize supernatural power to be universal and to inhabit all natural phenomena. Snake power, bear power, lightning power, or yucca power appears to a person and offers its use and the songs or ceremonies that make its application effective. The man or woman who accepts the power must agree to assume its implicit awesome responsibilities and the potential dangers involved in its use. Two fundamental steps are involved in the acquisition of shamanistic status: one must accept as a possession the supernatural power that appears in a "power dream"; subsequently, the claim to power must be credited by culture mates. The power may then be used for good (shamanistic) or bad (witchcraft) purposes (Boyer 1983:238).

The power function is central to the healing process among Apaches. The recognition of dependence and a willingness to put oneself into the hands of the healer are basic prerequisites to the healing process.

> An Apache who seeks shamanistic help has to humble himself to a point which would be unacceptable unless he were prepared to put himself unreservedly in the hands of the practitioner. The sufferer or a relative who speaks for him must approach the shaman in the most obsequious fashion. He must call him by a relationship term, whether or not the shaman is a relative, lay a ceremonial cigarette at his foot, tell of his great need and of his absolute dependence upon the particular shaman's ceremony. "Only you can help me. Do not fail me now" is the closing plea. The shaman ponders the matter. He mutters something about the ingratitude of a former patient or the pressure of duties. After a sufficiently significant pause he stoops with fine condescension, picks up and smokes the cigarette, and so indicates that he will take the case. (Opler 1959:1375)

The traditional healer may exercise social power—the power of channeling, resolving, or utilizing the social conflicts embedded in the tribe or community. Diviners, healers, and witch doctors in Africa function as conflict experts who detect the active agents of conflict situations and exercise the power to control or direct them. The *nganga,* in Zaire, is seen as the great peacemaker and guardian of the community. His individual interventions of healing are seen as barometers of the public health.

The traditional healer of central Africa has a wide knowledge of such things as the history of familial lineages, the origin of villages, the relationships among clans, the roles and psychologies of each member of the community, and past, present, and potential conflicts. He uses these data to restore or maintain the necessary equilibrium in community relations. He does this on three levels: ancestral tradition—the spirits; familial relations—the clan and its clashes; and the cultural context—enemies and social competitors (Sow 1980:89–90).

The *nganga* has highly developed psychotherapeutic and sociotherapeutic intervention skills. When persons become ill, he sees it as symptomatic of the festering relations in the lineage and calls the kin together to discuss their problems and concealed feelings and make peace publicly. The catharsis, in a dramatic discharge of aggressiveness, frequently settles differences and resolves social discord.

The Healing Process

The two universals of non-Western psychiatry are confession and suggestion (Kiev 1964:36,110). To this have been added faith and group support (Edgerton 1971:271). Compare these with Case Study: Witchcraft Death.

Faith is a generalized expectation by the patient that the treatment being offered can be effective.

Catharsis through *confession,* ventilation, and physical expression

CASE STUDY: Witchcraft Death (Nigeria)

Mondolo came to the pastoral counselor in a state of acute anxiety. She had not eaten or slept for three days. She insisted that she was about to die and must stay awake to avert it. With patient encouragement, she finally reported the following circumstances.

Two neighbors, her close friends, had quarreled bitterly a week previously. One of these women, upon returning home after the verbal battle, was terrified to find a little girl in her bedroom standing at the head of her bed. This was clearly an evil sign, since a bedroom is a very personal and private place, and a non-family member intruding into such a place is suspected of doing witchcraft. This was doubly fearsome since the little girl was the daughter of her opponent in the conflict. The woman went into shock and died during the night. Upon learning of this, Mondolo became extremely anxious because it was common knowledge in the neighborhood that she strongly agreed with the dead woman in her complaints against the neighbor, who was now considered by all as responsible for her opponent's sudden death. Mondolo was convinced that she would be next to die and was afraid to return home, lest she see some omen signaling that her time had come.

The pastoral counselor listened carefully to her fears and offered understanding and support as they were fully expressed. He then reassured her that the power of Jesus Christ was greater than that of witchcraft. After they had prayed together, the two agreed to go to the suspected woman to work at reconciliation between them and to express acceptance of her in the community by this visit. The conversation ended with the two accepting each other as friends again. Mondolo's anxiety was dissipated, and communal solidarity was affirmed by her action.

may be nonverbal—in the form of ecstatic dancing to total exhaustion —or verbal—in confession and apology for wrongful acts, thoughts, and hidden desires.

Group support may vary from a renewal of the social network or inclusion in a therapeutic "healing" community to participation in an elaborate "discharge ceremony that ritualizes the patient's cleansing of illness, death, and rebirth into a new life" (Prince 1974:143). Among the Ndambu of northern Zimbabwe, the patient's kin may join with a hostile patient in a kind of group therapy complete with catharsis of the aggressive impulses and social reintegration (Turner 1964:262).

Suggestion takes many forms. Among the Yoruba, the curer may give "a continuous barrage of suggestions at all levels from the most intellectual to the most concrete and primitive" (Prince 1964:111). There may be indirect communication through allegory, simile, or traditional stories; or use of trance by either the patient or the curer or both to communicate suggestions by supernatural powers; or the impact of special effects through legerdemain, ventriloquism, sleight of hand, or magic; or a change in consciousness through drumming, dancing, and fatigue; or bodily contact such as rubbing, sucking, bathing, anointing or steaming, burning, whipping, or cutting; or the enactment of potent rituals with highly dramatic and magical symbolism; or the use of simple devout prayers for supernatural guidance, intervention, and healing; or the uses of herbal medications that may contain *Cannibis sativa* or various mushrooms with consciousness-altering properties—all of which can heighten the power of suggestion (Edgerton 1971).

The effective healer unites the powers of faith, confession, group support, and positive suggestion and communicates these to the deepest levels of the client that are available. If this is not sufficient to break through the illness process, the healer may seek to address even deeper levels. In a culture where actions speak to the core of the person rather than words, this movement toward the center may take the form of deeper acts of devotion and self-discipline.

The use of the unconscious is present implicitly or explicitly in all healing processes. In his classic study *The Discovery of the Unconscious* (1970:6–9), Henri Ellenberger notes that healers, from shamans and medicine men of primitive societies to contemporary psychoanalysts, have always made therapeutic use of the unconscious in two ways. First, the healer brings out aspects of the patient's unconscious and uses them to produce a cure. Exorcists did this when they caused a supposedly latent possession to appear and cast out an induced spirit along with the disease. In the second use, the healer cures the patient by using a state of ecstasy brought about within the self. This is the method of the shaman who travels in the spirit world to recapture a soul supposedly escaped from its body. The unconscious process of either the patient or the healer may be a source of power.

Mr. Naidu, a Kali healer in the Guiana region of South America, has an impressive record of healing psychosis, kidney disease, cancer, and other illnesses. His system is deceptively simple—he prays with the patient, tries to discover how the patient is "living wrong," and urges him to "live right." He does not accept his fee unless the patient gets well. If the patient does not respond to the initial consultation, Mr. Naidu prays and fasts for several days. If there is yet no response, he prays, fasts, and walks on coals. In the last instance, the patient almost without exception gets well (Jourard 1974:318).

"In faith healing, diagnosis is fundamentally irrelevant and recovery depends on supernatural forces. Its therapeusis uses exhortation and mobilizes religious and personal fervor, often in an effort to induce altered levels of consciousness in order to diminish the patient's use of rational thought," reports L. Bryce Boyer (1983:239), in critique of the movement into the middle zone from his own preferred scientific paradigm. "The role of suggestion is paramount and the patient's submission is obligatory. The therapist's effort . . . is to maintain emotional hold over the patient, that is, to exploit transference and subjugate the patient to continuing dependency. In faith healing, reliance on evidence is in itself irreligious."

There are striking similarities between modern psychotherapies and many elements we have noted in traditional forms of healing. Psychiatrist Mansell Pattison (1977:17) concludes that we must see folk healing as parallel to, not inferior to, our "scientific models."

> The same process of discovering and integrating the symbolization of reality can be found in [Western psychiatry and] in the therapies of indigenous folk healers. I believe that the ethnographic evidence indicates that we have sold the folk healers short. We have interpreted their therapies solely as simpleminded magic rituals; whereas the potency and efficacy of their therapies may be every bit as efficacious with their culture as psychoanalytic therapy is in our culture. And perhaps with the same failures as well.

The X Factor in Healing

The activity of all those in the helping professions—healers, therapists, counselors, physicians—depend either on endogenous self-righting mechanisms for healing to occur or on exogenous experts or substances. In Western cultures, there is limited faith in the "inner healer" and an immediate and sustained dependence on exogenous healing specialists and on external substances and processes. In traditional cultures with fewer formal healing institutions, there is more dependence on endogenous self-correcting processes such as dreams, sleep, or rest, altered states of consciousness, religious experience, or even the transformative power of psychotic experience as a healing resource. These self-righting mechanisms do work effectively in many forms of psychiatric disorder (Prince 1976:155).

Frank (1961), Kiev (1964), and Prince (1964) have each stressed the contributions of faith, hope, belief, and sympathetic union (producing high suggestibility) as central factors in the effectiveness of traditional cultural curative approaches; they see these as a point of contact for comparing and contrasting traditional and Western methodologies.

Faith, hope, belief, and suggestibility—along with (1) relief from alienation and shame and (2) catharsis of anxiety and guilt—are central to the therapeutic process of folk healer and shaman and to the therapeutic process of the psychologist, psychiatrist, and pastoral counselor as well. Although the aura and intensity of religious healing is rarely produced or desired in a Western context, suggestibility, persuasion, and the power of basic trust are profoundly important therapeutic forces.

Shapiro (1971:438) examines this in research on the placebo effect in therapy—meaning a nonspecific effect produced by belief in the efficacy of the therapy rather than its specific content or agent—which creates a floor of healing trust between client and counselor. The placebo effect has been most carefully examined in relation to drug therapy, when the healing power of the ingested substance depends solely upon the potency of belief in the medication and faith in its effects rather than upon the inert substance. The factors that appear most important in producing this effect in Western therapy are (1) newness of the approach and its intellectual, emotional, and financial status, fame, and popularity; (2) the prestige or status of the therapist; (3) the therapist's interest and attitude toward the patient, toward the treatment relationship, and toward expected outcomes of the treatment; (4) the degree of suggestibility of the patient; and (5) the congruence or concordance between the therapeutic approach and the patient's worldview, attitudes, and biases as molded by social class and cultural forces.

"The symbolic component of medical treatment is highly significant," concludes Moerman (1979:60–62). "Some studies demonstrate that a placebo is fully 30 to 60% as effective as an active medication, thus perhaps half the effectiveness of *any* medication may be due the symbolic concomitants of the healing act. The *form* of medical treatment can be effective medical treatment."

Kleinman and Sung (1979:7–26) speak of the phenomenon of "cultural healing" that occurs automatically when any medical system gets to work in defining the disease, mobilizing defenses, and administering treatment.

The close correspondence of these factors to the high esteem of the shaman, the cultural belief and total trust in the healing process, the depth of religious awe and faith, the radical openness of the patient in willing outer-directed suggestibility, and the perfect contextual congruence is undeniable. But the willingness to observe these same effects in Western psychiatry, Shapiro concludes (1971:439), is strangely lacking.

> This [placebo effect as a concept in therapy] is not popular because psychotherapy is frequently believed to be a modern treatment based on scientific principles, while the placebo effect is viewed as a superstitious response to a drug. Adamant claims that psychotherapy is not susceptible to placebo effects conform to the principle that every placebo once accepted was vigorously defended as a non-placebo. Medical history clearly demonstrates that despite the sensitivity of many practitioners to the non-specific or placebo effect of others, they were usually insensitive to their own.

Torrey (1972:1) makes this point even more inclusively by concluding:

> Witchdoctors and psychiatrists perform essentially the same function in their respective cultures. They are both therapists; both treat patients using similar techniques; and both get similar results. Recognition of this should not downgrade psychiatrists; rather it should upgrade witchdoctors.

Torrey (1972:7–8) summarizes the essential features of psychological healing shared by folk and scientific healers as (1) comparable concepts between healer and patient in regard to the causation of symptoms, (2) desirable personal qualities of the healer such as firmness and maturity, (3) expectation that the culturally defined treatment produces improvement, and (4) effective technique. He concludes that only certain physical therapies—chemotherapy and electroconvulsive shock therapy—can be defined as purely scientific on the basis of accurate cause-and-effect outcome predictions. He then insists that "in overstatement [reviewers comment, that] the techniques used by Western psychiatrists are, with few exceptions, on exactly the same scientific plane as the techniques used by witchdoctors. If one is magic then so is the other. If one is prescientific, then so is the other."

> All medical systems have developed etiological theories consonant with local worldview, technological competencies, and social structure. The healer—whether calling upon the help of the supernatural, performing a complex "sociopsy" designed to reveal the broken threads in the social fabric, gazing into a glass of water to endow it with his own grace, or reading the printout of a blood-gas analysis—automatically reflects the cultural/symbolic functions of the medical system of which he (she) is part. (Press 1982:184)

Turner (1964) describes the complex and extensive "sociopsy" performed by the African Ndembu healer, who interviews a number of the patient's kinfolk in an attempt to identify the social or moral disjuncture that led to the illness being treated. Part of the cure involves orchestrated confrontations between the patient and others with whom he or she has experienced animosity or distrust.

A major problem in transcultural pastoral psychotherapy is a discrepancy between the expectations of therapist and counselee about the outcome of the sessions. In a culture in which all cure comes through faith healing, the conscious or unconscious expectations of change may be through submission to the counselor's powers. In order for the therapist to understand the counselee's expectations, he or she must know the functions and principles of shamanistic practices in that culture, the mythology and folklore that is taught to children through storytelling, the verbal and nonverbal allusions to legendary events, all of which reinforce faith in the indigenous healing practices that are a living part of the person's past and present. These expectations exist as highly charged emotional "power fields" in the person's understandings of sickness, healing, and health (Boyer 1983:240).

The complexity and mystery of these cultural depths frequently require that the therapist be of the same cultural tradition; otherwise, co-therapy is essential. A wise man or woman may function as a healer-facilitator in co-therapy. For expatriates or bicultural therapists, such a partner in the healing process can be invaluable—indeed, revelatory.

Cooperation and Collaboration Between Healing Traditions

In many different countries, there is creative dialogue between psychotherapists working from Western psychological and theological models and healers working from traditional understandings of human nature and community. These relationships have taken various forms: *cooperation*, as the two work in parallel, with each holding a unique worldview and its consequent practice of healing; *collaboration*, as the two approaches have been allowed to complement, correct, and augment each other; and, in a few settings, *co-creation*, as a new theoretical base, practical application, and therapeutic program have emerged, drawing on the best of each and finding a third way that goes beyond either.

The first step toward mutuality is recognizing the strengths that exist in traditional healing approaches (what have been called "indigenous folk healers"). Writing from his research and field observation, John Janzen (1978:228) lists some personal qualities of the practitioners of traditional healing—physical, emotional, spiritual—in Zaire.

> The expertise of good inspirational diviners in resolving conflict and alleviating anxiety is remarkable. Many people seek their counsel. These practitioners have an uncanny gift for second-guessing their clients' problems and a disarming manner of laughing sympathetically at fears not founded in fact. But they react in moral indignation to foolish folks' abuse of one another or themselves, and scold them like a loving parent might. They have the temerity of spirit to probe deeply into dreams, to lay bare hidden motives in tacky situations. The best ones do not stir up conflict in the analysis of conflict. They know when to ease the séance away from direct interpersonal encounter to projected social symbols such as an ancestor or a genealogically remote set of twins. In short, they are significant agents of social integration.

Traditional diviners and healers have been accepted as collaborators by health treatment institutions in Zaire, Zimbabwe, Nigeria, Uganda, Tanzania, and Kenya, and in India, Pakistan, and Malaysia, as well as in other settings where experiments in collaboration, consulting, and referral have taken place. Western-trained physicians and village-trained healers have combined or cooperated in treatment programs, to the strengthening of each.

> The "Chikore experiment" incorporated a pastor with the gift of divining and counseling into the staff of the large Chikore Hospital in Rhodesia. He was provided with a grass-roofed palaver house in the hospital compound near the wards. Patients' families freely consulted him about kinship problems, witchcraft suspicions, guilt feelings, and other typical issues accompanying disease, while the sufferer simultaneously received Western medical care nearby. (Donaldson 1967:8)

The most widely published experiment is that of psychiatrist T. A. Lambo. Speaking of his "unorthodox collaboration" with traditional healers, he writes (1964:450), "We have discovered throughout long practice in Africa that it is essential to the scientific understanding of persons and their social environment to work in close collaboration with other disciplines." Lambo sought to supplement his British training by drawing on psychiatric traditions in the Nigerian culture. He created a therapeutic liaison center in a village near Ibadan University, where he served on the faculty. Patients were housed in this center and diviners from the area were paid a stipend to see and help them, while receiving supervision from Lambo. The collaboration allowed the patient to draw on the familiar sources of help while assimilating the strange, and to deal with the myths, beliefs, and values of the village while encountering new belief systems in modern psychiatry.

Where psychiatrists and traditional healers work conjointly, the sanctioning strength of friends, kin, and clan can be called on to reinforce the therapy, much like network therapy is attempted in a few Western settings.

> In the *psychopalavre,* begun by Dr. Bazinga at the Neuropsychiatric Insti-
> tute of Kinshasa, the sufferer participated alone initially while learning to
> role-play and gain detachment from the setting that had caused his distress.
> When he was strong enough to meet his familial or job situation again,
> kinsmen were invited to participate in the *psychopalavre.* The therapy
> management group of kinsmen was thus utilized by Western medicine to
> sanction improvements experienced by the sufferer during group therapy,
> a technique not unlike that used by certain healing cults and prophets.
> (Janzen 1978:229)

Pastoral counselors in various African countries have led in the dialogue between and cooperation of pastoral therapists and traditional
healers. The "healing communities" of Zairian healers offer a blend of
group therapy, individual therapy, and the milieu approach of people
living, working, and risking relationships with each other.

The wisdom of traditional methods of intervening in personal and
interpersonal crises has been recognized by a number of key pastoral
theologian-therapists. In Zaire, Jean Masamba Ma Mpolo early took the
position that since therapists function out of a cultural complex of values,
myths, and views of human nature, of maturity, normality, and health,
there are multiple traditions that can be used therapeutically: the classic
Greek myths united with empirical analysis as set forth by Freud; the
supra-cultural mythologies integrated with Western philosophy by Carl
Jung; the blend of naturalism, humanism, and existentialism of Rogers,
Perls, Maslow, Fromm, May, and others; the unitary understandings of
nature, humanity, and being that are the legacy of African healing traditions; the centuries-old wisdom of Chinese philosophy, psychology, and
healing arts; or many other wisdom traditions around the world.

Masamba Mpolo's leadership in reclaiming historic traditions of healing fragmented, divided, and disintegrating personalities (see Case Study:
Mafwana) has invited therapists in the African setting to look to their
roots to find models for understanding persons, relationships, and identity in community.

The meeting of traditions that are theological in their depths provides
a multidimensional interface, since they seek to integrate the past (history), the future (destiny), the divine (transcendence), the truly human
(nature, nurture), and the goal of life and growth (meaning). As a Zairian
healer, Nganga Masamba, said to a Western physician, "You are a
doctor of the land, but I am a doctor of the water," which, freely
translated from the metaphor of the tribe and the mood of the moment,
means, "You and your medicine are great, but they are temporal; ours
is the eternal medicine of the ancestors" (Janzen 1978:229).

The work of integration between traditional and empirical, between
national heritage and innovation from other cultures, is an extremely
demanding and difficult task. It is not a utilitarian eclecticism but a new
structuring and revisioning of both therapies.

CASE STUDY: Mafwana (Africa)

Mafwana, female, 28, divorced, is referred to Masamba Ma Mpolo by a European pastor who cannot understand her problem. Mafwana is convinced that the failure of her marriage is due to marrying against the wishes of her parents back in the ancestral village. One month after her separation from her husband, she became anxious, tormented in conscience, and troubled by dreams of punishment, evil sexual acts, and persecution by male friends.

The crucial dream brought an encounter with her dead grandfather, who pressed her to kill a pig to make peace with her uncle (who died five weeks after her marriage) and to go to the cemetery and pour wine on his tomb in a traditional rite of forgiveness. Mafwana refused, seeing such rituals as contradictory with her Christian faith.

After seven sessions of therapy, Mafwana chose to return to the village for a family palaver and the rituals of reconciliation. In the presence of her family she acknowledged the error of not consulting her family before marriage and the three-fold "sin" admitted—a marriage without family consent and dowry was considered adulterous, the polygamous union violated her Christian church's values, and after the separation the man had taken the child, as dictated by the patriarchal customs of his tribe, the Luba. Mafwana's ethnic group, the Kongo, trace descendance matriarchally, but she was separated from her daughter because of the quasi-legal status of the union.

The family review of the case revealed ancestral indignation expressed in her dreams. Libations were made at the uncle's and maternal grandfather's tombs. Mutual forgiveness was proclaimed. An expiatory goat was killed and eaten in a feast by both maternal and paternal clans.

A village delegation met with the pastoral counselor for two sessions of negotiation with the ex-husband's family, which resulted in her regaining physical custody of the daughter, financial support, and the planning of a village worship service for a Christian blessing on the new start for both mother and daughter.

This resulted in a complete cure of Mafwana's anxiety, reconciliation with both the living and the dead family clan, and reintegration of both the personal and the collective ego. This reconciliation process symbolized her dynamic world vision and reconnected her solidarity with familial tribal values on both conscious and unconscious levels.

(Masamba Ma Mpolo 1985:315)

The fact that a pattern of seeking healing is "traditional" does not make it immune to criticism. The reclaiming of traditional patterns by national groups who experienced the cultural genocide of the old imperialism is a necessary, even imperative, task. But methods of healing must be evaluated in terms of their effectiveness or ineffectiveness or a new imposed injustice replaces the old when traditional medicine is all that is supplied to tribal groups. Diabetes is the failure of the pancreas to supply insulin and it is only treatable by insulin—traditional, herbal, ritual, or magical rites notwithstanding.

A marriage partner who employs a healer to put a curse on the spouse to deal with jealousy, rather than see a marriage counselor using a rational approach of talking therapy, is making a choice between ways of intervening. A value-free attitude of relativism evades the central issue of choosing what therapeutic approach is most appropriate, most effective, and most liberating and healing for both persons.

Not all systems are neutral bases for developing systems of intervention in human crises. Some are rooted in socially recognized "fields of creative good," and others draw their power from "fields of destructive evil." Where the healing method is rooted in fear, imposes the coercive power of anxiety, and draws on understandings of the demonic, the negative character and charisma support alienation and disintegration of humanness. When the healing methodology is grounded in the wholeness of persons, relationships, and communities, it is life enhancing and moves toward the reconciliation of what is estranged, the reconnecting of what is severed.

Possession as a Multicultural Phenomenon

Spirit possession and mediumship are among the most widespread and intriguing phenomena in the literature of religious studies, research into healing practices, and explorations into human conflict resolution. Under such names as ecstasy, demon possession, devil dancing, shamanism, pythonism, spiritism, spiritualism, geomancy, occult practice, and witchcraft, they have been the subject of writings extending over three thousand years. From ancient Babylonia, Sumeria, and Egypt, or from the classical Greek reports of Dionysiac cults in which worshipers possessed by the god saw visions and performed extraordinary feats, to present-day Western witchcraft; or from early Chinese accounts of hungry ghosts to the present geomancy rituals, divination, and protection against spirits from home to marketplace, the obsession with possession is one of humankind's oldest phenomena.

The vision of a middle zone or mesocosmos filled with spirits has been traced in the history of virtually all cultures, and in much of the world it is still the dominant vision of reality. As Geertz describes the Indonesian worldview (1960:159):

> Bangsa alus, memedi, gendruwo, lelembut, setan, jin tuyul, demit, danyang —this flood of bald children, white tigers, and foot-shuffling chickens— provide for those who believe in their existence a set of ready-made answers to the questions posed by puzzling experiences, symbolic pictographs of the imagination within whose framework even the anomalous seems inevitable. Has older sister Suwarni just recovered from a week of splitting headaches?

It is because when she squatted down on the toilet there was a lelembut already seated there—in his anger and chagrin he slapped her across the eyes. Has Haji Abdullah, having lost a brother and a wife within a year, now suddenly gotten rich? The combination of circumstances strongly suggests a tuyul. The spirit world is the social world symbolically transformed. One class of spirits lords it over another, one racial group of spirits follows that group's behaviors.

In all continents, there are groups in which particular persons at specific times undergo startling and dramatic changes of personality— trembling, sweating, groaning, speaking with strange voices or in unintelligible sounds, assuming a different identity, claiming to be a spirit and not a human being, asserting authoritative leadership with commands, or foretelling the future.

The nature of spirit possession, as viewed by an anthropologist who observed it in Ghana in over thirty-five years of study, follows these well-defined lines:

The dissociated state in spirit possession (often called "trance") is of brief duration, usually an hour or two, very seldom as long as a whole day. When normal consciousness is regained the subject has no recollection of what he did, said, observed, or felt while possessed. The possession fit, or trance, exhibits two distinct phases. There is a short opening phase of dazed, mute inaccessibility and a second, longer phase of excitement with great activity —dancing, singing, leaping, running, miming, "prophesying," and so on. Both beginning and ending of the excited phase are abrupt. The person loses the abstracted, mask-like expression and regains awareness.

The possessed person is in a state of dissociated personality whereby a split-off part of the mind possesses the whole field of consciousness, the rest being in complete abeyance. Splitting of the stream of consciousness is familiar to anyone who can "do two things at once" such as playing the piano and simultaneously planning a summer holiday, or driving a car "automatically" while thinking about something quite different. It is the total banishment of all but one stream which is the essential feature of dissociation. It is not true of the possessed person that, as Africans have it, "something has come to him"; rather it is that something has *gone* from him. (Field 1969:3–4)

In certain forms of hypnotic states, the entire group functions as the hypnotist or a socially recognized signal serves to induce a particular pattern of hypnotic behavior without any additional induction procedures. The phenomenon of a mass-induced hypnotic state is directly related to the rhythmic incessant drumming and continuous dancing. These techniques may induce "possession" states or "dissociational" behavior, as in the voodoo rituals of Haiti, the *zar* cults of northeast Africa, and the fire-walking rituals of Southeast Asia. The group expectation that trance states will occur in certain persons in specific occasions mobilizes the dissociative capacity inherent in every individual, and the resulting group atmosphere gives both permission and motivation to those who are the focus of the group excitement.

Trance behavior can function as a socially "normal" means of coping with sudden fright, such as Alberle noted with Siberian tribespeople who become possessed as a way of dealing with crisis situations. Malay women were triggered by a startle reaction into a possessed hypnotic state in which they identified with the aggressor and responded with echolalia—repeating what others said as if echoing them—and echopraxia—mimicking the actions of others in a physical mirroring. Adelman observed a Malaysian man who went into shock when surprised by a tiger and, in possession, so identified with the animal psychologically and behaviorally that the tiger was frightened into immediate flight (Devereaux 1966:273).

The forms that possession takes vary widely from culture to culture. People cut themselves with knives, walk on hot cinders, climb ladders of razor blades, bathe in boiling oil, or even enucleate eyes while in trance. Or possession may take highly verbal forms of speaking, singing, or prophesying to an audience; or there may be cursing, blaspheming, scatological language, and threatening in hostile behavior.

The outward manifestations of spirit possession vary widely—from fainting, trances, glossolalia, rigid postures, violent dancing, acts of extreme agility such as climbing down treetrunks head first, chewing broken glass, gripping hot irons, walking over glowing coals. At the end of the trance state most people are amnesiac, recalling little or nothing. The quality of possession varies from one individual to another. Some enter it simply with prayers or giving offerings; with others there is a marked loss of control and consciousness. The subjects vary from culture to culture. In Bali possession occurs only among the young; in Haiti it is more common among adults (Kiev 1972:32).

Possession may serve social functions such as the healing trance of a shaman and ritual celebrations such as fire walking and group dances, or it may fulfill individual needs such as catharsis and release. Trance states may function as a defense against deeper mental illness and latent disorders. In early stages of psychiatric illness, persons often seek dissociative experiences in the hope that religious belief, ritual, or conversion will provide conjunctive solutions and forestall the disintegration of personality that is threatening them from within. For some persons the permission to ventilate, express, and act out forbidden and suppressed impulses in a communally approved setting may forestall the involuntary eruption of such material in day-to-day relationships.

Possession as a means of meeting communal needs is described by Sow (1980:109) as a social spectacle that takes place within forms and boundaries fixed by tradition. The body of the possessed person becomes the stage for a community affair, a drama that serves the group by allowing its unconscious to speak. The person possessed is not demeaned but honored by serving as guide. It is a privilege to be the channel of discovery, guidance, and revelation.

Possession makes it possible to expand the dialogue with the invisible forces in the depths of one's being. The possessed person, who acts like "a mare mounted by a rider genie," allows these forces to take possession of his or her body, temporarily taking the place of the subject's personal-

ity. The possessed person may then be questioned by the master technician in the trance ceremony. "When questioned, the genie (subconscious-
unconscious) replies through the mouth of the person possessed, making
diagnosis and suggesting solutions for settling the conflict" (Sow 1980:
110).

> A well-ordered séance constitutes real-life theater. The theatrical and psy-
> chodramatic qualities of these public sessions, with a cast of professional
> players attuned to the real-life culture, promote catharsis, the discharge of
> tensions, and the resolution of conflicts. One may rightly speak of genuine
> psychodrama. (Sow 1980:111)

Possession, Social Oppression, and Transition

In societies that are highly oppressive of females, possession serves as
the sole means of liberation available to an abused woman. There can be
social prestige as well as attention to injustices gained by being possessed
by a devil or a god, a demon or an ancestor. The possessed person is
suddenly able to be aggressive or prophetic, insulting or awe-inspiring,
hostile or regally commanding. Possession can be a socially accepted
form of self-assertion, or compensation for a position of insignificance,
of confrontation on needs that cannot be expressed in normal communication. African studies have examined the function of these liberation
dramas in (1) competition among multiple wives, (2) demanding goods,
services, and fairer treatment for self or for children, and (3) obtaining
attention and treatment for other illnesses or physical problems.

Among the Muslim tribes of Somalia, I. M. Lewis (1971:75) studied
the *zar* spirits, who "are thought to be consumed by envy and greed, and
to hunger especially after dainty foods, luxurious clothing, jewelry, per-
fume, and other finery." He describes the dominant pattern:

> The prime targets for the unwelcome attention of these malign spirits are
> women, and particularly married women. The stock epidemiological situa-
> tion is that of the hard-pressed wife, struggling to survive and feed her
> children in the harsh nomadic environment, and liable to some degree of
> neglect, real or imagined, on the part of her husband. Subject to frequent,
> sudden, and often prolonged absences by her husband as he follows his
> many pastoral pursuits, to the jealousies and tensions of polygyny which
> are not ventilated in accusations of sorcery and witchcraft, and always
> menaced by the precariousness of marriage in a society where divorce is
> frequent and easily obtainable by men, the Somali woman's lot offers little
> stability or security.

In a strongly patrilineal and patriarchal society, possession becomes
a means for asserting these requests, as Lewis notes, "which are voiced
in no uncertain fashion by the spirits speaking through the lips of the
afflicted women, and uttered with an authority which their passive recep-
tacles rarely achieve themselves." The result is an interpretation by a
female shaman, a dancing fiesta, gifts, and other necessities for relieving
the possession.

Zar cults function as religious and social gatherings for release of tensions, anxiety, and anger at oppression; *zar* doctors who have come to terms with the possession utilize the trance state to diagnose and prescribe cures for illnesses. Possession thus has many uses—economic, marital, social, recreational, medical, and religious.

The use of possession as a tool is well developed in Ethiopia, Egypt, the Sudan, Saudi Arabia, and other Muslim areas of Africa. Parallel phenomena occur in Southeast Asia, South America, and the Caribbean Islands, especially Haiti, where trance phenomena and possession are used instrumentally in familial, social, and political relationships and are scheduled for tourism profits.

In Malaysia, northeast Africa, and the Middle East, the phenomenon of possession and exorcism is associated with *marginality*. In central Africa, whether in the rites-of-passage possession dances or in the stress situations along the transition lines from village to city, possession is associated with *liminality* (Langley 1980:226). Victor Turner (1969:95) has taken the concept of liminality as a rite of passage in the human developmental cycle and applied it to liminal periods of history when old structures are passing and a new order has not yet taken firm shape. Africa in the mid-twentieth century is a land of liminality, and the various cults function as movements to support, define, and direct through the conscious and unconscious uncertainties as a tribe is fragmented and a new nation seeks to emerge.

When a society is in transition and a people must exist on its margins, liminality and marginality create a group ready to be possessed. The loss of sociocultural rooting, the anxiety of being between identities, opens one to possession. Where the society has been corporate and outer-directed, the dissolving of these boundaries that ensured safety and security through solidarity are an open invitation to outer-directed possession experience.

Yap (1966:114) studied sixty-six Hong Kong cases of persons who believed they were possessed, either by gods or demons. These cases, predominantly women of ancestral worship or spirit-medium backgrounds, were sorted into three distinct groups. The first exhibited neurotic characteristics. In these, Yap observed the function of the spirit possession in dramatization of fantasies and wish fulfillment of persons with long-term existing conflicts in their lives. Members of the second group were clearly depressed, and in the demon voices their own voices were heard talking about sexual frustration and the morbidity of their depressive pain. Those in the third group were clearly psychotic. No observers looked on them as demon-possessed because of the marked signs of their disordered thinking processes. In their psychotic troubledness, they had taken the cultural patterns of possession to express their delusional thoughts. Those who claimed to be god-possessed were looking for an elevation in status, whereas those who were demon-possessed were asking for some suspension of criticism from their own selves and from others concerning their conflicts or their ongoing depression.

What Yap notes but does not see as central to these cases is that all of them came from the oppressed, the disenfranchized in the larger society. Bourguignon (1973:327) finds that the frequency of demonic possession in two-thirds world settings is strongly correlated with the occurrence of social oppression or societal stagnation. Carstairs and Kapur (1976:110–112) observe that in an Indian community possession appears in the most oppressed groups. Demonology is most intensely present in social situations where the structures are oppressive, the institutions ineffective, and the possibilities of liberation and change are out of reach. In such settings of outer-directed external control and external responsibility (see chapter 3), evil becomes personified within the social system as evil demons (rather than recognized in the evil structures), and the symbolic drama of the accusations of oppression, experience of oppression, and liberation of the possessed are acted out in unconscious parody of the larger tragedy that cannot be liberated. The safe displacement of anger and revolution through possession of persons and liberation replaces the collective communal transformation that is so sorely needed with a personal reformation of individuals who bear the pain of the community in miniature within themselves.

Demonology and witchcraft distill the evil of the whole society and focus it in certain persons, as powerful people with negative charisma, or as the weak and powerless, who are then scapegoats for the evil of the whole community.

> Belief in witchcraft is one of the great fears from which mankind has suffered. It has taken its toll literally in blood. Witchcraft must be symbolic. It is a belief which helps to interpret and canalize the dis-ease of society. . . . [Witchcraft beliefs] resolve certain conflicts or problems; but I did not say that this is a good solution. The aggression invited by witchcraft beliefs is as harmful as anything a society can produce in the way of disruptive practices; the relief offered by witch-hunting and witch-punishing is no more than temporary and their capacity to allay anxieties no more illusory: for if witchcraft beliefs resolve certain fears and tensions, they also produce others . . . the kind of remedy which both becomes a drug and poisons the system. (Parrinder 1958:206)

In hierarchical cultures, the "real" is that which fits within the hierarchy, the "illusory" is any force which pulls persons outside their place or station in the chain of being. Demons are considered masters of deceit, perpetrators of the illusion that one can break out of the orders of existence and act individually. "Subversion of hierarchy is to substitute chaos for cosmos, illness for health, disorder for order, falsity for truth, pollution for purity, delusion for plain sensory evidence, vainglory for humility, solipsism for awareness of others, negation for affirmation of social interaction, and so on" (Turner 1983:x).

The demonic is the fatal inversion and negation of order within a culture. It embodies the destructive, the evil, the final contradiction of life: death. The demonic symbolizes the destructive possibilities within any given cultural or social order (Kapferer 1983:232).

The eruption of anger, greed, violent rage, passion, or desire in a structured hierarchical society is seen as personal, social, and cosmic disruption; it is the appearance of the demonic.

Psychoanalytic Interpretations of Possession

The psychoanalytic reinterpretation of possession was initiated by Sigmund Freud. In "A Neurosis of Demoniacal Possession" he wrote (1949:436):

> What in those days were thought to be evil spirits to us are base and evil wishes, the derivatives of impulses which have been rejected and repressed. In one respect only do we not subscribe to the explanation of these phenomena current in medieval times; we have abandoned the projection of them into the outer world, attributing their origin instead to the inner life of the patient to whom they manifest themselves.

Freud interpreted the possession of the soul of this demonically possessed person in a case history from 1669 by use of his hypothesis that the "Devil" was "chosen as a substitute for a father figure." Assuming that God and the Devil "were originally one and the same, a single figure which was later split in two bearing opposed characteristics," Freud concludes (1949:437):

> If the benevolent and righteous God is a father substitute, it is not to be wondered at that the hostile attitude which leads to hate, fear, and accusations against him comes to expression in the figure of Satan. The father is thus the individual protypable God and the Devil.

Following the lead of observable phenomena in particular cases—like the paranoid psychotic who externalizes an inflamed conscience and perceives it as persecution coming from outside—Freud generalizes the case into a series of inferences about universals. That God or Satan can function as a father substitute in a particular case is demonstrable; to infer that this reveals a universal explanation of cosmic good and evil is reducing the most complex issues to the simplicity of a psychical defense.

The Jungian interpretation characteristically turns inward for an understanding of the demonic rather than outward, as does Freud, to the loss of a loved object. The human psyche (as modeled in Figure 9-2) is not self-contained and isolated from others but is continuous with humanity through its depths in the collective unconscious. These historical and cultural legacies form patterns within the unconscious. The persona presented to the world is a compromise between the outer reality and the ego within. Beneath the self-awareness of the ego lies the shadow of all that is negated, denied, and repressed into the personal unconscious. Within the reserves of the unconscious is the cross-sexual pole of the psyche (the anima for males, the animus for females) which is the source of creativity and growth and the guide to completeness.

At the center is the self, which is rarely known before midlife, when the person turns inward in deeper self-understanding. Within the psyche

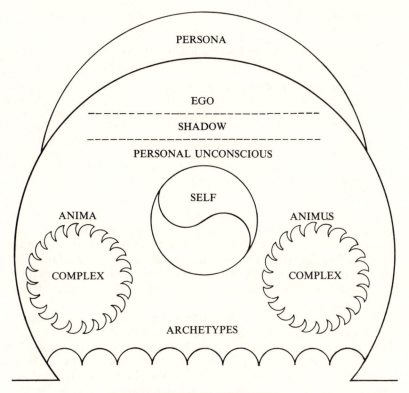

Figure 9-2. The Jungian model of the self.

Complexes, split off from consciousness, absorbing energy from the archetypes and the collective unconscious and allying with the cross-sexual pole (the anima or animus), may erupt with demonic malignancy.

float complexes that can claim a central position as a false self, a negative destructive center as the self fragments.

Within the psyche, these complexes exist with a degree of autonomy that can erupt into the personal unconscious and break through the shadow and threaten to overwhelm the entire personality. As Jung writes (1933:91):

> Whatever else may be taking place within the obscure recesses of the psyche —and there are notoriously many opinions as to this matter—one thing is certain: it is first and foremost the so-called complexes (emotionally toned contents having a certain amount of autonomy) which play an important part there. The expression "autonomous complex" has often met with opposition, although, as it seems to me, unjustifiably. The active contents of the unconscious do behave in a way I cannot describe better than by the word autonomous. The complexes . . . come and go as they please. They have been split off from consciousness and lead a separate existence in the

unconscious, being at all times ready to hinder or reinforce the conscious intentions.

Possession is dissociation magnified to the creation of an alter- or counter-ego, suggests Gross (1963:185), following Jungian thought.

> The magnification of dissociation is increased in an atmosphere of belief in possessing spirits. We may assume that this is not only due to the presence of "suggestion" but to *what* is suggested. "Spirits" are the archetypical symbols for complexes. They have the connotation of independent psychic entities, so that when the unconscious accepts the idea of a possessing spirit, the splintering of the psyche is accentuated. This analysis suggests, further-more, that the quality or the nature of the possessing spirit will reveal the nature of the autonomous complex and will point to the source of the psychic conflict.

From the Jungian perspective, a complex may take on a demonic character as it becomes autonomously malevolent and emerges as "another personality," distinct from and directly opposite to the ego or the persona. The dissociation of the complex, the magnification of its malignancy, the investment with supernatural character (or recognition of it as a culturally defined spirit, god, or demon) all unite to endow it with extrahuman power and identity.

A complex may draw energy from the archetypes in the collective unconscious, ally itself with the most potent force in the psyche, the cross-sexual pole of anima or animus, and function "supernaturally" in inexplicable potency, malignancy, and diabolic destructiveness. When this complex and its allied forces within the psyche are identified as a spirit or demon by the culture or by significant persons within that culture, the belief gains power from its contextual congruence with the community's worldview.

Psychoanalytic thinkers of the object relations school understand the demonic in a way parallel to Jung's "complex." The personality may be dominated by a part process, by an ego introjection. In the de-velopmental process of internalizing objects—relationships, their emo-tional tones, the image of significant persons—destructive objects may be introjected and identified as an evil self. These good and bad ob-jects may take possession of the person in later crises. Fairbairn notes (1954:70):

> It is to the realm of these bad objects . . . that the ultimate origin of all psychopathological developments is to be traced; for it may be said of all psychoneurotic and psychotic patients that, if a True Mass is being cele-brated in the chancel, a Black Mass is being celebrated in the crypt. It becomes evident, accordingly, that the psychotherapist is the true successor to the exorcist, and that he is concerned, not only with the "forgiveness of sins," but also with "the casting out of devils."

Writing from the perspective of object relations theory, Henderson (1976:627) implies that therapist and exorcist are dealing with identical phenomena but with different techniques.

The religious view of emotional pain contains an important if imperfect truth which has been too long disregarded. The psychotherapist differs from the exorcist not so much in theory, although terminology is different, but in belief that the therapeutic process to be effective is apt to require a more painstaking process to dissolve the persecuting forces.

This object relations theory sees ego introjections of unconditional badness and unbridled commitment to evil returning in times of stress or crisis and taking possession of the total ego. Part process comes to dominate the whole; the evil incorporated in childhood with its concreteness, totalism, and cosmic malevolence later erupts in demonic form.

Possession as Hysteric Behavior

Possession in many cultures is a common phenomenon, treated with simple and concrete therapies. Newman (1965:84) has described such a case from the Gururumba of New Guinea. Among them, ghost possession is a state seen as dangerous to both the individual and the group.

> A party of men had gone into a mountain forest to search for wild pandanus nuts. While there, some of them decided to hunt tree-climbing kangaroos. BonGire, one of the hunters, became separated from the others, and burst into camp late at night, bleeding at the nose, his body badly scratched. Rushing to the campfire, he stood for a moment in silence; then suddenly he began shouting wildly and attacking bystanders until he was subdued and tied to a tree at the edge of the clearing. This unusual behavior was interpreted as ghost possession. The campfire was built up and smothered in wet leaves to create smoke; BonGire was suspended, hands and feet bound, from a pole and held in the smoke until he vomited. After five minutes or so of this treatment he cried out in his normal voice to be taken out of the smoke, thus indicating that his ghost had been exorcised and that he was again normal.

Possession as the experience of being controlled by alien intrusive powers can be viewed as the tyranny of a part of the emotional self over the whole. In Western thought this is understood as hysteria. In collective cultures it may be experienced as possession.

Hysteria, as an occasional behavior, as a personality disorder, or as a hysterical psychosis, shares in common the factors of intense repression and the misapprehension of a part of the personality as the whole. The person in repressing one emotion allows the self to be flooded by another. The exaggerated emotion is experienced in the absence of centered thinking and feeling and the exclusion of opposite emotions. Thus when angry the person sees the whole self and relationship as defined by that anger; when affectionate the affiliative feelings fill the total field of vision. Hysteria is thus a polar swing in response to intensely repressive internal-control strategies.

Hysteria, in Western diagnosis, is defined by its exaggerated deviations from inner control of and inner responsibility for choices and their consequences. In a culture that views the self as externally controlled by the situation or circumstances and sees responsibility as lying outside the self within the group, the identical process of hysteria is experienced in a reverse pattern.

The equivalent disturbance for hysteria, when experienced in an outer-directed culture, is possession (Table 9-1). Out of his studies of possession in Southeast Asian cultures, Langness has drawn on the similarities between inner-directed hysteric psychoses and the same functional process in outer-directed collective cultures. The two phenomena are functional equivalents, he concludes; both channel and exploit existing neurotic leanings and relieve mental stress. Hysterical psychoses and possessions are both sociocultural and individual phenomena. The presence of one in a culture, caste, or class is directly related to the absence of the other.

From this correlation of the two phenomena, Langness concludes (1976:62):

1. We should consider the possession phenomena in various cultures —*Malgri* in the Wellesley Islands, *wiitiki* in Ojibwa Indians of Canada, *latah* in Malaysia, *imu* in Japan, *negi* in New Guinea, *koro* in Southeast Asia—as members of the same class of behavior and equivalent to hysterical psychoses experienced in individualized cultures.

2. We should accept the word "possession" to describe the behavioral syndromes in which the culture has patterns for and ways of inducing the experience.

3. We should consider trance as a phenomenon apart from either possession or hysterical psychosis.

4. We should consider these latter two equivalent since (a) they are both episodes of brief duration although with recurrent episodes, (b) they are predictable in form, (c) they occur only in limited segments of the

---

Table 9-1. The Hysteria Model of Understanding Possession

Individual Hysterical Psychosis	Collective Possession
An individualized psychopathology occurring in a culture that sees its members as isolated units responsible for self and behavior.	A collective phenomenon occurring in a culture that sees its members as parts of the solidarity of family, kinship, and tribal systems sharing responsibility.
Hysteria is a culturally shaped private experience, a profane phenomenon individualized in the culture.	Possession is a culturally normative religious experience, a sacred phenomenon institutionalized in the culture.
Responses are individual, to unconscious conflicts within the isolated individual.	Responses are sociial, to unconscious conflicts within the culture.

population, (d) they are learned, and (e) they can both be seen as stemming from conflicts in the ethnic unconscious.

A psychosocial interpretation of demonology has been suggested by Robert LeVine (1973) by correlating the degree of cultural belief in possession with the individual's propensity to participate in possession process. Within the general culture of belief there will be degrees of potential for differing individuals to act out the community's beliefs of demonology, where the general belief of demonology is a culturally modal belief that serves to perpetuate, defend, and strengthen the sociocultural system and deepen its solidarity. In situations where the general belief in demonology is no longer a culturally modal belief, only those with specific psychological tendencies (phobic, hysteric, obsessive, or a histrionic personality disorder) are likely to use such beliefs in their ego defense, and a psychosis with strongly hysteric character and a past or present context of belief in demonology may be expressed in acting out clearly demonic possession.

The possession syndrome may strike an entire village, as in 1966, when an epidemic of possession occurred in a village near Ranchi, India. Measles and chicken pox had been raging for about a month. Such epidemics are explained even by educated people as a visitation of the goddess Kali or one of her avatars, so a rigid routine of prayer and fasting was being strictly followed throughout the village.

> A girl of eleven suddenly felt a peculiar sensation entering her body, began to sway dramatically, and announced "I have come—I am here." The village exorcist was called and was severely reprimanded by the girl for not recognizing her as Muruga. The exorcist ignored this and began to dance around her and shout, so the exasperated goddess snatched a handful of burning coals from a fire, and said, "Take this payment and annoy me no further." People saw that she was not burned and were convinced that she was indeed Muruga, so they bowed down and worshipped her. The goddess then said that promised sacrifices had not been given and she had come to claim her due. She then established herself in a neighbor's house and prophesied through the night. Great crowds gathered, and then others became possessed. A girl of eighteen claimed to be Kali; a boy of eight, Shiva; another woman an avatar; and then several more. After a week, all returned to their normal personalities. Psychiatric investigation of all indicated unresolved personality disturbances which they sought to escape through the religious symbolism. The so-called possession syndromes are in fact examples of the phenomenon of multiple personality . . . the result of unconscious dissociative processes. (Verghese and Abraham 1976:37–38)

Following a "possession epidemic" in a school in west Karnataka, India, a psychiatric team did an epidemiological study of thirty villages around the school. The high prevalence of the possession syndrome in children believing themselves inhabited by spirits and "ganas," or demigods, was correlated with a high belief in the existence of possession phenomena. Female sex, young age, and low education were found to predispose an individual to become possessed in response to this powerful religious atmosphere. The possession syndrome, they concluded, is a temporary induced phenomenon used by some to become healers and counselors, by others to take up the sick role and get help, and by others to enact religious ritual and gain attention and elevation. Some fail to gain anything and suffer (Venkataramaiah 1981:217–219).

The victims of possession states usually have psychiatric problems, and this is an opportunity for emotional abreaction in a socially sanctioned way. Dissociation states provide emotional catharsis, a sense of renewal, and an improved capacity for dealing with reality. They reinforce group values and group integration playing a formalized role in the native system of psychopathology (Verghese and Abraham 1976:131).

Yap (1966:114), studying possession in the Chinese population of Hong Kong, identified three traits necessary for this phenomenon to occur. The subject should be (1) dependent and conforming in character, (2) confronted with a problem of great importance with regard to her instinctual and emotional needs, and (3) responding in the presence of a group belief in the occurrences of possession.

The state of possession can be divided into three degrees. First-degree possession is complete. There is clouding of consciousness, skin anesthesia to pain, a changed demeanor and tone of voice, an inability to call the patient to reality, and subsequent amnesia. Second-degree or partial possession consists of mild clouding, partial anesthesia, no change in voice or demeanor, the possibility of recall, but partial amnesia. Third-degree or histrionic possession shows no clouding, anesthesia, change of voice, or demeanor; there is immediate recall and the seeking of attention, with mannerisms such as giggling or inviting behaviors.

As a summary definition after his studies of possession in multiple cultures, Kiev concludes (1961:133): "Spirit possession is a culturally sanctioned, heavily institutionalized, and symbolically invested means of expression in action for various egodystonic impulses and thoughts."

The regularity, consistency, and predictability of the possession syndrome in various cultures suggest to many psychiatrists that it should be seen as a category of behavior that is clinically recognizable and diagnostically clear. As Teja writes (1970:37), "Hysterical possession states provide a unique syndrome of hysteric behaviors and should be recognized as a diagnostic category under the hysteric psychoses."

Diagnosis of Possession

The incidence of possession symptoms in both Eastern and Western cultures, in less developed and in highly technological cultures, confronts the pastoral counselor with persons reporting oppression by external spirits in settings in which this would have previously been immediately considered psychotic symptomology.

Mansell Pattison writes of this increase in Western culture (1977:9):

> With an understanding of the social conditions which give rise to demonology, it is possible to see that contemporary social conditions are ripe in the western world for the re-emergence of supernaturalistic belief

systems, and even demonology. Society has been perceived as oppressive, trust in social institutions has disintegrated, social protest has been realistically dangerous, and a mood of helpless impotence has emerged. New hope, new meaning, and new purpose can be seen in the myriad of supernaturalistic systems now gaining devotees. So it should not surprise us that the evil society should again be personified and symbolized in demonology.

Many pastoral counselors in cross-cultural settings take a position of suspended judgment even while in active encounter with the convictions and beliefs of their clients. Their basic assumption is that, for what is perceived to be real, the consequences are real; for those who believe in spirit possession or demonic oppression, these powers are realities both of thought and experience. They neither affirm nor deny the existence of reality of the spirits and demons, but they trace and clarify the perceptions and understandings of the persons involved and support them in requesting prayer, liberation, and exorcism from their congregation or faith community. (See Case Study: Amerindian Possession.)

Interpathic co-experiencing of the fear, powerlessness, and sense of external oppression that holds the "possessed" person in a steel-gloved grasp allows the therapist to feel the consequences of this pain within himself or herself and to stand with the other authentically in the search for liberation and deliverance.

Regardless of whether the pastoral counselor perceives the demonic as ontologically, socially, culturally, or functionally evil, diagnosis of the oppression state is necessary for effective pastoral counseling, pastoral psychotherapy, or general pastoral care.

The diagnosis of possession and associated trance behaviors is a complex phenomenon. Pastoral counselors in many cultures struggle with differentiating between the symptoms of psychoses, neuroses, or personality disorders and the trance phenomena they perceive as destructive, evil, and indicating the demonic.

Historic Catholic and Protestant traditions of exorcism require the examination of the troubled person by psychiatric disciplines to differentiate between a psychic disorder and extrapsychic oppression; however, the criteria vary from one diagnostician to another. The pastor requesting consultation may encounter only mental health professionals, who begin from an assumption of unitary causation from natural intrapsychic disturbances.

Clinically trained pastoral counselors in India, Indonesia, and Hong Kong who consult with pastors on their decisions about troubled counselees report the following criteria: (1) Has there been any history of mental illness in the person over a period of years? (2) Is there any history of mental illness in the family system? (3) Is there evidence of a regular cyclical mood swing indicating an affective disorder? (4) Are there signs of a thought disorder—detachment from reality, delusions, hallucinations, loss of ego boundaries, loss of reality-testing skills? These indicate a psychiatric disturbance. The most prominent features are (1) a fixed opposition to moral, ethical, and spiritual values; (2) an intense hostility toward values, symbols, and persons that represent the sacred, the holy; (3) a loss of voluntary control of these behaviors; and (4) trancelike behaviors, evidenced in a counter-personality, alien voices, unexplained knowledge, claims, and evidences. All indicate oppression of evil in possession (Krisetya 1984).

The criteria cited are parallel to those used by pastoral diagnosticians in Western cultures, but in all settings clarity in diagnosis and in accuracy of assessment vary widely from clinician to clinician. The boundaries are rarely clear, because neurotic and psychotic symptoms frequently accompany those signs used to identify demonic incursions into the personality.

CASE STUDY: Amerindian Possession (United States)

Mary is a pretty, well-developed, adolescent thirteen-year-old girl from the Yakima Indian Reservation. The public health doctor has diagnosed "acute schizophrenic psychosis" after finding her incoherent, agitated, babbling, and muttering about ghosts.

Mary's problems began four months earlier at a summer camp for Indian girls. She and several girlfriends had stolen out at night to play in the moonlight among the tall fir trees. As they ran through the shadows they saw human figures up in the trees, which drifted down, and the girls recognized them as their tribal ancestors. The girls reported talking to and hearing words from the ghosts before they ran back to their cabin and hid beneath the covers. But a ghost followed Mary, jumped on her as she lay in bed, and tried to choke her. She struggled and screamed, gasping for breath. The counselors came running but could not calm her, so she was taken to the local hospital for a tranquilizing shot, then home to her parents.

For the following months, Mary attended high school in teenage clothes and was an honor student, a cheerleader, and a student body officer. But at home each evening she combed her hair into traditional braids, donned long-skirted Indian dress, and wandered about in a daze. She would see ghosts at the windows or, when walking out-of-doors, blood on the ground. She thought the ghosts had killed one of her friends and feared they would attack her family. She would become so anxious at these times that she would have to be taken to the emergency room for a shot, but the next morning she would get up and go to school like a normal schoolgirl.

The mother, reassured that the psychiatrist believed in religion, confided that her own father had been a witch doctor who had healing powers. He had healed her of severe facial burns, leaving no scars. For the first time she admitted that her father had told her that his powers would be passed on to a grandchild; that the oldest, this girl, would have his powers. The mother suspected that Mary's disturbance was related to this, although the family was now Presbyterian and did not believe in witchcraft.

"In old times," the mother reported, "someone receiving the powers of the spirits to become a witch doctor had to struggle with spirits until she proved that she could rule them. If the person did not want to accept the gift, a ceremony of exorcism would renounce the grandfather's legacy and set her free."

Mary, the mother, and the counselor agreed that the old women of the tribe should gather and conduct the ritual of exorcism that night. Following the ceremony, Mary's strange behavior disappeared. Her mood, behavior, and family relationships returned to normal.

> *Psychiatrist's Note:* An almost identical story is told in the account of Jacob's wrestling and gaining power over a night spirit (Gen. 32:24–31). *Psychodynamically,* one might see the mother as favored daughter of the father competing with her maturing daughter. The mother withholds approval of her daughter's sexuality; the daughter projects this disapproval onto hallucinatory ghost objects and on the incestuous grandfather. The resolution comes as mother and daughter ritualize the daughter's freedom, maturation, and right to become a woman. *Transculturally,* the particular psychodynamic of family life was acted out in a pattern provided by the culture, but the family was caught between cultures. The diagnosis of schizophrenia and the medications were understandable but inappropriate. The sanctioning by the psychiatrist of the indigenous cultural healing process relieved this bind and enabled the natural system to function. Family therapy or individual psychotherapy would probably not have been successful, because the problem, though deeply repressed in all family members, was embedded in the traditional Indian belief system. Encountering it as real allowed an intervention in the system that was real.

(Condensed from Pattison 1977:11–15)

In Figure 9-3 the diagnostic process is diagrammed on a decision tree as utilized in the DSM III diagnostic sequences. There are two main assumptions behind this pattern for differential diagnosis.

First, when there are clear physical, medical, or biochemical deficits or discernible personality or crisis determinants, these should be treated first before spiritual options are pursued. (As a hungry person needs meat before meaning because concern for physical needs is the meaningful way of addressing the felt need, so the person with biophysical deficits deserves medical and psychiatric or psychological clinical care before spiritual intervention.) Care for the full functioning of the organism is basic to care for the full mental, spiritual, and relational wholeness of the person.

The subpoints of this assumption are: (1) Mental illness and spiritual oppression by overwhelming evil can be differentiated and must be seen distinctly (so psychotic features should be identified and treated as thought disorders, not spiritual disorders). (2) The possession ideation that may accompany the thought disturbance occurring at mood-swing times in bipolar disorders should be treated as an affective disorder rather than spiritual highs and lows. (3) Factitious disorders, such as demonopathy in imitation of possession or malingering as an attention-seeking process should be clearly differentiated from involuntary oppression. (4) Indiscriminate categorizing of persons, and groups, religious functions of shamans and priests, individual and group mysticism, and hypnotic trance processes should be eliminated. (5) Long-term personality disorders such as the histrionic personality must be recognized; spiritual treatment of what is a developmentally learned and enduring personality tendency is rarely indicated because most of the determinants are unconscious and not available to volitional response (repentance) or transformation through surrender to transcendent power (conversion).

Second, a sense of being overwhelmed by the demonic, and signs of personality possession, may be indicated by (1) the explicit negations of core faith assumptions; (2) appositional behavior to moral, responsible, spiritual values; and (3) insistent blasphemous, scatological, self-consciously evil responses to affirmations of faith, hope, grace, and love from the surrounding group offering pastoral care.

The diagnostic pattern of Figure 9-3 is focused on careful identification of symptoms to differentiate possession from psychosis, neurosis, and personality disorders. However, it does not suggest that possession phenomena cannot occur in conjunction with other disorders and personality disturbances.

The intercultural counselor who prefers pastoral diagnosis from theological categories—grace, hope, love, vocation—may find clinical differentiation such as the decision tree unfamiliar or confusing. Interdisciplinary conversations between the various helping professionals are used in many different cultures to clarify the differences between the experiences of frailty, suffering, and disorder and the puzzling troubles understood as an incursion of evil and defined by the language of the mesocosmos.

In all diagnosis, one may look either for a primary cause or for multifactoral causes of emotional or spiritual troubledness. Emotional disturbance in a personality may be an opening for possession or a consequence of possession, or there may be no relationship at all between emotional disorder and possession.

Diagnostically, one may employ a viewpoint of either unitary or multiple causation. The unitary approach, which looks for a single cause, is exemplified either by those mental health professionals who *only* associate possession processes with mental illness or by shamans who *only* associate these same processes with demons. The multiple-causation view recognizes the possibility that eruptions from the unconscious may occur in emotional distress alone, or such distress may be present with a consciousness of overwhelming evil. Diagnosis may proceed in either/ or, both/and, neither/nor options (Southard 1984:4).

The multiple-causation viewpoint allows recognition of greater complexity and variety in emotional and spiritual pathology. It views posses-

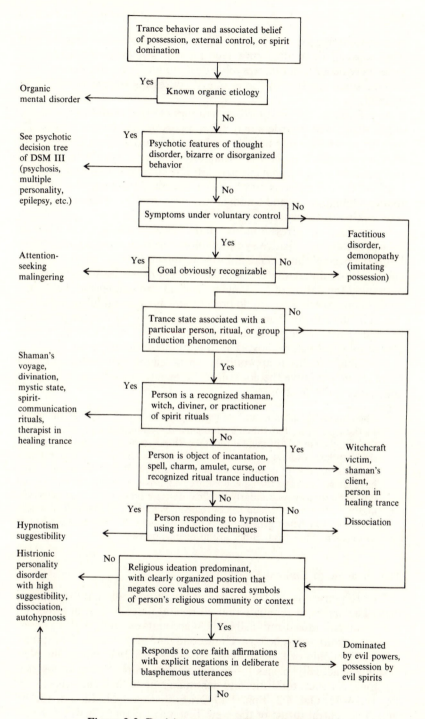

Figure 9-3. Decision tree for differential diagnosis of trance behavior and possession belief.

sion as occurring jointly with the other options listed on the decision tree. Thus a psychotic, malingering, factitious, or histrionic personality disorder may occur as an intrapsychic dysfunction in conjunction with an extrapersonal invasion by forces of evil oppressing the personality from without.

A multiple-causation approach assumes (1) that both internally and externally caused disorders may affect a personality simultaneously, (2) that the personality fragmenting in thought disorder or out of control in affective disorder may be vulnerable to domination by external evil, (3) that the individual without effective impulse control and subject to flooding from the unconscious may be more susceptible to possession, and (4) that psychopathology and demonic troubledness may be interrelated and interlocking disturbances.

Counselors who stress a unitive diagnosis note that signs of evil exist in a psychotic or affective symptomology (as it disrupts relationships, limits the person's human possibilities, or inflicts internal pain), but these can be clearly differentiated from the concept of possession. The task of discerning the nature of the human problem and diagnosing the disturbance being experienced should precede any moral or middle-zone explanation in any culture. Thus pastoral therapy must begin in the physical/scientific realm to diagnose the physical, cerebral, biochemical, or psychopathological before moving to the middle-zone diagnoses.

A flexible humility is appropriate when dealing with issues on which there are no definitive theological or therapeutic answers, as Paul Bach concludes (1979:24–25):

> The church should not confuse psychopathology with demonic influence. In the case of an individual's problems, the church should first consider them in the context of mental illness, with possession as a consideration of the very last resort. . . . First of all, there is no creedal statement which includes mention of demon possession or demons. If the framers of dogma have chosen to leave the issue unaddressed, it is not wise for us to be more dogmatic than they. Similarly, biblical description of possession behavior, and Christian belief which has developed as a result of the biblical narratives, are very heterogeneous, as is mental illness. Therefore, it is best not to overgeneralize from either group of phenomena.

The Demonic in Biblical Literature

Two responses to the biblical literature on possession are most common. The first is to conclude that all mental illness was seen as demon possession and thus dismiss all biblical accounts as mythological, superstitious, primitive psychology. The second tendency is to see the primary locus of demonic evil in troubled persons rather than where the New Testament actually places it—in social and political institutions that become idolatrous, totalistic, and dehumanizing to their subjects (1 Cor. 2:6; 15:24–26; Gal. 4:3; Eph. 1:19–21; 6:12; Col. 1:13, 16; 2:8, 15, 20; etc.). The central thrust of the New Testament is that Christ has delivered humankind from elemental powers of taboo, superstition, and fearful bondage; that he has received authority over social, political, structural, and national powers that abuse, misuse, betray, and bind humankind.

Many experts in human sciences declare that the ancients saw all mental illness as demonic in nature and causation. They point to the biblical records as a case in point, but the fact is that the biblical documents reveal a clear concept of "madness" differentiated from the concept of possession.

Nebuchadnezzar, warned by Daniel of the megalomanic self-image, of arrogant pride, and of his insatiable ego, refused to change his ways and a year later was smitten by madness, seven years of delusional thinking followed by the king's being ostracized from civilization. Daniel, amid Chaldean colleagues skilled in magic, divination, and the demonic, makes no attempt at such an explanation. Instead it is irrationality—the loss and regaining of reason—that is noted.

David (1 Sam. 21:13–15), in danger of his life in the Philistine city-state of Gath, feigned insanity. "He changed his behavior before them, and feigned himself mad in their hands, and made marks on the doors of the gate, and let his spittle run down his beard. Then said Achish to his servants, 'Lo, you see the man is mad; why then have you brought him to me? Do I lack madmen, that you have brought this fellow to play the madman in my presence?' "

David, Achish, the Hebrews, and the Philistines shared a common concept of madness and its characteristic behavior. Yet David was a refugee from his own king's wrath at this very time, and it was ascribed to "an evil spirit from the LORD." It was not Saul's possession but common madness that David mimicked.

Further references to madness occur in the Old Testament (Deut. 28:28; Eccl. 1:17; 2:2, 12; 7:25; 9:3; 10:13; Jer. 25:16; 50:38; 51:7; Zech. 12:4).

In the New Testament, madness and demon possession exist as separate categories as well. Festus (Acts 26:24) accuses Paul of irrationality; the Greek word used is the root of our term *manic*. Rhoda (Acts 12:15) is accused of being manic but not demonized, when she seems detached from reality. Paul uses the word to suggest how Corinthian citizens might regard Christians who speak in tongues (1 Cor. 14:23).

Jesus both cast out demons and healed physical diseases. At times physical illnesses were attributed to possession. Mark 9:14–29 indicates that both epilepsy and deafness were linked to demonic torment. Matthew 12:22–24 reports a deaf and blind man whose condition is attributed to an evil spirit. Yet Jesus confronted deafness, dumbness, and blindness on other occasions with no reference to demonic activity.

Demonic domination is, in contrast, a disintegration of the self, a fragmentation of its identity, a displacement of its sense of responsible agency. The symptoms of the demon-possessed recorded in the New Testament are self-hatred, self-destructiveness, fear, rage, withdrawal from human relationships, and generalized hostility (Mark 1:23–26; 5: 1–9; 9:14–29; etc.). The external locus of control, the sense of their being more sinned against than sinners, reveals a close parallel to the dissociation and hysteric personality patterns recognized in every culture as those of persons suffering thought and feeling disorders.

Jesus and the Mesocosmos

In the New Testament, as in all traditional cultures, there is the language of the macrocosmos—the realm of God—the language of the microcosmos—the world of humanity—and the language of the mesocosmos, with its unclean and evil spirits who provide explanation for physical illnesses and spiritual or emotional diseases. What is most striking is the restraint of these passages and the simplicity and directness of Jesus' response to the troubled persons brought to him. Several other conclusions are strongly supported by the data given.

1. All biblical references to possession are ascribed to demons, not to the devil. The two are not equated.
2. Jesus' encounter with those "possessed by demons" is totally different from the Jewish exorcism of his time. He used no spells, incantations, rituals, or invocations. Instead his method is the same with all illnesses and evil spirits.
3. The demons are described as the reverse of personhood, as antipersonal or nonpersonal forces. They are without name or identity.
4. The demons are evil powers or destructive forces that trouble persons, and these powers are perceived or interpreted differently in each culture and age. The encounter with the unseen and inexplicable will be conceptualized uniquely in each culture's language, experience, and interpretation of the nonrational.
5. The power Jesus gave to his disciples was the power to heal diseases of both internal and external cause. There is no mention of separate powers to heal and to exorcise. Expressions used to address illnesses are interchangeable with those used to command possession.

The encounter with the middle zone of human experience—the mesocosmos—occurs in both Old and New Testaments, but its near absence is more striking than its presence.

The sphere of the demonic in the Old Testament is restricted to the few references to practices in the surrounding nations. The three references to Satan (1 Chron. 21:1; Job 1–2; and Zech. 3:1–2) all refer to him as an actor in dramatic portrayals of God's sovereign administration of the world.

In the New Testament, the cosmic battle between the powers of evil and the appearance of the Christ form the context of the various references. The devil appears to tempt Jesus (Matt. 4:1–11; Mark 1:13) and his disciples (Matt. 6:13; 1 Cor. 7:5). Some cases of physical, mental, and emotional illness (Matt. 12:22; Mark 5:1–20; 9:17) but not all (Mark 1:29–31; 2:1–12; John 9:1–7), are attributed to the demonic. The primary goal of evil forces in the New Testament is not to oppress individuals but to corrupt and combat the community of the Spirit, the church (2 Cor.

2:11; 12:7; Eph. 6:11; 1 Thess. 2:18; 1 Peter 5:8). Jesus saw conscientious Pharisees as the sons of Satan (John 8:44), not prostitutes or tax collectors. It was his friend Peter whom he called Satan, not his enemies who killed him (Mark 8:33).

Biblical scholars vary from those who interpret these passages as referring to a literal devil and demons as personal representatives of evil, to those who see these references as symbols that draw analogies from human experience to express how evil impacts upon human beings. Those who see these as "personal" are tempted to place responsibility for human sinfulness outside of human volition, or to focus on their impact on individuals rather than on the social, political, and cultural spheres the New Testament calls "principalities and powers." Any literal interpretation must not create equal and opposite forces in apposition to God or endow their "personal nature" with the full personhood possessed only by God and humans created in God's image. Those who interpret the devil and the demonic as symbolizing evil dare not lose the full respect for the mystery and immensity of evil or seek to minimize its effect on all levels of human society—political, social, communal, familial, and psychological.

The symbolic interpretation is characteristic of the biblical theology of many pastoral theologians since it (1) accepts the great problem of evil without the reductionism of much demonology; (2) applies the demonic to the many ways in which evil permeates social, personal, and political systems; (3) affirms the destructive nature of the demonic and diabolic as nonbeing, as negating all good, as the absence of truth, virtue, and righteousness; (4) gives a name to the conflicts with evil that people face within, between, and among them in their communities; and (5) uncovers the realities of evil hidden beneath the conscious defenses of the person, the surface concealments of systems, the public faces of institutions.

Interviews with pastoral counselors in Asia, Africa, South and Central America, Oceania, Europe, and the Middle East contribute to and shape the following guidelines.

1. The pastoral counselor must use culturally adaptive syntonic language, concepts, and explanations in both psychological and theological diagnoses. Emic constructs (from within a given culture), not etic ones (from without), and contextually congruent, not incongruent, theory, are necessary. And this is especially crucial in working with middle-zone issues.

2. The Western-trained pastoral counselor must recognize the conceptual vacuum in both theory and theology. The paradigms of Western scientific thought offer an empty epistemology for unraveling experiences of possession by alien personalities, collective influence of group hypnosis, and the power of rituals, spells, incantations, and the like in tribal life.

3. The pastoral counselor must be willing to see the client within her or his context, understand the personality in its relational network, and respect the person's theology in its cultural integrity. This requires flexi-

bility in one's own theological framework and a willingness to enter another's experience interpathically.

4. The counselor must be open to other traditions of healing, to learn from the other culture's healing practices, to respect those methods that are integrative, conjunctive and reconciling, and to confront those that are fragmenting, disjunctive, and alienating.

5. The pastoral counselor follows the tradition of the prophets in demystification of the natural world. Where wind, storm, fire, pestilence, and earthquake were seen as the work of animistic gods or demonic powers, the Old Testament prophets declared that these were natural forces under the dominion of the Creator. This process of reframing the middle zone can result in secularization, as more and more is included in the zone of natural science, or it may sacralize, as all of life is seen as sacred, all of creation as entrusted to our care, and all natural forces as evidence of the Creator's work.

Summary

The intercultural pastoral counselor functions with an expanded worldview that accepts middle-zone experience without imposing a single-level scientific perspective. Recognizing the role of metaphorical feelings, language, and explanations in problem resolution and healing, the counselor is flexible in drawing on and cooperating with traditional healing processes and communal, tribal, and religious expectations and beliefs of each counselee or family.

Cooperation with traditional healers, religious leaders, and communal spokespersons strengthens the counselor's ability to intervene in and influence most cultures of the world.

Possession experience occurs in all known cultures. It is particularly marked in groups in transition or those experiencing social oppression. Possession can be usefully viewed from psychoanalytic, behavioral, cultural, and religious paradigms since it serves functions in all these domains. Effective pastoral care requires (1) careful diagnosis, which differentiates what are mental, social, and spiritual phenomena and (2) responsible intervention that takes evil as well as illness seriously.

The intercultural pastoral counselor, as a representative of the faith community, encounters both counselees and context, persons and their healing assumptions, traditions, and potentials, with interpathic warmth, authenticity, and insight. Faith in the ultimate power of God can direct the destructive into constructive change, the demonic toward liberating and redemptive transformation.

10

Mental Health and Mental Distress Across Cultures

A Theology of Human Frailty

"Let us define mental health as the adjustment of human beings to the world and to each other with a maximum of effectiveness and happiness. Not just efficiency, or just contentment—or obeying the rules of the game cheerfully. It is all of these together."

—Karl Menninger, 1955

"The reasonable [person] adapts . . . to the world; the unreasonable one persists in trying to adapt the world to himself. Therefore all progress depends on the unreasonable."

—George Bernard Shaw

"I am beginning to realize that 'sanity' is no longer a value or an end in itself. The 'sanity' of modern man is about as useful to him as the huge bulk and muscles of the dinosaur. If he were a little less sane, a little more doubtful, or a little more aware of his absurdities and contradictions, perhaps there might be a possibility of his survival."

—Thomas Merton, 1966

THE BLACKSMITH AND THE KING
BAGANDA TRIBE, UGANDA, EAST AFRICA

There was once, a long time ago, a blacksmith named Walukaga. He was the chief of the king's blacksmiths, and he could make hoes, knives, spears, axes, and hooks. And he could make wonderful figures of iron for the king.

One day the king summoned Walukaga and said, "Walukaga, you are the most skillful of all blacksmiths. I have a task which you alone can fulfill." Walukaga made obeisance, touching his forehead to the ground. The king clapped his hands, and attendants came bringing a great quantity of iron ready for the working. "Walukaga," said the king, "take this iron and forge it into a man, a real man of iron who can walk and talk, who has blood in his veins, knowledge in his head, and feelings in his heart."

Walukaga heard the king's words with despair. He knew not only that the request was impossible but that he must obey or lose his head and the heads of all his family. The king has taken leave of his senses, he thought, but he did not dare say it aloud.

For days Walukaga puzzled over what he could do. He asked counsel of all his friends. They suggested he take his family and flee to a far country. One night as he was returning home through the bush, he met a friend who had gone mad and was living in the wild. The man greeted him quite rationally, so they sat down and talked of this and that. Then Walukaga told him his story. The man said, "The king has gone mad, he has asked you for the impossible, and you must do no less. Go to the king, tell him that you must have special charcoal to stoke the fire and special water. He must order all the people to shave their heads and burn the hair to make one thousand loads of charcoal, and weep until there are one hundred pots of tears."

Walukaga knew immediately that the madman's advice alone could cure the king's madness and save his family. He went to the king and bowed low, then made the special requests. The king was so obsessed with his desire for an iron man that he readily agreed to give him whatever he needed.

All throughout the kingdom the subjects shaved and wept, but when all heads were smooth and all eyes squeezed dry there was not even one load of charcoal and one pot of tears.

The king sent for Walukaga and said, "Walukaga, do not try any more to make the iron man. I cannot give you the charcoal and water."

Walukaga bowed until his head touched the ground; then he looked up and said, "Master, you could not get these for me because it was impossible, just as impossible as it is to make an iron man who thinks and speaks and has feeling in his heart."

And all the people said, "Walukaga speaks the truth."

"One sixth of all people are suffering from the profound distress that is commonly called mental illness," the World Health Organization reported in 1975. That is about one person in every family, if they were evenly distributed. However, distribution and frequency vary from family to family, culture to culture, and country to country.

At least one fourth of all illness is mental illness, but 90 percent of the developing world receives little or no mental health care from professionals. Yet the culture, clan, or family may provide support, intervention, and "therapy" in ways that relieve symptoms and integrate the person into life with greater speed and effectiveness than Western practices produce.

The major patterns of abnormal behavior recognized by Western psychiatry are found throughout the world. However, there are important variations in the form, frequency, distribution, and social implications of this behavior.

Or, conversely, one might say, the major patterns of mental distress throughout the world can be labeled by the nomenclature of Western psychiatry, but the forms that certain symptoms take, the frequency of their occurrence, the preference a particular culture seems to have for a certain set of symptoms, and the way these symptoms are valued or disvalued in the community vary widely.

Attempts to compare the various types of mental disorders cross-culturally have generally been unsuccessful. One major difficulty is in separating what may be termed "primary symptoms" from "secondary symptoms." Primary symptoms—for example, those that are basic in characterizing depression—are those that occur early and constitute the actual disorder, such as loss of energy, sleep disturbance, and loss of affect. Secondary symptoms are the individual's reactions to the disorder—shame and self-punitive guilt in the West, lethargy, laziness, and avoidance of responsibility in other world settings. These secondary symptoms develop as the person attempts to come to terms with his or her changed behavior, and in an individualistic culture they are dealt with primarily by retroflection in self-reproach; in a collective society they may be attributed to external forces or projected onto a hostile environment. These secondary elements are thus strongly cultural, and the counselor must have sufficient familiarity with the world of the client to be able to distinguish the primary from the secondary problems.

As an introductory overview, it is helpful to note Draguns's conclusions after surveying psychological disorders of clinical severity (1980: 156).

No disorder is immune to cultural shaping.

No disorder is entirely traceable to cultural characteristics.

Psychoses are less influenced by culture than nonpsychotic disorders.

Affective disorders are more culturally shaped than the schizophrenias.

Variations of psychoses are meaningfully related to social, economic, technological, religious, and other features.

Differences are more marked on the plane of symptom than of syndrome.

Among symptoms, those of cognition, perception, and affect are less influenced by culture than those pertaining to rule and social behavior.

Both psychotic depression and schizophrenia appear to be characterized by a few symptoms that appear to be culturally unchangeable.

While the cultural plasticity of patient characteristics has been over-

estimated, the cultural plasticity of those involved—family, associates—
has been universally underestimated.

A great deal of the disagreement over the similarities and differences
in Eastern and Western views of mental illness comes from the tendency
to think in diagnostic terms and to compare views of etiology and the
ensuing labels. If attention is focused on comparing and correlating
symptom patterns instead of diagnostic categories, a great amount of the
cross-cultural confusion disappears. Searching for symptoms should precede any attempt to verify or duplicate any culture's categories of mental
illness.

Pastoral counselors, as responsible diagnosticians, must be well aware
of their own categories for understanding mental distress and equally
cognizant of the understandings of the persons, groups, and cultures in
which they are ministering. The ability to observe specific behaviors
rather than infer patterns that match familiar diagnoses, and to note
particular symptoms rather than intuit standard categories, will aid in
more discrete clinical work, because even the most common difficulties
in one's home culture may take significantly different form in another.

Labeling in Cross-Cultural Perspective

In recent years, the impact of labeling a pattern of behavior as "mental
illness" has been lessened by the suggestion that "what is viewed as
normal in one culture may be seen as quite aberrant in another" and so
the process of labeling is destructive. "Once the label of schizophrenia
has been applied, the diagnosis acts on all—patient, family, and relatives
—as a self-fulfilling prophecy. Eventually the patient accepts the diagnosis, with all of its surplus meanings and expectations, and behaves ac-
cordingly" (Rosenhan 1973:250,254).

This perspective on the dysfunction of labeling offers the following
description of the relationship between behavior patterns and the label
of "mental illness": (1) These behaviors represent deviations from what
is considered normal in a particular group, (2) the norms against which
the deviations are identified are different in different groups, (3) like
other deviations they elicit reactions of disapproval and stigmatization,
(4) the label once affixed tends to become fixed, (5) the person thus
labeled mentally ill is thereby encouraged to learn and accept the role
identity that perpetuates the stigmatizing behavior pattern, (6) individuals who are more powerless in a social group are more vulnerable to this process than are others, because (7) social agencies in modern industrial society contribute to the labeling process, which has the
effect of creating problems for those they treat rather than easing them
(Murphy 1976:1019).

Labeling theorists express a thorough dissatisfaction with the concept of mental illness, pointing out that it is a vague and euphemistic
metaphor and connects phenomena that are neither "mental" nor "illness." They note that the term came into use to protect people who

would otherwise have been burned at the stake as witches (Sarbin 1969:11,15). From this view, the label "mentally ill" is a stigmatizing and brutalizing assessment in any society, particularly those of the West. It robs the person of identity through profound mortification and depersonalization and forces an ascribed role with an extremely difficult exit.

A non-Western parallel is suggested by death practices among the Melanesians. Persons who are so old or so seriously ill that they are likely to die are labeled *mate,* which means "dead person." They then become subjects of a ceremonial live burial. The labeling process is a social fiction, in which the living are defined as dead, literally "mortified," perceived "as if dead," and then buried. Through the word *mate* the person is deprived of the right to life, although their understanding is that the person is relieved of a worn-out earth life and hastened on to a higher status in a spiritual afterlife. Thus the therapeutic intervention is motivated by caring intentions and a commitment to mutual aid (Rivers 1926:38–48).

The Melanesian myth of death is a parallel construct to the Western myth of madness, according to labeling theorists such as Scheff (1966), Szasz (1961, 1976), Sarbin (1969), and Goffman (1962). Their studies have challenged the reification of diagnostic language into permanent categories rather than heuristic metaphors and have exposed the tendency of theorists to propound *trait theories* (of unchanging attributes) out of data which suggest *state theories* of temporary or transitional nature. The more basic hypothesis is that in a culture where phenomena are not labeled "mental illness" they are screened out of the perception of the people who speak that language or are seen in other frames of reference as alternate forms of behavior.

In her comparative study of the Eskimo and the Yoruba tribespeople of Nigeria, Murphy (1976) noted that neither group have words that parallel our understandings of senility, neurosis, or depression or of a more general classification of mental illness. Yet the Yoruba lexicon has words for "unrest of mind which prevents sleep, terror at night, intense shame, fear of being among people, tenseness, overeagerness." The Eskimo have words for "worrying too much until it makes one sick, too easy to get afraid, crying with sadness, head down and rocking back and forth, shaking and trembling all over, afraid to stay indoors." In terms of sickness labels, these go unlabeled. Yet they exist, they are considered something the healer or shaman can cure, and they disqualify people for certain tasks, such as captain of a hunting boat. Murphy concludes (1976:1024):

> The answer to the question whether phenomena we label mental illness go unlabeled elsewhere is thus, yes. These Eskimos and Yorubas point out a large number of psychological and behavioral phenomena which we would call neurosis but which they do not put together under such a rubric. The consequence is not, however, a reduction in the number of persons who display the phenomena or great difference in how they are treated . . . the phenomena exist independently of labels.

In general terms, the treatment of troubled persons shows significant parallels from culture to culture. The Yoruba have no word for senility, but they observe older persons who become incapable of caring for themselves, talk to themselves, or wander away and get lost. In such cases they are watched, protected, and provided for in a way similar to that of a Western nursing home. And the common range of possible responses to the mentally ill—confinement, restraint, or exclusion from the community or allowing people to exclude themselves—happens in both Western and African nations. The helpless tend to receive help, the foolish are laughed at, the noisy are calmed with herbs or with medication, the violent are restrained. The styles vary widely, but the attitude is the same, best described as ambivalence—neither strongly negative in judgment and stigma nor positive in concern and understanding. There is fear and yet compassion.

In traditional China, the sense of stigma attached to mental illness led to the concealment of persons undergoing distress. Family members of persons with major mental illness still have a strong tendency to deny the fact. The severe stigma attached to mental illness can "arouse a great deal of shame and a sense of having failed one's family" (Sue and Sue 1973:641), leading to suppression and somatization, as we will observe in later discussion. Thus attitudes do vary widely, but the ambivalence of concern with mixed with confusion, of caring and avoidance, are common across cultures.

Thus, we may conclude, labels can be self-fulfilling prophesies that apply stereotypical roles and impose limitations, and they can also assist in naming, limiting, and identifying the nature, pattern, and predicted progression of an emotional disorder. They are part process, and not the central or causative part. Diagnoses are useful when employed heuristically and advisedly and when they are applied not with the hard determinism of a geologist identifying static specimens but with systemic and organismic definitions.

The classic parable of three umpires conversing about their art illustrates the varied attitudes of other diagnostic arts. "I calls 'em as I sees 'em," said the first. "I calls 'em as they is," said the second. "They ain't nothing till I calls 'em," said the third. At its worst, the label theorists have noted, diagnosis is like the third umpire. At its best, it follows the first.

That diagnostic language varies across cultures goes without saying, but similarities may occur, with the humor of surprise, as Leighton reports in a conversation with a Yoruba healer in Nigeria (1969:182).

> On one occasion a healer said to me, through an interpreter, "This man came here three months ago full of delusions and hallucinations; now he is free of them." I said, "What do these words 'hallucination' and 'delusion' mean? I don't understand." I asked this question thinking, of course, of the problems of cultural relativity in a culture where practices such as witchcraft, which in the West would be considered delusional, are accepted. The native healer scratched his head and looked a bit puzzled at this question, and then he said, "Well, when this man came here he was standing right

where you see him now and thought he was in Abeokuta" (which is about thirty miles away). "He thought I was his uncle, and he thought God was speaking to him from the clouds. Now I don't know what you call that in the United States, but here we consider that these are hallucinations and delusions."

What Is Normal, What Is Normative?

Effective mental health is measured by self-reliance, self-sufficiency, inner-directed responsibility for oneself, and an internal sense of personal identity—in the West. In Eastern cultures these traits are considered undesirable, abrasive, and disruptive of harmonious social relationships.

In the West, rugged individualism is still stressed as the model of mature personhood. As an ideal, individualism begins with a commitment to self-reliance. Persons in all societies express appropriate self-sufficiency, but individualism demands more—the belief that one controls one's own destiny without need of the assistance of others. This results in competitiveness and, surprisingly, conformity. In a climate of competitive climbing, the individualist must belong to status-giving groups, conform to their customs, and use these relationships to move toward success (Hsu 1983:4–5).

In sociocentric cultures mental health is measured by effective interpersonal relationships, the ability to maintain smooth harmonious group membership, responsibility to others, and accountability for one's own work and role in community. The person's center is not within the self but on the boundary between self and others.

> Certainly there are people who would be considered mad in any cultural setting; but there are others who show patterns of thinking, mood, speech, attitude, perception, and behavior perfectly acceptable in one [culture] but not so in another culture. A belief in spirits, considered perfectly normal in one group, becomes a delusion when expressed by a person belonging to another more "rational" culture. A degree of rebelliousness which is acceptable as normal in a Western adolescent can be seen as very distressful and odd when displayed by his counterpart in an orthodox Hindu family. (Carstairs and Kapur 1976:12)

"Mental health," according to the World Health Organization, "is the capacity of an individual to form harmonious relationships with others and to participate in or contribute constructively to changes in the social environment."

For African traditional groups, the social solidarity of person and community is essential for the health of the individual and the harmony of human relationships.

> Concepts of health within the framework of African culture are far more social than biological. In the mind of the African, there is a more unitary concept of psychosomatic interrelationship; that is, an apparent reciprocity between mind and matter. Health is not an isolated phenomenon but part of the entire magico-religious fabric; it is more than the absence of disease. Since disease is viewed as one of the most important social sanctions,

peaceful living with neighbors, abstention from adultery, and keeping the laws of gods and men are essentials in order to protect oneself and one's family from disease. (Lambo 1964:446)

In the traditional tribal worldview, the surrounding world is seen as hostile and threatening, an invading and destructive environment.

The external is aggressive. If man does not conquer it, it destroys man, and makes him a victim of tragedy. A sore which is neglected does not heal, but becomes infected to the point of gangrene. A child who is not educated goes backward. A society which is not governed destroys itself. (Kane 1961:79)

Violence is waiting to invade from without or to erupt within the community unless there are practitioners with power to inhibit or control these forces of disruption. Illness is only an epiphenomenon; the true cause of sickness is of a moral or relational or social order. The immediate mechanical, chemical, or other physical cause explains nothing. It is only a coincidence arranged by hidden conflicting forces that caused the fundamental conflict (Sow 1980:63).

The concepts of health and disease in African culture constitute a continuum from interior self to the wholeness of the environment with virtually imperceptible gradations. As Burstein notes (1952:77), "Medicine . . . is only one phase of a set of processes to promote human well-being; averting the wrath of gods or spirits, making rain, purifying streams or habitations, improving sex potency or fecundity or the fertility of fields and crops—in short, it is bound up with the whole interpretation of life."

What, then, is normal mental health within a culture, between cultures, or in a transcultural perspective? The problem of defining normalcy is intense, multifaceted, complex. "Normal" is routinely defined by a range of values clustered around the mean of a distribution curve in a general population. This is easily done for weight or height, but it is extremely complicated in defining personality.

Culture-free definitions of sanity are equally problematic. We may define a healthy person in any culture as one who is (1) pursuing a course of action with (2) the capacity to assess the behavior expected of him or her and the rewards or punishments for the personal choices made and (3) a willingness to accept the consequences or pay the price for those choices.

Can a total society become insane as it pits culture against person, forcing the performance of actions contrary to what is best for the human condition? If our criteria for making such judgments are found only within the present society or culture that has rendered the members human, the concept of "the human condition" is relative to the particular observer. When multiple cultural groups are used as a data base, a broader definition of the human condition can be achieved. When not only present universals but also the historical experience of the human community are included in formulating criteria, then a transcultural referent can be utilized. But even this may not offer us the accurate picture of what is normative humanness.

The pastoral counselor, when a Christian theologian, sees normative humanness as defined in a particular person chosen historically by a community, which recognized the normative character of that individual life as "revelatory" of a transcendent referent point. When the pastoral counselor represents Judaism, normative humanness is found in the biblical vision of the image of God. The usage of normality (prescriptive) as contrasted with a statistical norm (descriptive) is present in every caring discipline, although it is explicit with the religious therapist and implicit if often unarticulated by secular therapists.

Abnormal Behavior and Culture

Culture and psychopathology have developed a rich mythical relationship of romantic philosophical character that is not supported by clinical evidence. Consider these three examples.

1. The belief persists that some cultures protect their members from mental illness while others engender disorder. The oft-quoted belief is that nonindustrial cultures, which emphasize spiritual values, being, and harmony, have less illness, while industrialized cultures emphasizing materialism, doing, and competition generate more disorders. Each culture has its bonding and its alienating processes; each has conjunctive and disjunctive forces. The differences are in degree of stress, not in the absence of disorders in one group vs. another.

2. The view that primitive cultures are more healthy and developed cultures are more troubled by psychopathology finds more support in Enlightenment philosophy than in hard data. The judgment that insanity is part of the price we pay for civilization, made by many post-Enlightenment writers, including Sigmund Freud, was based on "the noble savage" assumption, not on clinical data. No cultural group has been found that is free of mental disorders. Each cultural group has greater differences within than between groups, which supports stress as the pivotal factor, not culture. Each cultural group makes certain subgroups lead more stressful lives. No culture avoids placing some subsets of people in psychologically noxious positions (Leighton 1982: 217). All cultures are flawed. All offer privilege to some groups and individuals, and all impose suffering and stress on some categories of persons.

3. The view that cultures are relatively stable, self-correcting, and self-integrating in cyclical patterns of change, growth, and evolution is a selective perception. Cultures can and do disintegrate, creating psychologically toxic and physically dangerous environments. When change accelerates beyond the adaptive abilities of human social systems and their members, the developmental processes are distorted by fragmenting parental processes, the stress levels of persons throughout the life cycle create dysfunctions, and the sociocultural matrix disintegrates. This may occur in visible disruptions of self-destructive violence, genocide, or oppression, or in slow, insidious distortion, dysfunction, and disintegra-

tion of social trust, institutional integrity, and the internal content of a culture's spirit, moral sensitivity, and will to meaning.

The relationship between culture and psychopathology has been most frequently studied by comparing symptoms or symptom clusters to note their differences. The next step is to note the similarities or identify which phenomena are identical.

Differences become meaningful and submit to interpretation as they are perceived as regular occasions in human experience. The movement must be from the idiographic (individual instance) to the nomothetic (natural law) in an ongoing rhythm of contact and concept. From this, it is hoped, a unifying law or principle may define a generic relationship between the psychological disorder and its cultural milieu.

Draguns (1975:119–120) suggests three possibilities concerning the nature of this relationship between a culture and its characteristic forms of mental disturbance.

1. Abnormal behavior represents an exaggeration of the typical adaptive behavior of a given culture. It is a caricature of its tendencies, or the cultural pattern reduced to the absurd. Compulsivity becomes the perfection of performance valued by a group exaggerated beyond the possible; hysteria is the dramatic element of relationship inflated from melodrams to daily theater.

2. Abnormal behavior stands in contrast to its culture. It is the path of greatest resistance expressed through doing the unexpected, the confusing, the culturally shocking, the deliberately unintelligible. Thus it makes the easy difficult, the simple complex, the concerned apathetic, the inconsequential into an obsessive concern.

3. Abnormal behavior varies irrationally from culture to culture. Its manner, meaning, and forms are independent of normal variations both within and between cultures. Thus it is neither reducible to nor predictable from culturally typical behavior patterns. This view would support the traditional medical model, which sees psychopathology as disturbed behavior best understood as illness, as irrationality, as disordered response.

Any of these three relationships can be used to explain the irregular responses of personality disorders or of psychological distress. Still, a variety of intriguing questions remain.

1. Are abnormal behaviors parallel to the normal variations between cultures? For example, in comparing Argentine psychiatric clients with Americans, the former show a marked passivity in symptom expression. In research on normal populations, a parallel passivity is substantiated for Argentine and for virtually all Latin-American populations (Diaz-Guerrero 1967:79).

2. Does abnormal behavior simply take the themes, concerns, illusions, and fears of its time and place? Studies done over the past century in European countries—Austria, Czechoslovakia, Italy, Germany—

demonstrate that the social and political ethos of the time is reflected in distorted forms in psychiatric symptoms. An Austrian psychiatrist has demonstrated that the common paranoid delusion of electrical control first appeared shortly after the first uses of electricity (Lenz 1964). The pathology of Japanese persons follows their own worldview, just as Western depression is shaped by Western views of reality, space, time, the physical body, and human activity.

Schizophrenic symptoms among Africans in Queensland included auditory and visual hallucinations of mythological content as well as delusions of grandeur, such as becoming a chief or doctor, and of being poisoned or bewitched. But European expatriates' delusions were of thought control through electricity, telepathy, and hypnotism (Laubscher 1937:221–224).

3. Does abnormal behavior act out the myths, types, and archetypes of its cultural milieu? From the folk rituals of Africa, the possession beliefs of Indonesia, the ancestral spirit, wind, and water beliefs of China, or the Horatio Alger or Hollywood-starlet myths of American success, each culture has its fantasies of fulfillment. Does the troubled person act out what the normal person dreams about, or do such persons resist defensively what the others strive to achieve?

4. Does the society have pre-patterned roles prepared for the persons they unconsciously select? Are there familial, clan, or communal scapegoats, persons who function as a safety value for the cultures accumulating stress? Perhaps the ways of perceiving troubledness are so stereotyped that no matter what the behavior of the individual in stress, the reactions, sanctions, stigma, avoidance, judgments, and special treatment channels the abnormal reaction down the well-traveled pathways of known and accepted psychopathology.

5. Psychopathological behavior may vary across cultures as a function of different understandings of the patient role. Patient roles were examined in Japan and the United States by Yamamoto (1972) and by Katz and Sanborn in Hawaii (1973). Both studies revealed that patient behavior is directed by the assigned "roles of sickness" blueprinted by the society. Cultural patterning for being sick, and especially for being mentally ill, socially deviant, or chronically troubled, is visible in every culture examined in such comparative research.

However we sort out this multifactorial, intricately interrelated relationship between what is the norm for a society and what is not normal, it is clear that the person, the community, and the designated healer are all actors in a drama with a long history, a well-defined script, a series of acts and intermissions, and an expected denouement for each variety of mental distress in each particular community.

Thought Disorders

Culture affects the symptom content in thought disorders. Although form and process are universals, the ideas and beliefs that are distorted or exaggerated in delusional formation are derived from the culture's values.

In traditional societies such as India or Mexico, persecutory ideas often center in mothers-in-law, members of the extended family, or spirits of the dead. These are stress points in all cultures but more intensely so in traditional vertical societies.

The social and emotional withdrawal seen among schizophrenics in Asia parallels the Hindu and Buddhist teaching of detachment as the way of reacting to difficulty. The high frequency of catatonic rigidity, negativism, and stereotypy among Amerindians is a like pattern of the passive-aggressive tradition of response to threat. The persecutory paranoia more prevalent with Europeans may stem from the low tolerance for aggressive impulses in the West as compared to the East (Kiev 1972:51).

There is evidence to suggest that paranoid schizophrenia is more common in the technologically developed countries; catatonic and hebephrenic schizoid disorders prevail in the less developed countries. Auditory hallucinations and systematic delusions are more common in cultures stressing verbal and abstract development, while aggressive behavior is more visible in more primitive cultures. In outer-directed groups, the pathology will focus on rapport with the deities, ancestors, spirits, or other forces; in inner-directed cultures the rapport with the ideal self, the conscience, and the moral laws of God will dominate consciousness. Hysteria and conversion of anxiety is thus much more common in less developed societies and particularly among less educated persons, whereas depression is more frequent within developed and Westernized cultures.

> The most common form of schizophrenic presentation in the African is catatonia or acute excitement. Catatonia is usually manifested in posturing, mutism, facial grimaces, and mannerisms. When the patient is brought in with acute excitement, a mistaken diagnosis of hypomania is quite possible. There are associated delusions of grandeur, loquacity, and hyperactivity. (Amara 1967:48)

Cultural variations in expressive styles of schizophrenia do show some significant tendencies. For example, Indian schizophrenics show catatonic rigidity, negativism, and stereotypy; their withdrawal may be related to the formal hierarchical culture pattern, which values introversion and emotional controls. Aggressiveness and expressiveness are common in patients from southern Italy, which fulfills the culture's valuing of extroversion, expressiveness, and emotionality. African patients show catatonic withdrawal or acute excitement with a tendency to be silent, offering few verbal clues. But the general similarity of the central cluster of symptoms surrounding a thought disorder strongly suggests that the nuclear features of schizophrenia are not culturally determined.

The International Pilot Study of Schizophrenia, begun in 1966 as a large-scale cross-cultural collaborative project carried out simultaneously in nine countries differing considerably in their sociocultural characteristics, included China, Colombia, Czechoslovakia, Denmark, India, Nigeria, the Union of Soviet Socialist Republics, the United Kingdom, and the United States of America. The 1,202 persons investigated in the nine countries were traced again, both two and five years after the initial examinations. The findings are highly significant.

> Patients diagnosed as schizophrenic on the basis of standardized assessments and clearly specified diagnostic criteria demonstrated very marked variations of course and outcome over a two-year period. Schizophrenic patients in the centres in developing countries had on the average considerably better course and outcome than schizophrenic patients in the centres in developed countries. Part of the variation of course and outcome was related to sociodemographic (e.g., social isolation, marital status) and clinical (e.g., type of onset, precipitating factors) predictors, but another larger part remained statistically unexplained. This suggests that variables usually used to describe psychopathology, the environment and history of psychiatric patients in European and North American cultures, may not be sufficient to account for cross-cultural differences. (Sartorius and others 1977: 540)

Schizophrenic patients in centres in developing countries, particularly in Ibadan (Nigeria) and Agra (India), had a better course and outcome on all variables than the schizophrenics in the centres in developed countries, with particularly sharp contrast to London, Moscow, Prague, and Washington.

Evidence gathered so far supports the thesis that there is a relationship between variables linked to culture and social environment and the prognosis of schizophrenia. The central hypotheses are the size of family group and the nature of interaction between its members (the nuclear vs. the joint family), the existence or absence of crystallized social stereotypes of the schizophrenic, and the extent of availability of specialized medical and social welfare services that might reinforce such stereotypes (Sartorius and others 1977:540).

Differences in the intensity of the family bonds, in the type of family structure, or in the socioeconomic features of the culture may make it remain in remission. When returning to a rural community where there is considerable familial and communal support, and in which there is less competitive stress than in a highly industrialized society, a person has greater likelihood of successful reentry and stabilization.

It is also possible that the treatment process is less traumatic, less subject to stigma, less cut off from family solidarity, and more likely to initiate involvement of and change in the family of the patient in the developing nations than for those in industrialized, individualized, and more alienated societies (IPSS 1979:371).

Affective or Feeling Disorders

Affective disorders are marked by significant mood changes, which may occur as a depressive reaction, a bipolar reaction, or various patterns of unipolar and bipolar changes in sequence. Reactive depressions, in response to an external crisis, loss, or change, are differentiated from primary or endogenous depressions, which are constitutional or genetic in origin and are linked with no precipitating events.

The frequency and distribution of affective disorders varies significantly between cultures. Bipolar, or manic-depressive, disorders are relatively similar across cultures, but depression is not.

In his study of the Yoruba tribe in Nigeria, Leighton found a number of gaps in the expected disorders—a near absence of obsessive-compulsive and phobic symptoms and a complete absence of depressive symptoms as defined in the West—although components of the syndrome, such as loss of interest in life, extreme worry, sapped vitality, low energy, came up in other contexts (Leighton 1969:184).

Leighton's observation is supported by clinicians throughout many of the developing countries where similar physical changes are not experienced in the familiar Western depressive illness pattern.

This raises the question of whether depression may not be predominantly a Western phenomenon. Clearly, energy loss is experienced in very different ways and may be labeled differently from one culture to another. In inner-directed Westerners, guilt feelings, self-punitive thoughts, and morbidity are all experienced, along with the acute energy change of an affective disorder.

African psychiatrist T. A. Lambo writes (1960:470):

> Depression is found in those cultures that enforce social control by way of abstract and situation-centered moral teachings predicated on moral obligation. The individualistic, competitive, and aggressively striving Protestant cultures may specifically produce unusual psychological stress, and belief in original sin may intensify oppressive self-reproach.

It is plausible to argue that "depressive disease," as a biochemical disorder of the brain's bioamine neurotransmitters, is a universal phenomenon, but "depressive illness," as a personal and social experience of depressive disease, is culture-specific (Kleinman 1978a:295).

> Disease in the Western medical paradigm is malfunctioning or maladaptation of biological and psychophysiologic processes in the individual, whereas illness represents personal, interpersonal, and cultural reactions to disease or discomfort. Illness is shaped by cultural factors governing perception, labeling, explanation, and valuation of the discomforting experience, processes embedded in a complex family, social, and cultural nexus. Because illness experience is an intimate part of social systems of meaning and rules of behavior, it is strongly influenced by culture: it is culturally constructed (Kleinman 1978b:251).

Definitions of depression vary from describing physical symptoms such as energy loss and sleep disturbance to seeing depression as an expressed mood. If the latter definition is used, the rates of depression in many developing countries would be virtually zero, not only because the guilt feelings, self-recrimination, and depressive affect are totally absent but also since mood states are not labeled in those societies.

Marsella (1978:350) raises serious questions about the validity of the concept of depression across cultures.

> It may well be the case that depression is a disorder of the western world and is not universal. Or perhaps it would be more accurate to say that depression is a disorder associated with cultures that are characterized by particular epistemological orientations: specifically, cultures which tend to "psychologize" experience. In these instances, experiential states become labeled and interpreted psychologically and this adds the components of depressed mood, guilt, self-depreciation, and suicidal ideation. At this level, the experience of depression assumes a meaning which is clearly different from that associated with a purely somatic experience of the problem.

No universal conception of depression exists, and there is a strong likelihood that different labels will be used in some cultures, although technological change, urbanization, the breakup of the joint family, the pressure toward individualism, and the gradual internalization of a more atomistic sense of autonomy may bring about the gradual shift toward the greater incidence of Western-style depressiveness even in settings where it was previously quite rare.

The recognition of a particular symptom as an illness requiring treatment depends on the degree of disability it poses to the sufferer and the degree of tolerance by the social group to which the person belongs. Lambo (1956) suggests this may account for the lower incidence of reported depression in Nigeria. Teja and Narang (1970) saw it as explanatory of differences in rates of depression from one area of India to another that varied as widely as from 4 to 21 percent of the populations seen in psychiatric clinical centers.

The ways of responding to the loss of affective energy is as varied as are other cultural patterns. Loss of energy and fatiguability is obviously more of a problem for field workers in an agrarian society or factory workers in an urban technical situation than in an urban slum with high unemployment or a traditional village with low demands for production.

Where depressive sentiments are accepted as normal responses to fate, to the nature of life, or to a pessimistic worldview, they are seen as characteristic of adult thought. In severe economic, political, or social oppression, consciousness-raising may be necessary before one can recognize the emotional state as depressed. The mood is appropriate to the mode of life but out of proportion to even the painful reality. Mild depressive disorders are unrecognized because they are so similar to the apathy and lassitude that accompany malnutrition, parasitism, and intense poverty.

In all cultures, diurnal mood changes, insomnia, early morning awakening, and loss of interest in the social environment are universally recognized as core symptoms of depression. Westerners include fatigue, self-punitive ideas, and loss of interest in both sex and food, but persons from developing countries do not. The guilt, self-reproach, and suicide common with Western disorders are replaced by low energy, hallucinations, somatic symptoms, and conversion to other problems.

Based on an extensive review of cross-cultural literature on depression, Marsella (1983:238) reached the following conclusions: (1) Depressive experience and disorder vary considerably as a function of sociocultural factors—"depression" takes very different forms in different cultures. (2) The epidemiology of depression is not known because of limitations in research methods, but there is reason to believe that the frequency of depression is higher in Western societies—some cultures show high rates, others low, but the differences in experience, in concepts, in labels suggest that we know relatively little about rates. (3) The experience and manifestation of depression differ as a function of Westernization. Cultures evidencing a subjective epistemological orientation (Table 10-1) tend to avoid psychologizing of experience and show fewer psychological and existential symptoms. (4) Depression assessment methods are highly ethnocentric and need to give greater attention to somatic and interpersonal aspects of depressively disturbed processes in many cultures. (5) Personality correlates of depression vary across cultures with respect to presence or absence of guilt, self-concept discrepancy, and body-image dissatisfaction. (6) Sociocultural theories of depression are descriptive but not explanatory or predictive—we do not yet understand how the context influences the person in producing depressive experiences.

Depressive responses to life, in many settings, are understood as normal recognition of the difficulties in what are truly uncongenial circumstances. In research in a Mexican rural village, Romanucci-Ross (1983:269) found that in her three years of residence no one in the village was considered insane by others. Much behavior occurred that people considered a natural response to depressing circumstances, leading to strategies for countering depression that could be seen as preventing or avoiding "mental illness." But the persons were not identified as depressed. Not only is this related to the recognized predominant use of denial as a defense mechanism in Mexican culture, it is also connected to the negative expectations of life. Life is viewed as a long, hard task, offering insufficient and infrequent rewards and providing meager resources in an environment of scarcity and adversity. Interpersonal relationships frequently lead to frustrations, deprivation, alienation, and disappointment. Yet persons are expected to accept these experiences as inherent to all life and to ward off or compensate for depression.

Romanucci-Ross summarized her findings on the relationship between low expectations—depressive context—and individual depression —depression content—in feeling disorders (1983:270):

> The term "depression," of course, has several meanings, both for the professional and the lay person. However, whether or not depression is experienced subjectively depends upon levels of expectation, both positive and negative. In the village, expectations for good outcomes were set so low (improbable), and for bad outcomes so high (probable), that real-life experiences, however harsh, would never exceed these upper and lower limits. Such pessimistic attitudes were culturally established. This resulted

Table 10-1. Depressive Disorders in Different Cultures

Individuated Culture *(autonomous self)*	*Sociocentric Culture* *(familial self)*
Central elements	*Central elements*
1. Language is abstract verbal sequential.	1. Language is metaphorical, visual, spatial.
2. Reality is mediated through description, definition, argumentation.	2. Reality is mediated through images and pictures.
3. Orientation of thought is primarily objective.	3. Orientation of thought is largely subjective.
4. Locus of control is internal.	4. Locus of control is external.
The depressive disorders that emerge in such individuated cultures are *symptomatically* expressed in affective existential, cognitive, and somatic areas of functioning.	The depressive disorders that emerge in such collective cultures are *symptomatically* expressed primarily in somatic areas of functioning.
Experientially, the person experiences increased sense of isolation, detachment, separation.	*Experientially,* the person remains attached to diffused self and familial identity.
If a culture labels negative experience in psychological terms, a "Western" picture of depression emerges.	If a culture labels experience in somatic terms, a much lower rate of depression appears.

(Adapted from Marsella 1983:275)

in a constriction of patterns of the permissible, with all behavior predicted on low expectations. All of the fantasy, both social and personal—including proverbs, stories, ballads, humor, and films—helped persons growing up in this culture to set their reference levels of expectation. Tragedies emphasized separation from the mother, from children, from the group, indeed from life itself, but these were treated lightly, as though one could profitably exchange the whole lot "for a drink of tequila." So in the process of becoming a member of the culture, the individual in this way also internalized the mechanism for calibrating and dampening the resonance of events.

Therefore, in this folk culture, the repertoire considered normal by the group included a wide variety of both depressive and manic behavior.

The peasant wisdom of Haiti as shown in its proverbs offers incisive examples of the subjective experience of low expectations in a chronically depressive context—economic deprivation, exploitation by social and political systems, powerlessness to obtain justice before oppressive landowners.

"A cockroach has no rights in front of a chicken."
"The fish trusts the water, but in the end the water boils the fish."
"When the chicken's heart is happy the hawk is not far away."

These "realistic" expectations of life form the norm of existence for large groups in the lower socioeconomic social strata. Though normal for the context, they are not normative humanness by the values of the group, or the aspirations of its members from their understandings of authentic humanness.

Culturally Bound Syndromes

Cultures have their unique definitions of, explanations for, and interventions into forms of mental distress. Such local variations are illustrated by Seguin's comparison (1970) of explanations of disease and distress of Peruvian Indians living in the Amazon jungle with those of people living on the coast. In the jungle, distress, is assumed to come from natural forces; it results when the soul is stolen by mountains or rivers. On the coast of Peru, distress is presumably caused by people who produce harm. Seguin infers that in the jungle one must fight for survival against nature, while on the environmentally benign coast the major threat is from other humans. Thus the form, the content, and the attribution of the cause of distress are shaped by time and place.

The connection between culture and the structure of psychiatric illness is often illustrated or substantiated by studies of culture-bound disorders, with their exotic symptomology. These culturally conditioned responses are compensatory patterns that ritualize the basic symptoms known in Western societies as anxiety, hysteria, obsessive-compulsive neurosis, phobias, depression, and dissociation.

Anxiety states. Koro in Southeast Asia, *susto* in Latin America, bewitchment in Nigeria are only three of many anxiety states that focus on fear of death, castration, loss of potency, and harm by black magic, evil eye, or "soul loss."

Hysterical disorders. Called *latah* in Southeast Asia, the same syndrome has at least eighteen other names in various tribal groups in Siberia, Japan, Africa, and South and Central America.

Obsessive-compulsive states. Frigophobia, which leads a northern person to keep adding or changing clothes out of fear of cold; and *shinkei-shitsu,* obsessive fears and rituals among young Japanese males, are two of many compulsive states.

Phobic states. The evil eye is feared in a wide variety of societies on every continent; voodoo curse and death appear in Africa and the Caribbean.

Depressive states. The *hiwa-itck* among the Mohave Amerindians, the *windigo* psychosis among Canadian Indians; and malignant anxiety among West Africans are all variants of outer-directed depression.

Dissociative states. Amok in Southeast Asia, *hsieh-ping* among Chinese who identify with the dead in a dramatic seizure, *piblokto* among Eskimos, and spirit possession in cultures around the world are all periodic dissociative processes that may be brief episodes or lasting disorders.

The most frequently discussed culture-bound syndromes are listed for quick reference in Table 10-2. What is most striking is the similarity of human anxieties, defense mechanisms, regressive-defensive strategies, and means of compensating for internal conflict and feared fragmentation.

Pathology Across Cultures

Although there are wide variations and disparities in the prevalence rates of neuroses and personality disorders, the occurrence of schizophrenia is very similar across cultures—about 2 or 3 per thousand. The clinical manifestations vary greatly from culture to culture, but the regular incidence suggests that the etiology is a universal phenomenon, not a culture-bound one.

In Western studies, the rate of psychiatric disturbance increases with age, although in Eastern studies there is a tendency for it to come down after the age of 60. Whether this is a statistical change due to differences in life expectancy in the hemispheres or related to the more significant roles of older adults in the East is not clear.

It is universally reported that psychiatric disturbance is more frequent among those in the lower socioeconomic classes, as assessed by literacy, occupation, and income. The drift hypothesis suggests that individual or familial disturbances causes persons to be downwardly mobile. The stress hypothesis suggests that pressures of life in the lower socioeconomic groups may be responsible. The drift hypothesis is more frequently linked to schizophrenia and organic states, the stress theory to personality disorders.

Almost all Western studies indicate higher psychiatric disturbance among singles; in India the rate is higher among married people. The most commonly accepted explanation is that morbid personality traits reduce the likelihood of marriage in the West and in India lead to greater familial pressure to marry, with the assumption that this will be beneficial. The additional stress of marriage precipitates existing tendencies (Verghese and Abraham 1976:123).

Migration is strongly associated with an increase in psychiatric disturbance. Rapid acculturation increases vulnerability. Mental illness rises as a consequence of rapid sociocultural change. Okinawans, for instance, although known for a relatively low incidence of mental illness on their home island, apparently found migration to Hawaii enormously stressful. In this new home, they developed rates of psychosis significantly higher than any other major group in the islands (Maloney 1945:391–399).

In indigenous Australia, Cawte (1974:11) noted the emergence of

Table 10-2. Characteristic Psychiatric Symptoms
Specific to Certain Cultures

Syndrome	Symptoms	Occurrence
Amok	A sudden unprovoked outburst of rage and violence causing the person—always a male—to run about, indiscriminately attacking, maiming, or killing all men and animals encountered until he is overpowered or killed. Usually preceded by depression, followed by amnesia.	Malaysia, Africa, and other tropical countries; Laos in recent years
Dhat	An acute male anxiety reaction usually associated with frequent masturbation or coitus. The person fears he has lost all vitality, is impotent, will suffer some serious disease.	India
Koro	An acute anxiety reaction. Men fear penis is shrinking into the body and death will follow, so it is tied or clamped. Women fear nipples or vulva are shrinking inward. Precipitated by fear of sexual excess, coitus with prostitutes.	Malaya China
Latah	Two forms. (1) A startle reaction in response to some stimulus. The person exhibits inappropriate motor and verbal behavior or obscenity over which there is no voluntary control. (2) Echo-behavior in imitation of any observed behavior—echopraxia, echolalia, automatic obedience. Person is aware but has no control.	Malaya Borneo
Piblokto	"Arctic hysteria." Victim shouts, disrobes, imitates animals or birds, is hyperactive for one to two hours, then quiets, has amnesia about the episode. A dissociative reaction predominantly among females.	Eskimos
Possession	Dissociation states—trance, identification with the dead, temporary belief in divine occupation, convulsions. Provides emotional catharsis, reinforces group values in a formalized role. Both males and females, in some cultures sex-linked.	India China Indonesia Malaya Egypt Central America South America South Africa
Susto	Acute anxiety reaction. Belief that the soul has left the body, is kidnapped by Earth. "Soul loss" may be accompanied by hyperventilation, fever, chills. Adolescents, children.	Peru Colombia Central America
Windigo	Acute anxiety and delusion. The person, afflicted in starvation times, fears transformation into the cannibal monster Windigo. Withdraws, commits suicide, or is killed by community.	American Indian

mood disorders—intrapunitiveness leading to depression—much more prominantly in transitional than in stable societies. The full syndrome was a forced replacement of the extended family by the Western conjugal family, the loss of objects that sustain the person's self-esteem and identity, repression of familiar moral codes, and, in the crisis of stress, a general affect of guilt.

Indian migrants to Trinidad and Surinam have disabling conflicts between the ties of the family and ethnic community and the desire to join the "outside" modern community. A flamboyant alcoholism mixed with periods of depression and suicidal tendencies was associated with this rebellion against the duties and obligations to the traditional family and religion (Angrosino 1974:129).

Urbanization has been associated with an increase in psychiatric disturbance. Rapidly urbanized Africans who discard their native culture but fail to readily assimilate the second culture show increased disturbance (Lambo 1968).

In his survey "Trends in Psychiatry in Black Africa," Allen German offers a clear summary of the significant differences between African and European psychopathologies (1975:417). The major differences are:

1. The frequency with which easily precipitated and recurrent transient amorphous psychoses are encountered. (Sudden onset, florid symptoms, and short duration mark these "acute psychotic episodes," which appear as a frequent feature in African clinical psychiatry.)

2. The somewhat better social prognosis of process schizophrenia. (Social acceptance and inclusion in family and community provide support and group solidarity, in sharp contrast to the labeling, discrimination, and exclusion of other cultures.)

3. The relative absence of self-directed and self-centered symptoms such as notions of worthlessness and guilt and obsessional-compulsive behaviors. (Depressive phenomena are outer-directed in persecutory forms rather than intrapunitive pain. The group obsessional rituals allow for ritualized release of anxiety without the construction of personal obsessive or compulsive rituals.)

4. The widespread use of projective mechanisms manifesting themselves in paranoid thinking of a persecutory type. (Group identification rather than self-identification increases projective mechanisms and decreases intrajective ones.)

5. The high frequency of hysterical symptoms and states, often in the setting of anxiety reactions of psychotic intensity, which certainly contribute to the problem of "acute transient psychoses." (Conversion states and dissociative states are very frequently encountered. Trance and possession states are culturally sanctioned and expected in tribal and religious contexts.)

6. The widespread tendency, particularly among preliterate patients, to express any state of psychic pain or conflict in somatic terms. (Conversion of anxiety into various somatic disorders is frequent and conceptually congruent with social concepts of illness and healing.)

Abnormal Behavior in China

China, since the revolution, has made a remarkable change in the rate of occurrence of mental illnesses. For the first half of this century, China was referred to as "the sick man of Asia." Tertiary syphillis was one major cause of mental illness, opium addiction was another. Now there are no cases of tertiary syphilis, and it appears that China is the first country in the world free of drug addiction. Other mental illnesses affect far fewer people than in the West—about 6 per thousand people, as compared to 150 per thousand in the United States. Of these, only two to four are schizophrenics, which is about one fifth of the incidence of schizophrenia in the West. (Livingston and Lowinger 1983:31–38).

Two explanations for this phenomenal change seem to be well supported. These are (1) the externalization of stress into strong environmental supports and (2) its internalization into somatization. These two, far from being contradictory, support each other in the personal and interpersonal management of distress.

1. The externalization of stress into the powerful communal supports offered by the socialist society utilizes and appropriately fits the traditional personality patterns. The tradition of familism rather than individualism creates persons with familial identity rather than individual identity. The patterns of valuing external control rather than internal control and accepting external responsibility rather than an internal sense of private personal responsibility combine to facilitate the redirection of stress into the communal structures rather than focusing it on the individual psyche.

The strong relationship between the person and the environment reduces stress and supports mental functioning from the simple levels of daily decisions to the complex levels of personal crises. In the West, our love of privacy is inherently crazy-making through its isolation and loneliness. In China, there is neither a word for, concept of, nor practice of privacy. Sleeping four to a room, living in a small apartment, interacting with an extended family, integrated into communal life, protected and directed by the courtyard committee in the apartment, the neighborhood committee on the street, and the work committee on the job provide security and immediate troubleshooting of marital, parental, familial, and interpersonal difficulties in constructive reconciliation.

Neighborhood committees assist families in the practical resolution of living problems. If a mother of preschool children wishes to work, a nearby grandmother is given work as a child minder, and the interlocking need satisfaction is supportive to both. The mental diseases of old age —involutional depression, senile psychosis—are almost nonexistent in China.

Social policy supports the recovery and reintegration of the mentally ill. If a worker is hospitalized, the job is held open for months at full pay. If the illness goes on past a year, 70 percent salary continues. On reentry, the colleagues are formed into a supportive network to reduce stress and celebrate the person's meaningful return to work in rebuilding the nation. As one ex-patient described the new attitude, "In the old society I would have disappeared; in the new society I can recover" (Livingston and Lowinger 1983:103).

2. The internalization of stress by somatization has an equally long history in Chinese personality patterns. The protection of family face and the severe stigma against mental distress both led to suppression of introspective awareness and expressive communication on stress and to somatization of anxieties. "The most common findings among Chinese counselees are psychological desires expressed in somatic symptoms such as peptic ulcer, insomnia, and headaches" (Hsu and Tseng 1972:704).

For centuries, the Chinese have seen mood and physiological state as more than just interrelated; the former directly causes the latter. Both the characteristics of socialization, with oral indulgence and exaggerated physical concern, and the Chinese social structure, which demands suppression of affect, contribute to internalizing stress in somatization. Illness functions as escape, as severe protest, as an excuse for release from obligations, or as a displacement of deep, unacceptable psychic conflicts (Wang 1983:298).

Traditional Chinese mental health systems operated on the concept of balance between body and emotion. When the body was ill, emotional abreaction was triggered. When emotions were troubled, the body was treated. This suggests the need for continuing research on internalization and somatization and on the interpersonal problems and coping strategies of the Chinese. Other cultures have much to learn from the Chinese experience, as well as significant things to offer them (Wu 1982:299).

A Theology of Human Frailty

Human beings are mentally, emotionally, and spiritually both durable and fragile, tough and brittle, resilient and frail. Theological interpretations of humanness have stressed responsibility as an active agent and accountability as a social being, but they have had little to offer in understanding the nature of mental, emotional, and spiritual disorder. Much has been written of sin—willful disobedience or apathetic indifference—but much less of moral inability. Volumes of theology and philosophy have explored the rational and emotional capabilities of the human mind and heart but devoted much less time to thought and feeling disorders.

The theologically oriented counselor must have thought deeply about the relationship between health and unhealth, normality and abnormality, the good and the evil in life, and the understandings of theodicy.

In the face of human suffering, the pastoral counselor seeks to embody grace. In the dilemmas of disaster and disease, the counselor offers presence and compassion. In the binds of injustices, injuries, and human insensitivity, the counselor works for justice and release from oppression. But suffering is endemic to existence, disaster and disease inescapable, and injustice universal. A theology that reveals the meaning in human pain and makes sense of the existence of good and evil in everything is needed by all persons in the helping professions.

In this section we shall look at abnormality as related to stressors in the human situation, as rising from structural weakness in the essential nature of humans, as caused by imbalance of various human functions, or as experienced evil. Necessarily, we shall finally examine a pastoral theology of evil and theodicy.

Abnormality and Stress

Mental, emotional, and spiritual illness are seen by some theologians, psychologists, and philosophers to be caused primarily, if not solely, by external stressors, hostile environments, and anomic atmospheres. Rather than intrinsic weakness in the person, the extrinsic malevolence of family and society is cited.

For the first half of the twentieth century, most behavioral scientists and theologians alike theorized that psychopathology was a reaction to external stress—psychosis occurring as a reaction to severe stress, neurosis and personality disorders from more minor stress. Further research suggests that multiple etiological factors (biological, psychological, and sociocultural) contribute to the formation of psychopathology. Biological factors are more crucial in psychosis, psychological and sociocultural stress to neuroses.

Sociocultural stress is stimulated by three cultural processes: cultural content, cultural atmosphere, and cultural change (Wittkower and Prince 1974:539–541). All three may occur in concert and create anxiety in combined malevidence.

1. *Cultural content* includes (a) taboos that may frustrate essential needs; (b) value saturation, such as obsessive exaggeration of a value (such as achievement in Japan, success in the United States, or racial purity in Nazi Germany); (c) value ambiguity, when antagonistic values conflict in the society or within the person; (d) loss of role (such as retirement) or denial of role (as from discrimination against minorities), and (e) culture-bound sentiments, such as prejudices, jealousy, or fear of spirits. It is the task of a theology of value to assess and correct the contents of culture, since culture is the form and meaningful faith is the content.

2. *Cultural atmosphere* is a major factor in stress. A stressful atmosphere of anomie results from a lack of integration in the society, often evidenced in poverty, migration to urban life, unemployment, failure or absence of education, and racial, sexual, or ethnic alienation. A stressful atmosphere in political and social life rises as rigid structures dominate the individual, coerce conformity, and impose uniformity. It is the task of a pastoral theology to renew the atmosphere, reintegrate those excluded, and reconcile the alienated.

3. *Cultural change* creates problems of cultural shock and stressful acculturation, with both frequently accompained by poverty. Major

shifts in social status and rapid change in social cues combine to increase shock geometrically. It is the task of a prophetic theology to transcend and direct in the midst of change and to offer stability in continuing political and social evolution.

In summary, stress is evoked by cultural demands, intensified by determinations that limit behavior range, and shaped by the culture's own definitions of anxiety and abnormality. Yet these same factors may provide security, which alleviates stress, for some persons. What is stress-producing for some personalities is stress-reducing for others. However, exaggeration of these factors (demands, determinations, and definitions) appears to be consistently stressful in most cultures. Mental health and mental illness occur side by side in cultures when stress factors converge with biological predisposition and psychological vulnerabilities.

Abnormality as Structural Weakness

Abnormal behavior arises not only in response to political and socio-cultural stressors outside the person but in obedience to organismic factors—both biological and psychological—that are a part of the essential structure of humanness. The potential for good or evil is inherent in us all, not only in our behavioral directions but in our personalities, their cognitions, perceptions, and emotions.

Created as free yet finite, responsible yet fallible, capable yet limited, self-aware beings yet always becoming, we have the potential for pathology—mental, social, moral—present in core self and social self. Mental and emotional illness is not a foreign process but an extension, exaggeration, or distortion of our essential humanness.

Henry Ey, the French philosopher and psychiatrist, has formulated a series of three hypotheses (1969:111–161) on the nature of mental illness that are helpful in sensing the relationship between health and pathology in the human personality. They recognize pathology as potentials present within humans as finite beings.

1. Mental illness is implied in the organization of the psyche, in the genetic developmental progression of the child through sequential tension states, which inevitably achieve only a partially functional synthesis, and in the structural stratification of the psyche, which inevitably contains splits, divisions, tension, imbalances.

2. Mental illness is essentially negative or regressive in structure. It is a shrinking back, a returning to an earlier "safety," a flight from present and unavoidable realities; it is a rupture of communication and interrelationships that are necessary for perception, comprehension, accommodation to the environment; it is an unstructuring of reality.

3. Mental illnesses, psychoses, and neuroses are typical forms—by their dynamic structure and their evolution—of various levels of developmental failure or dissolution of psychic organization. The various processes indicate the breakdown of the strata and structures of the developing and functioning psyche. "To be mentally ill is therefore for

a person to fall under the influence of the determinism of his/her organism."

We may add to Ey's original three hypotheses, (4) mental illnesses are thought and feeling consequences of biological processes that impact on the organization of the psyche, its developmental progression, its structure of reality, and its advancing organization or retreating dissolution. Biochemical imbalances are demonstrably more closely related to psychoses—thought disorders—and depressions—feeling disorders—than to neuroses and living disorders.

Abnormality as Imbalance

A theological perspective on emotional disorder formulated by Søren Kierkegaard in the nineteenth century continues to be a useful means of examining the relationship between faith and psychopathology.

Emotional disorder is most clearly understood as the experience of extreme despair, what Kierkegaard called "the sickness unto death." "To despair over oneself, in despair to will to be rid of oneself, is the formula for all despair" (Kierkegaard 1941:44). In Western fashion he applied despair particularly to self-rejection, but the concept when viewed from other cultures is much more inclusive, as we shall see.

Despair results from a loss of self—however self is visualized and experienced within the particular culture. To despair is to be overwhelmed by self-rejection. Such despair is due to imbalances in at least three major polarities of the human self. These are, as diagrammed in Figure 10-1, the polarity between (1) a sense of infinitude, of being able to transcend life and its limitations, and a sense of finitude, of being lost in the mundane, the faceless, the mechanics of life; (2) a sense of necessity, where all is given, required, hopeless, and unchanging, and a sense of possibility, in which everything is possible so one loses reality in the dream world of fantasy; and (3) an obsession with consciousness through self-examination and its inverse, living in unconsciousness without reflection and self-examination.

When balanced, these three polarities are the source of both emotional and spiritual health. In imbalance, they produce psychological pathology as well as spiritual despair. "Health consists essentially in being able to resolve contradictions. So it is bodily or physically; a draft is indifferently cold and warm, disparate qualities undialectically combined; but a healthy body resolves this contradiction and does not notice the draft. So it is with faith" (Kierkegaard 1941:46). In the balanced development and flexible utilization of the strengths on both ends of these polarities, the person finds the means of being authentically grounded in the life situation yet capable of transcending it; of actively dealing with the daily necessities of existence yet envisioning possibilities; of living with the free, joyous naïveté of childhood yet with a deep consciousness of self, of others, and of life.

The forms these polarities take will vary with the corresponding values of the society. Indian mysticism may exaggerate infinitude and, at the

Infinitude

One can become so
intoxicated with infinitude
that any thought of
weakness, fallibility, or
limitation drowns the soul
in despair. Perfectionism,
self-judgment, exaggerated
pretensions are utterly
discouraging, depressing,
filled with despair.

Consciousness

To be overwhelmed by
consciousness is to be too
aware of oneself, of
others, of relationships
and their meanings. As
self-consciousness
increases, the more
threatening is the despair
of the overexplored life.
This may lead to the
defiant despair of willing
conscious, isolated
self-sufficiency.

Possibility

The despair of possibility
comes from the loss of
awareness of what is truly
necessary. In ignoring
obedience, submission, and
limits one may live in a
wishful yearning dream
world or in a melancholy
world of malevolent
fantasy. The despair of
possibility may thus result
in either unrealistic hopes
or unrealistic dread.

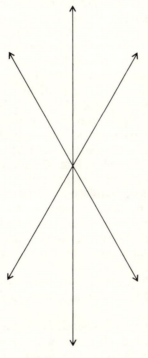

Necessity

The despair of necessity
rises as one is defeated by
submitting to the
pressures of circumstance,
of yielding to
overwhelming situations.
Hope is lost in the
obsession with fitting the
present situation, with
obeying the inevitable.
Fatalism, a sense that all
is hopeless, unchanging,
and meaningless, drowns
the person in despair.

Unconsciousness

One can live in innocence,
in a naïveté that does not
know of despair. Nor does
the unexplored life
recognize the true self
within. Such a person is
essentially spiritless. The
despair may come from
not willing to be a self out
of fear of consciousness,
or discovery of inadequacy
and weakness.

Finitude

One can become swamped
with finitude, of being not
a self but a number, a link
in the human chain of
faceless imitations of the
crowd. By losing oneself
in total conformity, one
may be a success in
business, in community
life, in being an atom of
the human mass, yet
despair of any significance
or personal worth.

Figure 10-1. Three major polarities of the human self.

Health is balance; unhealth is an exaggeration of one or more poles.

same time, require increased necessity and limited consciousness in order to fit within the hierarchical structures of the social order. Chinese pragmatism may stress necessity and finitude to the loss of infinitude and possibility, yet call for a heightened sense of social and self-consciousness. Within each culture the whole spectrum of possible imbalances can occur, although both content and form tend to follow the current stories and values of the society.

Religious faith and emotional health both occur along these same polarities and are two parallel and interlocking processes. Faith that is intoxicated with the transcendent becomes lost in infinitude. This is loss of all sense of realistic limitations. As the person is confronted by the ultimate infinity of God, despair over limitations, imperfections, and weaknesses may result. Or such despair may be concealed in a compensatory reaction that pretends a perfection beyond possibility or assumes a hypernormal personality that is all-sufficient, all-knowing, and all-absorbed in super-spirituality. The reverse pole of finitude can produce an extremely literalistic, rigid, obsessive faith, which as Kierkegaard says is "desperately narrow-minded and mean-spirited." Or the faith may become totally outer-directed, extrinsic, and be lived out in conformity to others' demands, in absorption into the group faith patterns without internalized values, beliefs, or commitments.

Faith that exaggerates possibility is "so heavenly it is of no earthly good." The loss of reality results in living in a world of dreams, illusions, fantasies while couching this in the language of faith. Lost is the realistic centering of faith in lived action; missing is the willing obedience that combines possibility and necessity in authentic commitments of life.

Faith at the reverse pole has lost all hope and serves the "god of necessity." Unable to hope, the person is also unable to pray, unable to reach beyond the self in service to others, unable to live freely and joyfully.

Faith that is focused on expanded self-consciousness becomes too introspective, analytic, and self-absorbed. Its tendency is toward defiant self-sufficiency, while at the opposite pole one lives in an unaware innocence that denies spirit and destroys spirituality.

Jean-Paul Sartre (1959:22–23) describes the faith dilemma of the person who discarded infinitude but discovers the frightening universe of possibilities without any moral necessities:

> The existentialist . . . thinks it very distressing that God does not exist, because all possibility of finding values in a heaven of ideas disappears along with him . . . everything is possible if God does not exist, and as a result man is forlorn, because neither within him nor without does he find anything to cling to. . . . We find no values or commands to turn to which legitimize our conduct. So in the bright realm of values, we have no excuse behind us, nor justification before us. We are alone, with no excuses.

Cognition, feeling, and faith all require a balance of each of these dimensions for vital health and emotional and spiritual depth—or, to say it inclusively, for full humanness.

Abnormality as Experienced Evil

Abnormality, as the personal experience of evil, is interpreted in each culture by its own myths and stories. Good and evil are universal categories, and in every culture the fragmentation of the personality is viewed as either the evidence of forces of good or the intrusion of powers of evil. Evil, as the fragmentation of the self, the alienation of relationships, or the destruction of family and community, may be ascribed to internal forces of decay and disruption or to external powers that invade and subvert.

Evil is not to be confused with suffering, although the two are interrelated.

> The problem of suffering passes easily into the problem of evil, for if suffering is severe enough it usually, though not always, seems morally undeserved as well, at least to the sufferer. But they are not, however, exactly the same thing. . . . For where the problem of suffering is concerned with threats to our ability to put our "undisciplined squads of emotion" into some sort of soldierly order, the problem of evil is concerned with threats to our ability to make sound moral judgments. (Geertz 1973:105–106)

What is central to the problem of evil is not the management of our affective resources in the face of suffering but the balancing of our cognitive and affective resources to provide an ethical process to guide our actions. The vexation here is the contradiction between things as they are and as they ought to be if our conceptions of right and wrong are valid. What our moral values decree that certain actions and individuals deserve and what we actually observe that they receive are far apart. The inconsistency between what "is" and what "ought" troubles every culture.

> Nor is it necessary to be theologically self-conscious to be religiously sophisticated. The concern with intractable ethical paradox, the disquieting sense that one's moral insight is inadequate to one's moral experience, is as alive on the level of so-called primitive religion as it is on that of the so-called civilized. (Geertz 1973:106)

In theological thought we speak of evil as natural or moral evil to differentiate between the evil that is an essential part of existence in a world of circumstance and the evil we cause by our choices and acts. Natural evil includes the tragedies and disasters we humans are heir to —floods, storms, earthquakes, disease, accident, biochemical imbalances, and organic mental or emotional disorders. Moral evil is the evil we humans cause ourselves or others. It includes the misuse of freedom, the abuse of self and others, the intention, volition, and commission of evil, and the omission of good (Jackson 1981:146).

Evil may also be differentiated between intrinsic evil and instrumental evil. Intrinsic evil is "anything, all things considered, without which the universe would have been better" (Griffen 1976:22). Rape, child violation, and war are intrinsic evils. Instrumental evil points to the effects of an act that of itself may be well-intentioned. The overprotection of a parent that creates excessive dependency, or the affectionate care of a dominant husband that denies the wife's freedom to express her own initiative and realize her own gifts—these exemplify instrumental evil at its well-intentioned best.

Dialogue on the nature of evil between the fields of theology and Western psychology has been difficult because each discipline begins from a contrasting perspective: theology focusing on evil as injustice and unloving action as defined by transcendent and universal values; psychology preferring a value-free universe in which evil is seen as the inappropriate, the dysfunctional, the repressed. In Western psychotherapy, evil has been flattened, losing its nature of affront to the transcendent good. It is reduced from its eternal significance to a temporal issue. It has been shrunk from its truly communal nature to an individual problem.

The troubled person is seen by most counselors as sinned against rather than sinning. From early childhood deprivation, distortion, and disparagement, the person develops as one misused and abused, as sinned against more than sinful. Developmental psychology has a rich vocabulary for those who have been victimized, but little language to describe those who pursue evil.

Evil is not a category in diagnostic lexicons. We speak of malingering when there is obvious intentional deceit; we identify certain forms of narcissism as morally self-absorbed and resulting in consistent and deliberate choices for the self against others; we identify sociopathic personalities that are morally incapable. But social, relational, and developmental explanations, not moral ones, are preferred.

The intercultural pastoral counselor recognizes the need for a deep understanding of intrinsic natural evil that sees tragic events, the unavoidable abnormalities of human dysfunction, and the pain of human existence as inescapable parts of life as it is and, at the same time, as tragedies that must be faced, resisted, and, where possible, changed. Such evil occurs not in an uncaring universe of mechanical regularity but in a creation, upheld by and sustained by a Creator whose essential nature wills love and justice for all.

Yet this understanding of God as one who wills justice and love for all creation stands in continuing contradiction to the suffering endemic to all human existence. The task of reconciling these two realities—good and evil—is called theodicy in theology and goes nameless in the field of psychology. Yet the ambiguities and contradictions of existence perplex both, because all humans seek to comprehend the incomprehensible and are forced to accept the unacceptable.

Good and Evil, God and Humanity

Three theological models of evil are offered by the major world religions: monism, polar dualism, and tragic dualism.

Monism envisions evil as the inevitable shadow of good. For good to be known, there must be evil; for life, death; for creation, destruction; for growth, decay; for health, sickness; for righteousness, sin. The distinctions between such inseparable aspects of the one monistic reality are all illusions. The unity of all things must be embraced in true enlightenment. Monism, characteristic of Buddhism and Hinduism, is present in Christian Science and many other contemporary philosophies and religions.

Polar dualism perceives good and evil as distinct entities that complete and fulfill each other. Both good and evil are created by a good Creator. Each pole is necessary to the other. Free will is dependent upon having authentic options between good and evil, so the Creator permits evil as necessary to freedom and responsibility. Evil, as Martin Buber concluded, "is the yeast in the dough, the ferment placed in the soul by God, without which the human dough does not rise" (Buber 1953:94). Jungian psychology and some streams of Judaism exemplify this perspective. Both good and evil are thus within the control and intentions of God.

Tragic dualism perceives good as God's intention and design for creation and evil as the tragic result of human rebellion. Evil is a cancer in the social body which, by nature of God's own noncoercive way of love, is outside divine control. This has been the classic Christian formulation of the problem, seeing God as willing only good but seeking to work out such good providentially within a world in revolt.

Monism sees God as either both good and evil or beyond such illusory distinctions. Polar dualism unites the two in the paradox of God's working out of freedom and responsibility within an authentically moral context. And tragic dualism struggles with the irresolvable and nonlogical dilemmas of a God of goodness in a world that is visibly tortured by evil. The pastoral counselor, daily confronted by evil both natural and moral, both extrinsic to and intrinsic in the counselees, seeks some resolution for personal integration as well as spiritual and therapeutic direction.

Four logical options exist in our attempts to understand the goodness of God and the presence of evil: (1) God is neither all-good nor all-powerful; (2) God is all-good but not all-powerful; (3) God is all-powerful but not all-good; (4) God is both all-powerful and all-good. The first is usually excluded as less than God; the last is the traditional Judeo-Christian-Muslim solution, but it leaves us with the contradiction between the existence of God and the presence of evil.

The problem may be stated in brief: God is creator (the world, matter, energy, and spirit are God's handiwork), God is omniscient (capable of visualizing all possible worlds), God is omnipotent (able to create any possible world), God is perfectly good (choosing to create the best of all possible worlds), but the world contains massive evil.

A wide number of theodicies have been constructed, of which the main options are: (1) What we may perceive as evil is necessary for the greater good. (2) Evil is an inevitable byproduct of an essentially good world. (3) Evil, properly perceived, has no reality; it is nonbeing. (4) The universe is imperfect; God is drawing it toward perfection. (5) The whole question of evil is semantically meaningless. (6) The meaning of evil is a mystery God hides from our knowing. (7) Suffering tests, instructs, purifies, and matures us. (8) Suffering punishes us for our sins. (9) Evil is solely the result of sin, which rises from the exercise of free will. (10) God permits evil to achieve the greater good of freedom (Russell 1981:17).

The last is the most frequently argued position, but it leaves itself open to several severe objections. Why is the degree of unlimited evil necessary —the genocide, war, holocausts, and destruction of persons on such an ultimate scale? How does it account for natural evils such as floods, tornadoes, plagues, cancer, and the mental anguish of disorders? Clearly a God who would not permit the innocent to suffer does not exist.

It has been suggested that in the best of all possible worlds, not of all ideal worlds, it is necessary that the good outweigh the evil but not necessary that evil not exist at all. This is possible in our world, and in the life of each person within it, if existence is not limited to this life but has another dimension. This theodicy demands an afterlife as the fulfill-ment of justice (Paterson 1979:23).

Process theism sees God forming a good cosmos out of eternal un-formed matter—primal chaos—and evil arising from the resistance of matter to the will of God. This suggests that God is not all-powerful but is limited by the external principle of matter.

If another principle exists besides God, is there a prior fundamental or Ur-principle? If the two are coeternal and balanced, the universe would be static. If not balanced, one is greater in all eternity and would prevail. If God is greater, why the delay? There is no way here to relieve God of responsibility for creation.

The hypothesis that God is not all-good is puzzling, even frightening, but it is logical and coherent. "If by God we mean a being who would not permit torture, genocide, and concentration camps, that being obvi-ously does not exist. If we observed a human—let us say a head of state —who had the power to prevent torture, genocide, and concentration camps in the nation and refused to do so, we would not call such a ruler good. We can scarcely hold God less accountable than a human. Thus if God exists, God cannot be good in our sense of the word" (J. Russell 1981:227).

The argument from free will does not resolve the dilemma. Free will may be necessary for moral good to exist, but it is possible to conceive of a universe in which creatures of free will are able to do only limited harm to each other, even a cosmos in which creatures of free will freely choose the good.

If God exists, then God is not good in the traditional sense of the word. God's goodness is different from ours. So the problem of theodicy can be stated:

God is. God is all-powerful. God is good, but with a different goodness than we know. God creates a world with evil, in our sense of the word. So the existence of evil does not contradict the existence of God.

Is this a word game with the word "good" that empties it of linguistic meaning? We must then assume that God ultimately loves creation and creatures but in a way beyond our understanding (Job 38; Isaiah 55).

For Christian pastoral counselors, the key element in resolution of this conflict is the fact that Christ—God-with-us—suffered as a human. The incarnation silences the charge that God is aloof, impassive, and cruel. The presence of God-with-us shows the way in which God is involved compassionately and ultimately to the depths of human suffering. As God presented Godself to us in human form that we can apprehend and understand, so God has communicated goodness to us in the life, teaching, and death of Jesus in ways we can grasp. Divine goodness and human goodness are thus analogous but not identical; they are similar and yet distinct. God has created a world in which evil exists; God joins us in fighting it and leads the way in rejecting it and choosing what is ultimately good.

Pastoral counselors are truly pastoral as they are present with others in their pain or as they are available to others in the midst of disorder. In being the face of God to one who is in pain, the counselor embodies the only transhistorical and transcultural answer we have to the insolvable problems of theodicy—God-with-us. The God who has come, is come, and shall come to share with us in future pain is not the answerer of our philosophical and theological despair; this God is the answering One who suffers with us in our hurting and supports us in our healing.

Summary

The intercultural pastoral counselor is aware of the cultural shaping and labeling of mental illness. What is normal and normative in each culture varies significantly, as does what is abnormal behavior in each setting. Thought disorders show greater similarity between cultures than do affective and personality disorders. Some syndromes are culturally bound, such as the unique forms hysteria takes in various cultures. Pathology is similar yet distinct in traditional and modern cultures.

The pastoral counselor sees human frailty and suffering as rooted in the structural weaknesses of humanness, in the imbalances due to arrested or exaggerated development and to relational difficulties and environmental stressors. The evil of human alienation from both the self and from others is understood as universal, inevitable, and yet not necessary and therefore alterable. Human suffering, fragmentation, and illness are tragic parts of creation which must be understood with a theodicy that takes the realities of evil, human freedom, and responsibility and the possibilities of healing and reconciliation with equal seriousness.

11

Pastoral Psychotherapy
Across Cultures

Models of Pastoral Counseling
and Theology

"Western psychotherapy has engaged in the self-illusion that we offer a culture-free, value-free, ideology-free cure under the universal rubric of mental health."

—Mansell Pattison, 1977

THE HEALING OF THE MIND
JEWISH FOLKTALE

In a distant land, a prince lost his mind and imagined himself a rooster. He sought refuge under the table and lived there, naked, refusing to partake of the royal delicacies served in golden dishes— all he wanted and accepted was the grain reserved for the roosters. The king was desperate. He sent for the best physicians, the most famous specialists; all admitted their incompetence. So did the magicians. And the monks, the ascetics, the miracle makers; all their interventions proved fruitless.

One day an unknown sage presented himself at court. "I think that I could heal the prince," he said shyly. "Will you allow me to try?"

The king consented, and to the surprise of all present, the sage removed his clothes and, joining the prince under the table, began to crow like a rooster.

Suspicious, the prince interrogated him. "Who are you and what are you doing here?"—"And you," replied the sage, "who are you and what are you doing here?"—"Can't you see? I am a rooster!" —"Hmm," said the sage, "how very strange to meet you here!"— "Why strange?"—"You mean, you don't see? Really not? You don't see that I'm a rooster just like you?"

The two men became friends and swore never to leave each other.

Then the sage undertook to cure the prince by using himself as example. He started by putting on a shirt. The prince couldn't believe his eyes. "Are you crazy? Are you forgetting who you are? You really want to be a man?"—"You know," said the sage in a gentle voice, "you mustn't ever believe that a rooster who dresses like a man ceases to be a rooster." The prince had to agree. The next day both dressed in a normal way. The sage sent for some dishes from the palace kitchen. "Wretch! What are you doing?" protested the prince, frightened in the extreme. "Are you going to *eat* like them now?" His friend allayed his fears. "Don't ever think that by eating like man, with man, at his table, a rooster ceases to be what he is; you mustn't ever believe that it is enough for a rooster to behave like a man to become human; you can do anything with man, in his world and even for him, and yet remain the rooster you are."

And the prince was convinced; he resumed his life as a prince. (Wiesel 1972:170–171)

Counseling has many metaphors. The word pictures vary intriguingly from culture to culture.

A Samoan woman, innocent of medicine's specializations, was referred by her family doctor, who told her she was going to see a psychiatrist. In her first visit she asked the question that was puzzling her. " 'Doctor' I know, 'baby doctor' I understand, 'bone doctor' I once meet, but I never know a psychia—what do you call it?—yeah, psychiatrist. What kind of doctor are you?"

The therapist, understanding the Samoan preference for physical expression and human relationship rather than abstraction and intellectual discussion, answered, "I am a heart doctor. I help people with worry in the heart."

"Then I'm seeing the right kind of doctor, because my heart has lots of worry" (Tseng 1981:260).

At the end of a first session, a man asked the pastoral counselor, "Just what is a *pastoral* counselor, anyway?"

The counselor, knowing the man understood "pastor" as a person committed to leadership in the Christian community, reflected on how to answer. "All healing happens through acceptance from some human community," he said, "and the pastoral counselor is someone who identifies her or his community by name in the very first word, so you know where she is accountable, or where he draws his strength."

"It's like putting your values up front rather than keep me guessing?"

Our metaphors reveal the truth of our relationships, our understandings of ourself and others, and the values and beliefs that connect us.

Advisers, advocates, brothers or sisters, behavioral modifiers, carers, coaches, consultants, counselors, critics, defenders, dream interpreters, educators, elders, enablers, facilitators, family helpers, feelers, fellow travelers, friends, guides, gurus, headshrinkers, healers, helpers, hypnotists, interpreters, judges, listeners, meddlers, mediators, participant observers, pastors, peacemakers, problem solvers, referees, saviors, shamans, surrogate parents, therapists, trainers, troublemakers, understanding supporters, witch doctors, wounded healers—the list is much longer, the roles fulfilled much more broad, the relationships more varied and complex than any of these. In some cultures one may be many or almost all of the above in the course of a counseling relationship.

The metaphors we use shape both the theory and process of pastoral psychotherapy: they are the crucial elements forming the structure of our definitions. Cross-cultural definitions employ a rich variety of metaphors, and we shall examine these in constructing both our definition of and direction for cross-cultural psychotherapy. We will explore the metaphors of hide-and-seek, choice and change, sanctioned retreat, teacher and student, scientific technique and skill, therapeutic communication, healing relationship, human transformation, the healing community, host and guest, and the wounded healer.

Hide-and-Seek

"To provide a theoretical model that fits all kinds of psychotherapy, ancient and modern, East and West, one that is deceptively simple, I propose that the essence of psychotherapy is 'hide-and-seek,' " writes Takeo Doi, the University of Tokyo psychiatrist.

Hide-and-seek is virtually the most primitive and the most international children's game. Only one other precedes it: peek-a-boo, or *fort-da* in German, or *inai-inai-bah* in Japanese, which means "now gone, now gone, here now." This disappearing-reappearing play indicates that the infant is beginning object relations, differentiating self and other. Hide-and-seek requires a higher level of psychological development, including a capacity for duplicity, a kind of lying—an innocent lying—for the sake of preserving one's separate self, one's secrets and one's ability to be in secret.

> When I say that the essence of psychotherapy is hide-and-seek, it is because the patient is induced to look for the secret of his [her] illness by the therapist. But since the secret of the illness, which they work together to find out, lies hidden in the patient [her] himself, the psychotherapeutic hide-and-seek is really played within the patient. That is why it is so difficult and the therapist's help is needed. If the patient is within the neurotic range, he [she] can rather easily be made interested in discovering the secret of the illness. But if psychotic, it is hard to engage him [her] in the psychotherapeutic hide-and-seek. He is either in no mood to play the game or is feeling terrified because he is convinced that his "secrets" are out, that is, he feels exposed and defenseless. . . . There is also a subtle difference in the meaning of "secret," for what strikes the patient as well as the therapist as secret is not really one's inner secrets, but rather what makes us transcend them: in other words, the therapy itself becomes shrouded with the sense of secret, or perhaps mystery. A sense of mystery is, of course, pronounced . . . in all religiously inspired therapies or healing. (Doi 1976:274–275)

Western psychoanalytic therapies seek for the secret within the individual's past; rational therapies look for the enigma hiding in the faulty thinking. Self therapies hunt for the secret in the self-system of the person. Family therapy, along with many non-Western therapies, looks more broadly for the secret: to the family system, the social network, or the community conflicts that place the person in a bind.

For Morita therapy, the secret is the patient's *toraware,* the state of being bound up with one's physical and mental conditions and driven by the instinct for self-preservation. For Naikan therapy, the secret is one's hidden guilt and the unacknowledged indebtedness to parents. In shamanistic therapies, the secret is revealed (or created) by what the shaman divines. In both Japanese and traditional African psychotherapies, the focus is less on seeking the hidden secret and more on finding the person entrapped in his or her hiding place and bringing the isolated back into community.

The Japanese, Doi notes, are more inclined to play the disappearing-reappearing game than to choose hide-and-seek; or, if playing the latter, they are likely to come out from hiding to be found or wait and grieve if no one comes to find them. Western people, who stress the worth and individuality of a human soul, may become too preoccupied with the search for secrets and the fascination with finding out the hidden elements of the self. They want to be "it" when it is time to get on with caring for others.

As a metaphor, hide-and-seek captures the process and the story of therapy in a provocative way. The parallel theological metaphors of a seeking God, the pastoral tasks of seeking the lonely and alienated, and the necessity for relationship and community for full humanness are all brought into connectedness.

Choice and Change

A second universal metaphor for counseling and psychotherapy has been suggested by Jerome Frank in *Persuasion and Healing.* Psychotherapy is one of many methods for getting people to change their minds or mend their ways. There is probably nothing more universal than attempts to achieve the goals of choice, change, and correction; thus this approach offers a useful starting point for intercultural comparison. The definition of evoking a change of mind or a change of behavior is broad enough in scope to incorporate various helping methods without destroying their unique distinctions, yet it is comprehensive enough to provide a common basis for examining universal features of counseling across cultures.

A succinct statement of this perspective on counseling theory from a Western perspective defines the purposes of counseling as threefold: (1) *choice,* such as whether to marry, divorce, change jobs, get more education; (2) *change,* such as the need to acquire new social skills, learn new ways of relating and resolving conflict, alter one's daily routine of activities, give up limiting dependencies, habits, addictions, or face a terminal illness; and (3) *clarity,* the need to reduce confusion by gaining a realistic view of one's abilities and vocational possibilities, to reorient one's life while coming off drugs, or gain new perspectives on boundaries, responsibilities, and conflictual or entangled relationships (Gilmore 1973:44). Choice, change, and clarity are ends in most psychotherapy, although the choice may be located in the person or in the group (depending on the culture), the change may be internal to the person or external in the context, and the clarity may be more imposed than evoked. Yet these elements provide three dimensions of psychotherapeutic movement that do occur in all counseling.

Frank's cross-cultural comparisons involve several interactive sets of forces: (1) a sociocultural context that provides criteria, definition, value, healing capacity, and social recognition to (2) certain individuals possessed of healing powers, to whom all concerned believe it right and proper for (3) the sufferer to present himself or herself to obtain relief for certain classes of difficulties. So arrangements are made for (4) some regularized, even ritualistic, contacts between therapist and patient, which occur in an atmosphere heavy with hope, faith, and concern for change to occur in the patient's condition. These social forces are instrumental in stimulating change—whether by substantive alteration of internal or external components or by eliciting a placebo effect.

Originally, Frank considered the placebo effect as the manifestation of a suggestion reaction provoked by the personal influence (power, charisma, status, mystique) of the healer, with certain social characteristics of the patient (suggestibility, dependency) and of the social context in which the healing occurs (belief systems, trust in the persons and process, faith in transcendent powers at work). In later writing Frank calls this a nonspecific aspect of psychotherapeutic healing, which he sees anchored in the interpersonal relationship between the therapist and client. A special human relationship is necessary for effective counseling and psychotherapy, but it alone is not sufficient for healing. Change in both thought and behavior requires a conjunction of factors brought together by the relationship itself, including (1) a belief and thought system (2) shared by patient and therapist, which gives a basis for (3) comprehending disturbance and its therapy, (4) modifying the patient's knowledge, (5) enhancing the patient's expectations of being helped, (6) providing meaningful success experiences, and (7) facilitating the patient's capacity to experience emotions within and between self and others (Frank 1971: 360).

From this point of view, it matters less what technique or methodology the therapists may use. What is important is that they are endowed with culturally defined and socially empowered therapeutic qualities and conduct themselves as the counselee and the society expect they will in an enabling relationship.

For the pastoral counselor these metaphors are parallel to theological presuppositions that *being* is more essential to enabling growth than *doing,* that *presence* is more evocative of change than *strategy,* that calling persons to change (repentance), choice (responsibility), and clarity (integrity) are central to the counseling task.

Sanctioned Retreat

A third universal metaphor is that of the sanctioned retreat—a respite from life tasks, social accountability, communal expectations, and personal responsibility—to allow for reorganization of one's life process and a reintegration of values. This retreat-release-renewal process goes by many names, with positive and negative connotations. In some settings it is defined as a "sick role," which permits a period of recognized irresponsibility and flexibility in a context routinely rigid and prescribed.

Anthropologist Victor Turner, in his study of therapeutic rituals (1969:94–107), offers a language for illuminating the nature of this healing process of release from the prescribed to choose new patterns of being and becoming. Most primitive rituals of psychic healing can be divided into three phases—the phase of separation, the liminal phase, and the phase of reincorporation.

In the phase of separation, one divests the self of former roles and familiar processes of identification. In the liminal phase, the person enters a period of undifferentiated utopian equality. Former roles, commitments, and values are abandoned, and an aura of innocence and an atmosphere of rebirth provide a context for transformation. Liminality is a phase of transition, of being in movement from one state to another. As the person leaves the liminal state and moves back into responsible participation, there is a reincorporation into the life of the community, but with renewed health and vitality. The basic commitments, tasks, and responsibilities, suspended during the liminal period, now become operative again. The transitional stage was temporary. The goal was reincorporation, reintegration, renewed and strengthened participation in the life of the community.

These three stages—separation, liminality, reincorporation—are phases in all social rituals; they are in particular the sequence of periods in healing rituals of therapeutic change.

In most primitive societies, the period of liminality was always viewed as transitional and temporary and invariably led to reincorporation into the group's social, moral, and relational standards; but in more complex and individualistic societies, liminality has become an alternate life-style in psychological adjustment and a central goal in many forms of religion. The free, unrestricted, unobligated state of amoral values and uncommitted options that is necessary for the healing process is extended to offer an existential, here-and-now way of unstructured living typical of many of the humanistic therapies with an ethic of encounter, immediacy, and responsibility within the present moment. In religious liminality, the person practices an individual private piety without reference to the covenanted ethical structures and the responsible acceptance of and conformity to the norms of the religious community. Such private pietism may take the form of the I-Thou relationships of existential faith or the believer who participates in the faith community as a consumer and spectator but not as an integral member in social and moral solidarity with others.

In every society, suggests Turner (1969:139), there is a dialectical movement between the structured community and the free-floating community he calls "communitas." This twofold movement is absolutely necessary for the survival and health of any society.

> What is certain is that no society can function adequately without this dialectic. Exaggeration of structure may well lead to pathological manifestation of communitas outside or against "the law." Exaggeration of communitas, in certain religious or political movements of the leveling type, may be speedily followed by despotism, over-bureaucratization, or other moves of structural rigidification.

Talcott Parsons has written of a "sanctioned retreat" to describe this period of liminality. Therapy gives a time of release from the structural demands of the social-occupational-religious-moral institutions so the person can have the distance and leisure to reconstruct life, regather energies, and assimilate new learnings for a more effective reentry. When a person finds that he or she no longer has the emotional energy, capacity, and resilience to perform the previously chosen social role, then society, seeing this as "illness," recognizes the appropriateness of a "sanctioned retreat," with the expectation that the therapist or group offering support for this time of reconstruction will seek to bring the person back into the network of social responsibilities that comprise human existence in community. This sanctioned retreat is from the public world of the religiously sanctioned ethic, and the return is to the public world of the religiously defined ethic. So, in actuality, even secular psychotherapy is a morally defined interlude in the society's moral-religious process (Parsons 1964:319–320).

Browning's analysis of this sanctioned retreat (1976:33) is insightful in offering an understanding of Western psychotherapy.

> Parsons' thesis is also helpful for locating the sociological significance of certain features of most counseling and psychotherapy. Talk about the internal therapeutic process as being permissive, as exhibiting unconditional positive regard and acceptance, as not being moralistic and judgmental, as prizing all the feelings of the patient, and as accepting negative attitudes, would be understood from this perspective as having to do with transitional techniques and attitudes employed by the counselor to create the sanctioned retreat needed for the patient to analyze the self and reorganize the inner life. They were temporary expedients designed to get the patient to relax long enough to explore his [or her] unhappiness or incapacity.

Whether one thinks of the pause in the person's life project for reconstruction as a "sanctioned retreat" or as transitional liminality, the pastoral counselor is concerned about both the person needing released time from the normal social obligations and for the social, spiritual, and communal context to which the counselee must eventually return. If there is no moral context from which to distance oneself in times of personal transformation, and none to rejoin, then both counselor and counselee suffer from confusion, isolation, and a loss of healing power.

For the pastoral counselor, the metaphor of sanctioned retreat has many theological parallels. The rhythm of withdrawal and reengagement, of concern for both time in the wilderness and return to the world, of solitude in spirituality and healing as well as return to life in community, are concerns for those who see life as a balanced whole between personal integrity and communal solidarity.

Teacher and Student

A fourth universal metaphor is that of education. There are elements of learning, unlearning, and relearning in all therapy, so the particular commonalities of learning processes become useful meeting points for cross-cultural comparison, especially in drawing on the learning theories developed in various Western schools of thought and in the guru–chela relationship of the East.

The goals of treatment in most Western therapy range from symptomatic treatment of things such as tics and phobias to "massive personality overhauls" but it is, in a sense, specialized reeducation. The person is encouraged to develop a new self-image, with greater self-esteem, to be relieved of subjective feelings of pain, anxiety, and stress, perhaps to achieve greater independence, and to function more effectively in society. These are educational goals, a relearning of thought, feeling, and behavior (Kennedy 1973:1174).

But only in some therapies are learning models strongly espoused—behavioral learning, social learning, rational emotive therapy, and reality therapy, to name a few. Yet learning theory and therapeutic theory are different points on the same continuum—though with different ratios of responsibility assigned to the teacher (therapist) and the student (patient).

In the Indian culture, the guru–chela relationship has been held up as an appropriate therapeutic model. In contrast to the premium placed on personal independence in Western thought, Indian societies see maturity as a satisfying and continuous dependency relationship; in fact, independency longings can produce neurotic anxiety.

> The guru-chela relationship is *sui generis,* and ideally does not represent another, mundane, relationship (such as the parent-child relationship, which transference, for example, is believed to represent). The major paradox of psychotherapy is that, if the psychotherapist stands with society and works for the individual's adjustment to it by modifying and coaxing the latter's unconscious drives and tendencies into social respectabilities, then he/she can become the obedient instrument of rancid traditions, decaying systems, and disintegrating institutions. If, on the other hand, he/she stands with the individual, really interested in helping, he/she is forced into social criticism. The guru solves this paradox by becoming the paradox . . . in this world yet not of this world . . . emancipated from the bondage of social conditioning yet without discarding it, living not for self . . . but for others. The guru-chela paradigm appears particularly tenable where self-discipline rather than self-expression is the cherished goal. (Neki 1977:5–6)

The guru is the more active, responsible, directive, advisory, controlling party; the chela is the more passive, dependent, adaptive, teachable, and obedient person in the transaction. The psychotherapeutic tradition is to build a temporary ad hoc relationship; the guru–chela relationship is a permanent abiding commitment. Therapy is for the hour and the period of contract; the guru–chela relationship embraces all of life, inside and outside the therapeutic hour, and in open-ended commitment for life and beyond.

The Western therapist sees dependency as "a feeling of helplessness, over-valuation of the strengths of others, seeking restoration by dependence, blind faith, and desire for the constant presence and undivided attention and esteem of the person depended on" (Maslow and Mittelman 1943:151). The Eastern perspective accepts dependency, fosters it, and through this relationship works on the disciple's life pattern, awakens self-value, and leads to confident dependability and appropriate independence.

> Cultures are like jigsaw puzzles; any given culture's institutions fit each total cultural pattern as would pieces of a particular puzzle. One can't borrow a piece from one culture and fit it into another. The Western psychotherapist—with such weaponry as free association, dream interpretation, and working through—is a product of an overly expressive culture; while the guru—with his meditational, contemplative, and other "mind-quieting" procedures—is an evolute of a suppressive culture. The guru thus holds out an image that is emotionally acceptable to people in a predominantly suppressive culture, while a psychotherapist projects an alien image. (Neki 1973:764)

The educational model is useful in correlating Western, Japanese, Indian, and some African therapies, but many traditional healing processes in the two-thirds world deal little with reeducation, ego-strengthening, and personality modification. Rather, they are pragmatic perspectives, with immediate goals of tension reduction or the alleviation of symptoms that are troubling persons or getting them in trouble with others. Even though patients may spend weeks or even months with a curer, the process does not depend on verbal exchanges for the achievement of insight in the patient. Instead, the verbal exchanges may be with the spirits that are thought to be affecting the person, and the questions asked do not anticipate a direct, conscious reply. The common element may be in ventilation, confession, or catharsis—a discharge process—rather than in learning and integration of insight.

Pastoral counseling across cultures shares a great deal with educational models and learning theories. The recognition that values, worldviews, belief systems, life goals, and a sense of meaning are integral parts of each person's quest for health and wholeness makes the pastoral counselor less willing to settle for symptom reduction without asking what place and function the particular symptom serves in the person's orientation in living.

Scientific Technique and Skill

A fifth metaphor for cross-cultural counseling is the experimental "scientific" model of technique and skill. Counseling approaches vary in their emphasis on technical skill and specific therapeutic techniques as over against the focus on the importance of "the human relationship" in psychotherapy. Until quite recently, behavioral and psychoanalytic approaches have been seen as stressing technique and methodology and minimizing the human side of the counselor-counselee process. However, research on effective vs. ineffective therapy has consistently demonstrated that personal, relational, affiliational factors have always been central, whether recognized as such or taken for granted in the theoretical statements (Truax and Carkhuff 1967; Combs and Syngg 1949).

The high importance given to scientific methodologies as a universal common denominator is consistent with the spirit of the age. In the twentieth century, the only truly universal ideology with global legitimacy is science. If there is any believable cross-cultural faith, it is science. Yet in spite of its universality and the nearly unanimous support it receives from ruling elites, military powers, and recognized officialdoms of each society, science is only cautiously trusted, frequently suspected, largely feared as well as praised. In other words, the attachment to science of every society—East, West, or third world—is ambivalent (Cohen in Rouner 1983:223–224).

This universal love-hate relationship with science becomes a deep commitment in developing countries, which place a high premium on technological development. With science embraced as the one transcultural language and ideology, the older values—cultural, religious, economic—can be discarded as outdated.

Chinese communists, for example, became strongly anti-Confucian and anti-Christian because both religions were viewed as passé cultural relics that must necessarily be eliminated as anachronisms in a scientific age. If Christianity can be exposed as medieval, then "one can wave goodby to Confucian China without deserting China" (Levenson 1965: 21).

The universal faith in the efficacy of the scientific method has supported the conviction that technique may be the common link, that skill may provide an empirical, measurable, replicable process for the treatment of discomforts, disorder, or disease.

Strupp, in seeking to identify the specific features of therapeutic influence, originally hoped to devise specific techniques for individual persons and their unique symptoms. He discards this mechanical conception, noting, "We are beginning to recognize and take seriously the extraordinary complexity of the therapeutic influence." Later he states that "the search for highly specific techniques . . . is probably futile" (Strupp 1973:275,313).

Strupp concludes (1973:283) that therapeutic influence is composed of two fundamental factors: one consists of the nonspecific, basic, general effect that is present in the interpersonal relationship; the second consists of specific techniques employed by the therapist. But these techniques are operative only through the medium of relationship, and all effects can be attributed, to a large part, to such human qualities of the therapist as "interest, understanding, respect, dedication, empathy . . . which instill trust. . . . Therapeutic techniques are anchored in and potentiated by . . . the establishment and maintenance of a proper healing relationship."

For pastoral counselors, effective technique and facilitative skills are secondary. The primary pastoral concern is for uniting doing and being. Clarity in process must be united with authenticity in presence. In any forced choice between technique and relationship, it is in relationship that the power of the pastoral resides.

Therapeutic Communication

A sixth metaphor for counseling is that of communication. This universal process of exchanging and correlating meanings is a common thread uniting all visions of cross-cultural therapy.

Communication is a meeting of meanings that occurs in a dynamic ever-widening spiral of interchanges between parties. It combines facial, postural, gestural, verbal, tonal, situational, positional, and indefinable relational elements. It involves co-perception, co-confusion, co-interpretation, communication, and co-experiencing as its goal, but each of these is possible only in part.

Psychotherapy is primarily interaction through conversation, and the effectiveness of the communication is the major variable in determining its productivity. In effective communication, both persons move toward each other in adjustment and adaptation. The client may change expectations, alter ways of perceiving, learn new cognitive and affective language, and even dream clinically appropriate dreams to match the therapist's theoretical bent, but the primary communicative obligation is for the therapist to move toward the client in communication style, cultural images, and therapeutic agenda. The conceptual differences must be reduced, the communication disparity dealt with clearly and openly.

The psychotherapeutic process is, in essence, conversation and other communication about communication. Much of the conversation focuses on clarifying meanings and making conscious and explicit what is indirect, subtle, covert, and unaware in the counselee's communication. These multilevel meanings reveal the conflicts within the self and the conflicts with the culture that are binding to this particular person. In meta-communication (communication about communication), awareness of what is repressed and insight into what has been denied or concealed are brought into the open for exploration and experiencing.

In any conversation, participants must possess a common set of symbols, come to agreement on their meanings, choose a mutually agreeable subject, and explore it in continuing interchange. When the focus of the conversation is on the conflicts that trouble the personality or soul, that person's uniquely personal symbol system, metaphors, and the feelings that accompany them must be explored by both. It happens in a language known, in essence, only by one person yet fully understandable only when two—the perceiver and a participant observer—tease out its entangled strands together.

If communication is to flow between persons within a tolerable range of error, the basic frame of reference of each party must overlap sufficiently to provide awareness of each other's view of human beings and their nature, of the world and its working, of the boundaries of natural events and the supernatural, and of the social context in which all these come together. This frame of reference, or worldview, should be shared, but it need not be identical. Some disparity always exists and is not only tolerable but desirable. The recognition of communication gaps, the clarification of differences, and the negotiation of disagreements provide the stuff of testing out relationship and building skills for understanding oneself in the presence of another and understanding the other in depth comparison with one's own values. "The typical psychology of a given nation can be learned only through familiarity with its native language. The language comprises everything which is intrinsic to the soul of a nation and therefore provides the best projective test there is for each nation" (Doi 1973:15).

The pastoral counselor, grounded in a theology of incarnation, values communication as central to the task of promoting healing relationships. Incarnation includes (1) presence, (2) self-disclosure, (3) openness to the other, (4) sharing in suffering, (5) reconciliation of alienated relationships, and (6) mutuality as a goal of human community. These are the central issues of communication theory and practice as well. The pastoral task of embodying such graciousness seeks to elevate communication to communion.

Healing Relationship

The seventh and most frequently utilized metaphor for cross-cultural counseling and therapy is the healing relationship. Since all psychotherapy involves at minimum a therapist and a client interacting in a special way, many have identified the common factors in this relationship as the essential universal ingredients. The emphasis on the curative power of the relationship has been strong in existential and humanistic approaches, but it is also present in differing degrees and diverse forms in virtually all healing transactions.

In the oft-quoted study of effectiveness in Western psychotherapy, the evidence indicated that a person may be made better or worse depending greatly on the therapist's capacity to provide central therapeutic elements of "empathy, nonpossessive warmth, and genuineness." These characteristics are positive reinforcers, as Truax hypothesizes (Truax and Carkhuff 1967:150).

> These three "therapeutic conditions" have their . . . effects in the following
> four modalities: (1) They serve to reinforce positive aspects of the patient's

self concept, modifying the existing self concept and thus leading to changes in the patient's own self reinforcement system; (2) they serve to reinforce self-exploratory behavior, thus eliciting self concepts and anxiety-laden material which can potentially be modified; (3) they serve to extinguish anxiety or fear responses associated with specific cues, both those elicited by the relationship with the therapist and those elicited by patient self-exploration; and (4) they serve to reinforce human relating, encountering, or interacting, and to extinguish fear or avoidance learning associated with human relating.

The much-researched trinity of warmth, empathy, and genuineness, which appear to the Western patient as authentic caring, are evidence of weakness and incompetence to the Burmese. The openness, mutuality, and egalitarianism of a client-centered approach that fosters trust in the West may be misinterpreted as lack of interest in a hierarchically structured setting such as Thailand or China, where the therapist is expected to demonstrate involvement by taking clear, firm, concerned positions.

> One universal fundamental feature of psychotherapy is an emotionally special interpersonal relationship created and managed to foster personal change in the client. Despite this universality, it is possible, and even probable, that the constituent elements of "the good relationship" are different in one culture than they are in another. (Wohl 1981:146)

We can say with certainty that while a special kind of human relationship is necessary for psychotherapy, the specialness that will create the desired hope and trust in the counselee is significantly different, and the time required for the therapist to be perceived as "caring" is smaller in the West than in other settings.

Our general Western concept of a good therapeutic relationship includes acceptance, unconditional positive regard, emotional warmth, congruence and authenticity, concern for the other's integrity, respect for boundaries on the part of the therapist, respect for the other's status and ability, trust in the therapist's reliability, and attraction to the other as a significant person. Even if, in most cultures, these qualities are desirable in general human relationships, they may not always characterize what is wanted from an "expert," "healer," or "adviser."

> The contrast in behavior of Western and traditional therapists also is striking. Whereas the former should not become involved personally with the patient, he (or she) is expected to be empathetic, nonjudgmental, warm, and human, exhibiting behavior that leads to the patient's involvement with the therapist through the phenomenon of transference. The Western therapist is, obviously, quite different in approach to the patient from the ordinary physician. In contrast, a non-Western mental therapist involved in major curing rites behaves very much as when treating physical illness. He "cloaks himself in a powerful impersonal role," exercising authority, charisma, and often feats of legerdemain. "Though he may know the patient well, during treatment he moves into an impersonal role dimension," rarely if ever encountering the "transference" phenomenon. (Kennedy 1973:1173–1174)

Western therapists place a high premium on the quality of unconditional regard offered the client—for an hour of undivided attention.
Outside the therapeutic setting, the high valuation assumedly continues,
but the availability of the counselor is normally limited to emergency
situations, and these contacts are not encouraged. In some cultures, the
therapist becomes available for continuous care and support. Such
shared living arrangements offer maximum availability for intervention
in the patient's distress. Prince has described treatment among the
Yoruba of Nigeria (1974:143). Psychotic patients "live in" with the
healer, for an average of three or four months, cared for by a family
member who remains with them. Generally they are shackled for the first
few weeks of their stay, until they can be trusted not to run away. Various
herbal medicines are used, and animal sacrifices may be carried out upon
admission. When the patient is deemed ready for release, a "discharge
ceremony" may be held on the banks of a river, involving blood sacrifice,
symbolic cleansing of the patient of his illness, and perhaps symbolic
death and rebirth into a new life.

In Vellore, India, pastoral counselor Carlos Welch utilizes the "therapeutic family" approach in the treatment of dysfunctional persons. Up
to five persons are accepted into the therapist's home for periods of one
month to six months. The spontaneous regression that occurs in the
structured environment may require total care until the person grows
through the early developmental stages into adolescence. As soon as they
are capable, persons are assigned a daily schedule of work. The secure
structure and clear contractual agreements invite responsible participation.

> The therapeutic family system requires a very high degree of commitment
> on the part of the therapists. Also required is a support group who are
> trained in restraining methods and willing to provide supervision of highly
> disturbed persons until they develop social control. . . . Psychological
> counseling is not advising or advice giving, which is the usually understood
> meaning of the word "counseling" in India. Rather the process is a facilita-
> tive and supportive experience for working through the trauma and utiliz-
> ing personality resources for resolving the crisis. (Welch 1979:73–74)

The high demands on relationship in many traditional cultures require
a commitment of the therapist of greater amounts of time and emotional
energy. The concrete evidence of caring in open availability is the crucial
factor in trust and responsivity.

> As compared to his Western counterpart, the Indian patient is more ready
> to accept overt situational support, less ready to seek intrapsychic explana-
> tions; more insistent and importunate with regards to personal needs and
> time; more ready to discard ego-bounds and involve the therapist in direct
> role-relationships; and finally to receive guidance and support as from the
> joint-family elder. (Surya and Jayaram 1964:3)

In attempting to isolate four universals in psychotherapy, Torrey
(1972) listed as essential (1) a worldview shared by therapist and patient,
(2) a close interpersonal relationship, (3) the patient's expectation of

being helped, and (4) specific techniques. Torrey's confidence that these four factors are universally present and essential is matched by an equally strong conviction that overcoming cultural barriers between therapists and patients is extremely difficult. He argues that cultural commonality within all four of these aspects is so critical that a cultural gap of any significant distance between partners in therapy provides almost insurmountable barriers to the therapeutic work. The cruciality of the common worldview, the delicacy of sustaining a close trusting personal relationship when cues and expectations become so easily confused, the wide variation in expectations, and the variety of appropriate techniques contain so many variables that the delicacy of therapeutic work is rendered impossible.

The more sensitive the counselor is to the expectations of the client, and the more aware of the cultural expectations that support and surround the individual's expectations, the more capable he or she will be of utilizing these expectations for the advancement of the therapeutic process. The less aware the counselor is of these expectations, the more dysfunctional will be the communication, the interpersonal transactions, and the emerging relationship. The expectations of the client have powerful effects on every aspect of the therapeutic relationship. Personal, familial, and cultural expectations must be assessed early in the process of any work across a cultural gap. An early attempt to reduce the disparity between what the counselee expects and the actual therapeutic procedures that are likely to be used can free both parties to work more effectively.

Expectations of persons, as well as cultures, can be usefully conceived as influencing or determining the "frame of mind" or "set" of the counselee. The set describes both cognitive and affective expectancies that define agenda, focus interest, direct motivation, and inhibit or activate various behaviors.

B. E. Collins (1970) has summarized five sets common to clients in many cultures (see Table 11-1): complex units of thinking-feeling-acting that direct the person toward (1) data gathering, (2) seeking affiliation, (3) orienting by status authority and legitimacy, (4) placing the self on trial for rewards or punishments, and (5) striving for consistency and perfection. These sets are described in Western language, but they are familiar to counselors in many cultures.

The aware counselor recognizes the expectational set and establishes contact within its constructs before exploring the discrepancy between the anticipated and the actual. The discovery of one's attitudinal set is best facilitated by the evoking of awareness (affective discovery), not the offering of insight or analysis (cognitive discoveries). Meeting the client within the initial set and working through rather than contradicting expectations invites the greatest growth. In cross-cultural counseling, the interpathic counselor may choose to work within a set for an extended period of time, because it may be contextually congruent with the life situation of the person and its maintenance may serve a significant function in the person's surrounding community.

Table 11-1. Psychological Sets of Counselees

The Problem-Solving Set: Information orientation
The client is concerned with obtaining correct information (solutions, outlooks, skills) that has adaptive value in the real world. Information is accepted or rejected on the basis of perceived truth or falsity; Is it an accurate representation of reality? The processes tend to be rational, logical, analytic, problem-oriented. The counselor must be truthful and credible to reach this set.

The Consistency Set: Integrative orientation
The client is concerned with resolving cognitive dissonance by changing an opinion, belief, or behavior to make it consistent with other opinions, beliefs, or behaviors. The basic assumption is that the world is consistent and inner tensions must be resolved to produce inner consonance with what is without. People are not necessarily rational beings but rationalizing ones. The conviction is that "good people do good things and bad people do bad things," consistent with their character of nature. The counselor must be consistent with perceived reality to reach this set.

The Economic Set: Reward or Punishment orientation
The person is influenced by the perceived rewards or punishments the source is able to deliver, so may change in deference to the other's greater power. This may ensure behavioral compliance but does not guarantee private acceptance. It requires constant surveillance, because the person is likely to revert to old methods or modes of behavior when it is removed. The counselor must be powerful to reach this set.

The Identity Set: Identification orientation
The individual desires identification and solidarity with a reference group or an influential person held in high esteem. Since much of one's identity is drawn from the reference group admired, to which the person aspires, their characteristics, beliefs, values, and behaviors are adopted and assimilated. So the person, through identification, accepts beliefs and conforms to the group's standards or norms. The counselor must be attractive to reach this set.

The Authority Set: Legitimacy orientation
The person views those with status or position as possessing legitimate right to prescribe attitudes or behaviors. Certain authorities are seen as having the right to demand compliance or to recommend the expected or accepted norms of behavior for the person or the group. The counselor must be authoritative or have the power of status or position to reach this set.

These sets frequently interact, and any number of them can be operating at the same time.

(Collins 1970:26–33)

Expectations may also be viewed as sequential stages of development in therapeutic relationship. There are three familiar stages in the therapist–client relationship during much psychotherapeutic process. They are the initial magical relationship, the parental relationship, and the realistic relationship. The length of time spent in each of these periods is both an individual and a cultural variable.

> Indian patients bestow omnipotence on the [therapist]. The cultural norm of respect for the elderly and the authoritarianism of the hierarchically oriented society produce consequent dependence on elders, or those with higher social status. This can prolong the parental stage of relationship for a long time. In some, this stage may be continued without any disadvantage. A realistic relationship should foster interdependence and balance individual growth within the bounds of family welfare. (Ananth 1981:124)

The central element, from the perspective of the relational metaphor, is the contact achieved, the interpathic feeling and understanding experienced, the genuine caring communicated. For the pastoral counselor, such presence, acceptance, and love is the core quality of grace that makes counseling authentically pastoral. As Indian pastoral counselor Dayanand Pitamber writes (1979:24):

> Pastoral counseling tries to communicate love through interpersonal relationship. It does not mean that interpersonal relationship is used as a mere technique to communicate love, but rather it is an expression of love in itself . . . a genuine encounter in which the person is able to experience love . . . not only human love but also divine love.

Human Transformation

An eighth universal metaphor for cross-cultural counseling is human transformation. In both Eastern and Western cultures such deep change proceeds in a series of polar steps. In one culture we may identify more strongly with one role almost to the elimination of—and impoverishment of—the other. But human wholeness occurs as there is creative assimilation of each, or in some cultures an integration of both into a synthetic unity. Naranjo (1972:122) calls this process one of healing—enlightenment—development in his description of parts of this integration. The process is an alternation within, a creative tension of, a unifying assimilation of, and an integration between the following experiential poles. It calls for the simultaneous increase in both.

1. Identity of self as a distinct center *and* identification with other selves.
2. Awareness of objective reality *and* appreciation of subjective vision.
3. Detachment from group mind and ethos *and* participation in community.
4. Personal freedom to choose *and* capacity and willingness to surrender.
5. Differentiation within and between *and* unification within and be-

tween (intrapersonal/interpersonal, body/mind, thought/feeling, subject/object, human/divine).

6. Self-acceptance *and* self-denial.

7. Consciousness, insight, knowledge *and* intuition, awareness, understanding.

Western psychotherapy is skewed toward the left column of polarities; Eastern therapies tend toward the right. Both are essential to humanness, but the basic assumptions of the particular heritage biases the development of both person and culture. Western psychology has tended to see the right column as immature—childhood identification, subjectivity, surrender, unification, self-denial, intuitive hunches. The left column was seen as evidence of maturation—distinct identity, objectivity, freedom of choice, differentiation, self-acceptance, rational consciousness. Western male development, with its exaggeration of left-column values and impoverishment of the right, was frequently and erroneously used to project a normative model of humanness. Not only are the full ranges of human experience as both female *and* male necessary to understanding of existence, both Eastern and Western visions, both traditional and technologically developed perspectives, are indispensable for human transformation and growth.

Philemon Choi, the outstanding pastoral counselor in Hong Kong, writes (1980:13) of the need for therapists who belong to the culture served:

> Because of the complexity of each individual culture, it would be more feasible for any counselor from a different culture to make significant contributions at the level of research, training, and consultation rather than direct service. With efforts from both sides, the task of crossing the cultural gap would be made much easier. This would help to promote the development of counseling in non-Western cultures, at the same time stimulating growth in the field of cross-cultural counseling.

The pastoral counselor working in multicultural settings will most frequently do therapy with persons of his or her own culture or with those who are bicultural. "Bicultural" refers here to persons who live in a third culture that develops between or on the boundary of two adjoining cultures. These bicultural citizens may feel equally at home in either world or alienated from either or both. The development of interpathic cross-cultural insight and awareness is highly necessary to work on this boundary, to consult with and refer to therapists within the adjacent cultures, and to assist clients whose positions in bicultural experience, intercultural marriage, or multicultural relationships create tensions both intrapersonal and interpersonal. At the end of his study on theory and practice of intercultural therapy, Julian Wohl concludes (1976:205): "The occasional Western engaging in intercultural therapy is at best doing therapy to learn the culture so that he [or she] can better do research or perform training and consultative functions for the direct delivery of service."

The perspective on the nature of humans that underlies Western psychology emphasizes individuality, the self-contained encapsulated psyche or subjective world. This post-Enlightenment view is continuous with the political-social philosophy which assumed that human satisfactions and goals are fundamentally personal and individual.

Each individual has a unique, idiosyncratic experience of life. Each lives in a unique subjective world, pursuing personal pleasures and private goals, dreams and fantasies. Each person constructs a lifeline which, when the allotted time is over, will vanish. The function of the family of origin is to launch the developing individual; of the family of marriage to provide individual need fulfillment without limiting the autonomy of the person; of the community to provide a secure, open social context for individual achievement and self-realization; of the state to preserve and provide for the possibility of individual fulfillment.

Asian psychologies begin not from an individual model but from a relational one (Table 11-2). The person is not a monad but at least dyadic, triadic, or more. (The personal nature is derived interpersonally, the personality is constituted of relationships, the affects are multipersonal emotional fields that connect with positive or negative energies, and one is emotionally troubled when in trouble in relationships with family, community, ancestry, nature, or cosmic orders.)

Table 11-2. Comparison of Psychotherapy, West and East

Western Psychotherapy	*Asian Psychotherapy*
The individual model concentrates on the *text* of psychic disturbance—the decoding of symptoms, the awareness of the person's history, the analysis of the intrapsychic dynamics —from which the disorder springs.	The relational model concentrates on the *context* of the disturbance—the disordered relationships symbolized in the feelings of despair, shame, guilt, confusion, and isolation—in which the disorder is embedded.
The sources of strength lie in the individual's capacity to be self-directing, to claim autonomy and responsibility, and to use a scientific theory of the self to regain inner direction and control.	The sources of strength lie in the integration of the person in the social and cosmic order, a polyphonic social drama that triggers a ritual restoration of the dialogue with family, community, and tradition.
The individual approach is based on the self-regulating wisdom of the organism of the counselee. The empathy, warmth, and genuineness of the counselor are intense, authentic, but intended to be temporary and, as soon as possible, unnecessary for individual self-determination, definition, and direction.	The relational approach is based on the quality of the relationship the counselor and counselee create: the empathy, support, compassion, nonverbal acceptance, recognition, presence, seeing and being seen, dependency and dependability in an ongoing inclusion in the network of relationships.

(Adapted from Kakar 1984:10–13)

In the relational model, the needs for affiliation, attachment, connectedness, and interdependence are the primary and predominant motivational push and pull in the person rather than the press of sexual and biological drives. Thus the person is not an individual but is dividual: that is, a divisible part of the primary social unit of which the self is created.

The body image is not clearly etched, with impermeable boundaries, but lives in a constant interchange with the physical, social, and spiritual environment. The self is not a distinctly bounded, relatively constant, stable entity, an internal agent who is an object among other objects in the social universe, but a dynamic, fluid, enlarging, or contracting experience of human-being-with-others.

The Healing Community

The ninth metaphor, the healing community, is both metaphor and reality. As metaphor, it is a phrase used to describe those family systems, neighborhood groups, health care systems, committed support groups, and creative churches that surround persons with care. As a reality, healing community is any positive network of persons that enables health, growth, or human transformation.

Negative community provides only maintenance needs or, worse, allows its people to live in deprivation, oppression, or exploitation. Positive community creates an atmosphere of security and safety for its members, which allows growth, maturation, and fulfillment. Such community is concerned about physical, emotional, and spiritual needs among its members.

In outer-directed cultures, community plays a more obvious role in the person's development and personality adjustment. In inner-directed settings, community is internalized, and although it is just as crucial to the person's development, it is less visible. The significant people of one's life are internalized to form an internal community of reference that remains central all life long. In every culture, the significant persons without as well as the significant relationships that are sustained within form the two poles of healing community (or malevolent community) that nurture humanness.

The power of healing is owned by community. It is community which can guarantee justice where one has been oppressed or exploited. It is community which goes beyond the mistreatment or misuse of its member families or persons to affirm the worth and dignity of every member. It is community which recognizes those who have the gift of evoking healing, which confers authority to intervene in the pain of those who suffer. It is community which must receive, support, and integrate the ill back into healthful roles and relationships. Healing and health are rooted in the networks of persons that validate and invigorate personhood. Every person needs a network of from twenty to thirty persons to create a healthful community of support, nurturance, and fulfillment. This is composed of subgroups of persons—family, fellow workers, club or team members, neighbors, congregation, and so on. These groups are significantly interrelated and mutually interdependent to some degree. A troubled network has only ten to twelve people, and these are only superficially related. A deeply troubled person has a four- or five-person system of significant people. The numbers of persons in personal networks vary from tribal to industrial societies, from individualist to sociocentric groups. But the need for a supportive community is constant across all human boundaries.

The attitudes toward community are strikingly opposite in East and West. The loose communities of Western life are a sharp contrast to the traditional, intentional, or communal networks of the East.

In the West, privacy is guarded as a treasure; in China there is no word for privacy. In the West, loneliness is epidemic, mental stress is hidden, distress is covered in silent desperation and anxiety, depression and despair are fought clandestinely. In China, it is difficult to be lonely in the tiny apartment, or the four-to-a-room sleeping quarters of the commune. For each apartment block there is a courtyard committee, for each street a neighborhood committee. They are not there to see that the lights are off or the water available; they do their special form of pastoral care. If a couple is in conflict, they offer immediate help. If children are anxious about family tensions, they may confide in the committee. Friends will intervene by talking with each parent, then the couple, then the family, then the extended or three-tiered family of multiple generations. This family therapy—new, expensive, hard to find in the West— is immediate, ordinary, and free in China.

In contrast, Western individualism leaves the task of creating a supportive community to each person's initiative or to his or her good or bad fortune.

Most Western psychotherapy is grounded in the basic premise of the autonomy of the individual. From this the following assumptions emerge:

The individual can create personal meaning independent of social entanglements

The personality can separate itself from its binding family emotional heritage

The individual has the power to look unafraid at the insecurities of a helpless childhood

The individual has the transcendence to review the crises of life objectively and dispassionately

The individual has the capacity to channel sexuality, aggression, rage, egotism, and greed toward creative goals

Freedom and growth come from cutting loose from imperfect parents, siblings, and family roles

The individual can face suffering without avoidance, death without denial

And all this rises from the individual powers of the fully realized autonomous self

Yet the greatest need of persons, in the West as well as in the East, is to belong to a network that can support where they are weak, include when they are lonely, and accept where they feel unacceptable.

The pastoral counselor possesses what every therapist longs for—a community that surrounds the counselor and reaches to support and include the counselee. The pastoral person is a representative of the community of the spirit that offers a multidimensional network of caring, of moral discernment, of meaningful life direction, of significance through service to others. To be included in such community is to be in the healing context of true humanness.

Host and Guest

The tenth and most intriguing metaphor for pastoral counseling across cultures is that of host and guest.

In all counseling and psychotherapy, it is the counselee who is the host and the counselor who is the guest.

It is the host, not the guest, who owns the life story and human experience that are shared in the counseling situation. The boundaries, the center, the possibilities, the pain are all possessions of the host, not the guest. Counseling theories that see the counselor as definitive in the counseling situation—the person who sets the boundaries, defines the goals, creates the atmosphere, induces change—are missing the most basic element of the process. All therapy takes place on the turf of the recipient, in the life, the emotional world, and the opening future of the person desiring healing or growth.

The counselee host may hold single title to his or her life process (Western individualism), or the life experience may be held in joint ownership with the family (familiocentric personality) or with the tribe or caste (sociocentric personality). The entering guest is being welcomed not only into the story of the one person being encountered but into the story of the group, confronting not just the individual's role but the whole cast in the familial, communal drama.

The guest is present by invitation, not intrusion, so honoring the rules of the house (cultural values) and the rules of the community (moral values) are necessary. The guest is not an intruder, invader, or spy but an honorary though temporary member of the family. The house etiquette, rituals, secrets, and privacy will all receive respect.

The guest, as visitor, remains within the turf assigned by the host. He or she owns only what has been brought along as necessities or received as gifts.

The guest does not claim ownership of the other's story, so confidentiality is respected; the responsibility of persons for their own choices and their consequences are guarded. The guest never forgets whose turf, whose house, it is.

The guest does not overstay his or her welcome; the privilege of being in another person's world is not taken lightly.

Henri Nouwen has described this host-guest relationship using the biblical metaphor of hospitality (1975:51). Hospitality means receiving each other and respecting each person's difficulties and struggles, weaknesses and strengths.

> Hospitality, therefore, means primarily the creation of a free space where the stranger can enter and become a friend instead of an enemy. Hospitality is not to change people, but to offer them space where change can take place. It is not to bring men and women over to our side, but to offer freedom not disturbed by dividing lines. It is not to lead our neighbor into a corner where there are no alternatives left, but to open a wide spectrum of options for choice and commitment. It is not an educated intimidation with good books, good stories, and good works, but the liberation of fearful hearts so that words can find roots and bear ample fruit. It is not a method of making our God and our way into the criteria of happiness, but the opening of an opportunity to others to find their God and their way.

When counseling in a second culture, one dare never forget who is host and who guest. The imperialism of the counseling room, the couch, and the chair is unacceptable. The appropriate metaphors are those of an open door, an open self, an attitude of hospitality, and a mutual willingness to receive as well as give, to learn as well as teach, to be served as well as to serve.

For the pastoral counselor, the images of incarnation as dwelling with others in vulnerability and openness to hear, receive, and share in suffering are as central as the person of Christ. The way of Christ is the way of enfleshment, of embodying the realities shared, of truly being there *for* others and *with* others.

The Wounded Healer

The eleventh metaphor for pastoral counseling across cultures is the wounded healer. "The fundamental archetype of all life is wound and healing," wrote C. G. Jung. Woundedness is the inevitable price of life in a vulnerable environment (Table 11-3), healing is the necessary process of life in renewing itself in the ongoing cycles of daily metabolism and periodic transformation. Both wound and healing are implicitly present in both persons in any human transaction, but they become explicit as central elements in the counseling relationship (Guggenbühl-Craig 1976:92).

If the counselor denies the woundedness and takes on the persona of the healer, the relationship is incomplete. Any attempt to meet a need or resolve the pain of another by supplying their lack from the counselor's resources of insight or power is ultimately useless and powerless. As the "healer persona" acts as helper and rescuer in claiming responsibility for the other's healing and change, the intervention only decreases the other's ability to respond. Moving too easily and too casually into another's pain will inadvertently and unknowingly confuse the counselor's life with theirs, substitute the counselor's healer for theirs, and so hinder the other's inner healer.

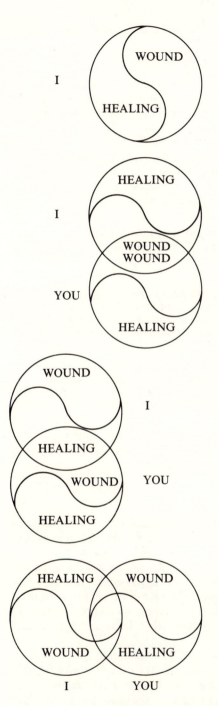

In every person there is both wound and healing. My woundedness will respond only to my inner healer; your healer cannot restore my woundedness nor mine yours.

If we meet wound to wound, I reliving and sharing my woundedness as I respond to your hurt, our identification may only intensify the pain and the problem as I pour my woundedness into your wound.

If we meet healer to wound, I becoming a helper rescuer, taking full responsibility for you, my intervention may decrease your ability to respond. I may block your inner healer.

When we meet wound to wound *and* healer to healer, my woundedness will not infect yours but will stand with you in presence and understanding; my healer will not rush to rescue your present sense of powerlessness but will call out the healing forces within you.

Figure 11-1. The wounded healer.

When wound meets wound there is empathy and compassion; when healing calls to healing, there is awareness, repentance, and growth.

Table 11-3. Wounds

Loneliness. Loneliness is a deep wound, cutting to the core of the self. Maturity is making peace with my aloneness so that I can be alone even in the presence of other people. As aloneness becomes affirmed as solitude, the need to escape or avoid loneliness diminishes. Religious faith does not take away our loneliness, it guards and values it as a gift.

Individuation. Becoming one's self is an experience of sadness. Maturing is taking the dependent attachment feelings for the most important people in your life, separating these feelings from them, integrating the ideals and values into the core of one's self, then reaching out with them to make contact with others in community.

Losses. Growth is a sequence of union and separation followed by union and separation. The pain of loss, the grief of the tragic, the sadness of the many deaths that fill and end our lives is ours to accept, appreciate, and integrate into our whole self.

Angers. The energies of my arousal in response to the invasions, violations, and irritations of living with others can be used in self-destructive pain or annihilating rage, or it can be affirmed as arousal to life's tensions and frustrations and directed toward contact, clarification, and re-creation of relationships.

Powerlessness. Impotence in the face of injustice and oppression and subjection to violence, coercion, and systematic inhumanity wound one deeply. Faith does not offer a magic cure or an escape into future promises, but the strength to be here, now, struggling for justice.

Unlived life. Unchosen options, unexperienced passion, undiscovered relationships leave the pain of incompleteness. Faith is the ability to cancel demands on what cannot be, to take action toward what can be, and to be at peace with what is here and now.

If the counselor is in touch with or flooded with his or her own woundedness in response to the other's wound, the suffering of one may compound the other. Simple identification—"my wound is just like your wound"—only increases the suffering. Sympathy as an involuntary joint pathos may confirm the hopelessness and helplessness; empathy as a voluntary shared pathos can direct the wound toward healing; interpathy as a parallel and yet interacting pathos can call out the healer in another who is truly other from another cultural world.

When we meet wound to wound *and* healer to healer, the counselor's woundedness will not infect or contaminate the other's wound. Rather it will enable the two truly to stand with each other in mutual awareness of their hurting humanness. In such presence, the counselor's healer will not rush to rescue the counselee's temporarily powerless inner healing, but will call out and nourish those healing forces within the soul. When wound meets wound, there is interpathy and compassion; when healing calls to healing, there is awareness, insight, repentance, change, and growth.

Meeting wound to wound is the basis of truly human encounter. It is not a kind of spiritual exhibitionism, a social flashing of going public with one's own pain to affirm solidarity with another who is suffering. The attitude of "Don't feel so bad about your 'problem'; I have felt the same confusion, depression, hopelessness as you feel" only adds despair to despair, little faith upon little faith. Meeting wound to wound while in balance with one's inner healer means being at peace with one's own woundedness, at home with one's own human condition, at one with suffering humanity. Such open vulnerability and authenticity is not without risk, as Nouwen writes (1972:92): "No one can help anyone without being involved, without entering with his [her] whole person into the painful situation, without taking the risk of becoming hurt, wounded, or even destroyed in the process."

As counselor, one becomes open to explore, experience, and accept one's own wounds as one is willing to enter one's own pain and know it fully, one's own fear and feel it deeply, one's own aloneness and claim it authentically. As the woundedness is uncovered, the hurt and the healing within it can be recovered, the suffering and the celebration reclaimed, the folly and the wisdom discovered. When one is at peace with one's own pain, at home with failing, finitude, suffering, and limitations, then truly standing with another in pain becomes possible. One can be touched deeply by another's tragedy, and be in touch with surprising tenderness.

When meeting healing to healing (as well as wound to wound) the illusion that wholeness can be given by one person to another is dispelled. Healing is not a gift to be given, it is life awakened, strengthened, nourished. When one suffers a physical injury, the best medications can protect from infection, reduce invasion, or support reconstruction, but they are finally powerless to heal unless the inner healer responds and cell reunites with cell.

Participating in another's healing does not take the pain away, it makes peace with it and directs it toward wholeness. "Pain that is shared is no longer paralyzing but mobilizing, when understood as a way to liberation. When we become aware that we do not have to escape our pains, but that we can mobilize them into a common search for life, those very pains are transformed from expressions of despair into signs of hope" (Nouwen 1972:93).

For the work of the pastoral counselor, the central model is the seer and the suffering servant for the Jewish tradition, and Jesus the wise yet wounded healer for the Christian. When God came among us, God came as a wounded healer. As the servant was wounded for us and by his wounds we are healed (Isaiah 53), so it is in the suffering, dying, rising, and transforming presence of the Christ that God's woundedness and healing became fully accessible to us. "This is the central archetype of all creation and recreation," said Jung, as he recognized that the essential biblical metaphor is rooted in biological reality, enacted in all social reality, and central to all spiritual reality in culture after culture.

The wounded healer, in the Christian path, sees the other as irreducibly valuable, as one to be prized and served as an embodiment of Jesus Christ. "Whatever you do in service to the least esteemed person, you do it to me," said Jesus. This willingness to care for another as the human face of God is the central metaphor of Christian service.

Indian Sikh journalist Khushwant Singh reported (1975:119) on his questioning of Mother Teresa, " 'Mother, tell me how have you trained yourself to touch people with loathesome diseases like leprosy and gangrene? Aren't you revolted by people filthy with dysentery and cholera vomit?'

"She looked me squarely in the eye and replied, 'I see Jesus in every human being. I say to myself, "This is hungry Jesus, I must feed him. This is sick Jesus, this one has gangrene, dysentery, or cholera. I must wash him and tend to him." I serve them because I love Jesus.' "

Summary

The intercultural pastoral counselor recognizes that many metaphors of psychotherapy exist in various cultures. No one image of healing, change, or growth satisfactorily defines or describes these processes as they occur in all cultural settings.

The metaphors of hide-and-seek, choice and change, sanctioned retreat, teacher and student, scientific technique and skill, therapeutic communication, healing relationship, human transformation, the healing community, host and guest, and the wounded healer offer aspective windows into the complex process of therapy and growth. The pastoral theologian sees each of these as an expression of grace, as an experience of integrity, as an encounter that invites wholeness.

In summary of the trajectory of the total argument of this book, we can affirm that the intercultural pastoral counselor is:

1. Culturally aware, interpathically skilled, and authentically present in dialogue with persons of other cultures, values, and faiths.

2. Culturally sensitive to what is universal, cultural, or individual, and valuing humans as essentially, culturally, and individually of ultimate worth.

3. Conscious of both individuality and solidarity with others in his or her self-identity, in its infinite variety in other cultural, familial, and personal identities, and seeing the individual-in-community as the basic unit of humanness.

4. Sensitive to the wide variation of human controls in the different human contexts, respecting the positive as well as negative functions of each emotion and its moral as well as functional content.

5. Aware of values—their nature, universality, uniqueness, variety, and power in directing life—and sensitive to the core values of culture, group, and person.

6. Concerned with essential human groups—family, marriage, and

kinship groups—as well as individuals, and sees relationships of integrity as essential to personal integration and health.

7. Aware of the inequities of gender roles, sensitive to the exploitation and abuse of women, and committed to work for justice and the liberation of all who suffer oppression.

8. Aware of the moral character of human choice, reasoning, and behavior, of the constancy of form and contrasts in content in ethical stories and storytellers.

9. Sensitive to worldviews which accept middle-zone experience, utilize metaphorical, mythical, and supernatural explanations for human pain, tragedy, and disorder, and demand power confrontations with evil and the demonic.

10. Aware of the cultural shaping and labeling of mental illness, recognizing the wide variation in what is normative and normal in each culture and seeing human frailty and suffering with insight and compassion.

11. Recognizes that many metaphors for psychotherapy exist in various cultures, seeing each as an expression of grace, an experience of encounter inviting integrity and wholeness.

These key elements are integral to the effective work of the intercultural pastoral counselor and caregiver. The counseling and giving of care will take many forms with richly varied content. We end this study not with the construction of a single integrative model but with the recognition of the need for as many models as there are cultural contexts, and the call for pastoral counselors to work creatively, flexibly, humbly, and redemptively on the boundaries, where crossing over and returning enrich and transform our vision of human life and destiny.

Bibliography

Abelson, R. R. 1968. *Theories of Cognitive Consistency: A Sourcebook.* Chicago: Rand McNally.

Aberle, D. F., A. Cohen, A. Davis, M. Levi, and F. Sutton. 1950. "The Functional Prerequisites of Society." *Ethics* 60:100–111.

Abraham, W. E. 1966. *The Mind of Africa.* Chicago: University of Chicago Press.

Abrahams, Roger D. 1983. *African Folktales.* New York: Pantheon Books.

Ackerknecht, Erwin. 1971. *Medicine and Ethnology.* Baltimore: Johns Hopkins Press.

Adegbola, E. A. D. 1969. "Le Fondement Théologique de la Morale." In Kwesi Dickson and Paul Ellingworth, eds. *Biblical Revelation and African Beliefs.* Maryknoll, N.Y.: Orbis Books.

Adeyemo, Tokunboh. 1979. *Salvation in African Tradition.* Nairobi: Evangel Publishing.

Akahoshi, Susumu. 1968. "Unity and Union in Psychotherapy and Salvation." *International Review of Missions* 54:175, 184.

———. 1975. "Japanese and Western Religiosity." In Kenneth Dale, *Circle of Harmony.* Tokyo: Seibunsha.

Akutagawa, Ryunosuke. 1952. *Rashomon and Other Stories.* New York: Liveright Publishing Corp.

Alexander, W. M. 1980. *Demonic Possession in the New Testament.* Grand Rapids: Baker Book House.

Al-Issa, Ihsan. 1980. *The Psychopathology of Women.* Englewood Cliffs, N.J.: Prentice-Hall.

Allport, G. W. 1954. "The Historical Background of Modern Social Psychology." In G. Lindzey, *Handbook of Social Psychology,* vol. 1. Cambridge: Addison-Wesley Publishing Co.

Amara, I. B. 1972. "Psychiatric Problems—Observations in Sierra Leone and Liberia." Quoted in *Transcultural Psychiatry. See* Kiev 1972.

Amirtham, Samuel, ed. 1977. *The Nature and Destiny of Asian Man.* Madras: SCM Press.

Ananth, J. 1981. "Is Western Training Relevant to Indian Psychiatry?" *Indian Journal of Psychiatry* 23(2):120–127.

Angrosino, Michael. 1974. *Outside Is Death: Community Organization, Ideology, and Alcoholism Among East Indians in Trinidad.* Winston-Salem, N.C.: Wake Forest Press.

Arieti, Silvano, et al., eds. 1975. *New Dimensions in Psychiatry: A World View,* vol. 1. New York: John Wiley & Sons.

As, Berit. 1981. Quoted in *The Female World,* p. v. *See* Bernard 1981.

Bach, Paul. 1979. "Demon Possession and Psychopathology: A Theological Relationship." *Journal of Psychology and Theology* 7(1):22–26.

Baker, Hugh. 1979. *Chinese Family and Kinship.* London: Macmillan Publishing Co.

Bam, Brigalia, and Lotika Sarkar. 1979. *New Perspectives for Third World Women.* Bangalore: CISRS.

Barry, Herbert, Margaret Bacon, and Irvin Child. 1957. "A Cross-Cultural Survey of Some Sex Differences in Socialization." *Journal of Abnormal and Social Psychology* 55:327–332.

Basseches, M. 1981. "Dialectical Schemata: A Framework for Empirical Study." In *Social Psychology. See* Gergen and Gergen 1981.

Bateson, Gregory. 1936. *Naven.* Stanford, Calif.: Stanford University Press.

———. 1972. *Steps to an Ecology of the Mind.* New York: Random House.

Battle, E., and J. Rotter. 1963. "Children's Feelings of Personal Control as Related to Social Class and Ethnic Group." *Journal of Personality* 31:482–490.

Beattie, John, et al. 1969. *Spirit Mediumship and Society in Africa.* New York: Africana Publishing Corp.

Bellah, Robert. 1970. "Father and Son in Christianity and Confucianism." In William A. Sadler, Jr., ed., *Personality and Religion.* New York: Harper & Row.

Benedict, Ruth. 1946. *The Chrysanthemum and the Sword.* New York: Meridian Books.

Berger, Peter, and Hans F. Kellner. 1981. *Sociology Reinterpreted: An Essay on Method and Vocation.* Garden City, N.Y.: Doubleday & Co.

Bernard, Jessie. 1981. *The Female World.* New York: Macmillan Publishing Co., Free Press Book.

Berns, Walter. 1971. "Pornography vs. Democracy—A Case for Censorship." *The Public Interest* 22 (Winter): 3–24.

Berreman, Gerald. 1972. "Race, Caste, and Other Invidious Distinctions in Social Stratification." *Race* 13 (4):385–414.

Berry, J. W., and W. J. Lonner. 1975. *Applied Cross-Cultural Psychology.* Lisse, Netherlands: Swets and Zeitlinger.

Bettelheim, Bruno. 1973. "Personality Formation in the Kibbutz." In C. E. Nelson, ed., *Conscience.* New York: Paulist/Newman Press.

Bhatti, Ranbir, and S. M. Channabasavanna. 1979. "Social System Approach to Understanding Marital Disharmony." *Indian Journal of Social Work* 40(1): 79–88.

Biestek, Felix. 1967. "Problems in Identifying Social Work Values." In *Values in Social Work.* Monograph 9. New York: National Association of Social Workers.

Binnie-Dawson, J., et al. 1981. *Perspectives in Asian Cross-Cultural Psychology.* Lisse, Netherlands: Swets and Zeitlinger.

Bloch, Sidney, and Paul Chodoff. 1981. *Psychiatric Ethics.* Oxford: Oxford University Press.

Bloodworth, Dennis, and Ching Ping. 1977. *The Chinese Machiavelli.* New York: Dell Publications.

Bochner, Stephen. 1982. *Cultures in Contact.* Oxford: Pergamon Press.

————, ed. 1981. *The Mediating Person: A Bridge Between Cultures.* Boston: G. K. Hall & Co.

Bock, Philip K. 1980. *Continuities in Psychological Anthropology.* San Francisco: W. H. Freeman & Co.

Bond, Michael, and Peter W. H. Lee. 1978. "Face Saving in Chinese Culture." Social Research Center, Chinese University of Hong Kong.

Bonhoeffer, Dietrich. 1965. *Ethics.* New York: Macmillan Co.

Bourguignon, Erika. 1973. *Religion, Altered States of Consciousness and Social Change.* Columbus, Ohio: Ohio State University Press.

————. 1976. *Possession.* San Francisco: Chandler & Sharp, Publishers.

————. 1980. *A World of Women: Anthropological Studies.* New York: Praeger Publishers.

Bowen, Murray. 1978. *Family Therapy and Clinical Practice.* New York: Jason Aronson.

Boyer, Bryce. 1983. "Approaching Cross-Cultural Psychotherapy." *Journal of Psychoanalytic Anthropology* 6(3):237–245.

Brain, James. 1973. "Ancestors as Elders in Africa." *Africa* 43:122–133.

Brandt, Conrad, B. Schwarz, and John K. Fairbank. 1952. *A Documentary History of Chinese Communism.* London: George Allen & Unwin.

Brislen, Richard W. 1981. *Cross-Cultural Encounters.* New York: Pergamon Press.

———— et al. 1973. *Cross-Cultural Research Methods.* New York: John Wiley & Sons.

Browman, David L., and Ronald A. Schwarz, eds. 1979. *Spirits, Shamans, and Stars.* New York: Mouton Publishers.

Brown, P., and S. Levinson. 1978. "Universals in Language Usage." In B. Goody, *Questions and Politeness.* Cambridge: Cambridge University Press.

Browning, Don S. 1966. *Atonement and Psychotherapy.* Philadelphia: Westminster Press.

————. 1976. *The Moral Context of Pastoral Care.* Philadelphia: Westminster Press.

Bruner, E. M. 1961. "Mandan." In Edward H. Spicer, ed. *Perspectives in American Indian Culture Change.* Chicago: University of Chicago Press.

Buber, Martin. 1953. *God and Evil.* New York: Charles Scribner's Sons.

Burris, Barbara. 1972. "The Fourth World Manifesto." In Anne Koedt and S. Firestone, eds., *Notes From the Third Year: Women's Liberation.* Geneva: World Council of Churches.

Burstein, S. R. 1952. "Public Health and Prevention of Disease in Primitive Communities." *Advancement of Science* 9(33):75–81.

Buss, Arnold, and Robert Plomin. 1975. *A Temperament Theory of Personality Development.* New York: John Wiley & Sons.

Butterfield, Fox. 1982. *China: Alive in the Bitter Sea.* New York: Times Books.

Caldarola, Carlo. 1979. *Christianity: The Japanese Way.* Leiden: E. J. Brill.

Cannon, W. 1957. "Voodoo Death." *Psychosomatic Medicine* 19:182–190.

Caplan, N., and S. D. Nelson. 1973. "On Being Useful—The Nature and Consequences of Psychological Research on Social Problems." *American Psychologist* 28:199–211.

Carstairs, G., and R. Kapur. 1976. *The Great Universe of Kota: Stress, Change, and Mental Disorder in an Indian Village.* Berkeley, Calif.: University of California Press.

Carstairs, M. 1957. *The Twice Born.* London: Hogarth Press.

Cawte, John. 1974. *Medicine Is the Law: Studies in Psychiatric Anthropology of Australian Tribal Societies.* Honolulu: University Press of Hawaii.

Channabasavanna, S. M., and R. S. Bhatti. n.d. "A Study of Interactional Patterns and Family Typologies of Mental Patients." Bangalore: NIMHANS.

Chesler, Phyllis. 1972. *Women and Madness.* Garden City, N.Y.: Doubleday & Co.

Chiu, L. H. 1972. "A Cross-Cultural Comparison of Cognitive Styles in Chinese and American Children." *International Journal of Psychology* 7:235–242.

Choi, Philemon. 1980. *Counseling—A New Frontier in Asia.* Hong Kong: Chinese Christian Association.

Chomsky, Noam. 1966. *Cartesian Linguistics.* New York: Harper & Row.

Chung, Helen Hee-Kyung. 1981. "Women in Chinese Experience." *See* Herzel 1981.

Clasper, Paul. 1982. *Eastern Paths and the Christian Way.* Maryknoll, N.Y.: Orbis Books.

Clinebell, Charlotte H. 1976. *Counseling for Liberation.* Philadelphia: Fortress Press.

Clinebell, Howard. 1984. *Basic Types of Pastoral Care and Counseling.* Nashville: Abingdon Press.

Cohen, Robert S. 1983. "Reflections on the Ambiguity of Science." *See* Rouner 1983.

Cohen, Rosalie. 1969. "Conceptual Styles, Cultural Conflict and Nonverbal Tests of Intelligence." *American Anthropologist* 71:828–855.

Cole, Michael. 1974. *Culture and Thought: A Psychological Introduction.* New York: John Wiley & Sons.

Collier, Helen. 1982. *Counseling Women: A Guide for Therapists.* New York: Free Press.

Collins, Adela. 1985. *Feminist Perspectives on Biblical Scholarship.* Chicago: Scholars Press.

Collins, B. E. 1970. *Social Psychology.* Reading, Mass.: Addison-Wesley Publishing Co.

Combs, Arthur, and Donald Syngg. 1949. *Individual Behavior.* New York: Harper & Brothers.

Cragg, Kenneth. 1956. *The Call of the Minaret.* New York: Oxford University Press.

Crapanzano, V., and V. Garrison. 1977. *Case Studies in Spirit Possession.* New York: John Wiley & Sons.

Crawford, Cromwell. 1974. *The Evolution of Hindu Ethical Ideals.* Calcutta: Firma K. L. Mukhopadhyay.

Croll, Elisabeth. 1978. *Feminism and Socialism in China.* London: Routledge & Kegan Paul.

Dale, Kenneth. 1977. "Transforming Barriers Into Bridges." *Japan Christian Quarterly* 43:3.

Darmaputera, Eka. 1982. *Pancasila and the Search for Identity and Modernity in Indonesian Society.* Unpublished dissertation. Newton Center, Mass.: Andover Newton Theological School and Boston College.

Das, M. S., and P. Bardis, eds. 1978. *The Family in Asia.* London: George Allen & Unwin.

Das, Soman. 1979. "The Concept of Dharma in Hindu Ethics." *Religion and Society* 26(3):55–71.

Davis, Kingsley. 1949. *Human Society.* New York: Macmillan Co.

Dawis, Rene. 1978. "A Paradigm and Model for the Cross-Cultural Study of Counseling." *Personnel and Guidance Journal* April 1978: 463–466.

Dawson, John, and Walter Lonner, eds. 1974. *Readings in Cross-Cultural Psychology.* Hong Kong: International Association for Cross-Cultural Psychology, Hong Kong University Press.

Dentan, R. K. 1968. *The Semai: A Nonviolent People of Malaysia.* New York: Holt, Rinehart & Winston.

Desai, I. P. 1956. "The Joint Family in India—An Analysis." *Sociological Bulletin* 5(2):147ff.

de Silva, Lynn A. 1981a. *The Problem of the Self in Buddhism and Christianity.* New York: Barnes & Noble Books.

———. 1981b. Quoted from a speech given at an Asian conference. *See* Rousseau 1981.

Devereaux, George. 1956. *Normal and Abnormal.* Washington, D.C.: Anthropological Society of Washington.

———. 1966. "Cultural Factors in Hypnosis and Suggestion." *International Journal of Clinical Experimental Hypnosis* 14:273–291.

DeVos, George. 1980. "Afterword." *See* Reynolds 1980.

Diaz-Guerrero, R. 1967. "Sociocultural Premises, Attitudes, and Cross-Cultural Research." *International Journal of Psychology* 2:79–88.

Doi, Takeo. 1973. *The Anatomy of Dependence.* Tokyo: Kodansha International.

———. 1976. "Psychotherapy as 'Hide and Seek.' " In W. P. Lebra, ed., *Culture-bound Syndromes, Ethnopsychiatry, and Alternate Therapies.* Honolulu: University Press of Hawaii.

Donaldson, Franklin. 1967. "Sister Buck Memorial Hospital Project in Spiritual Healing." Chikore, Zimbawe.

Draguns, J. G. 1975. "Resocialization Into Culture." In Richard W. Brislin and others, eds., *Cross-Cultural Perspectives on Learning.* New York: Russell Sage Foundation.

———. 1980. "Psychological Disorders of Clinical Severity." *See* Triandis 1980.

Draper, Patricia. 1977. "!Kung Women: Contrasts in Sexual Egalitarianism in Foraging and Sedentary Contexts." *See* Reiter 1977.

Dueck, Al. 1983. "American Psychology in Cross-Cultural Context." *Journal of Psychology and Theology* 2(Fall):3.

Duke, James. 1976. *Conflict and Power in Social Life.* Provo, Utah: Brigham Young University Press.

Dumont, Louis. 1970. *Homo Hierarchicus.* Chicago: University of Chicago Press.

———. 1971. "Religion, Politics and Society in the Individualistic Universe." *Proceedings of the Royal Anthropological Institute* 1971:31–41.

Dunne, John S. 1972. *The Way of All the Earth: Experiments in Truth and Religion.* New York: Macmillan Publishing Co.

Durkheim, Emile. 1951. *Suicide.* Glencoe, Ill.: Free Press.

———. 1966. *The Division of Labor in Society.* New York: Free Press of Glencoe.

Eberhard, Wolfram. 1965. *Folktales of China.* Chicago: University of Chicago Press.

———. 1967. *Guilt and Sin in Traditional China.* Berkeley, Calif.: University of California Press.

Ecclesiam Suam. 1964. Vatican City.

Edgerton, Robert. 1971. "A Traditional African Psychiatrist." *Southwestern Journal of Anthropology* 27:259–276.

Ellenberger, Henri. 1970. *The Discovery of the Unconscious.* New York: Basic Books.

England, John. 1981. *Living Theology in Asia.* London: SCM Press.

Erickson, Milton, and Lawrence Kubie. 1939. "The Permanent Relief of an Obsessional Phobia by Means of Communications with an Unsuspected Dual Personality." *Psychoanalytic Quarterly* 8:471–509.

Erikson, Erik. 1963. *Childhood and Society.* New York: W. W. Norton & Co.

———. 1964. *Insight and Responsibility.* New York: W. W. Norton & Co.

———. 1979a. "Introduction." *See* Kakar 1979a:26.

Evans-Pritchard, E. E. 1976. *Witchcraft, Oracles, and Magic Among the Azande.* Oxford: Clarendon Press.

Ey, Henri, and E. W. Strauss. 1969. *Psychiatry and Philosophy.* New York: Springer Publishing Co.

•

Fairbairn, W. R. 1954. *An Object-Relations Theory of Personality.* New York: Basic Books.

Farley, Margaret. 1985. *Feminist Consciousness and the Interpretation of Scripture.*" *See* Russell 1985.

Fieg, John. 1979. "Concept of Oneself." *See* Smith and Luce 1979.

Field, M. J. 1969. "Spirit Possession in Ghana." *See* Beattie 1969.

Field, Tiffany. 1981. *Culture and Early Interactions.* Hillsdale, N.J.: Lawrence Erlbaum Associates.

Fiorenza, Elisabeth Schüssler. 1975. "Feminist Theology as a Critical Theology of Liberation." In Walter Burkhardt, *Woman, New Dimensions.* New York: Paulist Press.

Firth, Raymond. 1957. *Elements of Social Organization.* New York: Franklin Watts.

Fontana, A., and B. Noel. 1973. "Moral Reasoning in the University." *Journal of Personality and Social Psychology* 27:419–429.

Foster, George. 1962. *Traditional Cultures, and the Impact of Technological Change.* New York: Harper & Brothers.

——— and Barbara Anderson. 1978. *Medical Anthropology.* New York: John Wiley & Sons.

Foster, J. M. 1964. *Psychological Counseling in India.* Bombay: Macmillan Co.

Fox, Robin. 1971. "The Cultural Animal." In J. F. Eisenberg and W. S. Dillon, *Man and Beast: Comparative Social Behavior.* Washington: Smithsonian Institution Press.

Frake, C. 1961. "The Diagnosis of Disease Among the Subanun of Mindanao." *American Anthropologist* 63:121.

Frank, Jerome D. 1961. *Persuasion and Healing.* Baltimore: Johns Hopkins Press.

———. 1971. "Therapeutic Factors in Psychotherapy." *American Journal of Psychotherapy* 25:359–361.

Frazier, Edward F. 1939. *The Negro Family in the United States.* Chicago: University of Chicago Press.

Freire, Paulo. 1970a. *Cultural Action for Freedom.* Cambridge, Mass.: Harvard University Press.

———. 1970b. *Pedagogy of the Oppressed.* New York: Herder & Herder.

Freud, Sigmund. 1949. "A Neurosis of Demoniacal Possession in the 17th Century." In *Collected Papers.* London: Hogarth Press.

———. 1958. *New Introductory Lectures in Psychoanalysis.* London: Hogarth Press.

Freytag, Walter. 1958. *The Gospel and the Religions.* London: SCM Press.

Friedl, Ernestine. 1975. *Women and Men, an Anthropologist's View.* New York: Holt, Rinehart & Winston.

Fromm, Erich. 1947. *Man for Himself.* New York: Rinehart & Co.

———. 1972. *Psychoanalysis and Religion.* New Haven, Conn.: Yale University Press.

Gardner, John W. 1964. *Self-Renewal: The Individual and the Innovative Society.* New York: Harper & Row.

Gaw, Albert, ed. 1982. *Cross-Cultural Psychiatry.* Littleton, Mass.: John Wright/PSG.

Gbadamosi, Bakare. 1969. "A Wise Man Solves His Own Problems." In O. R. Dathorne and Willfried Feuser, *Africa in Prose.* Baltimore: Penguin Books.

Geertz, Clifford. 1960. *The Religion of Java.* New York: Free Press of Glencoe.

———. 1968. *Islam Observed.* Chicago: University of Chicago Press.

———. 1973. *The Interpretation of Cultures.* New York: Random House.

Geertz, Mildred. 1961. *The Javanese Family.* New York: Free Press of Glencoe.

Gergen, Kenneth, and Mary Gergen. 1981. *Social Psychology.* New York: Harcourt Brace Jovanovich.

Gerkin, Charles. 1984. *The Living Human Document.* Nashville: Abingdon Press.

German, Allen. 1975. "Trends in Psychiatry in Black Africa." *See* Arietti 1975.

Gibran, Kahlil. 1918. *The Madman.* New York: Alfred A. Knopf.

Gifford, Carolyn De Swarte. 1984. "Which Issues Are Women's Issues?" *Daughters of Sarah* 10(2).

Gigliesi, Primrose. 1982. *The Effendi and the Pregnant Pot.* Beijing: New World Press.

Gilligan, Carol. 1982. *In a Different Voice.* Cambridge, Mass.: Harvard University Press.

Gilmore, S. K. 1973. *The Counselor in Training.* Englewood Cliffs, N.J.: Prentice-Hall.

Gingrich, Ann K. 1985. "Networking as a Form of Female Therapy." Unpublished paper.

Glenn, Edmund. 1981. *Man and Mankind: Conflict and Communication Between Cultures.* Norwood, N.J.: Ablex Publishing Corp.

Goffman, Erving. 1962. *Asylums.* Chicago: Aldine Publishing Corp.

Goldschmidt, Walter. 1966. *Comparative Functionalism.* Berkeley, Calif.: University of California Press.

———. 1971. *Exploring the Ways of Mankind.* New York: Holt, Rinehart & Winston.

Goode, William J. 1963. *World Revolution and Family Patterns.* New York: Free Press of Glencoe.

Grant, C. David. 1984. *God the Center of Value.* Fort Worth, Tex.: Texas Christian University Press.

Griffen, David. 1976. *God, Power, and Evil.* Philadelphia: Westminster Press.

Gross, D. H. 1963. *A Jungian Analysis of New Testament Exorcism.* Unpublished dissertation, Harvard University.

Guggenbühl-Craig, Adolf. 1976. *Power in the Helping Professions.* Zürich: Spring Publications.

Gurin, P., G. Gurin, R. Lao, and M. Beattie. 1969. "Internal-External Control in the Motivational Dynamics of Negro Youth." *Journal of Social Issues* 25:29–54.

Gustafson, James. 1981. *Ethics from a Theocentric Perspective.* Chicago: University of Chicago Press.

Hall, Brian. 1976. *The Development of Consciousness: A Confluent Theory of Values.* New York: Paulist Press.

Hall, David. 1973. *The Civilization of Experience: A Whiteheadian Theory of Culture.* New York: Fordham University Press.

Hall, Edward. 1976. *Beyond Culture.* Garden City, N.Y.: Doubleday & Co., Anchor Books.

Hammond, Dorothy, and Alta Jablow. 1976. *Women in Cultures of the World.* Menlo Park, Calif.: Cummings Publishing Co.

Han Sung-Joo. 1984. "Trying to Erase Bad Memories." *Newsweek,* Sept. 17, 1984, p. 14.

Hanvey, P. 1979. "Cross Cultural Awareness." *See* Smith and Luce 1979.

Hastings, Adrian. 1973. *Christian Marriage in Africa.* London: SPCK.

Hauerwas, Stanley. 1974. *Vision and Virtue.* Notre Dame, Ind.: Fides Publishers.

Heisenberg, Werner. 1958. *The Physicist's Conception of Nature.* London: Hutchinson & Co.

Henderson, D. J. 1976. "Exorcism, Possession, and the Dracula Cult: A Synopsis of Object-Relations Psychology." *Bulletin of the Menninger Clinic* 40:603–628.

Herzel, Susannah. 1981. *A Voice for Women.* Geneva: World Council of Churches.

Hiebert, Paul. 1971. *Konduru.* Minneapolis: University of Minnesota Press.

———. 1976. *Cultural Anthropology.* Philadelphia: J. B. Lippincott Co.

———. 1982a. "The Bicultural Bridge." *Mission Focus* 10(1):1–5.

———. 1982b. "Folk Religion in Andhra Pradesh." In Samuel Vinay, *Evangelism and the Poor.* Bangalore: Partnership in Mission—Asia.

Hitchcock, John, and Rex L. Jones, eds. 1976. *Spirit Possession in the Nepal Himalayas.* Forest Grove, Ore.: International Scholarly Book Services.

Ho, David. 1974. "Face, Social Expectations, and Conflict Avoidance." *See* Dawson and Lonner 1974.

Hoch, E. M. 1966. "Family Mental Health Risks." In R. W. Taylor et al., *The Changing Pattern of Family in India.* Bangalore: CISRS.

Hsieh, T., J. Shybut, and E. Lotsof. 1969. "Internal vs. External Control and Ethnic Group Membership: A Cross-Cultural Comparison." *Journal of Consulting and Clinical Psychology* 33:122–124.

Hsieh Yu-wei. 1962. "Filial Piety and Chinese Society." In Charles Moore, ed., *Philosophy and Culture East and West.* Honolulu: University Press of Hawaii.

Hsu, Francis. 1949. "Suppression Versus Repression: A Limited Psychological Interpretation of Four Cultures." *Psychiatry* 12(3):223–242.

———. 1963. *Clan, Caste, and Club.* Princeton: D. Van Nostrand Co.

———. 1970. *Americans and Chinese.* Garden City, N.Y.: Natural History Press.

————. 1972. *Psychological Anthropology*. Cambridge, Mass.: Schenkman Publishing Co.

————. 1978. "Passage to Understanding." *See* Spindler 1978.

————. 1983. *Rugged Individualism Reconsidered*. Knoxville, Tenn.: University of Tennessee Press.

Hsu, J., and W. S. Tseng. 1972. "Intercultural Psychotherapy." *Archives of General Psychiatry* 27:700–705.

Hu Hsien-chin. 1944. "The Chinese Concept of Face." *American Anthropologist* 46:45–66.

Hunt, Robert. 1967. *Personalities and Cultures*. Garden City, N.Y.: Natural History Press.

Hutter, Mark. 1981. *The Changing Family: Comparative Perspectives*. New York: John Wiley & Sons.

Iglitzin, Lynne, and Ruth Ross, eds. 1976. *Women in the World: A Comparative Study*. Santa Barbara, Calif.: ABC-CLIO.

International Pilot Study of Schizophrenia (IPSS). 1979. *Schizophrenia: An International Follow-Up Study*. Geneva: World Health Organization; New York: John Wiley & Sons.

Jackson, Gordon. 1981. *Pastoral Care and Process Theology*. Washington, D.C.: University Press of America.

Jahoda, Gustav. 1982. *Psychology and Anthropology*. London: Academic Press.

Janzen, John M. 1978. *The Quest for Therapy in Lower Zaire*. Berkeley, Calif.: University of California Press.

Janzen, Rick. 1985. Interview. Associated Mennonite Biblical Seminaries, Elkhart, Ind.

Jewett, Paul. 1975. *Man as Male and Female*. Grand Rapids: Wm. B. Eerdmans Publishing Co.

Jones, E., D. Kanouse, H. Kelley, R. Nisbett, S. Valins, and B. Weiner. 1972. *Attribution: Perceiving the Causes of Behavior*. Morristown, N.J.: General Learning Corp.

Jones, J. M. 1972. *Prejudice and Racism*. Reading, Mass.: Addison-Wesley Publishing Co.

Jourard, Sidney. 1974. *Healthy Personality*. New York: Macmillan Publishing Co.

Jung, C. G. 1933. *Modern Man in Search of a Soul*. New York: Harcourt, Brace and Co.

Jung, Marshall. 1984. "Structural Family Therapy: Its Application to Chinese Families." *Family Process* 23:365–374.

Kakar, Sudhir. 1978. *The Inner World: A Psychoanalytic Study of Childhood and Society in India*. Oxford: Oxford University Press.

————. 1979a. *Identity and Adulthood*. Delhi: Oxford University Press.

————. 1979b. *Indian Childhood: Cultural Ideals and Social Reality*. Delhi: Oxford University Press.

————. 1982. *Shamans, Mystics, and Doctors*. Delhi: Oxford University Press.

————. 1984. "Psychological Counseling: Is There an Asian Model?" Address, APECA Conference, Bangalore, India, Oct. 10–17, 1984.

Kane, Cheikh Hamidou. 1961. *Ambiguous Adventure*. New York: Walker & Co.

Kapadia, K. M. 1966. *Marriage and Family in India.* London: Oxford University Press.

Kapferer, Bruce, ed. 1983. *A Celebration of Demons.* Bloomington, Ind.: University of Indiana Press.

Kardiner, Abram. 1945. *The Psychological Frontiers of Society.* New York: Columbia University Press.

Kashiwagi, Tetsuo. 1980. *The Theory and Practice of the Care of Patients Facing Death.* Nagoya: Nippon Soken Shuppan.

————. 1985. Interview, Osaka.

Katoppo, Marianne. 1981. *Compassionate and Free: An Asian Woman's Theology.* Maryknoll, N.Y.: Orbis Books.

Katz, M., and K. O. Sanborn. 1973. "Multi-Ethnic Studies of Psychopathology and Normality in Hawaii." In B. Brown and E. F. Torrey, eds., *International Collaboration in Mental Health.* Washington, D.C.: U.S. Government Printing Office.

Katz, Robert. 1985. *Pastoral Care and the Jewish Tradition.* Philadelphia: Fortress Press.

Keats, D. M. 1981. "The Development of Values in Adolescents." *See* Binnie-Dawson et al. 1981.

Kelsey, Morton. 1978. *Discernment: A Study in Ecstasy and Evil.* New York: Paulist Press.

Kennedy, John. 1973. "Cultural Psychiatry." In J. J. Honigmann, *Handbook of Social and Cultural Anthropology.* Chicago: Rand McNally College Publishing Co.

Kessler, Evelyn. 1976. *Women: An Anthropological View.* New York: Holt, Rinehart & Winston.

Keynes, John. 1981. *The Scope and Method of Political Economy.* London: Macmillan Publishers.

Kierkegaard, Søren. 1941. *The Sickness Unto Death.* Princeton, N.J.: Princeton University Press.

Kiev, Ari. 1961. "The Theory and Practice of Psychiatry in Haitian Voodoo." *Proceedings of the Third International Congress of Psychiatry,* 1961.

————, ed. 1964. *Magic, Faith, and Healing.* New York: Free Press of Glencoe.

————. 1972. *Transcultural Psychiatry.* New York: Free Press.

Kimper, Frank. 1971. Lecture Notes, School of Theology at Claremont.

Kimura, Ryukan. 1927. *A Historical Study of the Terms Hinayana and Mahayana and the Origin of Mahayana Buddhism.* New York: AMS Press.

King, Douglas. 1978. "Christian Ethics as Moral Theology: Toward the Contextualization of Ethics in a Southeast Asian Culture." *Southeast Asia Journal of Theology* 19(2):26–37.

Kirschenbaum, Howard. 1977. *Advanced Value Clarification.* La Jolla, Calif.: University Associates.

Kleinman, Arthur. 1978a. "Culture and Depression." *Culture, Medicine and Psychiatry* 2:295–296.

————. 1978b. *Culture and Healing in Asian Societies.* Cambridge, Mass.: Schenkman Publishing Co.

————. 1980. *Patients and Healers in the Context of Culture.* Berkeley, Calif.: University of California Press.

———— and Lin Tsung-yi. 1981. *Normal and Abnormal Behavior in Chinese Culture.* Dordrecht: D. Reidal Publishing Co.

———— and L. Sung. 1979. "Why Do Indigenous Practitioners Successfully Heal?" *Social Sciences and Medicine* 13B:7–26.

Kluckhohn, Clyde, and Henry Murray. 1948. *Personality in Nature, Society, and Culture.* New York: Alfred A. Knopf.

Koffka, K. 1962. *Principles of Gestalt Psychology.* London: Routledge & Kegan Paul.

Kohlberg, L. 1969. "Stage and Sequences: The Cognitive-Developmental Approach to Socialization." In D. Goslin, *Handbook of Socialization Theory and Research.* Chicago: Rand McNally & Co.

———— and R. Kramer. 1969. "Continuities and Discontinuities in Childhood and Adult Moral Development." *Human Development* 12:93–120.

———— and E. Turiel. 1971. "Moral Development and Moral Education." In G. Lesser, *Psychology and Educational Practice.* Glenview, Ill.: Scott, Foresman and Co.

Köhler, Wolfgang. 1938. *The Place of Value in a World of Facts.* New York: Liveright Publishing Corp.

Kopp, Sheldon. 1971. *Guru, Metaphors from a Psychotherapist.* New York: Bantam Books.

Koyama, Kosuke. 1974. *Waterbuffalo Theology.* Maryknoll, N.Y.: Orbis Books.

————. 1977. *No Handle on the Cross.* Maryknoll, N.Y.: Orbis Books.

Kraft, Charles. 1979. *Christianity in Culture.* Maryknoll, N.Y.: Orbis Books.

Krisetya, Mesach. 1984. Interview at Universitas Kristen Satya Wacana, Salitiga, Indonesia, Sept. 1984.

Kübler-Ross, Elisabeth. 1969. *On Death and Dying.* New York: Macmillan Co.

Kuhn, D., J. Langer, L. Kohlberg, N. Haan. 1977. "The Development of Formal and Logical Operations in Moral Judgment." *Genetic Psychology Monographs* 95:97–198.

Lacy, Creighton. 1965. *The Conscience of India.* New York: Holt, Rinehart & Winston.

Lagacé, Robert. 1977. *Sixty Cultures: A Guide to the HRAF Probability Sample Files.* New Haven, Conn.: Human Relations Area Files Press.

Laing, R. D. 1961. *Self and Others.* New York: Pantheon Books.

Lambo, T. A. 1956. "Neuro-Psychiatric Observations in the Western Region of Nigeria." *British Medical Journal* 2:1388.

————. 1960. "The Concept and Practice of Mental Health in African Cultures." *East African Medical Journal* 37:464ff.

————. 1961. "A Form of Social Psychiatry in Africa." *World Mental Health* 13(4):190–203.

————. 1964. "Patterns of Psychiatric Care in Developing African Countries." See Kiev 1964.

————. 1968. "Schizophrenia, Its Features and Prognosis in the African." *Second Colloquium of African Psychiatry.* Paris: Audecam.

Landy, David, ed. 1977. *Culture, Disease, and Healing.* New York: Macmillan Publishing Co.

Langford, Thomas A., and William H. Poteat. 1968. *Intellect and Hope.* Durham, N.C.: Duke University Press.

Langley, Myrtle. 1980. "Spirit Possession, Exorcism, and Social Context." *Churchman* 94(3):226–245.

Langness, Lewis. 1976. "Hysterical Psychosis and Possession." in W. Lebra, *Culture-Bound Syndromes.* Honolulu: University of Hawaii.

Laubscher, B. 1937. *Sex, Custom, and Psychopathology.* London: Routledge & Kegan Paul.

Leacock, Eleanor. 1981. *Myths of Male Dominance.* New York: Monthly Review
  Press.
Lebra, Joyce, et al. 1976. *Women in Changing Japan.* Boulder, Col.: Westview
  Press.
Lebra, T. S. 1972. "The Social Mechanism of Guilt and Shame: The Japanese
  Case." *Transcultural Psychiatric Research Review* 9:21–23.
———. 1976. *Japanese Patterns of Behavior.* Honolulu: University Press of
  Hawaii.
Lee, Jung Young. 1979. *The Theology of Change: A Christian Concept of God in
  an Eastern Perspective.* Maryknoll, N.Y.: Orbis Books.
Lefcourt, H. 1966. "Internal Versus External Control of Reinforcement: A
  Review." *Psychological Bulletin* 65:206–220.
Leff, Julian. 1981. *Psychiatry Around the Globe.* New York: Marcel Dekker.
Lehmann, Paul. 1963. *Ethics in a Christian Context.* New York: Harper & Row.
Leighton, Alexander. 1969. "A Comparative Study of Psychiatric Disorder in
  Nigeria and Rural North America." *See* Plog and Edgerton 1969.
———. 1982. "Relevant Generic Issues." *See* Gaw 1982.
Lenero-Otero, Luis. 1977. *Beyond the Nuclear Family Model.* Beverly Hills,
  Calif.: Sage Publications.
Lenz, H. 1964. *Vergleichende Psychiatrie.* Vienna: Maudrich.
Lerner, Daniel. 1958. *The Passing of Traditional Society.* New York: Free Press.
Leslie, Robert. 1979. *Counseling Across Cultures.* New York: UMHE Mono-
  graph.
Levenson, H. 1974. "Activism and Powerful Others." *Journal of Personality
  Assessment* 38: 377–383.
Levenson, Joseph. 1965. "The Communist Attitude Towards Religion." In W.
  Klett, ed., *The Chinese Model.* Hong Kong: Hong Kong University Press.
LeVine, Robert A. 1973. *Culture, Behavior, and Personality.* Chicago: Aldine
  Publishing Co.
Levinson, David, and Martin J. Malone. 1980. *Toward Explaining Human Cul-
  ture.* New Haven, Conn.: Human Relations Area Files Press.
Lewis, C. S. 1952. *Mere Christianity.* London: William Collins Sons & Co.
———. 1970. *God in the Dock.* Grand Rapids: Wm. B. Eerdmans Publishing
  Co.
Lewis, Helen. 1971. *Shame and Guilt in Neurosis.* New York: International
  Universities Press.
Lewis, Ioan M. 1971. *Ecstatic Religion: An Anthropological Study of Spirit Posses-
  sion and Shamanism.* Middlesex: Penguin Books.
Lian, Yeow Geok. 1981. "Filial Piety in Contemporary Society." *South East Asia
  Journal of Theology* 22(2):39–44.
Lieban, Richard. 1962. "Qualifications for Folk Medical Practice in the Philip-
  pines." *Philippine Journal of Science* 91:511–521.
Little, David, and Sumner Twiss. 1978. *Comparative Religious Ethics.* New
  York: Harper & Row.
Litwiller, Kenneth. 1985. Unpublished paper. Elkhart, Ind.: AMBS.
Livingston, Martha, and Paul Lowinger. 1983. *The Minds of the Chinese People.*
  Englewood Cliffs, N.J.: Prentice-Hall.
Lonner, Walter J. 1980. "The Search for Psychological Universals." In Harry
  C. Triandis and Alastair Heron, *Handbook of Cross-Cultural Psychology,* vol.
  1. Boston: Allyn & Bacon,
Lowen, Alexander. 1975. *Pleasure: A Creative Approach to Life.* New York:
  Penguin Books.

Luzbetak, L. J. 1970. *The Church and Cultures.* South Pasadena, Calif.: Carey Library.
Lynd, Helen M. 1958. *On Shame and the Search for Identity.* New York: Harcourt, Brace and Co.

MacCormack, Carol, and Marilyn Strathern. 1980. *Nature, Culture, and Gender.* New York: Cambridge University Press.
McGoldrick, M., J. K. Pearce, J. Giordano. 1982. *Ethnicity and Family Therapy.* New York: Guilford Press.
MacLeod, Ian. 1982. "The Dynamics of Shame and Guilt." In Carl Beck, *Can the Gospel Thrive in Japanese Soil?* Tokyo: Hayama Missionary Seminar.
McLuhan, Marshall. 1962. *The Gutenberg Galaxy.* Toronto: University of Toronto Press.
Macquarrie, John. 1983. *In Search of Humanity.* New York: Crossroad Publishing Co.
Mace, David, and Vera Mace. 1960. *Marriage: East and West.* Garden City, N.Y.: Doubleday & Co.
Malinowski, B. 1944. *A Scientific Theory of Culture, and Other Essays.* Chapel Hill, N.C.: University of North Carolina Press.
————. 1948. *Magic, Science and Religion.* Glencoe, Ill.: Free Press.
Maloney, Arnold H. 1945. *Pathways to Democracy.* Boston: Meador Publishing Co.
Margolis, Joseph. 1966. *Psychotherapy and Morality: A Study of Two Concepts.* New York: Random House.
Marsella, Anthony. 1978. "Thoughts on Cross-Cultural Studies on the Epidemiology of Depression." *Culture, Medicine and Psychiatry* 2:343–357.
————. 1983. "Depressive Experience and Disorder Across Cultures." *See* Triandis and Draguns 1983.
———— and others. 1979. *Perspectives on Cross-Cultural Psychology.* New York: Academic Press, 1979.
———— and G. White. 1982. *Cultural Conceptions of Mental Health and Therapy.* Dordrecht, Netherlands: D. Reidel Publishing Co.
Maruyama, Magoroh. 1970. "Toward a Cultural Futurology." American Anthropology Association National Meeting, Training Center for Community Programs, University of Minnesota.
———— and others. 1978. *Cultures of the Future.* The Hague: Mouton Publishers.
Masaaki, Kosaka. 1967. "The Status and the Role of the Individual in Japanese Society." In Charles Moore, *The Japanese Mind.* Honolulu: University Press of Hawaii.
Masamba Ma Mpolo, Jean. 1972. *Psychotherapeutic Dynamics in African Bewitched Patients.* Claremont, Calif.: Unpublished dissertation.
————. 1982. "The Holy Family." *New Internationalist* 118 (Dec.).
————. 1984. *Family Profiles: Stories of Families in Transition.* Geneva: World Council of Churches.
————. 1985. "African Symbols and Stories in Pastoral Care." *Journal of Pastoral Care* 39(4):314–326.
Maslow, A., and B. Mittleman. 1941. *The Principles of Abnormal Psychology.* New York: Harper & Brothers.
Matthews, Ellen. 1982. *Culture Clash.* Chicago: Intercultural Press.
May, Rollo. 1969. *Love and Will.* New York: W. W. Norton & Co.
Mbiti, John. 1970. *African Religions and Philosophy.* Garden City, N.Y.: Doubleday & Co.

―――. 1980. "A Change in the African Concept of Man Through Christian Influence." *See* Robinson 1980.

Mead, Margaret. 1940. "Warfare Is Only an Invention—Not a Biological Necessity." *Asia* 40:402–405.

Menninger, Karl. 1955. *The Vital Balance.* New York: Viking Press.

Merton, Thomas. 1966. *Raids on the Unspeakable.* New York: New Directions.

Miller, Jean Baker. 1976. *Toward a New Psychology of Women.* Boston: Beacon Press.

Mintz, S. W. 1971. "Men, Women, and Trade." *Comparative Studies in Society and History* 13:247–268.

Moerman, Daniel. 1979. "Anthropology of Symbolic Healing." *Current Anthropology* 20:59–66.

Monroe, Ruth, and Robert Monroe. 1975. *Handbook of Cross-Cultural Human Development.* New York: Garland Pub.

Montagu, Ashley. 1964. *Man's Most Dangerous Myth: The Fallacy of Race.* Cleveland: World Publishing Co.

Morley, Peter, and Roy Wallis, eds. 1978. *Culture and Curing.* London: Peter Owen.

Morris, Charles W. 1956. *Varieties of Human Value.* Chicago: University of Chicago Press.

Morrow, D. L. 1972. "Cultural Addiction." *Journal of Rehabilitation* 38(3).

Mulder, Niels. 1978. *Mysticism and Everyday Life in Contemporary Java.* Singapore: Singapore University Press.

Murdock, George P. 1945. *Outline of World Cultures.* New Haven, Conn.: Human Relations Area Files Press.

―――. 1961. *Outline of Cultural Materials.* New York: Taplinger Publishing Co.

Murphy, Jane. 1976. "Psychiatric Labeling in Cross-Cultural Perspective." *Science* 191:1019–1028.

Murphy, Robert. 1979. *An Overture to Social Anthropology.* Englewood Cliffs, N.J.: Prentice-Hall.

Myers, Lamar. 1983. Interview in La Cayes, Haiti.

Naipaul, V. S. 1981. *Among the Believers.* New York: Random House, Vintage Books.

Nakamura, H. 1964. *Ways of Thinking of Eastern Peoples: India-China-Tibet-Japan.* Honolulu: East-West Center Press.

Nakane, G. 1970. *Japanese Society.* Berkeley, Calif.: University of California Press.

Naranjo, Claudio. 1972. *The One Quest.* New York: Ballantine Books.

Neki, J. S. 1973. "Guru-Chela Relationship: The Possibility of a Therapeutic Paradigm." *American Journal of Orthopsychiatry* 43:755.

―――. 1977. "Presidential Address." *Indian Journal of Psychiatry* 19:1–10.

Nelson, James. 1971. *Moral Nexus.* Philadelphia: Westminster Press.

Newbigin, Lesslie. 1981. "The Basis, Purpose, and Manner of Inter-faith Dialogue." *See* Rousseau 1981.

Newman, Philip L. 1965. *Knowing the Gururumba.* New York: Holt, Rinehart & Winston.

Newmark, Eileen. 1980. *Women's Roles: A Cross-Cultural Perspective.* New York: Pergamon Press.

Ng, Chae-Woon. 1982. "Filial Piety in Confucian Thought." *Northeast Asia Journal of Theology* 28/29:13–48.

Niebuhr, H. Richard. 1963. *The Responsible Self.* New York: Harper & Row.

Niebuhr, Reinhold. 1964. *The Nature and Destiny of Man,* vol. 1. New York: Charles Scribner's Sons.

Noble, Lowell. 1975. *Naked and Not Ashamed: An Anthropological, Biblical and Psychological Study of Shame.* Jackson, Miss.: Jackson Printing.

Norbeck, Edward, and George DeVos. 1972. "Culture and Personality: The Japanese." *See* F. Hsu 1972.

Nouwen, Henri. 1972. *The Wounded Healer.* Garden City, N.Y.: Doubleday & Co.

———. 1975. *Reaching Out.* Garden City, N.Y.: Doubleday & Co.

Oden, Thomas C. 1966. *Kerygma and Counseling.* San Francisco: Harper & Row.

———. 1969. *The Structure of Awareness.* Nashville: Abingdon Press.

——— and others, eds. 1974. *After Therapy What?* Springfield, Ill.: Charles C Thomas.

Oesterreich, T. K. 1974. *Possession, Demonical and Other.* Secaucus, N.J.: Citadel Press.

Olney, James. 1972. *Metaphors of Self: The Meaning of Autobiography.* Princeton, N.J.: Princeton University Press.

Ong, Walter. 1969. "World as View and World as Event." *American Anthropologist* 71:4.

Opler, Marvin, ed. 1959. *Culture and Mental Health.* New York: Macmillan Co.

Outka, Gene. 1972. *Agape: An Ethical Analysis.* New Haven, Conn.: Yale University Press.

Palgi, Phyllis, and Henry Abramovitch. 1984. "Death, a Cross-Cultural Perspective." *American Review of Anthropology* 13:385ff.

Pande, S. 1968. "The Mystique of Western Psychotherapy: An Eastern Interpretation." *Journal of Nervous and Mental Disorders* 146:425–432.

Panikkar, Raymond. 1964. *The Unknown Christ of Hinduism.* London: Darton, Longman & Todd.

Papajohn, John, and John Spiegel. 1975. *Transactions in Families: A Modern Approach for Resolving Cultural and Generational Conflicts.* San Francisco: Jossey-Bass.

Parrinder, G. 1958. *Witchcraft, European and African.* London: Faber & Faber.

Parsons, Talcott. 1964. *Social Structure and Personality.* New York: Free Press.

Patai, Rafael. 1967. *Women in the Modern World.* New York: Free Press.

Paterson, R. K. 1979. "Evil, Omniscience, and Omnipotence." *Religious Studies* 15:1–29.

Paton, David. 1984. "Twelve Assumptions About Confessing the Faith in the Global Village." *East Asia Journal of Theology* 2(2):308–310.

Pattison, Mansell. 1977. "Psychosocial Interpretations of Exorcism." *Journal of Operational Psychiatry* 8(2):5–21.

Peck, Scott. 1983. *People of the Lie.* New York: Simon & Schuster.

Pedersen, Paul. 1977. "Asian Personality Theories." In R. Corsini, *Current Personality Theories.* Itasca, Ill.: F. E. Peacock Publishers.

———. 1981. "Alternative Futures." In A. Marsella and P. Pedersen, *Cross-Cultural Counseling and Psychotherapy.* New York: Pergamon Press.

——— and others. 1981. *Counseling Across Cultures,* rev. ed. Honolulu: University Press of Hawaii.

Perls, F. S. 1969. *Ego, Hunger, and Aggression.* New York: Random House.

Piaget, Jean. 1932. *The Moral Judgment of the Child.* London: Routledge & Kegan Paul.

Piers, Gerhart, and Milton Singer. 1953. *Shame and Guilt.* New York: W. W. Norton Co.

Pitamber, Dayanand. 1979. "Mental Health and Pastoral Counseling." *Religion and Society* 16(2):21–33.

———. 1980. "Psycho-Social Implications of Gandhi's Satyagraha for Personal Liberation in Human Community." *See* Robinson 1980.

———. 1982. "Psychosocial Enquiry Into the Phenomenon of Physical Violence Against Harijans," Bangalore, India, unpublished paper.

Plog, S. C., and R. B. Edgerton, eds. 1969. *Changing Perspectives in Mental Illness.* New York: Holt, Rinehart & Winston.

Potter, Ralph. 1969. *War and Moral Discourse.* Richmond: John Knox Press.

Prashantham, B. J. 1983. *Empowerment for Development.* Velore: Christian Counseling Center.

Press, Irwin. 1982. "Witch Doctor's Legacy: Some Anthropological Implications for the Practice of Clinical Medicine." In Noel Chrisman and Thomas Maretzki, *Clinically Applied Anthropology.* Dordrecht: D. Reidel Publishing Co.

Price-Williams, D. R. 1975. *Explorations in Cross-Cultural Psychology.* Corte Madera, Calif.: Chandler & Sharp.

Prince, Raymond H. 1964. "Indigenous Yoruba Psychiatry." *See* Kiev 1964.

———. 1974. "Indigenous Yoruba Psychiatry." In E. Hegeman and L. Kooperman, eds., *Anthropology and Community Action.* Garden City, N.Y.: Doubleday & Co., Anchor Books.

———. 1976. "Psychotherapy as the Manipulation of Endogenous Healing Mechanism: A Transcultural Survey." *Transcultural Psychiatric Research Review* 13:155–233.

Pruyser, Paul. 1968. *A Dynamic Psychology of Religion.* New York: Harper & Row.

Queen, Stuart. 1974. *The Family in Various Cultures.* Philadelphia: J. B. Lippincott Co.

Quiambao, Jacob. 1966. *The Asian Family in a Changing Society.* Manila: EACC.

Radcliffe-Brown, A. R., and Daryll Forde. 1970. *African Systems of Kinship and Marriage.* London: Oxford University Press.

Radcliffe Richards, Janet. 1980. *The Skeptical Feminist.* Boston: Routledge & Kegan Paul of America.

Rahner, Karl. 1978. *Foundations of Christian Faith.* New York: Seabury Press.

Ramanujam, B. K. 1978. "Studies of Change at the B. M. Institute of Mental Health." Ahmedabad, India, unpublished.

Ramseyer, Robert. 1983. "Christian Mission and Cultural Anthropology." In Wilbert Shenk, *Exploring Church Growth.* Grand Rapids, Mich.: Wm. B. Eerdmans Publishing Co.

Rawlings, E., and D. K. Carter. 1977. *Psychotherapy for Women.* Springfield, Ill.: Charles C Thomas.

Rees, John C. 1971. *Equality.* London: Macmillan Co.

Reeves, Nancy. 1971. *Womankind: Beyond the Stereotypes.* New York: Aldine Publishing Co.

Reiter, R., ed. 1977. *Toward an Anthropology of Women.* New York: Monthly Review Press.

Reps, Paul, ed. 1961. *Zen Flesh, Zen Bones: A Collection of Zen and Pre-Zen Writings.* Garden City, N.Y.: Doubleday & Co.

Rest, J., D. Cooper, R. Coder, J. Masanz, D. Anderson. 1974. "Judging the Important Issues in Moral Dilemmas—An Objective Measure of Development. *Development Psychology* 10:491–501.

Reynolds, David K. 1976. *Morita Psychotherapy.* Berkeley, Calif.: University of California Press.

———, ed. 1980. *The Quiet Therapies: Japanese Pathways to Personal Growth.* Honolulu: University Press of Hawaii.

Richardson, Edwin. 1981. "Cultural and Historical Perspectives in Counseling American Indians." *See* Sue 1981.

Ricoeur, Paul. 1971. "The Model of the Text: Meaningful Action Considered as a Text." *Social Research* 38.

Riezler, Kurt. 1951. *Man: Mutable and Immutable.* New York: Henry Regnery Co.

Rivers, W. R. 1926. *Psychology and Ethnology.* New York: Harcourt Brace & Co.

Robinson, G. 1980. *For the Sake of the Gospel.* Madurai: TTS.

Romanucci-Ross, Lola, and others. 1983. *The Anthropology of Medicine.* New York: Praeger Publishers.

Rosenhan, David. 1973. "On Being Sane in Insane Places." *Science* 179:250–258.

Rotter, Julian. 1966. "Generalized Expectations for Internal vs. External Control of Reinforcement." *Psychological Monographs* 80:1–28.

———. 1975. "Some Problems and Misconceptions Related to the Construct of Internal vs. External Control of Reinforcement." *Journal of Consulting and Clinical Psychology* 43:56–67.

Rouner, Leroy S., ed. 1983. *Foundations of Ethics.* Notre Dame, Ind.: University of Notre Dame Press.

Rousseau, Richard W., ed. 1981. *Interreligious Dialogue.* Montrose, Pa.: Ridge Row Press.

Ruether, Rosemary Radford. 1975. *New Woman, New Earth.* New York: Seabury Press.

Russell, Jeffrey B. 1981. *Satan: The Early Christian Tradition.* Ithaca, N.Y.: Cornell University Press.

Russell, Letty M. 1973. "Women and Liberation Theology." Unpublished paper.

———. 1974. *Human Liberation in a Feminist Perspective.* Philadelphia: Westminster Press.

———. 1979. *The Future of Partnership.* Philadelphia: Westminster Press.

———, ed. 1985. *Feminist Interpretation of the Bible.* Philadelphia: Westminster Press.

Safa, H. I. 1977. "Changing Modes of Production." *Signs* 3:22–24.

Safilos-Rothschild, Constantina. 1970. "Toward a Cross-Cultural Definition of Family Modernity." *Journal of Comparative Family Studies* 1:17–25.

Samples, Robert. 1976. *The Metaphoric Mind.* Reading, Mass.: Addison-Wesley Publishing Co.

Sanday, Peggy. 1981. *Female Power and Male Dominance.* Cambridge: Cambridge University Press.

Sanger, S. P., and H. A. Alker. 1972. "Dimensions of Internal-External Locus of Control and the Women's Liberation Movement." *Journal of Social Issues* 28:115–129.

Sarbin, T. 1969. "The Scientific Status of the Mental Health Metaphor." *See* Plog and Edgerton 1969.

Sartorius, N., A. Jablensky, and R. Shapiro. 1977. "Two-Year Follow-up of the Patients Included in the WHO International Pilot Study of Schizophrenia." *Psychological Medicine* 7:529–541.

Sartre, Jean-Paul. 1959. *Existentialism and Human Emotions.* New York: Philosophical Library.

Schachter, Shalomi. 1983. *Sparks of Light: Counseling in the Hasidic Tradition.* Boulder, Col.: Shambhala Publications.

Schacter, Stanley, and J. E. Singer. 1962. "Cognitive, Social, and Physiological Determinants of Emotional State." *Psychological Review* 69:379–399.

Schaffer, Kay. 1980. *Sex-Role Issues in Mental Health.* Reading, Mass.: Addison-Wesley Publishing Co.

Scheff, T. 1966. *Being Mentally Ill: A Sociological Theory.* Chicago: Aldine Publishing Co.

Scherer, Klaus, Ronald Abeles, and Claude Fischer. 1975. *Human Aggression and Conflict.* Englewood Cliffs, N.J.: Prentice-Hall.

Schlegel, Alice. 1977. *Sexual Stratification, a Cross-Cultural View.* New York: Columbia University Press.

Schneider, Carl. 1977. *Shame, Exposure and Privacy.* Boston: Beacon Press.

Schutz, William. 1967. *Joy, Expanding Human Awareness.* New York: Grove Press.

Schweder, R., and E. J. Bourne. 1982. "Does the Concept of the Person Vary Cross-Culturally?" *See* Marsella and White 1982.

Segall, Marshall. 1979. *Cross-Cultural Psychology: Human Behavior in Global Perspective.* Monterey, Calif.: Brooks-Cole Publishing Co.

Seguin, Carlos Alberto. 1970. *Introduction to Psychosomatic Medicine.* New York: International Universities Press.

Shah, Idries. 1967. *Tales of the Dervishes: Teaching Stories of the Sufi Masters Over the Past Thousand Years.* London: Jonathan Cape.

Shapiro, A. K. 1971. "Placebo Effects in Medicine, Psychotherapy, and Psychoanalysis." In A. E. Bergin and S. L. Garfield, *Handbook of Psychotherapy and Behavior Change: An Empirical Analysis.* New York: John Wiley & Sons.

Shenk, Calvin. 1983. *A Relevant Theology of Presence.* Valley Center, Calif.: MBM Books.

Singer, June. 1977. *Androgeny: Towards a New Theory of Sexuality.* London: Routledge & Kegan Paul.

Singh, Khushwant. 1975. *Gurus, God Men, and Good People.* New Delhi: Orient Longman.

Skinner, John. 1983. *The Meaning of Authority.* Washington D.C.: University Press of America.

Smith, W. Cantwell. 1962. *The Meaning and End of Religion.* New York: Macmillan Co.

Smith, Elise C., ed. 1979. *Toward Internationalism.* Rowley, Mass.: Newbury House.

Song, Choan-Seng. 1979. "New Frontiers of Theology in Asia." *South East Asia Journal of Theology* 20(1):13–33.

Southard, Samuel, and Donna Southard. 1984. "Demonizing and Mental Illness." Unpublished paper, Pasadena, Calif.

Sow, I. 1980. *Anthropological Structures of Madness in Black Africa.* New York: International Universities Press.

Spae, Joseph. 1976. "Theology and the New Maoist Man." In *Christianity and the New China.* South Pasadena: William Carey Library, Ecclesia Publications Book.

Sperry, R. W. 1965. "Mind, Brain, and Humanist Values." In J. R. Platt, *New Views of Human Nature.* Chicago: University of Chicago Press.

Spindler, George D., ed. 1978. *The Making of Psychological Anthropology.* Berkeley, Calif.: University of California Press.

Spiro, Melford. E. 1961. "Social Systems, Personality, and Functional Analysis." In Bert Kaplan, ed., *Studying Personality Cross-Culturally.* Evanston, Ill.: Northwestern University Press.

Spiro, Michael. 1978. "Culture and Human Nature." *See* Spindler 1978.

Stackhouse, Max. 1978. "Social Ethics: Some Basic Elements East and West." In S. Amirtham, *A Vision for Man.* Madras: CLS Press.

———. 1984. *Creeds, Society and Human Rights.* Grand Rapids: Wm. B. Eerdmans Publishing Co.

Stagg, Frank. 1973. *Polarities of Man's Existence in Biblical Perspective.* Philadelphia: Westminster Press.

Stewart, Edward C. 1972. *American Cultural Patterns: A Cross-Cultural Perspective.* LaGrange Park, Ill.: Intercultural Network.

———, J. Danielian, and R. J. Festes. 1969. "Simulating Intercultural Communication Through Role Playing." Alexandria, Va.: Human Resources Research Organization.

Strathern, Marilyn. 1972. *Women in Between: New Guinea.* London: Seminar Press.

Strickland, B. 1971. "Aspiration Responses Among Negro and White Adolescents." *Journal of Personality and Social Psychology* 19:315–320.

Strupp, H. 1973. "Toward a Reformulation of the Psychotherapeutic Influence." *International Journal of Psychiatry* 2:263–327.

Sue, Derald Wing. 1978. "Counseling Across Cultures." *Personnel and Guidance Journal* 56:451.

——— and others. 1981. *Counseling the Culturally Different.* New York: John Wiley & Sons.

——— and D. Sue. 1973. "Understanding Asian Americans: The Neglected Minority." *Personnel and Guidance Journal* 51:386–389.

Surya and Jayaram. 1964. "The Present-Day Indian Psychiatrist." Reported in J. S. Neki, Presidential Address. *Indian Journal of Psychiatry* 19:2, 3 (April 1977).

Swearer, Donald. 1977. *Dialogue: The Key to Understanding Other Religions.* Philadelphia: Westminster Press.

Swidler, Leonard. 1981. "Ground Rules for Interreligious Dialogue." *See* Rousseau 1981.

Szasz, Thomas. 1961. *The Myth of Mental Illness.* New York: Harper & Brothers.

———. 1976. *Schizophrenia.* New York: Basic Books.

Tan, Stephen. 1978. *Pastoral Care in Singapore.* Unpublished dissertation.

Tapp, J., and L. Kohlberg. 1971. "Developing Senses of Law and Legal Justice." *Journal of Social Issues* 27:65–92.

Taylor, Debbie. 1982. "Mum, Dad, and the Kids." *The New Internationalist* 118 (Dec. 1982).

Taylor, John V. 1963. *The Primal Vision: Christian Presence Amid African Religion.* New York: Oxford University Press.

Taylor, Kenneth. 1979. "Body and Spirit Among the Sanuma (Yanoma) of Northern Brazil." *See* Browman and Schwarz 1979.

Taylor, Richard W. 1966. *Society and Religion.* Madras: CCS.

Teja, J. S., and R. L. Narang. 1970. "Pattern of Incidence of Depression in India." *Indian Journal of Psychiatry* 12:37.

Teng, W. S., and J. Hsu. 1971. "Chinese Culture, Personality Formation, and Mental Illness." *International Journal of Social Psychiatry* 16:5–14.

Tillich, Paul. 1959. *Theology of Culture.* New York: Oxford University Press.

Tolstoy, Leo. 1877/1981. *Anna Karenina.* New York: Bantam Books.

Torrey, E. F. 1972. *The Mind Game: Witchdoctors and Psychiatrists.* New York: Emerson Hall Publishers.

Triandis, Harry. 1979. "The Future of Cross-Cultural Psychology." *See* Marsella and others 1979.

——— and J. Draguns, eds. 1983. *Handbook of Cross-Cultural Psychology,* vol. 6. Boston: Allyn & Bacon.

——— and William Lambert. 1980. *Handbook of Cross-Cultural Psychology,* vols. 1–6, Boston: Allyn & Bacon.

———, R. S. Malpass, and A. R. Davidson. 1972. "Cross-Cultural Psychology." *Biennial Review of Anthropology* 24:1–84.

——— and V. Vassiliou. 1967. *A Comparative Analysis of Subjective Culture.* Urbana, Ill.: University of Illinois Press.

Truax, Charles, and R. R. Carkhuff. 1967. *Toward Effective Counseling and Psychotherapy.* Chicago: Aldine Publishing Co.

Tseng Wen-shing and others. 1977. *Adjustment in Intercultural Marriage.* Honolulu: University of Hawaii, Department of Psychiatry.

——— and John McDermott. 1981. *Culture, Mind, and Therapy.* New York: Brunner/Mazel.

Tulkin, S. 1968. "Race, Class, Family, and School Achievement." *Journal of Personality and Social Psychology* 9:31–37.

Turiel, E. 1966. "An Experimental Test of the Sequentiality of Developmental Stages in the Child's Moral Judgments." *Journal of Personality and Social Psychology* 3:611–618.

Turner, Victor. 1964. "An Ndembo Doctor in Prache." *See* Kiev 1964.

———. 1969. *The Ritual Process.* New York: Aldine Publishing Co.

———. 1983. Foreword. *See* Kapferer 1983.

Van der Kroef, J. M. 1956. *Indonesia in the Modern World.* Bandung: Masa Baru.

Venkataramaiah, V., and others. 1981. "Possession Syndrome: An Epidemiological Study in West Karnataka." *Indian Journal of Psychiatry* 23:213–218.

Verghese, Abraham, and Annamma Abraham. 1976. *An Introduction to Psychiatry.* Madras: CLS.

Vivelo, Frank. 1978. *Cultural Anthropology Handbook.* New York: McGraw-Hill.

Wagner, Roy. 1981. *The Invention of Culture.* Chicago: University of Chicago Press.

Wallace, Anthony. 1961. *Culture and Personality: Studies in Anthropology.* New York: Random House.

Wang, Jen-Yi. 1983. "Psychosomatic Illness in the Chinese Cultural Context." *See* Romanucci-Ross 1983.

Welch, Carlos. 1979. "Mental Health Frontiers in India." *Religion and Society* 26(2):70–76.

White, C. B. 1975. "Moral Development in Bahamian School Children: A Cross-Cultural Examination of Kohlberg's Stages of Moral Reasoning." *Developmental Psychology* (11):535–536.

———, N. Bushnell, and J. Regnemer. 1978. "Moral Development in Bahamian School Children." *Developmental Psychology* 14 (1):58–65.

Whiting, B. B., and C. P. Edwards. 1973. "A Cross-Cultural Analysis of Sex Differences in the Behavior of Children." *Journal of Social Psychology* 91: 171–188.

Whyte, Pauline, and Robert Whyte. 1982. *The Women of Rural Asia.* Boulder, Col.: Westview Press.

Wiesel, Elie. 1972. *Souls on Fire.* New York: Random House.

Wittkower, E. D., and R. A. Prince. 1974. "A Review of Transcultural Psychiatry." In S. Arieti and G. Caplan, *American Handbook of Psychiatry.* New York: Basic Books.

Wohl, Julian. 1976. "Intercultural Psychotherapy: Issues, Questions, and Reflections." In Paul Pedersen and others, eds., *Counseling Across Cultures.* Honolulu: University Press of Hawaii.

———. 1981. "Intercultural Psychotherapy." *See* Pedersen and others 1981.

Wolfgang, A. 1973. "Cross-Cultural Comparison of Locus of Control." Proceedings of the 81st Annual Convention of the American Psychological Association 8:229–300.

Wong, Aline. 1978. "The Modern Chinese Family." In M. S. Das and P. Bardis, *The Family in Asia.* London: George Allen & Unwin.

Wren, G. C. 1962. "The Culturally Encapsulated Counselor." *Harvard Educational Review* 32(4):444–449.

Wrightsman, L. S. 1972. *Social Psychology in the Seventies.* Monterey, Calif.: Brooks-Cole Publishing Co.

Wu, David Y. H. 1982. "Psychotherapy and Emotion in Traditional Chinese Medicine." *See* Marsella and White 1982.

Yamamoto, K. A. 1972. "A Comparative Study of 'Patienthood' in the Japanese and American Hospital." In W. Lebra, *Transcultural Research in Mental Health,* vol. 2. Honolulu: University Press of Hawaii,

Yang, C. K. 1961. *Religion in Chinese Society.* Berkeley, Calif.: University of California Press.

Yap, P. M. 1966. "The Possession Syndrome: A Comparison of Hong Kong and French Findings." *Journal of Mental Science* 106:114–137.

———. 1969. "The Culture-Bound Reactive Syndromes." In W. Claudin and T. Y. Lin, *Mental Health Research in Asia and the Pacific.* Honolulu: East-West Center.

Yoder, J. H. 1983. "But We See Jesus: The Particularity of Incarnation and the Universality of Truth." In Leroy Rouner, *Foundations of Ethics.* Notre Dame, Ind.: University of Notre Dame Press.

Zimbardo, P. G., and F. L. Ruch. 1977. *Psychology and Life.* Glenview, Ill.: Scott, Foresman & Co.

Index of Subjects

Index of Names